# CAMBRIDGE
# Global English

Teacher's Resource

**6**

**Jane Boylan**
**and Claire Medwell**

CAMBRIDGE
UNIVERSITY PRESS

# CAMBRIDGE
## UNIVERSITY PRESS

University Printing House, Cambridge CB2 8BS, United Kingdom

One Liberty Plaza, 20th Floor, New York, NY 10006, USA

477 Williamstown Road, Port Melbourne, VIC 3207, Australia

4843/24, 2nd Floor, Ansari Road, Daryaganj, Delhi – 110002, India

79 Anson Road, #06–04/06, Singapore 079906

Cambridge University Press is part of the University of Cambridge.

It furthers the University's mission by disseminating knowledge in the pursuit of education, learning and research at the highest international levels of excellence.

www.cambridge.org
Information on this title: www.cambridge.org/9781107635814

© Cambridge University Press 2014

First published 2014
20  19  18  17  16  15  14  13  12  11  10  9

Printed in Great Britain by CPI Group (UK) Ltd, Croydon CR0 4YY

*A catalogue record for this publication is available from the British Library*

ISBN 978-1-107-63581-4  Teacher's Resource

..............................................................................................................................................

NOTICE TO TEACHERS
The photocopy masters in this publication may be photocopied or distributed [electronically] free of charge for classroom use within the school or institution that purchased the publication. Worksheets and copies of them remain in the copyright of Cambridge University Press, and such copies may not be distributed or used in any way outside the purchasing institution.

# Contents

# Map of the Learner's Book

| page | Unit | Words and expressions | Use of English | Reading/Writing |
|------|------|----------------------|----------------|-----------------|
| 6–19 | 1 Life experience | Free-time activities<br>Adjective and noun forms<br>Words connected with music<br>Sequencing words and phrases<br>Achievements<br>Verbs with prepositions | Wh- questions review<br>Present perfect simple<br>Past continuous | Read to understand general meaning<br>First-time experiences<br>A biography about JK Rowling<br>Literature: The story of Helen Keller<br>Paragraphs<br>Write a biography |
| 20–33 | 2 School | School subjects<br>Extra curricular activities<br>Collocations belong to; do chess; learn about; write for | Instead of / as well as + noun<br>1st conditional with if/unless | Read for specific information: A text about brain power and tips for studying well<br>Literature: Extract from a novel<br>Life at school<br>Create a poster on 'learning tips'<br>Use modals to be polite; ask permission<br>Write an email/letter |
| 34–35 | Review 1 | | | |
| 36–49 | 3 Sport | Sports<br>Sports equipment<br>Parts of the body<br>Football<br>Descriptive words | Reported speech<br>Reported Wh questions<br>Need/should/mustn't | Scanning<br>Articles about Paralymipian Hannah Cockroft and the London Marathon<br>Literature: Off Side<br>A bar chart and notes<br>A summary<br>Describe a sports event |
| 50–63 | 4 The big screen | Film types<br>Strong adjectives<br>Cinema history | Strong adjectives: absolutely/really<br>Passive (past simple)<br>Defining relative clauses with where, who and that | A film review<br>A storyboard<br>Literature: Jurassic Park<br>Guess meaning from context<br>Direct speech and reporting verbs<br>Create a storyboard |
| 64–65 | Review 2 | | | |
| 66–79 | 5 Inventions | Gadgets and equipment<br>Opinions and reasons<br>Adverbs | Used to for past habits<br>Will for prediction<br>2nd conditional | Use your own knowledge to understand a text: Lighting up the world; Wheels<br>Literature: Start Small, Think Big<br>A quiz on gadgets and inventions<br>Support your ideas with reasons<br>An essay about an important invention |
| 80–93 | 6 Explorers | Famous expeditions<br>Exploration of the Americas<br>Equipment<br>Descriptive words | Question forms: how many, what + noun<br>Linking expressions<br>Cardinal and ordinal numbers<br>Participle adjectives | Historical explorers<br>An explorer's blog<br>Literature: The Boy Who Biked The World<br>A quiz<br>Time references and dates<br>A blog/diary entry |
| 94–95 | Review 3 | | | |
| 96–109 | 7 Jobs and work | Compound nouns<br>Media jobs<br>Personal qualities<br>Clothes and uniform<br>Suffixes | Adjectives + prepositions + noun<br>Present continuous<br>Could + be | Skim a text<br>A TV presenter's job<br>Job adverts<br>Literature: You can be anything<br>Shortened sentences<br>Someone's job; a job advertisement |
| 110–123 | 8 Communication | Ways of communicating<br>Gestures<br>Negotiating | Present continuous for future arrangements<br>Polite requests | Gestures around the world<br>A class forum<br>Literature: Thank You Letter<br>Online communication<br>Online politeness<br>An online forum<br>Write a verse<br>A poster about communication<br>A discussion forum |
| 124–125 | Review 4 | | | |
| 126–139 | 9 Travellers' tales | Holiday activities<br>Descriptive adjectives<br>Nouns with -ing<br>Expressions with take | 2nd conditional<br>Prepositional verbs<br>Adjectives and prepositions | Use prediction to understand a text<br>An online review page<br>A poem: My dream holiday<br>Literature: The Light Beam That Got Away<br>Plan your writing<br>Post a comment/review<br>Write a poem: My dream holiday |
| 140–141 | Review 5 | | | |

| Listening/Speaking | School subjects | Pronunciation / Word study | Critical thinking / Values |
|---|---|---|---|
| Listen and talk about free-time activities; first-time experiences; inspiring people<br>Sequencing words/phrases<br>Give presentations: An inspiring person; a favourite book; an interesting experience | Maths: A pie chart | -tion/-cian | Attitudes to blindness and deafness<br>Analysing a pie chart<br>What makes some experiences special?<br>Who do we admire? Why?<br>Examining famous lives. |
| School life in different countries<br>Listen to students talking about different problems at school<br>Phrases: Giving advice<br>Emphasising words<br>Roleplay a problem at school | | Word stress for information<br>Silent letters | Value: Treating classmates fairly<br>Comparing school life<br>Considering good study habits<br>Creating and analysing solutions to problems |
| Listen for expression and emphasis<br>Reasons for liking sport<br>Listen to instructions to warm up<br>Talk about sports and equipment<br>Order and give instructions | Biology: Parts of the body<br>Maths: A bar chart | Emphasis | Teamwork<br>Interpreting information on a bar chart<br>Expressing opinions about sports events<br>Examining personal challenges and goals |
| Listen for specific information: A short history of cinema<br>Listen to film trailers<br>Listen to a film discussion<br>Make information interesting<br>Give presentations: A film review; talk about films | Maths: Currency | Dates (years) | Facing a problem<br>Describing films<br>Creating film scenes<br>Making deductions from inferences<br>Making predictions<br>Personal safety and looking after yourself |
| My favourite gadget<br>A new invention<br>Listen and speak about modern inventions<br>Prepare presentations: Know your audience<br>Give presentations: The history of an invention | Science: Thomas Edison | the a sound | Believing in yourself<br>Comparing and contrasting different gadgets<br>Making assumptions and predictions<br>Creating and describing an invention<br>Problem solving<br>Supporting opinions with reasons |
| Talk about what you know<br>The story of Columbus<br>Plans for an expedition<br>Use contractions<br>Give presentations: A historical explorer or expedition | Maths: Measurements<br>History: Explorers | the ch sound | Making visitors welcome<br>Making deductions<br>Selecting information from research<br>Creating a plan for an expedition<br>Making deductions from inferences |
| Describe job qualities<br>Pictures<br>Jobs that family/friends do; work uniforms<br>Give presentations: Present a design; a job you'd like | | Rhyming vowels | Working hard and setting goals<br>Express opinions about different jobs<br>Creating a uniform<br>Creating an advertisement |
| Key words for remembering whole sentences<br>Phone messages<br>A conversation with a teacher<br>Make notes before you speak<br>Role play: A difficult situation | Maths: How much to spend | Matching sounds | Saying thank you<br>Communication in different countries<br>Communicating in a difficult situation<br>Problem solving<br>Communicating appropriately online<br>Giving opinions |
| Holiday activities<br>Description of a special place: Pompeii<br>Interesting or surprising information<br>Activities you'd like to try<br>Give presentations: Describe a place | Science: The speed of light<br>Maths: Survey and report | the o sound | Learning from family members<br>Discussing positive and negative sides<br>Describing feelings about a special place<br>Imagining a dream holiday |

## Welcome to *Cambridge Global English Stage 6*

*Cambridge Global English* is an eight-level English course for young learners from the beginning of primary school to the end of junior secondary (roughly ages 6–13). The course has been designed to fulfil the requirements of *Cambridge Primary English as a Second Language Curriculum Framework*. These internationally recognised standards provide a sequential framework for thorough coverage of basic English concepts and skills.

The materials reflect the following principles:

- *An international focus.* Specifically developed for young learners throughout the world, the themes, situations, and literature covered by *Cambridge Global English* strive to reflect this diversity and help learners learn about each other's lives through the medium of English. This fosters respect and interest in other cultures and leads to awareness of global citizenship.
- *An enquiry-based language-rich approach to learning.* *Cambridge Global English* engages children as active, creative thinkers. As learners participate in a wide variety of curriculum-based activities, they simultaneously acquire content knowledge, develop critical thinking skills through tasks that encourage a personal response and practise English language and literacy. The materials incorporate a 'learning to learn' approach, helping children acquire skills and strategies that will help them approach new learning situations with confidence and success.
- *English for educational success.* To meet the challenges of the future, children need to develop facility with both conversational and more formal English. From the earliest level, *Cambridge Global English* addresses both these competencies. *Cambridge Global English* presents authentic listening and reading texts, writing tasks, and culminating unit projects similar to those students might encounter in a first language school situation. Emphasis is placed on developing the listening, speaking, reading, and writing skills students will need to be successful in using authentic English-language classroom materials. At Stage 6, learning strategies and tips for study skills are introduced and practised. This lays the foundations for developing effective study skills for future use.
- *Rich vocabulary development.* Building a large and robust vocabulary is a cornerstone to success in both conversational and academic English. *Cambridge Global English* exposes learners to a wide range of vocabulary through the text types and activities present in the materials. Many opportunities for revising these words and using them in personalised, meaningful ways are woven into the activities and lesson plans.

- *Individualised learning.* We approach learning in an individual way by both acknowledging the individual nature of the knowledge and background of each child and encouraging their specific input. We also provide for differentiated learning in the classroom by offering a range of activities of varying difficulty and extra challenges. Unit by unit support for this is provided in the unit notes in this book.
- *Integrated assessment.* Throughout the course, teachers informally assess their students' understanding of language and concepts. The Teacher's Resource provides suggestions for extending or re-teaching language skills based on learners' demonstrated proficiency. At the end of each unit, learners apply the skills and knowledge they have acquired as they work in groups to create and present a project of their choice. This provides teachers with an excellent performance assessment opportunity. An end-of-unit quiz in the Activity Book provides another evaluation measure: a quick progress check on learners' understanding of key ESL and literacy skills.

*Cambridge Global English* can be used as a stand-alone ESL curriculum, or it can be used as part of an innovative suite of materials created by Cambridge University Press for young learners at international primary schools:

- *Cambridge Primary Science*
- *Cambridge Primary Mathematics*
- *Cambridge Primary English (L1)*
- *Cambridge Global English.*

We encourage you to learn more about these complementary courses through the Cambridge University Press website: education.cambridge.org

We very much hope that you and your students will enjoy using these materials as much as we enjoyed developing them for you.

The *Cambridge Global English* team

## A Components

*Cambridge Global English* offers the following components:

- The **Learner's Book** provides the core input of the course. It consists of nine thematic units of study. Each unit contains six lessons developed around a unifying theme that is also linked to a main question at the beginning of the *Reflect on your learning* section of the main units. The materials feature skills-building tasks, including listening, reading, writing, speaking, as well as language focus, catering for the needs of learners studying in a primary context. In addition, we have included a strong vocabulary-building element. We also specifically explore ways of introducing basic learning skills and strategies, so that the children become aware of the act of learning and how it works through such features as:
  • Overt objectives at the beginning of each unit
  • Language and Writing tips
  • Listening and Reading strategies
  • Use of English
  • *Reflect on your learning*
  • *Look what I can do!*

  We try to aim our materials at the whole child with all the experiences that they bring to the classroom. We encourage the learners to see the moral and social values that exist in many of our texts and find opportunities for reflecting on these. We feel that the learner needs to be exposed to many different forms of text topics and styles in order to develop the skills of assessing, interpreting and responding appropriately. This means that the learners will see factual texts, imaginary text, dialogues, poetry, etc. on a range of different topics at the appropriate level.
- The **Audio CDs** include all the listening material needed for the Learner's Book and Activity Book. The listening material supports the Learner's Book with listening and pronunciation activities, as well as read-along stories. We recommend that learners use the Audio CDs at home to practise the stories and to show their parents what they know.
- The **Activity Book** provides additional practice activities, deepening learners' understanding of the language skills and content material introduced in the Learner's Book.

- The **Teacher's Resource** provides valuable guidance and support for using *Cambridge Global English* in your classroom. We understand that within each class there are children of different ability, particularly when children come from different pre-primary backgrounds. We think it is very important to support differentiated work in the classroom and we aim to do this through suggestions in the unit notes, with additional differentiation 'challenge' activities in the Activity Book. In addition, the production required in the project work can be graded in terms of ability.

  At the end of this book, we provide photocopiable activities for additional work. These are referred to in the unit notes. We also provide a selection of lesson-by-lesson spelling words which you can photocopy, cut out and give to the children to learn.

## B Learner's Book structure

*Cambridge Global English* consists of nine thematic units of study roughly set out to cover three units per term in most systems. The Stage 6 Learner's Book is organised as follows:

- **Main units:** Nine thematic units provide a year's curriculum.
- **Review pages:** Every two units we provide two review pages to revise and consolidate learning.

## C Unit structure

Each unit is divided up into six lessons. The length of lessons will vary from school to school, so we have not prescribed a strict time limit for each lesson. The lessons are organised as follows:

- **Lesson 1 Opening:** This lesson introduces the main topic, and prepares for the Big question which you will find at the beginning of the *Reflect on your learning* section. We also set out the unit objectives for the teacher to share with the learners. This overt teaching of objectives is part of the learning to learn strategy. The main lesson begins with a 'Talk about it' activity in which the children are expected to react to information, ideas or visuals. There is a contextualised listening or speaking text which leads to exploitation of vocabulary and grammar. A free-speaking activity usually ends the lesson.

- **Lessons 2–4 Skills:** In these lessons, we explore the topic in various ways using a variety of short listening and reading texts which do include cross-curricular topics. The lessons focus on the mechanics of reading, including spelling or pronunciation and use of English and integrate the four skills. Guided writing activities are included in these lessons.
- **Lesson 5 Literacy:** This literacy lesson involves reading authentic extracts, stories, poems and factual texts of longer length. It allows the learner to explore a variety of text types with the class and develop comprehension and writing skills through related activities. The literacy lessons can include some word focus and strategies for approaching new text types and usually include value-related activities.
- **Lesson 6 Choose a project:** This is the consolidation and production section of the unit in which the learners produce language related to some element in the unit. This lesson begins with the learners taking an active role in choosing a project, carrying it out and presenting it to the class. Then they reflect on their learning and do a short self-assessment activity: *Look what I can do!*

## D Activity Book

Each lesson in the Learner's Book is supported by two Activity Book pages which reinforce and extend the material introduced in the Learner's Book. It also provides opportunities for personalisation and creative work, as well as challenge activities to support differentiated classroom situations. In these activities, more confident learners can do additional work at a higher level. The last lesson of each unit offers additional assessment / self-assessment opportunities.

## E Customising your lessons

We provide support for planning each lesson in the unit pages of this book. We also clearly set out the teaching objectives. Please bear in mind the following:

- These are ideas and guidelines only and you should adapt them to your situation and the needs of your learner. Do not be afraid to change things and bring in additional elements.
- Monitor your learners. If they need additional support for some elements, tailor the material to their needs.
- Bring as much 'real' material into the classroom as possible in order to create more interest for the lessons.
- Be creative in developing extension activities and role plays. We offer suggestions, however there is much more that can be done.

- Encourage learning/teaching/showing between classes, even of different age groups.
- Don't forget to draw on parent support where possible.

When using the book, the following guidelines might be useful:

---

**Before using the Learner's Book**

- Warm up activities (songs, TPR, vocabulary games, alphabet chant, etc.).
- Pre-teach and practise key language that learners will encounter in the Learner's Book and Audio CDs. (Try to make learning experiences concrete, interactive, motivating.)

**While using the Learner's Book**

- Keep learners engaged in an active way.
- Use the illustrations as a conversation starter – ask learners to name everything they see; play *I Spy,* etc.
- Vary the group dynamics in the lesson: move from whole group response to individual response to pairwork, etc.
- Provide opportunities for learners to ask questions, as well as to answer them.
- Encourage learners to act out the language in the lessons.
- Encourage learners to use language structures and vocabulary to talk about their own ideas, opinions and experiences.
- In class discussions, write the learners' ideas on class charts. You can refer back to these charts in later lessons.
- Adjust your reading and writing expectations and instructions to suit the literacy level of your learners.

**Using the Activity Book and further suggestions**

- Use the Activity Book pages related to the Learner's Book pages.
- Depending on the ability of the learners, use the 'Additional support and practice' activities and/or 'Extend and challenge' activities suggested in the Teacher's Resource at the end of every lesson.
- Do a Wrap up activity or game at the end of every lesson. Suggestions are included in the Teachers' Resource.

---

We would strongly recommend that you supplement this core material with the following:

- An extended reading programme to provide the children with lots of practice of different types of books leading to reading independence. It is recommended that you regularly set aside time for the children to read books of their choice in class and that they are encouraged to read at home.

- Exposure to additional audiovisual material, such as television programmes, songs, film excerpts, so that the learners begin to feel confident in their ability to decode and understand a range of resources.
- Supplementary handwriting and phonics material to really help build on those skills at this crucial time.

## F Setting up the primary classroom

We know that there is not always a lot of flexibility in this, but, if possible, it would be useful to set up the classroom in this way:

- Have some open space where learners can do role plays, etc.
- Have a flexible seating arrangement, so that you can mix up the groups and pairs, and the learners become flexible about working in different ways.
- Make sure that you have display areas where you and the learners can bring in pictures and items linked to the themes you're working on. Also display examples of good work and creative work. Make small cards and display important words for the learners to remember.
- Change displays regularly to keep the learners interested and engaged.

## G Assessment

We recommend that you take the time and opportunity to observe and monitor the progress and development of your learners. We provide many opportunities for informal assessment through the projects, as well as self-assessment *(Look what I can do!)* in the main units of the Learner's Book. The Activity Book contains revision material at the end of each unit.

At the beginning of the year, create individual portfolio folders to keep work that shows how the children have been meeting the curriculum objectives. Use the portfolio to look over with the learners and create a feeling of progress and pride in what they have achieved. Keep this portfolio for parent–teacher meetings and send it home to show the parents/carers either at the end of each term or the end of the year. You might want to include a letter to parents/carers outlining what they have achieved.

If you would like further learner assessment opportunities, a table of how the Cambridge English Language Assessment exams for primary stages fits in with the *Cambridge Global English* levels is set out below.

### Cambridge English Language Assessment exam for primary stages

| Stage | Assessment | CEFR level |
|---|---|---|
| 6 | | |
| 5 | Cambridge English: Key (KET) | A2 |
| 4 | for Schools | |
| 3 | Cambridge English: Flyers (YLE Flyers) | |
| 2 | Cambridge English: Movers (YLE movers) | A1 |
| 1 | Cambridge English: Starters (YLE starters) | |

## H Home–school relationship

Support and encouragement at home is extremely important at this age. Encourage parents to become as involved as possible in their child's learning process by asking them what they have learned after every lesson, allowing children to 'teach' them what they have learned, taking an interest in what they bring home or want to perform for them and supporting any work the learners might try to do at home.

## I Icons

The following icons have been used to clearly signpost areas of special interest or as shorthand for specific instructions:

- Audio and track number reference. These appear in the Learner's Book, the Activity Book and the Teacher's Resource.
- Speaking opportunity / activity recommended for pairwork. These appear in the Learner's Book, the Activity Book and Teacher's Resource.
- Cross-curricular maths and science topics. These appear in the Learner's Book, the Activity Book and the Teacher's Resource.
- Links directly to Activity Book activity and references it. These appear in the Learner's Book and the Teacher's Resource.
- Activity to be written in the learner's notebook. These appear in the Learner's Book and the Activity Book.
- Activity to be done out of the book, in a more active classroom setting. These appear in the Teacher's Resource.

## Learning objectives from the Cambridge Primary English as a Second Language Curriculum Framework:
### Stage 6 correlated with Cambridge Global English, Stage 6

Below you will find a table setting out specifically where to find coverage of the framework objectives for Stage 6.

| Cambridge Primary English as a Second Language Framework: Stage 6 | CGE Unit 1 | CGE Unit 2 | CGE Unit 3 | CGE Unit 4 | CGE Unit 5 | CGE Unit 6 | CGE Unit 7 | CGE Unit 8 | CGE Unit 9 |
|---|---|---|---|---|---|---|---|---|---|
| **Reading** | | | | | | | | | |
| **R1** Recognise, identify and sound, independently, a wide range of language at text level | ✓ | ✓ | ✓ | ✓ | ✓ | ✓ | ✓ | ✓ | ✓ |
| **R2** Read and follow, independently, familiar instructions for classroom activities | ✓ | ✓ | ✓ | ✓ | ✓ | ✓ | ✓ | ✓ | ✓ |
| **R3** Read independently a range of short simple fiction and non-fiction texts with confidence and enjoyment | | ✓ | ✓ | ✓ | ✓ | ✓ | | | ✓ |
| **R4** Understand the main points of a wide range of short simple texts on general and curricular topics by using contextual clues | ✓ | ✓ | ✓ | ✓ | ✓ | ✓ | ✓ | ✓ | ✓ |
| **R5** Understand independently specific information and detail in short, simple texts on a wide range of general and curricular topics | ✓ | ✓ | | | ✓ | | ✓ | ✓ | |
| **R6** Recognise the difference between fact and opinion in short, simple texts on a range of general and curricular topics | | | | | ✓ | | | | |

| Cambridge Primary English as a Second Language Framework: Stage 6 | CGE Unit 1 | CGE Unit 2 | CGE Unit 3 | CGE Unit 4 | CGE Unit 5 | CGE Unit 6 | CGE Unit 7 | CGE Unit 8 | CGE Unit 9 |
|---|---|---|---|---|---|---|---|---|---|
| **R7** Recognise the attitude or opinion of the writer in short, simple texts on a wide range of general and curricular topics | | ✓ | | | ✓ | | | | ✓ |
| **R8** Use independently, familiar paper and digital reference resources to check meaning and extend understanding | ✓ | ✓ | ✓ | ✓ | ✓ | ✓ | ✓ | ✓ | ✓ |
| **Writing** | | | | | | | | | |
| **W1** Plan, write, edit and proofread work at text level with some support and a limited range of general and curricular topics | ✓ | ✓ | ✓ | ✓ | ✓ | ✓ | ✓ | ✓ | ✓ |
| **W2** Write, with some support, about factual and imaginary past events, activities and experiences on a growing range of general and curricular topics | | | | | ✓ | | | | |
| **W3** Write with some support about personal feelings and opinions on a limited range of general and curricular topics | ✓ | | ✓ | ✓ | ✓ | ✓ | | ✓ | ✓ |
| **W4** Use joined-up handwriting in all written work across the curriculum with appropriate speed and fluency | ✓ | ✓ | ✓ | ✓ | ✓ | ✓ | ✓ | ✓ | ✓ |
| **W5** Link sentences into a coherent text using a variety of basic connectors on a range of general and curricular topics when writing independently | ✓ | ✓ | ✓ | ✓ | ✓ | ✓ | ✓ | ✓ | ✓ |

| Cambridge Primary English as a Second Language Framework: Stage 6 | CGE Unit 1 | CGE Unit 2 | CGE Unit 3 | CGE Unit 4 | CGE Unit 5 | CGE Unit 6 | CGE Unit 7 | CGE Unit 8 | CGE Unit 9 |
|---|---|---|---|---|---|---|---|---|---|
| W6 Use independently appropriate layout at text level for a growing range of written genres on familiar general and curricular topics | ✓ | ✓ | ✓ | ✓ | ✓ | ✓ | ✓ | ✓ | ✓ |
| W7 Spell most high-frequency words accurately for a range of familiar general and curricular topics when writing independently | ✓ | ✓ | ✓ | ✓ | ✓ | ✓ | ✓ | ✓ | ✓ |
| W8 Punctuate with some accuracy, written work at text level for a range of general and curricular topics when writing independently | ✓ | ✓ | ✓ | ✓ | ✓ | ✓ | ✓ | ✓ | ✓ |
| Use of English | | | | | | | | | |
| UE1 Use a limited range of abstract nouns and compound nouns; use double genitive structures: a friend of theirs on a range of general and curricular topics | ✓ | | | | | | | | |
| UE2 Use quantifiers, cardinal, and ordinal numbers and fractions on a range of general and curricular topics | | | | | | | | | |
| UE3 Use a growing range of participles adjectives and a growing range of adjectives in correct order in front of nouns on a range of general and curricular topics | | | | | | ✓ | | | ✓ |

| Cambridge Primary English as a Second Language Framework: Stage 6 | CGE Unit 1 | CGE Unit 2 | CGE Unit 3 | CGE Unit 4 | CGE Unit 5 | CGE Unit 6 | CGE Unit 7 | CGE Unit 8 | CGE Unit 9 |
|---|---|---|---|---|---|---|---|---|---|
| **UE4** Use a range of determiners including neither, both on a range of general and curricular topics | | | | | | | | | |
| **UE5** Use a growing range of questions including how far, how many times, what + noun, on a range of general and curricular questions | ✓ | | | | | ✓ | | | |
| **UE6** Use a range of pronouns including relative pronouns who, which, that, whom, whose, on a range of general and curricular topics | | | | | | | | | |
| **UE7** Use simple perfect forms to express [recent, indefinite and unfinished] past on a range of general and curricular topics | ✓ | | | | | | | | |
| **UE8** Use a growing range of future forms including be going to [predictions based on present evidence] and will for predictions, on a range of general and curricular topics | | | | | ✓ | | | | |
| **UE9** Use a range of active and passive simple present and past forms and used to/didn't use for past habits/ states on a range of general and curricular topics | | | | ✓ | | | | | |

| Cambridge Primary English as a Second Language Framework: Stage 6 | CGE Unit 1 | CGE Unit 2 | CGE Unit 3 | CGE Unit 4 | CGE Unit 5 | CGE Unit 6 | CGE Unit 7 | CGE Unit 8 | CGE Unit 9 |
|---|---|---|---|---|---|---|---|---|---|
| **UE10** Use present continuous forms with present and future meaning and past continuous forms for background, parallel and interrupted past actions on a range of general and curricular topics | ✓ | | | | | | ✓ | ✓ | |
| **UE11** Begin to use simple forms of reported speech to report statements and commands on a range of general and curricular topics | | | | | | | | | |
| **UE12** Use a range of adverbs [simple and comparative forms], including adverbs of manner; use pre-verbal, post-verbal and end-position adverbs; on a range of general and curricular topics | | | | | | | | | |
| **UE13** Use a growing range of modal forms including would [polite requests], could [polite requests], needn't [lack of necessity], should, ought to [obligation], on a range of general and curricular topics | | ✓ | ✓ | | | | ✓ | ✓ | |

| Cambridge Primary English as a Second Language Framework: Stage 6 | CGE Unit 1 | CGE Unit 2 | CGE Unit 3 | CGE Unit 4 | CGE Unit 5 | CGE Unit 6 | CGE Unit 7 | CGE Unit 8 | CGE Unit 9 |
|---|---|---|---|---|---|---|---|---|---|
| **UE14** Use a growing range of prepositions preceding nouns and adjectives in prepositional phrases; begin to use dependent prepositions following adjectives on a range of general and curricular topics | | | | | | | ✓ | | ✓ |
| **UE15** Use the pattern verb + object + infinitive give/take/send/bring/show + direct/indirect object; begin to use common prepositional verbs; on a range of general and curricular topics | | | | | | | | | |
| **UE16** Use conjunctions while, until, as soon as in relating narratives if/unless in conditional sentences; on a range of general and curricular topics | | ✓ | | | | ✓ | | | |
| **UE17** Use if/unless in zero and first conditional clauses; use a range of defining and non-defining relative clauses with which, who, that, whose, whom on a range of general and curricular topics | | | | ✓ | | | | | |

| Cambridge Primary English as a Second Language Framework: Stage 6 | CGE Unit 1 | CGE Unit 2 | CGE Unit 3 | CGE Unit 4 | CGE Unit 5 | CGE Unit 6 | CGE Unit 7 | CGE Unit 8 | CGE Unit 9 |
|---|---|---|---|---|---|---|---|---|---|
| **Listening** | | | | | | | | | |
| **L1** Understand with little or no support, longer sequences of classroom instructions | ✓ | ✓ | ✓ | ✓ | ✓ | ✓ | ✓ | ✓ | ✓ |
| **L2** Understand more complex unsupported questions which ask for personal information | ✓ | | | | | | | ✓ | |
| **L3** Understand with little or no support, more complex questions on a range of general and curricular topics | ✓ | ✓ | ✓ | ✓ | ✓ | ✓ | ✓ | ✓ | ✓ |
| **L4** Understand, with little or no support, the main points in both short and extended talk on a range of general and curricular topics | ✓ | ✓ | ✓ | | ✓ | ✓ | | | ✓ |
| **L5** Understand with little or not support, specific information and detail in both short and extended talk on a range of general and curricular topics | ✓ | ✓ | ✓ | ✓ | ✓ | ✓ | | ✓ | ✓ |
| **L6** Deduce, with little or no support, meaning from context in both short and extended talk on a range of general and curricular topics | | | | | | ✓ | | ✓ | |

| Cambridge Primary English as a Second Language Framework: Stage 6 | CGE Unit 1 | CGE Unit 2 | CGE Unit 3 | CGE Unit 4 | CGE Unit 5 | CGE Unit 6 | CGE Unit 7 | CGE Unit 8 | CGE Unit 9 |
|---|---|---|---|---|---|---|---|---|---|
| **L7** Recognise, with little or not support, the opinion of the speaker(s) in both short and extended talk on a range of general and curricular topics | | | | | ✓ | ✓ | ✓ | | ✓ |
| **L8** Understand, with little or no support, both short and extended narratives on a range of general and curricular topics | | | | ✓ | | ✓ | | | |
| **L9** Identify rhymes, onomatopoeia and rhythm | | | | | | | ✓ | ✓ | |
| **Speaking** | | | | | | | | | |
| **S1** Provide detailed information about themselves and others at discourse level on a wide range of general topics | ✓ | ✓ | ✓ | ✓ | | | | ✓ | |
| **S2** Ask questions to clarify meaning on a range of general and curricular topics | ✓ | ✓ | ✓ | ✓ | ✓ | ✓ | ✓ | ✓ | ✓ |
| **S3** Give an opinion at discourse level on a range of general and curricular topics | ✓ | ✓ | ✓ | ✓ | ✓ | ✓ | ✓ | ✓ | ✓ |
| **S4** Respond, with increasing flexibility, at both sentence and discourse level to unexpected comments on a range of general and curricular topics | ✓ | ✓ | ✓ | ✓ | ✓ | ✓ | ✓ | ✓ | ✓ |
| **S5** Summarise what others have said on a range of general and curricular topics | ✓ | ✓ | ✓ | ✓ | ✓ | ✓ | ✓ | ✓ | ✓ |

| | | | | | | | | | |
|---|---|---|---|---|---|---|---|---|---|
| **S6** Link comments to what others say at sentence and discourse level in pair, group and whole class exchanges | ✓ | ✓ | ✓ | ✓ | ✓ | ✓ | ✓ | ✓ | ✓ |
| **S7** Keep interaction going in longer exchanges on a wide range of general and curricular topics | ✓ | ✓ | ✓ | ✓ | ✓ | ✓ | ✓ | ✓ | ✓ |
| **S8** Relate extended stories and events on a limited range of general and curricular topics | ✓ | | | | | ✓ | | | |

## 4 CEFR guidelines

The Cambridge Primary English as a Second Language curriculum framework is based on the Council of Europe's common European Framework of Reference for Languages (CEFR). For more information about the CEFR framework, please visit their website. The framework correlation to the *Cambridge Global English* stages (or levels) is set out in the table below. However, the material in the course may move more fluidly between levels since it has been written for an ESL context where it is difficult to have rigid conceptions about language level.

### CEFR levels for CIE stages

| | Cambridge Global English Stage | | | | | |
|---|---|---|---|---|---|---|
| | **1** | **2** | **3** | **4** | **5** | **6** |
| **Reading CEFR level** | Working towards A1 | Low A1 | High A1 | Low A2 | Mid A2 | High A2 |
| **Writing CEFR level** | Working towards A1 | Low A1 | High A1 | Low A2 | Mid A2 | High A2 |
| **Use of English CEFR level** | Low A1 | High A1 | Low A2 | Mid A2 | High A2 | Low B1 |
| **Listening CEFR level** | Low A1 | High A1 | Low A2 | Mid A2 | High A2 | Low B1 |
| **Speaking CEFR level** | Low A1 | High A1 | Low A2 | Mid A2 | High A2 | Low B1 |

# 1 Life experience

**Big question** What can we learn from our own and other people's life experiences?

## Unit overview

In this unit learners will:
- talk about free-time activities and life experiences
- do a presentation about someone they admire
- write a short biography
- read about the life of an inspiring person.

In **Unit 1**, learners will explore the notion of life experience: what we can learn from our own and other people's life experiences. Learners are presented with the Big question in **Lesson 1** and, in the course of the unit, will understand that tasks and projects in the unit answer the question. The unit begins by focusing on how people like to spend their free time, giving learners an accessible and familiar topic with which to start the unit and the Stage 6 course. Through looking at likes, dislikes and preferences for regular free-time activities, learners will practise communication and listening skills. They will then read short accounts of experiencing something significant for the first time and learn phrases to describe the impact of these experiences. They will learn to plan and deliver an oral presentation about someone they admire and explain why. They will write a short biography of someone who has done something inspirational, looking at lexical, grammatical and topical components included in this type of writing. Finally, they will read about someone who has had an inspiring, extraordinary life and discuss some social issues raised from the text.

Throughout **Unit 1**, learners are provided with numerous opportunities to apply and personalise what they have learned through discussion, interviewing and writing tasks.

The **Photocopiable activities** provide practice in: using present perfect simple forms to talk about personal experience **(1)**; past continuous forms to describe multiple events happening at the same time in the past **(2)**.

### Language focus

Question forms (review)

Present perfect forms (to describe experiences)

Past continuous forms (to describe continuous actions happening at the same time in the past)

**Vocabulary topics:** free-time activities; expressing preferences; noun/adjective forms; music; sequencing words; verbs with prepositions; verb/noun collocations reinstate

### Self-assessment
- I can talk about free-time activities.
- I can talk about life experiences.
- I can do a presentation about someone I admire.
- I can write a short biography.
- I can understand a life story about someone in the past.

### Teaching tips

Draw learners' attention to the idea of approaching a **reading** or **listening** text in *stages*, rather than trying to tackle all aspects of the text at once. The first step is to understand the general meaning (rather than details) by looking and listening for key words first. Make learners aware of what they do understand in the text and then pick out certain words (*key words*) that link closely with the main theme of the text and have strong images or associations with it. Images and headings around the text will also give clues to help identify general meaning and key words. Further guidance and practice is given on how to identify key words in this unit.

Review the learners' work and their own assessment of their progress, noting areas where learners demonstrate strength and confidence, and areas where they need additional instruction and practice. Use this information to select areas for review and specific focus, as you continue to **Unit 2**.

# Lesson 1: Life experience

Learner's Book pages: 6–7
Activity Book pages: 4–5

## Lesson objectives

**Listening:** An interview about preferences for free-time activities.

**Speaking:** Interview a partner to find out about preferences for free-time activities.

**Critical thinking:** Develop opinions about likes and dislikes and indicate preferences for free-time activities.

**Language focus:** *Wh-* question forms with *What, When, Who* and *Do you ...?* (a review).

**Vocabulary:** Free-time activities: *play video games, painting, play football, take photos, meet up with my friends, play the piano.* Expressing preferences: *quite like / can't stand / don't like / quite good at / hopeless at / prefer ... to*

**Materials:** poster paper or interactive whiteboard (IWB) slides.

## Learner's Book

###  Warm up

- To introduce the Big question, start by telling the class that this unit is going to be about life experiences. Explain that we can always learn something from our own and other people's experiences in life, including people from the past and well-known people. So the Big question is ... *What can we learn from our own and other people's life experiences?*
- Write the question on the board (for an electronic presentation, create a slide with interesting graphics). Tell learners that you are all going to do tasks and projects in the unit that will answer the question.
- Introduce the unit objectives to show learners what tasks are coming up. Present the objectives on a slide or large piece of poster paper to attach to the board.
- Tell learners that you will answer the Big question and look again at the objectives at the end of the unit. Keep the objectives slide/poster to revisit at the end of the unit.
- Tell learners that you are going to start by looking at *free-time activities.* You (the teacher) are going to mime an activity you like doing in your free time and they have to guess what it is. Choose one from the pictures in the book, mime it and elicit the whole phrase (e.g. *take photos*). Mime a couple more yourself, or ask learners to come to the front of the class and mime. The idea is to get learners thinking about the topic and to generate words and phrases that they already know.
- Focus learners on the first page of the unit and ask if they can see any of the mimed activities in the pictures.

## 1 Talk about it

Put learners in pairs and ask them to talk about the two questions. Model the activity first with a pair of learners in front of the class.

- **Additional support and practice:** Structure the pair work by giving each learner a letter. Ask the first question to Bs (and then swap over).
- Point learners to the second question and ask them to identify free-time activities that they do from the pictures.
- **Critical thinking:** Learners identify their own preferences from a choice of activities. Learners can be challenged by being asked to give reasons too.

> **Answers**
> Learners' own answers.

## 2 Word study

- Focus attention on the phrases in the box and ask learners to match them to the pictures.

> **Answers**
> a play the piano
> b take photos
> c play football
> d paint
> e play video games
> f meet up with my friends

## 3 Listen 2

- Tell the class that they are going to listen to a girl interviewing her classmates. Elicit from learners what they think the topic of the interview will be about (free-time activities).
- Focus learners' attention on the instruction in the book and ask them to tell you what they have to do while listening to the interview for the first time (write the activities that they hear in **Activity 2** in their notebooks).
- Play the interview; listen for and write the activities mentioned from **Activity 2**.

> **Differentiated instruction**
>
> **Additional support and practice**
> - Learners who need more support could write the activities first and then tick the ones they hear in the interview.
>
> **Extend and challenge**
> - Elicit other activities mentioned by the children in the interview (*play basketball; watch TV; draw cartoons; play guitar; watch movies/films; go to the park*). Ask learners which activities from the interview they talked about in **Activity 1**.

> **Answers**
> Meet up with my friends / play video games / take photos

**Girl:** Hi Hatem, Lucas ... Have you both got a minute?

**Hatem & Lucas:** Hi ... yeah, sure ...

**Girl:** I'm interviewing classmates for an article in the school magazine. We want to know what you all get up to when you're not at school. What do you like doing when you've got some free time?

**Hatem:** I really love playing basketball. There's a court near the block of flats where I live and I love meeting up with my friends and having a game. I really like being outside ... .

**Girl:** So, in general, do you prefer doing activities inside or outside?

**Hatem:** Outside, definitely! I don't like spending my free time inside. I quite like watching TV sometimes, but I can't stand playing video games or anything like that. They're too repetitive – they give me a headache!

**Girl:** Really? OK. Thanks, Hatem. What about you, Lucas?

**Lucas:** I don't mind being inside actually. I'm quite good at art and I love drawing cartoons, so I do a lot of that in my free time. I'm better at drawing and playing the guitar than sport. I'm hopeless at basketball – I keep tripping over and dropping the ball!

**Girl:** So Lucas ... when you go out, which places do you like going to?

**Lucas:** I love going to the park to take photos for my drawings, and watching films at the cinema. I prefer watching films on the big screen to watching DVDs at home.

**Hatem:** For me, it's the basketball court around the corner and the park.

**Girl:** And who do you spend your free time with?

**Hatem:** Mostly my friends who live in my block of flats and my older brother and his friends too.

**Lucas:** I go to the park with my two best friends usually and I spend a lot of time with my big sister. She's studying art at college and she helps me a lot with my drawing.

## 4 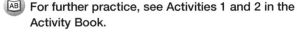 Listen 2

- Focus learners' attention on the phrases a–e. Tell them that they are going to listen again to complete the phrases. Before they listen, ask them to predict what words might be missing.
- Listen to check. Then complete the sentences in notebooks.

> **Answers**
> a quite/stand
> b mind
> c at
> d at
> e prefer/to

[AB] **For further practice, see Activities 1 and 2 in the Activity Book.**

## 5 [AB] Use of English

- Ask learners if they can remember any of the questions asked by the interviewer. Then focus attention on the **Use of English** box.

- Conduct a short review of *Wh-* question forms, focusing on the order of the components. Ask learners to tell you which words in the example questions are *question words* (**What/Who/Which**), then which words follow the question words (**do** + **you** + *verb*).
- Answer the question in **Activity 5** together as a class. To keep learners engaged, tell them to close/cover their books and then elicit the last two questions in the **Use of English** box word by word. If necessary mime or give clues to elicit each word (*Tell me a question word! Give me a preposition!*)
  1 *Who do you spend your free time with?*
  2 *Which places do you like going to?*
  Then elicit the main components of each question to show what happens to the order of the words.

> **Answers**
> 1 Question word (*Who*) + *do* (auxiliary verb) + *you* (subject) + verb (*spend*)
> 2 Question word (*Which*) + object (*places*) + *do* (auxiliary verb) + *you* (subject) + verb (*like*)

[AB] **For further practice, see Activity 3 in the Activity Book.**

## 6 Read

- Focus learners on the quotes in **Activity 6**. Conduct a quick reading race to keep learners focused and encourage them to notice key information. Ask questions like:
  *Who likes meeting up with his/her cousins?* (Answer - b)
  *Who likes being outdoors?* (Answer - d)
- Then ask learners to read the questions and match with a quotation. If your learners need more support, do the first one together as a class. The rest of the task can be done individually or in pairs.

> **Answers**
> 1 c   2 a   3 d   4 b

## 7 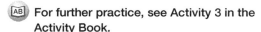 Talk

- Tell learners that they are now going to interview each other using the questions in **Activity 6**. First, practise the questions to ensure learners are confident with pronunciation.

> **Differentiated instruction**
>
> **Additional support and practice**
>
> - You could use the effective *backchaining* method to drill the questions, starting with the last word and building up the question from there, e.g. Question (4) could be drilled like this: *With?* (Learners repeat) *Time with? Free time with? Your free time with? Spend your free time with? Do you spend your free time with? Who do you spend your free time with?*
> - Split learners into pairs and tell them to interview each other using the questions in the book. They need to listen to their partner's answers and write short notes. Model the procedure first by asking a confident learner a question, and focus class

attention on which words you are noting down (on the board) from the answer. Point out to learners that you are only noting down the words that directly answer the questions. Keep the example on the board for **Activity 8**.

**Teacher:** *When you go out, which **places** do you like going to, Eva?*

**Eva:** *Well, I really like going to the **park** which is very **near my house**. It's very beautiful and there is lots of space ...*

**Notes:** *park     near     house*

- Stress to learners that this is a speaking activity and they should try and give full and interesting answers, even if their partner is only noting down basic details.

**Extend and challenge**

- To develop learners' fluency and to discourage them from simply reading the questions directly from the book, try a disappearing drill. Tell learners to close their books. Write each question on the board, eliciting the words from learners. Erase a couple of words and ask learners to repeat the question. Erase more words and ask them to repeat again; leave the partially completed question on the board and repeat the procedure with the other questions. Then tell them to interview each other, using just the words on the boards as question prompts.

 For further practice, see Activity 4 in the Activity Book.

## 8  Write

- Tell learners that they are now going to use their notes to write a short summary of their partner's answers to each question. Demonstrate by going back to the notes you made on the board in the previous stage. Elicit a full summary sentence from the notes, for example:

**Notes:** *park     near     house*

**Summary:** *Eva likes going to the park near her house.*

- Learners make their notes into summary sentences. They complete the activity individually, either in class or for homework.

 For further practice, see Activity 5 in the Activity Book.

## ↪ Wrap up

- To finish off, nominate learners to tell the class about activities that they had in common with their partner and ones that were very different.

## Activity Book

### 1 Vocabulary

- Learners complete short texts (speech bubbles) with a verb phrase or noun from the box.

**Answers**

| | |
|---|---|
| 1 playing football | 4 play the piano |
| 2 painting | 5 meet up with my friends |
| 3 take photos | 6 play video games |

## 2 Word study

- Learners read the texts in **Activity 1** and underline eight phrases that describe *preferences and abilities*.

**Answers**

| | |
|---|---|
| 1 really like | 5 love |
| 2 prefer | 6 quite good at |
| 3 hopeless at | 7 can't stand |
| 4 don't like | 8 hate |

## 3 Use of English

- Learners make questions with *Wh-* question words by rearranging jumbled words. They then match the questions to the answers (the speech bubbles) in **Activity 1**.

**Answers**

1 *How much free time do you have?* Response **c**
2 *What do you do at the weekends?* **d**
3 *Who do you like playing football with?* **a**
4 *Which activities do you prefer?* **b**

## 4 Word study

- Learners make their own sentences to describe their own activity preferences using prompts (in the form of the target phrases from **Activity 2**).

**Answers**
Learners' own answers.

## 5 📝 Challenge

- Learners write four *Wh-* questions that they would like to ask a famous person (of their choice). They imagine and write down the responses.

**Answers**
Learners' own answers.

# Lesson 2: A first time for everything

Learner's Book pages: 8–9
Activity Book pages: 6–7

## Lesson objectives

**Reading:** Understanding general meaning by identifying key words in a text.

**Speaking:** Expressing feelings about special experiences.

**Critical thinking:** What makes some experiences special? What feelings do they generate?

**Language focus:** Present perfect to describe experiences (time unspecified).

**Vocabulary:** Noun and adjective forms, describing emotions and feelings: *amazement/amazing; beauty/beautiful; terror/terrifying; pride/proud; bravery/brave; excitement/exciting; satisfaction/satisfying*

**Materials:** pictures reflecting a special experience you've had (for **Warm up**). Copies of **Photocopiable activity 1.**

## Learner's Book

###  Warm up

- Introduce the topic by telling the class briefly about a special experience you've had in your life, such as visiting a special place, or learning to do something for the first time (e.g. learning enough of a new language to have a conversation; learning a new sport, learning to drive, etc.). Show some pictures to elicit what you are going to talk about; tell the class briefly about your experience and ask them how they think the experience made you feel. Write any good suggestions on the board to come back to later; use this opportunity to introduce any words that later come up in **Activity 3.**

### 1 Talk about it

- Focus attention on the first two questions. Elicit responses from volunteers, or nominate learners and ask them the questions. Write any interesting words to describe feelings on the board to support learners when they talk in pairs in the next stage.
- Put learners in pairs and ask them to ask each other the questions.
- **Critical thinking:** Learners give a personal response and express personal feelings.

---

**Answers**
Learners' own answers.

---

### Reading strategy

- Draw learners' attention to the **Reading Strategy** and the idea of approaching a reading text in *stages*, rather than trying to tackle all aspects of the text at once. The first step is to understand the general meaning (rather than details) by looking for key words first. Make learners aware of what they do understand in the text and then pick out certain words (*key words*) that link closely with the main theme of the text and have strong images or associations with it. Images and headings around the text will also give clues to help identify general meaning and key words.
- Ask learners which approach they think makes more sense: to try and understand every word in a text the first time you read it, or approach the text step by step, first trying to understand the general meaning by picking out key words and then reading for detail if the task requires. Encourage learners to see that the second approach will support them better in managing reading texts.
- Further guidance and practice is given on how to identify key words in this unit.

### 2 Read

- Focus attention on the pictures and texts. Tell learners that they are going to read about when someone did something for the first time. Ask them to look at the pictures and quickly predict key themes in each child's story (i.e. *the sea; a rollercoaster; swimming*).
- Tell them that they are going to read the texts and explain the first reading task: while they are reading, they need to find key words and short phrases which show *what each child did*, *why it was special* and *how the experience made them feel*. Write these headings on the board to focus learners on the task.
- Before they read, demonstrate the task with the whole class. Write the first sentence of story 1 on the board and ask learners to identify the key words (in bold):
  *It doesn't seem so amazing now, but I remember the* **first time** *I saw the* **sea** *on a* **school trip**.
  (These words link closely with the main theme of the text.)
- Ask learners to complete the activity individually, then compare their choices of key words with a partner.
- **Additional support and practice:** Ask learners to read individually and then look for key words in pairs.
- **Critical thinking:** At the end, ask learners to respond to the children's experiences. *Which of these experiences have you had? How did you feel when you learned to swim? Did you feel like Cody? Can you remember the first time you saw the sea? How did it make you feel? Have you ever been on a rollercoaster? Did you have similar feelings to Santok?*

---

**Answers**
**Key words:** (Olivia) – first time / sea / school trip / amazement / beautiful / huge
(Santok) – rollercoaster / scared / exciting / terrifying / sense of pride
(Cody) – proud / learned to swim / excitement / satisfied / six years old / fear of water.

---

 **For further practice, see Activities 1 and 2 in the Activity Book.**

### 3 Word study

- Ask learners to copy the table in their notebooks; then read the texts again and find the corresponding adjectives and nouns. Do the first one together as a class; then have learners complete the rest, either individually or in pairs (for extra support if needed).
- Ask learners to find another adjective/noun pair in the last text (not included in the table) (Answer: *fear/ afraid*).
- Point out commonly used phrases (word chunks) that go with some of the nouns, e.g. *a sense of pride, feel proud of myself, a feeling of excitement, in amazement.*
- Any good suggestions that came up in the **Warm up** (for words to describe feelings) could be revisited here and added to this list. If learners suggested words/phrases that appear in the **Word study**, point this out so that they gain a further association to help them remember the words.

- Do some pronunciation practice to prepare learners for the next speaking activity by drilling the nouns and adjectives. Emphasise syllable stress by clapping (or similar) and ask learners to do the same.

**Answers**
| | |
|---|---|
| a amazement | e brave |
| b beautiful | f excitement |
| c terrifying | g satisfied |
| d pride | |

 **For further practice, see Activities 3 and 4 in the Activity Book.**

## 4 Talk

- **Critical thinking:** Tell learners that they are going to think of some experiences of their own to match the adjectives and nouns in **Activity 3**. Ask them some questions (as follows or similar) and tell them to write notes:
  *Write down something you've done that was **amazing**.*
  *When did you last feel **a sense of pride** about something you did?*
  *When was the last time you had **a feeling of excitement**?*
- Put learners in pairs and ask them to tell each other about an experience or feeling they have had, using their notes as prompts. Give a time limit.
- **Extend and challenge:** Ask early finishers to look at their table and think of more experiences or feelings to match the other adjectives and nouns.

**Answers**
Learners' own answers.

## 5 Use of English

- Write the three examples from the **Use of English** box on the board, leaving a space for the present perfect forms (e.g. _____ *you ever* _____ *the sea?*). Elicit the missing components from learners. Change 'you' to 'he' and elicit what happens to 'have'.
- Ask learners some concept-check questions to establish when the present perfect form is used in this context. E.g. *What are the sentences and questions talking about?* (Experiences/doing things) *Do we know exactly when the experiences happened?* (No)
- Focus learners on **Activity 5** and ask them to work out if the statements are true or false. If false, they need to correct the statements.
- Review the answers as a class. Clarify any confusions with the concept by presenting more example sentences and asking the concept questions again.

**Answers**
1 true
2 false – we use the present perfect when we <u>don't know</u> the time something happened, or if the time is not important.

 **For further practice, see Activities 5 and 6 in the Activity Book.**

## 6  Talk

- Ask learners to match questions a–c with the stories in **Activity 2**. Ask them which key words in

the questions helped them match with the stories (e.g. *felt really proud/ seen something ... amazing/ done something ... scared of*).
- Draw learners' attention to the secondary questions *What did you do?* and *What did you see?* and the tense (past simple). Ask why the tense changes in these questions (Answer: in the second question, we want to know specifically *when* something happened; in the first this isn't important).
- Tell learners that they are now going to write two more questions to ask their partner to find out about interesting experiences. Elicit a few examples from the class. To give more scope for suggestions, encourage learners to focus on something specific e.g. *Have you ever tried Japanese/Italian/Thai food?* Then elicit a follow-up question to find out more information, e.g. *When/where did you try it?*
- Give learners two minutes to write two more questions to ask their partner. Monitor and check learners are using correct forms.
- Put learners in pairs to ask and answer all five questions. Give them a time limit.
- **Additional support and practice:** To build learners' confidence in speaking, drill the first three questions. You could try a whispering drill to help learners gain confidence: ask them to repeatedly whisper the questions and then gradually raise their voices.

**Answers**
Learners' own answers.

## 7 Write

- Ask learners to choose one of their responses from **Activity 6** and write about it in their notebooks. They should use nouns and adjectives from **Activity 3** to describe how they felt.
- **Note:** This is a consolidation activity and can be done as a 'cooler' at the end of the class, or for homework.

**Answers**
Learners' own answers.

## Wrap up

- Ask learners to tell the class about interesting and surprising things they learned from their partner. Put prompts on the board, e.g. *The most unusual place visited/ the most exciting experience/ the scariest experience* (if appropriate), etc.

## Activity Book

### 1 Read

- Learners do a multiple-choice activity to support their understanding of the reading strategy. Then they read three comments about first-time activities and match to a picture.

**Answers**
1 b   2 c   3 a

## 2 Read

- Learners practise identifying key words in texts by finding key words and short phrases in the comments in **Activity 1**.

**Answers**

| | |
|---|---|
| Sumalee | *first time / elephant / terrified / never seen before / beautiful* |
| Jaya | *excited / learned / ride / bike / proud / four years old* |
| Callum | *rock climbing / first time / always / afraid / heights / satisfied / brave* |

## 3 Pronunciation 61 [CD2 Track 29]

- Learners identify stress patterns in target nouns and adjectives by listening to the words and choosing the correct stress pattern from a choice of two answers.

**Audioscript:** Track 61

1 terror

2 beauty

3 excitement

4 amazement

5 satisfaction

6 bravery

**Answers**
1 b   2 a   3 b   4 a   5 a   6 b

## 4 Word study

- Learners complete sentences in a gap-fill activity with target adjectives and nouns.

**Answers**

| | |
|---|---|
| **1** satisfied | **4** terrified |
| **2** excitement | **5** brave |
| **3** beautiful | |

## 5 Use of English

- Learners complete sentences with the correct form of the present perfect in a gap-fill activity.

**Answers**

| | |
|---|---|
| **1** has won | **3** has/been |
| **2** have/seen | **4** hasn't tried |

## 6 Challenge

- Learners write six sentences using the present perfect in their notebooks about things they have or haven't experienced.

**Answers**
Learners' own answers.

**For further practice using present perfect forms, see Photocopiable activity 1.**

# Lesson 3: Inspiring people

Learner's Book pages: 10–11

Activity Book pages: 8–9

### Lesson objectives

**Speaking:** Prepare and deliver a presentation about someone you admire.

**Listening:** Listen to a presentation and notice features of content and organisation.

**Critical thinking:** What kind of people do we admire and why?

**Vocabulary:** Words about music: *producer, talented, musician, admire, contract, perform*

**Sequencing words:** *since then, as well as this, to sum up.*

**Materials:** Pictures of idols and heroes (relatable or relevant to the country/culture in which you work).

## Learner's Book

### Warm up

- Put a selection of pictures on the board of well-known people, familiar to your learners, e.g. cultural icons (past and present), sports stars, people in entertainment. Make sure that these are people who have done admirable things, e.g. charity work, shown bravery or are good role models in sport (and not simply famous in their given profession).
- Ask learners to name the people and tell you something about what they have achieved. Establish that these are all people who have done good things and that we can call them *heroes* or *idols*.

## 1 Talk about it

- Ask learners, *Do you have a hero or an idol?* Point out to them that a hero or idol can be someone famous or someone they know (e.g. a member of their family or a friend). Elicit some responses and ask: *Why is this person your hero?* Write some responses on the board to build up some words and phrases to describe why we admire certain people.
- Ask learners to talk about the questions in pairs. Then nominate some learners to share their partner's responses with the class.
- Focus attention on the picture of will.i.am on page 10. Ask learners if they know who he is and, if so, what they know about him. Write any information that they offer onto the board in a spidergram (with will.i.am's name in the centre). This will help when learners listen to the presentation about will.i.am.

**Answers**
Learners' own answers.
will.i.am is a famous singer, musician and record producer

## 2 Listen 3

- Tell learners that they are going to listen to a presentation by Maria to her classmates about will.i.am, who is her hero. At this point, tell learners that later they are going to prepare their own presentation about someone they admire. First, they are going to look at Maria's presentation to help them when they prepare their own.
- Ask learners if they know why will.i.am could be Maria's hero (if they have not previously offered any information about his background or charity work).
- Tell learners that first, Maria wants to attract her classmates' attention to make sure they listen to her presentation. Ask them to listen to the first part and tell you how Maria does this. Tell them to concentrate only on this task and not to worry about trying to understand every word.
- Play the first part of the presentation; then pause and ask learners what Maria did to get the attention of her audience.
- **Additional support and practice:** If learners are slow to respond, read out the clues from the audioscript and ask what Maria wants her audience to do when they hear the clues. Elicit that she wants them to guess who she is going to talk about; in order to guess, her classmates have to listen to her clues. This mini-quiz gets her classmates' attention and makes them want to respond (as demonstrated in the audio).

**Audioscript:** Track 3

**Part 1**

**Maria:** Good morning everyone. Today I'm going to talk about a famous person that I admire. But first of all, I want you all to guess who it is. Here are some clues:

He is a famous musician but he also has lots of other jobs and projects.

His real name is William Adams and he was born in a poor part of Los Angeles in the USA.

He has performed for the US President, Barack Obama, and at a concert for the British queen.

He is a member of the group, the Black Eyed Peas ...

**Classmate:** I know! It's will.i.am!

**Maria:** Yes, that's right!

**Answers**
Maria asks her audience questions, which means they have to give a reply and this makes sure they are listening to her.

## 3 Listen 4

- Focus learners' attention on questions 1–4. Read them aloud to learners. If your class are familiar with will.i.am and his work, ask if anyone knows the answers already or point to any relevant information that was given in **Activity 1** in the spidergram (don't reveal yet whether any suggestions are correct). Then tell learners to listen to Part 2 and only focus on listening for the answers to the questions.
- Play the second part of the presentation, then pause and ask learners to discuss the answers in pairs.

- Elicit answers or listen again to check, if necessary.
- **Additional support and practice:** If learners are having difficulties, you could stop the audio after each relevant part and elicit answers 1–4, one by one.

**Audioscript:** Track 4

**Part 2**

**Maria:** So today I'm going to talk about the musician and songwriter, will.i.am. As I said in my introduction, he was born in East Los Angeles in the USA, in 1975. His family were quite poor, but his mum sent him to a school on the other side of the city, so he could get a better education.

At school, he became interested in music and he formed a rap group with two friends. This group signed a recording contract when will.i.am was just 18 years old.

Since then, will.i.am has become a world-famous musician. He is part of the successful pop group, the Black Eyed Peas and he has also worked with other famous singers such as Justin Bieber, Nicole Sherzinger, Britney Spears and Michael Jackson.

But will.i.am isn't just a singer, songwriter and musician. He is also a record producer, actor, DJ and a businessman. As well as this, will.i.am also gives a lot of his own money to educational projects, especially in science and technology. He has created an organisation called i.am.angel which helps poor students attend college.

**Answers**
1 will.i.am's mum.
2 He signed a recording contract.
3 He is also a record producer, actor, DJ and a businessman.
4 Science and technology.

## 4 Listen 5

- Focus learners' attention on the two questions and tell learners that they are going to listen for the answers in the last part. Check that they understand *admire*: if necessary, use the examples from the beginning of the lesson and point out that these are all people we *admire* (*think very well of because they have done something good*). Encourage learners to understand the word from the context it is presented in.
- Play the last part of the presentation; ask learners to listen out for one main reason why Maria admires will.i.am, and for how she finishes the presentation. Then ask learners to discuss the answers in pairs.
- Elicit answers or listen again to check if necessary.

**Audioscript:** Track 5

**Part 3**

**Maria:** To sum up, I chose to talk about will.i.am because I think he is very talented. He is good at lots of other things besides making music. I also really admire him because he uses his own money to help young people get a better education. He understands that young people are the future!

To finish my presentation, I'm going to play you my favourite Black Eyed Peas song ... *(audio fades)*

## 5 Listen

- Ask learners to look at the headings and to guess the order based on what they have just heard. If learners are sure of the order, then it shouldn't be necessary to play the whole presentation again at this point (there is an opportunity in the next activity); if they are unsure, then play it again.
- Go through the answers as a class, asking learners to remind you how Maria attracted her audience's attention in the first part.

**Answers**
Part 2, Part 3, Part 1

[AB] **For further practice, see Activities 2, 3 and 4 in the Activity Book.**

## 6 Word study

- Focus learners' attention on the words in the box. Ask them to repeat each one after you. Ask them if they remember hearing these words in Maria's presentation.
- Tell them that they are going to listen to the whole presentation again. When they hear one of these words, they have to raise their hands or stand up (make sure chairs are away from desks before the activity begins to avoid scraping interfering with the audio!).
- Play the audio; learners listen out for the words and raise hands/stand up when they hear them.
- After listening, ask learners to match the words with a definition.

**Answers**

| | |
|---|---|
| **1** contract | **4** producer |
| **2** musician | **5** admire |
| **3** talented | **6** perform |

## 7 Pronunciation 7

- Focus learners' attention on the words in **Activity 7** and ask them if they remember hearing these words in Maria's presentation. Ask them to practise saying the words themselves in pairs and try and identify which sound comes at the end of the words. Then play the audio for them to check and have them repeat the words. Ask again which sound they hear at the end of each word.

**Audioscript:** Track 7
1 musician
2 introduction
3 education
4 organisation
5 presentation

**Answers**
Sound heard at the end of these words is /ʃ.ən/

## 8 Use of English

- Focus learners on the sequencing phrases in the **Presentation tip**. Read them out and ask learners why these phrases are important in the presentation (they act as 'signposts' to help listeners follow the presentation).
- You could give them copies of the audioscript and ask them to underline or point to the phrases within the script. You could read the phrases aloud as they read, and have them put their hands up when they find them. Read the phrases in the order they appear, to reinforce the sequencing aspect. Alternatively, you could do the same activity without copies for learners. They listen to you reading the audioscript and put their hands up when they hear a sequencing phrase.
- Go back to the **Presentation tip** and ask learners to tell you which phrases are used at the beginning and end of the presentation.

**Answers**
Phrases at beginning: *Today I'm going to talk about ... / First of all ...*
Phrases at end: *To sum up ... / To finish my presentation ...*

### Present it!

- In preparation for learners delivering their own presentations, first, go through key points from Maria's presentation that they can draw on: 1) organising the presentation in sections using the headings in **Activity 5**; 2) attracting the audience's attention at the beginning with a question or *mini-quiz;* 3) using sequencing phrases to help listeners follow the presentation.
- Put learners into groups of three to prepare and deliver a presentation about one person they all admire. Together they research that person's life and work, and make notes under the headings in **Activity 5** (using the Internet or library). This can be done either in class time or at home. Learners could take a section each to research, but all should contribute their own views to the last section.
- Learners make slides or find other visual or audio aids to support their presentation (e.g. pictures, video clips, real objects, music).

- Ask learners to write out their presentation from their notes and produce one script per group, either in class time or at home. Check the scripts for grammar and vocabulary, although the emphasis is on organisation and quality of ideas rather than perfectly accurate scripts.
- **Extend and challenge:** As learners are delivering their presentations, note down main errors; either give to each group a note of the errors to correct themselves, or write up on the board at the end for a class error correction session (without stating which group or individual made the errors). **Note:** This would come after plenty of positive feedback regarding the presentations. Positive feedback must always come first and be emphasised.
- Give learners the opportunity to practise their presentations together. Each member of the group should deliver a part of the presentation. Monitor the groups, making sure you spend some time with each, helping with any pronunciation difficulties. Check that everyone has a part to present and that someone is responsible for visual prompts, operating slides, etc.
- **Critical thinking**: Before learners present to the class, give listeners a task by asking them to write down something they found interesting from each presentation. Tell them they can also ask any questions if they like.
- Have learners deliver their presentations in groups of three in front of the class. Introduce each group first and generate a supportive atmosphere by having learners applaud each group before and after each presentation. When each group finishes, make a positive comment about their presentation before welcoming the next group.
- **Additional support and practice:** Use of notes in delivery: stronger learners may be able to deliver without looking too closely at their notes; others may need to read from their notes at this stage. Use your discretion with regard to how much you allow this, taking into account ability and confidence levels in your class. Ultimately, in later years, learners need to be able to deliver oral presentations without reading word for word from notes. Ideally, we should encourage them to get into this habit as soon as possible, but learners will probably need the support of reading from their notes in these early stages.

## 👉 Wrap up

- Nominate learners to tell the class interesting facts that they noted from each presentation. Encourage learners to share other points that they liked about each other's presentations (e.g. visuals, music, the way someone delivered).

**Answers**
Learners' own answers.

## Activity Book

### 1 Word study

- Learners complete a paragraph with the target words from the box.

**Answers**
| | |
|---|---|
| **1** musicians | **4** producers |
| **2** performs | **5** admire |
| **3** talented | **6** contract |

### 2 Listen 62 [CD2 Track 30]

- Learners listen to a presentation and circle the correct answer (from two choices) in sentences about the presentation topic and components.

**Audioscript:** Track 62

**Gabi:** Today I'm going to talk about a group of people I admire, called the Recycled Orchestra. This special orchestra is a group of teenagers in Paraguay, South America, who make wonderful music with very unusual musical instruments. First of all, have a look at some pictures of the orchestra. Can you tell me what is different about the instruments? OK, you'll have to listen to find out!

As I said in my introduction, the Recycled Orchestra play very unusual musical instruments. They are special because they are all made out of recycled rubbish. The orchestra is part of a music school in a poor town near Paraguay's capital city. A huge landfill for rubbish sits near to the town and the Recycled Orchestra have turned the rubbish into a good thing. A few years ago, a carpenter made a beautiful violin out of the rubbish. He gave it to the music school because they didn't have enough instruments for all the children who wanted to play. After that, many more instruments were made out of the rubbish. This meant that more children could join the music school and the orchestra became stronger and stronger.

Since then, the orchestra has performed many concerts in their country and also in Brazil, Colombia and Panama. They play famous pieces of classical music and rock music too. As well as this, they have appeared in a film which tells their story and shows how music can improve children's lives and give hope for the future.

To sum up, I chose to talk about the Recycled Orchestra because their story shows how you can recycle rubbish into something really good. I admire the carpenter who had the clever idea of making instruments out of rubbish because his idea has given great opportunities to lots of children.

To finish, I'm going to play you a short video of some musicians from the Recycled Orchestra ...

**Answers**
| | |
|---|---|
| **1** a | **4** b |
| **2** b | **5** b |
| **3** a | **6** b |

## 3 Listen 62 [CD2 Track 30]

- Learners listen again and choose the correct sequencing phrases.

**Answers**
1 Today I'm going to
2 First of all,
3 As I said,
4 Since then,
5 As well as this,
6 To sum up,

## 4 Challenge

- Learners complete another model presentation with the correct sentences.

**Answers**
1 d   2 g   3 b   4 c   5 e   6 a   7 f

# Lesson 4: Extraordinary experiences

Learner's Book pages: 12–13
Activity Book pages: 10–11

### Lesson objectives

**Speaking:** Talk about characters from books and their authors, and how authors get their ideas. Discuss the issue of succeeding when life is difficult.

**Reading:** Read a biography of a well-known author.

**Writing:** Plan and write a short biography of a well-known person.

**Critical thinking:** Examining how the life of the author might have inspired a creative piece of work; looking at how a text is divided into paragraphs and the use of paragraph themes.

**Language focus:** Past continuous tense to describe past actions happening at the same time as another action.

**Vocabulary:** Verbs with prepositions

**Materials:** A picture of any well-known author familiar to your learners; a selection of story books; pictures of familiar well-known people who have achieved success despite adversity (optional). Copies of **Photocopiable activity 2**.

### Learner's Book

### ☞ Warm up

- Before learners open their books, play '*20 questions*' with your class. Choose an author that they know and like as your subject.
- Hold the author's picture so that the class can't see the image. Tell learners to ask you questions to guess the name of the well-known person in the picture. They can ask a maximum of 20 'yes/no' questions, for example: *Does this person live in* (country)*? Is it a man or a woman? Does he play a sport? Has she written a book?*, etc. You could make it into a competition and

give points to teams or individuals: e.g. a point for a question with correct grammar, an extra five points for guessing correctly.

- When learners have guessed correctly, talk a little bit about the author, e.g. *who are the characters in his/her books? What do you know about the author and his/her life?*

## 1 ☺ Talk about it

- For this stage, you could show learners some other books and ask if they know who the characters are and anything about the authors. Then focus on the first two questions and ask them to discuss their answers in pairs.
- Do some quick feedback, asking learners to tell the class which book characters they talked about. Then ask if anyone has any information about the authors themselves.
- **Critical thinking**: Ask learners if they have ever written a story (or refer to a specific story-writing activity that your class have taken part in). Ask them where they got their ideas for the characters. Then ask if they know, or can guess, where some of the authors they have just discussed got their ideas for characters.

**Answers**
Learners' own answers.

## 2 Read

- Focus learners on the picture of JK Rowling. Elicit any information that learners already know about her (including the answer to the first question, *Which famous story character did she create?*) and write suggestions on the board in a spidergram.
- Tell learners that they are going to read a short biography of JK Rowling. Elicit what a biography is (the story of someone's life, written by another person). Focus on the second question and read it aloud to learners (only focus on the first question if it has not been answered in the first stage). Explain that the learners are going to read the text quickly and that they are just looking for the answer to this question; they should not try to understand every word at this stage. Give learners a time limit of about two minutes.
- After reading, ask learners to briefly discuss the initial question/s in pairs and then elicit the answers.
- **Extend and challenge:** As well as the set questions, ask learners if the text mentioned any of the information that they offered in the first stage (recorded in the spidergram).

**Answers**
Harry Potter. 6 years

## 3 ✍ Read

- Focus learners on the statements (1–5). Read them together and ask if anyone already knows which are true or false. Then tell learners to read the text again, this time more slowly, and decide if the statements are true or false. After reading, they should discuss the statements with their partner and correct any that they think are false in their notebook.

**Answers**
**1** false. She was unknown/not famous.
**2** false. She studied at a UK university.
**3** true
**4** false. She is a world-famous author.
**5** false. Adults like them too.

## 4 🗣 Talk

- Ask learners to look at the questions. Check that they understand the word *inspiring* (someone or something who shows us that it is possible to do something very good) and ask what we can learn from JK Rowling's story (suggestions: she shows that it is possible to turn ideas into best-selling books; she never forgot about her ideas, even when she didn't have time to do anything with them; she never gave up on her dream of being a writer). Ask why it was difficult for JK Rowling to start writing the Harry Potter books before she did (she was a single mum with a small daughter to look after).
- **Critical thinking:** Ask learners to discuss the two questions in pairs, stressing that the focus here is to give personal opinions (they may disagree that JK Rowling is inspiring and have differing opinions about what constitutes a 'difficult life' and that is fine).
- **Additional support and practice:** If you think learners might struggle to think of examples, show the class a few pictures of examples, then ask or give clues to elicit what they have in common.
- Nominate some pairs to give feedback to the class about what they discussed.

**Answers**
Learners' own answers.

## 5 Read

- At this point tell learners that later they are going to write their own biography of a well-known person. Point out that this activity will help them organise their own biographies. Ask them to look at the text again and tell you how many paragraphs there are (numbered 1–4 in the text).
- Ask learners why they think texts are divided into paragraphs and elicit or tell them that paragraphs make the different themes in the text clearer and easier for the reader to follow. Draw their attention to the **Writing tip**. Read the themes a–d and ask learners to read the text again, matching a theme to a paragraph.
- **Additional support and practice:** Elicit or point out to learners the information in the paragraphs that matches each theme description (a–d).
- Draw learners' attention to the theme in (d). This is a common feature in conclusions or final paragraphs, and one that is often quite hard for learners to grasp when they are writing their own texts. Elicit from

learners what special message this text gives at the end (see last sentence of text).

**Answers**
**a** 3   **b** 1   **c** 2   **d** 4

 **For further practice, see Activities 1 and 2 in the Activity Book.**

## 6 📝 Word study

- Tell the class to look at the blue words in the text. Read each one out and ask what they notice about the words. What kind of words are they? (Verbs and prepositions) How many parts do they have? (2 or 3)
- Focus learners on the sentences 1–5. Ask them to read each one first and then decide which verb is needed to complete the sentence. Do (a) together as a class and ask if the form needs to be changed for this sentence (it doesn't).
- Ask learners to complete the activity in pairs. Point out that they need to: 1) choose the correct verb and 2) decide if the form needs to be changed.
- **Additional support and practice:** You could decide as a class first which verbs need a change of form and what form is needed, rather than leave learners to decide in pairs (in (c), (d) and (e) all verbs change to past simple form – *bring / brought up; sell / sold out; turn / turned into*).
- Point out to learners that multi-word verbs are best learned in 'chunks' (taking in all parts) and in context (focus on the meaning and association). Learners need to be encouraged to think of these types of verbs as whole units and learn accordingly.

**Answers**
**1** give up on
**2** think of
**3** brought up
**4** sold out
**5** turned into

### Use of English

- Ask learners to close their books. Write the first sentence from the **Use of English** box on the board (*While she was working full time ...*). You could try eliciting each word after *While* from learners to engage their attention, or ask them to find the sentence (starting with *While*) in the text and tell you what it is, although this will require learners to reopen their books to look at the reading text.
- Ask learners if they can remember what JK Rowling was doing *at the same time* as working full time. Elicit or tell learners that *she was bringing up her small daughter*.
- Ask learners how many actions there are in the two sentences (two) and if they are in the present or the past (past). Ask if one was happening *after* the other, or if they were happening *at the same time* (at the same time). Ask how we know they were happening at the same time and elicit or tell learners that we know because of the tense used (past continuous).

## 7 Use of English

- Focus attention on **Activity 7** and ask learners to complete the rule about forming the past continuous tense.

> **Answers**
> were/-ing

## 8  Write

- These activities can be done at home, if necessary. Elicit from learners which tense they need to use to complete the sentences (past continuous) and the reason why (because they are describing actions that were happening at the same time as other actions in the past). Draw their attention to the fact that these sentences need to be completed with their own ideas, recording real events about themselves.

> **Answers**
> Learners' own answers.

 **For further practice, see Activity 3 in the Activity Book.**

##  Write

- **Critical thinking:** Tell learners they are going to write their own biographies. Draw their attention to the suggested categories and the **Writing tip** about paragraph themes. Brainstorm ideas for biography subjects.
- Learners will probably need some time to research their subjects. This can be done outside of class. In this case, set this and the writing of the first draft for homework. You could then allow time in the next class for learners to polish up their drafts while you circulate and offer assistance. They then write a final draft.

> **Answers**
> Learners' own answers – Portfolio opportunity.

 **For further practice, see Activity 4 in the Activity Book.**

##  Wrap up

- When you have corrected the biographies, hand out to learners to read each other's work (one per learner). Ask them to make a note of who the biography is about and why the person is well known.

## Activity Book

### 1 Read

- Learners read a biography and put the paragraphs in order according to a list of headings

> **Answers**
> 1 b    2 d    3 c    4 a

## 2 Read

- Learners answer comprehension questions about the text.

> **Answers**
> 1 Fabrice Muamba.
> 2 During a football match, he had a heart attack in front of thousands of fans and nearly died.
> 3 The Democratic Republic of Congo, Africa.
> 4 11 years old.
> 5 He got excellent exam results in English, French and Mathematics.
> 6 In 2008.
> 7 No, he has stopped playing football.
> 8 The doctors who saved his life/helped him get better.

## 3 Use of English

- Learners complete sentences using the correct form of the past continuous with verbs from the box.

> **Answers**
> 1 was playing/were cheering
> 2 was lying/were working
> 3 was studying/was playing
> 4 was learning/was going
> 5 was getting/were celebrating

## 4  Challenge

- Learners write a biography of a well-known person using paragraph prompts.

> **Answers**
> Learners' own answers.

**For further practice in using past continuous forms, see Photocopiable activity 2.**

## Lesson 5: An inspiring life

Learner's Book pages: 14–15
Activity Book pages: 12–13

> ### Lesson objectives
>
> **Listening and reading:** Listen to and read a biography of an inspiring person from the past.
>
> **Speaking:** Discuss attitudes to blindness and deafness.
>
> **Writing:** Make a list of fair ways to treat blind and deaf people.
>
> **Critical thinking:** Compare attitudes to blindness and deafness in past and present times; establishing fair ways to treat blind and deaf people.
>
> **Vocabulary:** Verb–noun collocations, describing achievements: *give a speech, receive an award, do research, write an article, go to college, raise money*
>
> **Materials:** positive images associated with blind/deaf people (see **Warm up**), poster paper and pens.

## Learner's Book

###  Warm up

- Show learners some positive images associated with blindness and deafness that are relevant to the culture in which you work, e.g. a picture of a guide dog, something written in braille, signs seen in public places (shops, libraries, etc.) to indicate that assistance is available, a video clip or a picture of someone signing, etc. Ask learners to tell you what they understand from these images. Pre-teach *blind* and *deaf,* if necessary.
- Once you have established the association of the images, ask learners to tell you what day-to-day challenges blind and deaf people face. Then show how each item is used to address these challenges.

### 1 Talk about it

- Focus on the two questions and ask learners what they think life was like for blind and deaf people in the past. Elicit or give information yourself (if learners do not know) and write notes on the board. Then contrast with the information generated in the **Warm up** to show how things are different today. Keep your notes about past and present attitudes visible on the board (in preparation for the first reading activity).
- If necessary, search the Internet for websites giving information about historical attitudes to blind and deaf people, conditions and education.
  **Note:** Today, in many countries, people who are blind can be found in a variety of professions: judges, lawyers, accountants, secretaries, librarians, teachers, doctors. There are famous blind musicians, such as Stevie Wonder and Ray Charles and public figures like the British MP, David Blunkett. Facilities for blind and deaf people have improved immensely – in many countries people have guide dogs, public service provision and care in the home. There are national organisations that protect the rights of blind and deaf people, especially in the work place.

> **Answers**
> Learners' own answers.

### 2 Read 8

- Tell learners that they are going to listen to and read about a person from history who worked very hard to change attitudes towards blind and deaf people. If you think learners may have already heard of Helen Keller, give them a few clues from the text to elicit her name; if your learners won't have heard of her, tell them her name, nationality and that she was completely blind and deaf for most of her life. To generate interest, write the following statements on the board and ask learners to tell you if they think they are true or false:
  *1 During her life, Helen travelled all over the world.*
  *2 She met a US president.*
  *3 She spoke English and could read four other languages.*

**Audioscript:** Track 8
See Learner's Book pages 14–16.

> **Answers**
> **1** true
> **2** false – she met 12 US presidents!
> **3** true

- Tell the class to listen and read the whole text quickly, looking for the ideas that have already been mentioned in **Activity 1**. Draw learners' attention to the notes on the board about past and present attitudes. Stress to them that, at this point, they only need look for this information and not to worry about words they do not understand.
- Start the audio and tell learners to read the text while listening.
- After reading/listening, conduct a short feedback session pointing out information generated from **Activity 1** that also appears in the text.
- In preparation for learners reading the text again (to answer the comprehension questions), pre-teach the following words, paragraph by paragraph.
  **Part 1:** *dozen, respect, independent, vision*
  *When you can look after yourself* (independent)
  *A word that means 'twelve of something'* (dozen)
  *When you think very well of someone and listen to their opinions* (respect)
  *A word that means 'the ability to see'* (vision)
  **Part 2:** *manual, sign language*
  *A way of communicating for deaf people using hand gestures* (this may have come up in **Activity 1** and could be mimed here as a reminder) (sign language).
  *An adjective meaning 'by hand'* (manual).
  **Part 3:** *bent down, tapped* (these actions can be mimed, no definitions needed).
- Write the words on the board and ask learners to find the words in the text. Then read out the definitions and elicit the corresponding word.

> **Differentiated instruction**
>
> **Additional support and practice**
> - When pre-teaching the vocabulary, conduct a reading race: read the definitions in the order that the words appear in the text and ask learners to find the word, e.g. *Find me a word that means 'twelve of something'.* Do this one part at a time.
> - After learners have written the answers for questions 1–12, put them in groups of four to check their answers together.
> - Allow time for this before giving feedback on the answers. Where possible, use the pictures in the book to illustrate the answers.
>
> **Extend and challenge**
> - Learners could work in pairs to do the comprehension questions 1–12.
> - Tell learners that they are going to read each paragraph again to find more details. Draw their attention to the questions after each part. They should read and then answer the questions in their notebooks.

**Answers**
1 She became blind and deaf.
2 She taught the world to respect blind and deaf people.
3 a
4 They hired a teacher, Anne Sullivan.
5 She taught Helen how to spell words with her hands.
6 Helen didn't understand what the words meant.
7 Anne held Helen's hand under the water so she could feel it.
8 30 words.
9 By feeling her teacher's mouth as she talked.
10 a
11 a
12 b

 **For further practice, see Activities 1 and 2 in the Activity Book.**

## 3 🗨 Talk

- Keep learners in groups of four and ask them to look at **Activity 3**. Ask them to look at the text again and find five facts about Helen's life that surprised them. Then each person should choose one that surprised them the most.
- Do a quick class feedback session, nominating learners to tell the class about their choices.
- As a class, ask learners to tell you some important things that Helen did to help other blind people. Draw their attention in particular to the last paragraph of the text. Write their suggestions on the board.
- Tell them to discuss again in groups and decide on one example that they feel is the most important. Then ask one learner from each group to tell the class their answer.

> **Answers**
> Learners' own answers.

## 4 Word study

- Focus learners' attention on the verb/noun collocations in the box. Read each one aloud and ask learners to match them to the definitions in pairs. Tell them to find the words in the text to check their answers (most phrases are in the last paragraph; one is in the first (*go to college*) and another in Part 3 (*write an article*)).

> **Answers**
> 1 do research
> 2 give a speech
> 3 write an article
> 4 receive an award
> 5 raise money
> 6 go to college

 **For further practice, see Activity 3 in the Activity Book.**

## 5 🗨 Talk

- **Critical thinking:** Put learners in groups of four again and focus them on the question. Start by telling them that you (or someone you know) has achieved one (or more) of these activities and ask them to guess which one. Then ask if anyone in the class can give an example.
- Learners then think of their own examples in their groups. Circulate and help if necessary by asking individual groups questions to help them link the activities to real-life examples. *Do you have any older brothers, sisters or cousins who have gone to college or university? Did you read about that man in our town who won an award for ...? Why did Class X do the sponsored walk last year?*, etc.
- Conduct a class feedback session and try and elicit an example for each activity.

> **Answers**
> Learners' own answers.

## 6 🗨 Values

- Focus learners on the questions. If you feel it is appropriate, you could ask the class together if they know anyone who is blind or deaf and what they know about their life. However, be sensitive to the fact that some children may not be comfortable discussing someone close to them (e.g. a family member).
- **Critical thinking:** Ask learners to discuss the two parts of question 1 in pairs. Then conduct a short class feedback. You could ask learners to give you adjectives to describe what it might be like to be blind or deaf, as this might be an easier way for learners to respond to the second question.
- Focus learners on question 2. Check that they are clear about the meaning of *respect* (from earlier in the lesson: *treating a person with kindness, consideration, valuing who they are and treating them like an equal*). Ask them to think of three ways that we can all make sure we respect blind and deaf people.

> **Answers**
> Learners' own answers.

 **For further practice, see Activity 4 in the Activity Book.**

## 7 📝 Write

- **Critical thinking:** Put learners into groups of four again. Ask them to pool their ideas and make a list of fair ways to treat blind or deaf people, using the prompts (a) and (b). Tell them that this is a first draft that they will turn into a poster in the next stage. Monitor and circulate, giving support with grammar and vocabulary.
- Have learners refine their drafts into final sentences that they will put on a poster. Learners then make posters (one per group), adding visual images if they wish.

- **Additional support and practice:** To focus learners during group work, give them roles (or let them decide who does what). In this case, two learners could write the points and two could organise/draw the artwork and the layout of the poster. You could assign roles according to ability and interest, if appropriate.
- Display the posters on the wall and have learners walk around and read each other's, making a note of any different points that they didn't mention on their own posters.

> **Answers**
> Learners' own answers.

##  Wrap up

- Ask for volunteers to report back to the class about the points they noted.

## Activity Book

### 1 Read

- Learners read the biography about Helen Keller in the Learner's Book on pages 14–16 again and decide if sentences about the text are true or false. They correct the false sentences.

> **Answers**
> 1 false. It was difficult because there were few opportunities.
> 2 false. She was 18 months old.
> 3 true
> 4 false. Helen learned to speak when she was ten years old.
> 5 true
> 6 true
> 7 false. People could read her first book in 50 languages.
> 8 true

### 2 Read

- Learners complete sentences about the text with a number from the box. They then order the sentences to reflect the order of events outlined in the text.

> **Answers**
> a 20,/(Order) **6**
> b 100/**1**
> c 7/**3**
> d 18/**2**
> e 10/**5**
> f 39/12/**7**
> g 30/**4**

### 3 Vocabulary

- Learners complete sentences using the target verb/noun phrases from the box, using the correct form of the verb.

> **Answers**
> 1 gives a speech    4 raised money
> 2 go to university    5 wrote an article
> 3 received an award    6 doing research

### 4 Challenge

- Learners look at a range of signs found in public places and indicating support for blind and deaf people. They write down their ideas about what the signs mean and where they might see them.

> **Answers**
> Learners' own answers and following suggestions:
> **Meanings:**
> a blind person with stick; access and assistance available for blind people (this place is suitable for blind people to walk and travel).
> b ear symbol; equipment is available here to help/support people with hearing difficulties.
> c large print sign: copies of these books/leaflets are available in bigger writing.
> d two signing hands symbol: there is someone here who can communicate in sign language.
> e guide dogs allowed sign: you can bring your guide dog into this place / guide dogs are allowed here.
> f braille sign: copies of these books are available in braille.
>
> **Places:** You might see these signs in public places, such as schools, community centres, libraries, hospitals, shops and museums.

# Lesson 6: Choose a project

Learner's Book page: 18

### Lesson objectives

**Talk:** Deliver a presentation; conduct a survey; revise unit themes; discuss **Unit 1** Big question.

**Write:** Organise and prepare notes for a presentation; record survey responses and write a mini-report; revise unit themes.

**Critical thinking:** Apply new skills and language acquired in **Unit 1** to project work and revision activities.

**Language focus:** Recycling language points from **Unit 1**, i.e. question forms; present perfect; sequencing words.

**Vocabulary:** Recycling of new and reviewed vocabulary from **Unit 1**, i.e. free-time activities; phrases describing preferences; words about music; noun and adjective forms

**Materials:** paper; poster paper or IWB slides.

## Learner's Book

###  Warm up

- Put learners in small teams and play the *Stop the bus!* game to revise language and themes from **Unit 1**. Let learners choose a name for their team (e.g. a colour or animal). Give each team a piece of paper and ask them to nominate one member to be the writer. All other team members must contribute ideas which the writer records.

- Draw four columns on the board and write a topic in each column. Topics can be themes from the unit, language points or both. E.g. *A person you admire / a free-time activity / a word to describe feelings / a word about music.*
- Tell learners that you are going to give them a letter and they have to think of a word beginning with that letter for each of the themes. When a team has four answers (one for each column/theme) they shout *Stop the bus!* Everyone stops and the team gives their answers. Teams get a point for each correct answer (or you could give extra points for examples of good vocabulary or imaginative thinking – if an answer is a tenuous link to the topic, ask learners to explain and give extra points for persuasive reasoning!). Learners can give any words they know as answers, but you might like to give extra points if it is a new word remembered from **Unit 1**. e.g. Letter 'S'
*A person you admire / a free-time activity / a word to describe feelings / a word about music*
Shakira / swimming / satisfaction (extra point!) / saxophone
- Do a practice round first to make sure learners are clear about the rules of the game.
- After each round, record points on the board and declare an overall winner at the end. Remember to congratulate *all* teams on their efforts too.
- Tell learners they are now going to choose from the two projects and follow the instructions below for the one they have decided on.

## 1 A presentation

- Take learners through the step-by-step instructions presented in the Learner's Book. Spend time helping them to generate ideas for their chosen theme, e.g.
**Theme 1** Ask questions about recent local newspaper stories or a school newsletter; refer learners to these sources for more ideas and information. Learners could even arrange to interview their subject, if time permits.
**Theme 2** Encourage learners to find information about the author and any links between his/her life and the book characters.
**Theme 3** This could be linked with a holiday or school trip. Learners could bring in photos to stimulate ideas.
- When learners are drafting the presentation, make sure they use sequencing phrases to give structure to the piece, as well as following the other guidelines in **Lesson 3**.
- If learners need assistance with finding a device to attract the audience's attention, make the following suggestions: one or two direct questions to the audience to find out what they already know about the subject; a quick guessing game; using pictures; some 'amazing facts' or true/false statements.
- Give learners time to practise their presentation, ensure that each member has a part to say and that someone is responsible for organising the props (slides, pictures, etc.).

- **Portfolio opportunity:** When learners deliver the presentation, ask the audience to note down an interesting fact that they learned.
- Conduct a feedback at the end of the presentations where the audience shares points they found interesting.

## 2 A survey about favourite free-time activities

- Focus learners' attention on the pie chart and tell them to answer the four questions.
- Draw their attention to the percentages and ask them to think of other ways to describe these quantities, e.g. 40% – *almost half of the students …* 10% – *a few of them …*
They use a combination of these phrases and the percentages in their summaries (section 2).
- Learners then think of another question about free-time activities to conduct a survey with their classmates. Give them a number of classmates to interview (ideally a number that is easily divided, e.g. 20). Ask learners to share the interviewing, each asking an equal number of classmates the question.
- They put the results together and design the pie chart, calculating the portions to represent the answers. They then write the summary, using a variety of phrases to express the results.
- Tell them to make a small poster showing pie charts and summaries for display.

As an extension, you could ask learners to give a personal reaction to the results of their survey. Which results did they predict? Which surprised them? What were the similarities and differences with the pie chart in the example?

# Reflect on your learning

Learner's Book page: 19

## Reflect on your learning

- These revision activities can be approached in different ways, according to the level and character of your class.
Questions 1–7 could be used as a class quiz, with learners in teams and a time limit given to write answers to each question.
Alternatively, you could conduct a revision session – have learners work in pairs and take longer to think about and write down their answers. When pairs have finished the questions, they swap with another pair and correct each other's, with you monitoring and giving help and advice when needed.
You could set this task for homework/self-study.

## Look what I can do!

**Aim:** To check learners have fulfilled the objectives for **Unit 1** (and to what degree).

- Remind learners of the objectives from the start of the unit.
- Focus their attention on the 'can do' statements and read through together. You could put these on a slide or write on the board. Ask learners if they feel they can now do these tasks after completing **Unit 1**. By this point, you should have a clear idea yourself of how well your learners have completed the tasks. However, ask them to now do an initial self-assessment.
- Put learners in pairs and ask them to look through their notebooks and portfolios to find evidence of their work for each of the statements. Then they give themselves a rating as follows:

  ✓ Yes, I can – no problem!
  ? A little – I need more practice.
  X/☹ No – I need a lot more practice.

- Circulate and chat to learners about their self-assessment (some might be overly modest and you can point out that their rating could be higher). Make notes about areas that learners are not confident about (if you haven't already done so) for future reference (see **Teaching tip**).
- Conduct a general feedback at the end and find out which tasks learners found the most interesting/ useful/challenging, etc.

**Answers**
Learners' own answers.

### 📭 Wrap up

- As a class, look at the Big question again on a slide or written on the board: *What can we learn from our own and other people's life experiences?*
- Learners may need guiding to help them make the connection between the question and the unit themes and tasks. Write these prompts on the board (or put on a slide).

  **Prompts:**
  1 *Our reactions and feelings to things we see and do*
  2 *Ways to respect other people*
  3 *Our preferences – likes, dislikes*
  4 *What we are good at*
  5 *How people use their experiences to do good things*

- Ask learners: *What can we learn from doing free-time activities?* (Answer: 3 and 4)
  *What can we learn from doing things for the first time, seeing new things and going to new places?* (1)
  *What can we learn about the life of people like will.i.am?* (5)
  *What can we learn from the life of someone like Helen Keller?* (2)
  (Other answers also possible for some of questions, depending on viewpoint.)
- Alternatively, put learners in groups, print the prompts on different colour paper and give a set to each group; then call out the questions and have them hold up the answers.

## Activity Book

### Revision

- Learners complete sentences 1–12 by choosing the correct answer a–c. Sentences cover key grammar and vocabulary from **Lessons 1–6** in **Unit 1**.

### My global progress

- Learners think about their own responses to topics and activities in the units and answer the questions.

**Differentiated instruction**

**Look what I can do! A mini-awards system**
- At the end of each unit, you could give 'mini-awards' or 'unit awards' to individual learners, pairs or groups who have worked well in specific areas. These could be a mixture of serious and informal/humorous and could cover skills other than language to include learners of all levels and aptitudes, e.g.
  Good conversationalist/s
  Good writers
  Best biography
  Most improved pronunciation
  Best artwork/graphics
  Good presentation skills
  Most interesting presentation
  Most interesting first-time experience.

**Answers**
Learners' own answers.

# 2 School

**What can we learn in school besides school subjects?**

## Unit overview

In this unit learners will:

- talk about schools in different countries
- read about learning tips
- create a role play about school issues
- write an email asking for permission
- read about experiences at school.

In **Unit 2**, learners will look at the topic of school and explore a variety of ideas, experiences and issues that go beyond typical discussion of school subjects and lessons. What does school teach us besides school subjects? How can our experiences at school teach us important skills for other parts of our life, now and in the future? The Big question, which is presented to learners in **Lesson 1**, aims to encapsulate these ideas. Learners will understand that lesson tasks and projects will contribute to answering the question at the end of the unit.

The unit begins by asking learners to compare their school and school subjects to other schools both nationally and internationally. This gives learners an accessible and familiar topic with which to start the unit, while also encouraging them to consider school life in a wider global context. It also allows them to practise a range of skills, in particular communication and listening skills.

Following this, they read about good learning habits and behaviours and examine the language needed to express advice in this context. They create role plays to discuss common school problems with self-esteem and classmate behaviour. They look at appropriate ways to ask for something from someone in authority and write a semi-formal email, considering appropriate language and text organisation. Finally, they read an extract from a novel which will generate discussion about relationships in class.

The **Unit 2** topic of school gives great opportunities for learners to draw on their own experiences and use these to engage actively in personalisation tasks that develop key communication skills.

The **Photocopiable activities** provide grammar practice in the use of the 1st conditional (**3**) and modal verbs (**4**).

### Language focus

Linking phrases: *instead of*, *as well as* + noun

1st conditional with *if* and *unless* (to describe likely future events)

Modal verbs: *would, could, should* (in a semi-formal context)

**Vocabulary topics:** School subjects; verbs to describe behaviour; after-school activities (noun-verb collocations); verbs to describe body language.

### Self-assessment

- I can talk about my school and compare it with schools in other countries.
- I can describe ways to improve my brain power and study skills.
- I can prepare a role play about problems at school.
- I can write an email asking for permission to do something.
- I can understand a story about experiences at school.

### Teaching tips

**Researching information:** Numerous tasks throughout Stage 6 require learners to research a topic before a writing task, presentation or project work. In these cases, research needs to be focused on specific sources, rather than letting learners of this age research randomly and without direction.

**Non-digital resources:** Take learners to the school library and focus them on specific sections and publications to do their research. Know beforehand what individuals want to research and put them in pairs and groups with other learners with similar goals, so they can share the work load and support each other. Spend time with each group looking at contents pages and indexes, to focus their research from the onset. Likewise, resources can be brought into the classroom and learners organised in the same way. If learners are researching outside of school, talk to them beforehand about where they might find relevant and accessible information in public libraries and at home (types of magazines, newspapers, encyclopaedias, etc).

Similar points apply when using the Internet both inside and outside school. Focus learners on specific websites and search terms so that they can research safely and efficiently. If learners are going to be researching a topic at home, alert parents and care-givers, so they can monitor Internet use.

# Lesson 1: School

Learner's Book pages: 20–21

Activity Book pages: 16–17

## Lesson objectives

**Listening:** Listen to three children talk about school life in their countries; note down information for comparison.

**Speaking:** Compare aspects of your school life with other schools, nationally and internationally.

**Critical thinking:** Comparing and contrasting aspects of your school life; considering what you would like to change.

**Language focus:** Linking phrases for comparing and contrasting: *instead of, as well as* + noun

**Vocabulary:** *School subjects: National history, Arabic, Science, Art and Design, French, Islamic education, Social Studies, Spanish, Physical education*

**Materials:** poster paper or electronic slides; images of different schools in country and around the world.

## Learner's Book

###  Warm up

- To introduce the Big question, start by telling the class that this unit is going to be about school. Explain that, through school, we learn a lot of new things through school subjects and we also learn other important lessons from other experiences that we have at school. These lessons can help us in other parts of our lives now and in the future. Therefore, the Big question for **Unit 2** is ... *What can we learn in school besides school subjects?*
- Write the question on the board (for an electronic presentation, create a slide with interesting graphics). Tell learners that you are all going to do tasks and projects in the unit that will answer this question.
- Introduce the unit objectives to show learners what tasks are coming up. Present the objectives on a slide or large piece of poster paper to attach to the board:
- Tell learners that you will answer the Big question and look again at the objectives at the end of the unit. Keep the objectives slide / poster to revisit at the end of the unit.

### 1 🗨 Talk about it

- Start by showing learners a selection of pictures of other schools in their country. Choose images that show similarities and contrasts, (e.g. much bigger / smaller; inner city / rural; design of building, etc). Ask them to tell you first how they think their school is the same as the schools in the pictures. Elicit points such as hours of study, school subjects, uniform, etc. Write learners' ideas on the side of the board. Then brainstorm any differences, using the pictures to stimulate discussion.

- Point learners to the second question and ask them if they know anything about schools in other countries. Encourage any responses from learners who have personal experience of learning in another country or family members or friends that have studied abroad. Also encourage learners to imagine similarities and differences, even if they have no direct experience. If learners have no responses for this question, simply tell them that they are going to find out more about schools in other countries later in the lesson.
- **Extend and challenge:** Show your class pictures of schools and classrooms in other countries that show similarities and differences to your school. You could ask learners to guess first which country the schools come from, then elicit the differences from the picture. Extend by asking learners to imagine further similarities and differences based on the images and what they may already know about the country. This may be an opportunity to increase learners' awareness of and generate a discussion about conditions in schools in poorer nations.
- **Critical thinking:** Learners compare and contrast their experience of school with other national and international examples. They can be challenged by being asked to imagine what school life might be like in other places, if they have no direct experience.

> **Answers**
> Learners' own answers.

### 2 Word study

- Ask learners to close their books while you read out the list of school subjects in **Activity 2**. Ask them to raise their hands when you mention a subject that they study. At the end, elicit all the school subjects again – see how many they can remember from your list (without looking at their books).
- Focus learners' attention on the subjects listed in the Learner's Book. Ask them to read the list with a partner and identify again the subjects they study. Clarify any subjects that are unfamiliar to learners.

> **Answers**
> Learners' own answers.

### 3 Word study

- Focus learners on **Activity 3**. Ask them to work in pairs and note down other subjects that they study (not mentioned in **Activity 2**). Give a time limit of about a minute. The pair that comes up with the first full list reads it out to the class. The others check their list against it and amend / correct as appropriate.

> **Answers**
> Learners' own answers.

 **For further practice, see Activity 1 in the Activity Book.**

## 4 Listen 9

- Tell the class that they are going to listen to three children talking about school life in their countries. They need to listen and note down the school subjects that each child mentions from the list in **Activity 2**. Tell them that you will stop the audio after each speaker to give them a chance to write. Emphasise to learners that, at this stage, they need only listen for school subjects and they should not worry about trying to understand the other details.

---

### Differentiated instruction

**Additional support and practice**

- Learners who need more support could write the school subjects first and then tick the ones they hear in the listening task.
- After listening to the three speakers, ask learners to compare their answers with their partners and then tell you the school subjects that were mentioned from the list in **Activity 2**.

**Extend and challenge**

- **Activities 4, 5** and **6**. Elicit other school subjects mentioned by the children (Tian: *Language, Maths, Chinese;* Haniya: *Maths;* Mia: *Reading, Writing, Maths*). Ask learners which subjects were the same as the ones they noted down in **Activity 3**. If you are teaching in one of the countries featured in the listening task, ask your learners to do the activities as instructed but to compare the information given with their school. Then ask them to discuss similarities and differences between the given information and their school.

---

**Audioscript:** Track 9

**Tian:** Here in China, my school day starts at 7.30 am. We have a 2 hour lunch break and then finish school at 5 pm. It's a long day! I go to school from Monday to Saturday, and we have a day off on Sunday. At school we learn all the basic subjects such as language and maths, and also about our national history. I've learnt to write in Chinese. We use characters instead of letters. The characters are symbols that make words. Our school year is from September to July. During our summer break, we have summer classes to give us more help with our studies.

**Haniya:** In Bahrain, our school year is from September to July. We start the day at 8 am and finish at 2 pm, Thursday to Sunday. I'm in the sixth grade and this is an important year for me. I must get good grades so that I can go to the next stage of my basic education. After that, I will join the secondary stage, but not until I am 15 years old.

In school, we study lots of subjects including Islamic education, Arabic language, Science, Maths and Social Studies. At the moment we have the same teacher for most of these subjects. That will change next year when we will have a different teacher for each subject.

**Mia:** In Canada we start school at 9 am and finish at 3.30 pm, Monday to Friday. When I get home from school I start my homework straight away because I always have a lot to do. It's OK though, because we get a nice long holiday in July and August for the summer. Then we start the new school year in September. At school we learn reading, writing, science and math, as well as Canadian history and physical

---

education. We also learn French, because French is spoken in our country, as well as English. I guess my school is quite similar to a lot of American and European schools, although at my school we don't have to wear a uniform – I wear the same clothes at school and at home.

---

**Answers**

School subjects mentioned: National history / Islamic education / Arabic language / Science / Social Studies / Physical Education / French

---

## 5 Listen 9

- Focus learners' attention on the table in **Activity 5** and ask them to draw it in their notebooks.
- Explain to the whole class that they are going to listen again for the information needed to complete the table. Ask them to tell you exactly which information they are going to listen for from each speaker by having them read out the table headings (*School hours*; *days at school*; *the months of the school year*). Explain that you are going to stop after each speaker to give them time to write.
- Ask learners if they can remember any of the information from the first listening (but make it clear that this was **not** the task for the previous listening and it is OK if they can't tell you). If some learners can remember, ask them to listen again to check.
- Play the audio again, stopping after each speaker.
- After listening to the three speakers, ask learners to compare their answers with their partners and then conduct a class feedback to share the answers.

---

**Answers**

|  | School hours | Days at school | School year |
|---|---|---|---|
| **China** | 7.30 am–5 pm | Mon–Sat | September–July |
| **Bahrain** | 8 am–2 pm | Thursday–Sunday | Sept–July |
| **Canada** | 9 am–3.30 pm | Mon–Fri | Sept–June |

---

## 6 Listen 9

- Focus learners' attention on the questions in **Activity 6**. Read them together as a class and tell learners that they are going to listen again and answer these questions.
- Before listening, ask learners to go through the questions again in pairs and discuss if they already know any of the answers from the previous activities.
- Then play the audio again, stopping after each speaker, to allow learners time to write answers.
- After listening to the three speakers, ask learners to compare their answers with their partners and then conduct a class feedback.
- **Extend and challenge: Activities 4, 5** and **6**. If you are teaching in one of the countries featured in the listening task, ask your learners to do the activities as instructed but to compare the information given with their school. Then ask them to discuss similarities and differences between the given information and their school.

**Answers**

**a** A day off is a day free from work or school. In China, Sunday is the children's day off.
**b** Symbols that represent complete words.
**c** They do summer classes to help with their studies.
**d** Haniya needs to get good grades.
**e** When she's 15.
**f** French
**g** They wear their own clothes (no uniform).

## 7  Use of English

- Ask learners to tell you three subjects that they currently study (e.g. *Maths, Science, Computing*). Write a sentence on the board, such as: *We study Maths and Science _____ computer studies.*
- Focus learners on the linking phrases in the **Use of English** box. Read the information together. Then elicit which linking phrase can be used to complete the sentence (answer: *as well as*). Elicit what kind of word follows the phrase in the sentence by pointing at the word after the phrase (in this case, *computer studies* is followed by a noun).
- Follow the same procedure to give two more examples – another one for *as well as* and one for *instead of*. Have more examples prepared, in case your learners need further practice as a class.
- Now focus learners on the activity and ask them to complete the sentences with the linking phrases. If your learners need more support, do the first one together as a class. If learners have grasped the concept and the language without any issues, this could be done for homework. If they need further practice, ask them to do the task individually and then compare their answers in pairs.
- Conduct a class feedback to go through the answers. If there are any problems, show them more examples on the board, using information that is directly relevant to them.

**Answers**
**a** instead of
**b** as well as
**c** Instead of
**d** instead of
**e** As well as

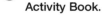 **For further practice, see Activities 2, 3, 4 and 5 in the Activity Book.**

## 8 Talk

- Put learners into groups of three or four to discuss the questions. Ask them to look at their answers for **Activities 4**, **5** and **6** and to make notes on similarities and differences.
- **Additional support and practice:** Less confident or reluctant speakers may find this task more manageable if you divide the questions up, giving one question to each group, according to ability (more confident or stronger learners could take question **c**).
- At this stage conduct a quick class feedback for questions **a** and **b**. If your learners are reluctant to speak in front of the class, ask them to appoint

a spokesperson (or choose one yourself) to give feedback on behalf of the group.
- **Critical thinking:** In question **c**, learners discuss things about their school that they would like to change, after hearing the examples from the other countries (e.g. school hours, length of holidays, etc).
- After discussion, conduct class feedback, establishing points in common and different ideas within each group. Ask learners to refer to the country where they got the idea from (e.g. *We would like to have long holidays like Canada*).

**Answers**
Learners' own answers.

## 9 Write

- Tell learners that they are now going to write a short summary describing school life in their country. Tell them to use the examples in the listening task as a guide. Project a copy of one of the speaker's accounts onto a screen or give learners a copy from the audioscript. Spend a few minutes looking at the example together and highlighting the aspects mentions (e.g. school hours, subjects, etc).
- Learners complete the activity individually in their notebooks in class or finish for homework.

## Wrap up

- To finish off, ask the class if there was anything that surprised them about school life in the other countries.

## Activity Book

### 1 Vocabulary

- Learners complete words for school subjects and answer questions about subjects in their own school and their preferences.

**Answers**
1 Islamic Education
2 Science
3 French
4 National History
5 Arabic
6 Spanish
7 Art and Design
8 Physical Education
9 Social Studies & Learners' own answers.

### 2 Read

- Learners read about school life in Egypt and compare with their own school day.

**Answers**
Learners' own answers (no written answer required).

### 3 Read

- Learners read the text again and complete a table comparing information about Egyptian schools with their own school.

## 4 Use of English

• Learners complete a short gapped text (linked to the reading text) with linking expressions, *as well as* and *instead of*.

Answers
1 instead of
2 Instead of
3 instead of
4 as well as
5 as well as

## 5 Challenge

• Learners write a short text comparing their school day with the example, using the linking expressions.

Answers
Learners' own answers.

# Lesson 2: What is brain power?

Learner's Book pages: 22–23
Activity Book pages: 18–19

### Lesson objectives

**Reading:** Find specific information in a text.

**Speaking:** Discuss and give advice about learning tips and study habits.

**Critical thinking:** Consider different advice for good study habits and what works for you.

**Language focus:** 1st conditional to express likely future events

**Materials:** pictures reflecting good and bad study habits (for **Warm up**); printouts of **Activity 2 quiz** for a running dictation activity (attached to the walls in your classroom); poster paper, coloured pens (for poster activity). Copies of **Photocopiable activity 3**.

## Learner's Book

###  Warm up

• Introduce the topic by showing learners some images that reflect good and bad study habits, (e.g. a huge burger and fries, a bottle of water, some fresh fruit, some chocolate, someone exercising). Present humorous images if possible (e.g. someone biting greedily into a burger) to generate interest. Ask learners to look at the title of the lesson and to tell you what the connection is with the images. Elicit that these images all show things that either improve or take away your brain power (and consequently your ability to study well) and that they are going to find out more later. Let learners speculate on which is which; don't give answers just yet.

## 1 Talk about it

• Focus attention on the two questions. Elicit responses from volunteers or nominate learners and ask them the questions. Put some answers on the board and use them to elicit comments around the class.
• **Critical thinking:** learners give a personal response and express personal habits and preferences.

Answers
Learners' own answers.

## 2 🗩 Talk

• Tell learners that they are going to do a quiz to find out more about brain power. If you want to energise your class or give them extra practice in all four skills, you could introduce the quiz as a running dictation. Let learners watch you fix the six statements from **Activity 2** on the classroom walls and tell you exactly where you are putting them (e.g. *by the window*; *next to the cupboard*) for extra language practice. Then divide them into A/B pairs and give A the task of 'runner' and B, 'writer'. (Make sure learners are clear about their role.) Then explain that A has to walk up to the statement, read it, remember as much as possible, go back and dictate it to B. B listens and copies. (A doesn't have to remember the whole line but should try and remember as much as possible. He/she can go back to check). If appropriate you can swap the roles half way by clapping your hands (make sure learners know beforehand that this is the signal to change). The objective is to write down the statements within a time limit or as fast as possible.

### Differentiated instruction

**Additional support and practice**

• If the running dictation activity is not appropriate in your classroom, you could read out the quiz statements to the class (ask learners to close their books first) and take a class vote on whether they are true or false. Then ask them to look at the statements again in pairs and record their answer in preparation for the next stage.
• When learners have done the dictation they can check their statements against the book and make any corrections.
• Learners then read the statements in **Activity 2** in the same A/B pairs and consider whether they are true or false (this will calm them down after the dictation). Ask them to record their answer in preparation for the next stage.

- **Finding specific information:** Draw learners' attention to the reading strategy on page 22 and the idea of focusing on finding *specific* information in a text, rather than trying to understand *all* of the information at once. Ask them which approach they think makes more sense: *try and understand all the information in a text the first time you read it* OR *approach the text step by step, first just looking for specific information.* Encourage learners to see that the second approach will support them better in managing reading texts. Remind them of the 'step-by-step' approach presented in **Unit 1** and point out that this approach links closely with that one.

[AB] **For further practice, see the Strategy check box in the Activity Book.**

## 3 [image] Read

- Go back to the quiz and tell learners that they are going to find out the answers in the reading text. Ask them to tell you which key words from the quiz they will be looking out for when they scan the text for the answers. Elicit one or two key words from each statement (e.g. *nuts / remember; sugary food / energy; chocolate; water / concentrate; memory / Activity; bed / late*). Focus attention on the pictures and remind learners that these give clues about major themes in a text.
- Ask learners to read the text to a time limit (about four minutes) to encourage them to just focus on finding specific information to answer the quiz statements.
- When they have finished reading ask them to check their answers to the quiz statements and then compare with a partner.
- **Extend and challenge:** Ask early finishers to think of tips to add to the list in the text.
- Conduct a class feedback, eliciting the answers and corrections for the false sentences.
- **Critical thinking:** At the end, ask learners to respond to the tips. *Which did you find interesting? Surprising? Which did you know already?*

**Answers**
1 true
2 false. Your energy will drop and you'll feel tired and unable to concentrate.
3 false. Only dark chocolate.
4 true

## 4 [image] Talk

- **Critical thinking:** Put learners in groups of three or four and ask them to find tips in the text that they follow already. Then ask each group to think of two more learning tips to share with the class. Give a time limit.
- **Extend and challenge:** Challenge learners (or give extra listening practice) by asking them to close

their books, then listen while you dictate these two questions. They copy them down and then answer. This is also an effective technique to re-engage learners whose attention might be wandering.
- Conduct a class feedback, asking each group to share their learning tips. Make a note of good ideas on the board in preparation for **Activity 8**.

**Answers**
Learners' own answers.

[AB] **For further practice, see Activities 1 and 2 in the Activity Book.**

## Use of English

- Write the two examples from the **Use of English** box on the board, leaving a space for the 1st conditional forms (e.g. 1: _____ you _____ plenty of water, you ____ ____ able to concentrate better in class, 2: *Your body* _____ _____ *as well,* _____ *you* _____ *plenty of sleep*). Elicit the missing components from learners if possible (or input yourself). Use different colours to highlight the target language.
- Explain that we use 1st conditional structures when we want to say that there is a *real possibility* of something happening. Point out to learners that, in the second sentence, 'unless' means 'if you don't'. Tell learners that 1st conditional sentences like these are often used to *give advice* (e.g. sentence 1) or to *warn* someone about something that we think is likely to happen (e.g. sentence 2).
- Focus learners on form. Show them that each sentence has two parts and that these can be swapped over (e.g. *Unless you get plenty of sleep, your body won't grow as well*). Change the pronoun (e.g. '*you*' to '*she*') and elicit any changes that occur in the *if/unless* clause; point out that '*will*' and '*won't*' stay the same.

## 5 [AB] Use of English

- Focus learners on the **Use of English** box and then on **Activity 5**. Ask them to match the sentence halves to complete the sentences.
- Review the answers as a class. Clarify any confusion with the concept by presenting more example sentences.

**Answers**
1 c   2 d   3 e   4 f   5 b   6 a

## 6 Use of English

- Focus learners on the activity and ask them to find more examples of 1st conditional sentences in **Activities 2** and **3**. They could do this activity in pairs. Alternatively, you could do the activity as a class and make it into a race by having learners read the quiz and text and put their hands up as soon as they find an example. All learners could then copy all the examples into their notebooks.

- Conduct a class feedback to check that learners have identified all the examples.

**Answers**
(From Activity 2 Quiz)
2 If you eat sugary food, you'll have enough energy to study for a long time
4 If you drink plenty of water, it'll help you to concentrate better.
(From Ex 3 Reading)
If you eat these foods, you'll get a quick energy lift ...
If you eat wholegrain food like brown rice and wholemeal bread, you'll have lots of energy throughout your school day.
... it won't do you good unless it's the dark kind.

## 7 Use of English

- **Activity 7** stretches learners more by requiring them to form their own 1st conditional sentences. It also prepares them for the writing activity in **Activity 8**. Ask learners to do the activity individually and then compare their sentences with a partner.
- Check answers together as a class.

**Answers**
a You'll be too tired to do homework unless you get enough sleep.
b If you eat fish and vegetables your brain will remember things more easily.
c You won't be able to concentrate if you eat too much white bread and sugar.
d You won't work well unless you eat healthy food.
e If you get enough activity, your memory will improve.

 For further practice, see Activities 3 and 4 in the Activity Book.

## 8  Write

- Put learners in groups of three and explain that they are going to make a learning tips poster. They need to write learning tips using the 1st conditional; they can get information from the quiz and text and also use their own ideas. Stipulate the minimum number of sentences you require (about eight – but adjust this according to the ability of your class). Stronger learners and early finishers can then add more sentences if appropriate. At the end, they will display their posters for others to look at and read.
- **Critical thinking:** Tell learners to write their favourite tips – ones that they feel are the most useful or interesting. Elicit a couple of examples first from the class. If you noted down any good answers on the board from **Activity 4**, refer learners to these now.
- Ask learners to write the tips first before making the poster. Monitor groups and help with language and vocabulary. Check that sentences are grammatically accurate before allowing learners to prepare the poster.
When learners have produced a series of satisfactory sentences, let them start the poster. Supply poster paper and coloured pens so learners can make the posters visually eye-catching. They could decorate with pictures (from magazines, or their own art work).

- **Additional support and practice**: You may feel it's appropriate to give learners roles in a group-work activity like this (e.g. two designers, one writer/copier). Early finishers can add more sentences to their poster.
- When everyone has finished, ask learners to walk around and look at each other's posters. They need to note down a tip from another poster that doesn't appear on their own and which poster they think is the most eye-catching.

**Answers**
Learners' own answers.

## ☞ Wrap up

- Take a class vote on the most eye-catching poster and nominate a few learners to tell the class about tips they noted down.
- **Critical thinking:** Ask each learner to choose two learning tips that they are going to follow from now on. Nominate a few learners to tell the class about the tips they've chosen and why.

## Activity Book

## Reading strategy

- Learners do a multiple-choice activity to support their understanding of the reading strategy.

**Answers**
- Look at any pictures. ✓
- Decide what information you want to find first. ✓

## 1 Read

- Learners complete four gapped comments about study tips.

**Answers**
1 b   2 c   3 d   4 a

## 2

- Learners write a comment about the study habits comments, identifying ones they already follow and which they think are the best.

**Answers**
Learners' own answers.

## 3 Use of English

- Learners choose the correct form of the 1st conditional components to complete sentences.

**Answers**
1 use
2 won't
3 make
4 will
5 find
6 can

## 4 📖 Challenge

- Learners form sentences about study habits with the 1st conditional, using pictures and word prompts.

**Answers**
1 If you sleep well, you'll study better.
  Unless you sleep well you won't study better.
2 If you drink plenty of / enough water, you'll concentrate better.
  Unless you drink plenty of water, you won't concentrate well.
3 If you do (enough / plenty of) activity, you'll (be able to) remember things well / better.
  Unless you do (enough / plenty of) activity, you won't (be able to) remember things well.
4 If you eat healthy food, you'll have energy (for studying).
  Unless you eat healthy food, you won't have energy (for studying).

**For further practice in using 1st conditional forms, see Photocopiable activity 3.**

# Lesson 3: A problem shared ...

Learner's Book pages: 28–29
Activity Book pages: 24–25

**Lesson objectives**

**Speaking:** Prepare and perform a role play about a problem at school.

**Listening:** Listen to two dialogues, identify specific information and features of language.

**Critical thinking:** Thinking of and analysing solutions to problems.

**Vocabulary:** Words to describe behaviour: *tell off; mess about; join in with; laugh at; bully*

**Materials:** film/video clip (for **Warm up**) (if available) or images showing problems at school.

## Learner's Book

###  Warm up

- You could introduce the topic of this lesson by showing learners a clip from a film or TV programme, depicting a problem at school (e.g. bullying; bad behaviour in class, etc.) to generate interest and initiate a discussion. Ask learners to watch and explain what problem is being played out on the clip. Alternatively, you could show learners images showing problems in a school environment or use the pictures in the Learner's Book. Ask them to speculate on what the problem might be by looking at the images.

### 1 Talk about it

- Focus learners on the questions in **Activity 1** and ask them to discuss briefly in pairs. If you haven't used the picture on page 24 in the warm up stage, ask learners to look at it and speculate what problem is depicted before moving on to the questions.

- Ask for volunteers or nominate some learners to share their ideas with the class. Note down ideas on the board to help learners with the next activity.

**Answers**
Learners' own answers.

### 2 Read

- Focus learners on the comments in **Activity 2** and explain that they all describe problems at school. Tell them to read the comments and look out for any that mention the same problems that they talked about in **Activity 1**. Refer them to the notes on the board as a reminder.

- Remind learners just to focus on looking for the specific information and not to worry about any unknown words at this stage.

- Give a time limit of about four minutes. Then conduct a class feedback, identifying common problems.

**Answers**
Learners' own answers.

### 3 Word study

- First, conduct this activity as a reading race with the whole class. Focus learners on the verbs highlighted in the texts, read out the definitions and ask them to match to a verb in the text.

- Check learners understand the meaning of the verbs by asking questions like: *Why did the teacher tell the children off?* (ref. comment 1); *Who is annoyed because her classmates waste time? What does she want them to do?* (ref. comment 3); *What is the child afraid of in number 4? Why?; What unkind things does the boy describe in number 5?*

- Ask learners to record the verbs and definitions in their notebooks.

**Answers**
a mess about
b laugh at
c tell s/o off
d join in with
e bully

 **For further practice, see Activity 1 in the Activity Book.**

### 4 Listen 🔟

- Tell learners that they are going to listen to two conversations about problems at school. At this point explain that later they are going to prepare their own role plays about the same topic. First, they are going to listen to these conversations to help them when they prepare their own.

- Focus learners on the gist task question in **Activity 4** and ask them to read it out to you. Make sure that they understand that they need to listen to identify which problems in **Activity 2** the children are talking about. Tell them that this time, they need to just listen to answer the question and that you will stop the audio after each conversation.

• Play the audio, stopping after each conversation. Elicit which problem the children are talking about.

**Audioscript:** Track 10

**1**

**A:** It's really annoying. Every time we work in groups Katie and I do all the work. Tara and Rachel don't do anything! They just mess about, talking and laughing. We're really tired of it!

**B:** OK, there are a few things you could do ... you could sit and do nothing, so *they* have to make the first move and start the activity ...

**A:** Mmm, not sure about that one. We'd probably never get started!

**B:** How about giving them specific jobs to do, like make notes or find pictures.

Or you could ask the teacher to mix up all the groups so you can work with someone new.

**2**

**A:** I don't know what to do. Three boys in our class are being really mean to Marcus for no reason. They call him names and laugh at him because he's small. And now they've started to push him around at break times. I've told them to leave him alone but they just laugh at me.

**B:** Why don't you tell the teacher?

**A:** Marcus says that if we tell the teacher, he will look weak. It will look like he can't stand up for himself.

**B:** It's OK to tell a teacher. If you don't tell someone, the bullying will probably get worse. I know! The teacher can say that he saw the boys bullying Marcus, not that Marcus has told him. How does that sound?

**A:** That's a great idea!

---

**Answers**
Conversation 1 is about comment 3 - attitudes to group work.
Conversation 2 is about comment 5 – bullying.

---

## 5 Listen 10

• Ask learners to copy the sentences, a – e, into their notebooks, leaving gaps for the missing words. Before they listen again, ask if anyone can remember the phrases from the conversations and can guess any of the missing words.

• Explain to learners that they have two tasks to do now – listen and complete the phrases and to tell you what solutions the friends suggest.

• Play the first conversation again, then give learners a few minutes to discuss in pairs the missing words in sentences a – c, and the suggested solution. Then repeat with the second conversation (sentences d – e).

• Conduct a class feedback, eliciting missing words and suggested solutions.

• **Critical thinking:** Ask the class what they think about the solutions; if they don't agree with them, why not?

• **Extend and challenge:** Start by asking learners what they think about the solutions given in the

conversations. Ask if these solutions would work if there were similar problems at their school. Use your discretion about how personal you make the discussion, especially if similar problems have occurred in your class. Extend the discussion further by asking learners to suggest other solutions for these problems.

---

**Answers**
**a** could
**b** How about giving
**c** could ask / to
**d** Why don't
**e** don't tell / will / get
**Solutions suggested by friends are:**
**Conversation 1** – to do nothing until Tara and Rachel take the initiative and start the activity; to give Tara and Rachel specific jobs to do; to ask the teacher to change the groups around so the girls can work with different classmates.
**Conversation 2** – to tell the teacher about the bullying; but ask the teacher to give the bullies the idea that *he* (the teacher) saw them bullying Marcus and not that Marcus had told him.

---

## 6 Pronunciation 11

• Draw learners' attention to the **Speaking tip** on page 25 and read it together. Then look at the sentences from the conversations in **Activity 5**. Ask learners if they can remember which word was emphasised in each sentence.

• Play the audio. Ask learners to listen, repeat the sentences and identify the stressed word in each sentence (or check if they had already remembered the stressed words). Make sure that learners are clear about which words are stressed and that they understand how the stressed words emphasise the points the speaker is making.

---

**Audioscript:** Track 11

**a** ... you could sit and do nothing, so they have to make the first move ...

**b** Marcus says that if we tell the teacher, he will look weak.

**c** ... The teacher can say that he saw the boys

---

**Answers**
**a** they
**b** he
**c** he

---

## 7 Pronunciation 11

• Focus learners on **Activity 7** and ask them to identify who the emphasised words refer to in the three sentences. Play the audio again if necessary and let them work in pairs to answer the question. You may need to remind learners who is who in the conversations (e.g. Katie is the girl who complains about Tara and Rachel; Marcus is the boy who is being bullied).

---

**Answers**
**a2** Tara and Rachel
**b3** Marcus
**c1** The teacher

---

### Present it!

- **A role play:** Explain to learners that they are now going to prepare and practise their own role plays. First, go through the problems that they discussed in **Activity 1** by referring them back to the notes made on the board (rewrite these if they have been removed, to help with this stage).
- **Critical thinking:** Put learners into pairs and explain that they are going to write a dialogue together, explaining what the problem is (Student A) and offering a solution (Student B). Tell learners that they need to think of a solution to the problem in their role play. Remind them of the functional language for suggestions, drawn from the audio in **Activity 4** and elicit the phrases again on the board.
- **Additional support and practice:** To give learners extra support in writing the role play, write part of one together as a class. Choose a problem to discuss (e.g. comment 4 from **Activity 2**) and elicit a simple dialogue line by line (learners can use the comments in **Activity 2** to help with language if necessary), e.g.
  **A:** *I don't know what to do, I'm scared to speak out in front of the class.*
  **B:** *Why are you scared?*
  **A:** *Because I'm afraid the other kids will laugh at me ...*
  **B:** *Why don't you ...?*
  Leave the dialogue on the board to give learners a structure. Or you could erase certain words, or just leave prompts, so they have to work a little harder to remember).
- Learners write their role play in pairs in their notebooks. Ask them to write about one or two problems depending on time and ability. Monitor the pairs, helping with language and vocabulary. Check the dialogues for grammar, vocabulary and organisation; however, the emphasis is on organisation and quality of ideas rather than perfectly accurate scripts. Ask learners to identify any words which could be emphasised to make a strong point.
- Now ask learners to choose a 'role': Student A has a problem, Student B is going to offer a solution or advice. Ask learners to practise their role plays in pairs. Again, monitor the pairs, helping with pronunciation and guiding them to noticing which words could be emphasised to make strong points.
- When learners have finished practising, you could either ask a few confident pairs to deliver their role plays in front of the class, or move all learners into groups of six and have three pairs perform for each other. While pairs are performing their role plays, ask listeners to note down the solutions offered for each problem because, at the end of the class, you are all going to vote on the best solution.
- **Extend and challenge**: As learners are delivering their role plays, note down main errors; either give to each pair a note of the errors to correct themselves, or write up on the board at the end for a class error correction session (without stating which learners made the errors).

**Note:** this would come after plenty of positive feedback regarding the role plays. Positive feedback must always come first and be emphasised.

> **Answers**
> Learners' own answers.

 For further practice, see Activities 1, 2, 3 and 4 in the Activity Book.

###  Wrap up

- **Critical thinking:** Learners should have noted down the solutions presented in each role play they listened to. Conduct a class round-up of problems and solutions presented and take a vote on the best solution to a school problem.

> **Answers**
> Learners' own answers.

## Activity Book

### 1 Vocabulary

- Learners complete a dialogue with the verbs describing behaviour.

> **Answers**
> 1 messes about
> 2 laugh at
> 3 tells us off
> 4 bully
> 5 join in with

### 2 Read

- Learners read about two school problems and identify what problem is being described.

> **Answers**
> 1 Dana feels very nervous about starting a new school.
> 2 Max got a bad result in his Maths test and is too scared to tell his mum.

### 3 Word study

- Learners complete answers to the problems described in **Activity 2** with a phrase. Then they match the answers with the problems in **Activity 2**.

> **Answers**
> 1 c; Problem 2
> 2 a; Problem 1
> 3 e; Problem 2
> 4 b; Problem 1

### 4 📝 Challenge

- Learners read about another school problem and write four suggestions for solutions.

# Lesson 4: Starting something new

Learner's Book pages: 26–27

Activity Book pages: 22–23

## Lesson objectives

**Speaking:** Talking about after-school activities.

**Reading:** Read an email asking permission to start an after-school activity.

**Writing:** Plan and write an email asking permission to start an after-school activity.

**Critical thinking:** Identify something new that your school needs and give reasons why; looking at how a formal email is divided into sections covering a different function.

**Language focus:** Modal verbs, *would*, *could* and *should* in formal emails

**Vocabulary:** After-school activities described in noun-verb collocations: *belong to a chess club / football club / computer club / music club*; *learn about how to use the Internet, act, dive*

**Materials:** Learner's Book, Activity Book. Copies of **Photocopiable activity 4**.

## Learner's Book

###  Warm up

• On the board, write a couple of after-school activities at your school that you know some of your learners attend. Elicit from learners what the words are describing (i.e. *after-school / extra-curricular activities*) and then ask who in the class goes to these activities. Ask a few more questions (e.g. *How often do you go? Which teacher runs the activity?*).

### 1 Talk about it

• Ask learners to tell you more after-school activities and write their suggestions on the board. Alternatively, if there is a large choice of after-school activities at your school, you could ask learners to think of one, write it down and mime it for the class to guess. Write all suggestions on the board to come back to later.

**Answers**
Learners' own answers.

### 2  Word study

• Choose an example of an activity from the choice on the board and ask learners: *Who belongs to the computer club?*, etc. Then elicit your question from learners and write it on the board, with '*belongs to*' highlighted clearly. Ask more questions to practise the verb + noun collocation, e.g. *Jose, which clubs do you belong to? Who belongs to the school choir?*

• Follow the same procedure again, asking learners, *What do you learn about at the Computer Club?* Elicit or input a response to produce, *We learn about how to* (*use the Internet ...*, etc.) and continue asking questions to encourage learners to produce the target phrases in sentences that talk about after-school activities they, their friends and / or siblings take part in.

• **Extend and challenge:** Extend this discussion about extra-curricular activities to include after-school / free-time events that are not connected to school.

• **Critical thinking:** Focus learners on the pictures in **Activity 2** and ask if there are any activities mentioned that don't exist at their school. Then ask if there are any new activities that they would like to see at their school. Make a note of any interesting ideas for reference later in the lesson.

**Answers**
Learners' own answers.

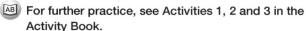 For further practice, see Activities 1, 2 and 3 in the Activity Book.

### 3 Read

• Focus learners on the email on page 26. Ask them to tell you who has written the email (Kareem Khan and Nathan Smith); who the boys are (Year 6 students) and who the email is written to (Mrs Miller). Ask them to read the email and tell you who they think Mrs Miller is. Give a time limit of about four minutes and tell them just to concentrate on the question you have asked them.

• Stop learners and ask who they think Mrs Miller is.

• Check learners understand the meaning of *newsletter* (a short letter that tells you interesting and important things that have happened recently) and show them an example if you can; also check they understand *permission* (when you ask someone if you can do something) and give them an example of a situation when you have to ask permission for something.

• Now conduct a reading race to establish some key points about the information in the email. As a class, ask learners to find the answers for:
*What do the boys want to do?* (Start a newsletter for Year 6)
*Why?* (Because there are a lot of exciting things happening in Year 6; their classmates are interested and would like to write for the newsletter too)
*How often do they want to produce the newsletter?* (Every 2 months)

*Where do they want to produce it?* (At Computer Club)
*Who has offered to help them?* (Mr Sanchez, their form teacher)

> **Answers**
> Mrs Miller is the head teacher.

## 4 Read

- Focus learners on the email text again and ask them how many different parts they can see (5). Make sure they are aware that the different sections are numbered.
- Go through the example together as a class. Ask the learners to read out the function heading (a *How they are going to produce it*) and go back to the text to see how this heading describes section 3.
- Ask learners to work in pairs to match the function headings with the email sections. Then conduct a class feedback.

> **Answers**
> a 3   b 5   c 4   d 1   e 2

### Writing tip

- To introduce the language in the writing tip, write the following sentence on the board:
  *we want to ask your permission ...*
  Tell learners (or elicit from them) that this sentence is not very polite (or too direct) when asking your head teacher for permission to do something. Ask learners what needs to change to make it more polite. Elicit:
  *We would like to ask your permission ...*
- **Additional support and practice**: Ask learners to find the target sentence, *We would like to ask your permission ...*, in the email in **Activity 3**; or write the sentence on the board, leaving gaps as follows, then elicit or input *would* + *like* (verb) and highlight the target language: *We _____ _____ to ask your permission ...,*.
- Write the following question on the board and follow the same procedure to illustrate *could*:
  *Can we come and see you?*
- Now write the following gapped sentence on the board. Ask them to find it in the email and tell you the missing words: *We _____ _____ you the newsletter before we send it.* Then complete the sentence, highlighting the target language.
- To check learners understand the meaning of *should* in this context, ask them, *Do the boys think it is a good idea or not a good idea to show the head teacher the newsletter before they send it?*
  Elicit that they think it is a good idea and explain that here, *should* expresses that *it is a good idea* to do something.
  Now highlight the form used in these sentences. Replace the pronouns (e.g. ~~we~~ → he / I / you) in the sentences and ask learners if you need to change the verbs too. Establish that the verbs don't change when the pronoun is changed. Highlight too that the verb after the modal verbs is without '*to*'.

## 5 Use of English

- Refer learners to **Activity 5**. Ask them what they think Mrs Miller's reply will be to the boys' request. Then ask them to read the text to find out and to choose the correct model verb to complete the reply. They should do the activity on their own and then check with their partner. If necessary, do the first one together.
- Conduct a class feedback. If you think your learners will have problems with this, have more similar examples to hand to illustrate how the modals are used.

> **Answers**
> a would
> b Could
> c should
> d should
> e Could
> f would

 For further practice, see Activities 4, 5 and 6 in the Activity Book.

### Write

- Tell learners they are going to write an email to their own head teacher to ask for something. Draw their attention to the suggested categories and put them in groups of four to brainstorm ideas of things to ask for. Then do a class feedback and put some ideas on the board as examples.
- **Additional support and practice**: In a mixed ability group, you could assign the categories for discussion and writing according to ability (rather than let learners choose a category). The 'new equipment' category is probably the most straightforward, then 'new activity group' and finally, 'organising an event' for stronger learners.
- Put learners in pairs to write the email. They need to choose a category and an idea. Then draw all learners' attention to the sections in **Activity 4** and elicit again the order of these sections in the writing model in **Activity 3**.
- Before allowing learners to start drafting their emails, clarify the structure of the text by going through the headings again:
  **1** elicit the greeting (*Dear ...*); **2** and the first line (*We would like to ask your permission to ....*); **3** then elicit what comes next (The reason why); then write on the board **4** *How ... ?* (it is going to happen); **5** What you need to do before starting; and finally, **6** the ending (*Best regards*).
- Now let learners start drafting the email. Circulate and offer assistance with ideas, grammar and vocabulary. When you are happy with the first drafts, let them write a final draft.
- **Critical thinking:** When learners have finished, put them in groups of four again and give them several emails from other class members to read. They then read and choose one idea that they think would make the biggest difference to the school.

> **Answers**
> Learners' own answers.

For further practice, see Activity 7 in the Activity Book.

 **Wrap up**

- Ask each group to share their chosen idea and list on the board. Then take a class vote on one idea that would make the biggest difference to your school.

## Activity Book

### 1 Vocabulary

- Learners read a factual text from a school brochure / website and circle the noun phrases to describe extra-curricular activities.

> **Answers**
> (go to) computer club / art, music and drama groups / a chess club /
> (join a) cookery group / write for the school newsletter / school choir

### 2 Read

- Learners answer questions about a pie chart on the topic of extra-curricular activities.

> **Answers**
> Computer club: 12 students Art club: 9 students School choir: 6 students No activity: 3 students

### 3 Recording information

- Learners look at information on another pie chart and convert numbers to percentages.

> **Answers**
> 1 Computer club: 35%
> 2 Drama club: 25%
> 3 Art club: 15%
> 4 School choir: 10%
> 5 No activity: 10%
> 6 Chess club: 5%

### 4 Read

- Learners read another model email text and match to a topic.

> **Answer**
> Organise an event

### 5 Use of English

- Learners complete the gapped model email text with modal verbs.

> **Answers**
> 1 would    2 would    3 would    4 would
> 5 would    6 should    7 could    8 should    9 could

### 6 Use of English

- Learners use the modal verbs, *would, could* and *should*, to write sentences from cues.

> **Answers**
> Learners' own answers.
> Suggestions:
> 1 We would like to ask for your permission to start an art club.
> 2 Could you help us organise the club?
> 3 We should ask for permission to use the art room.
> We should ask a teacher to help us organise the club.
> We should ask a teacher to help us run the club.
> We should say in the school newsletter that the club is starting next month.

### 7 Challenge

- Learners write an email to their head teacher asking for permission to start an after-school activity.

> **Answers**
> Learners' own answers.

**For further practice in using modal verbs, see Photocopiable activity 4.**

## Lesson 5: Classroom politics

Learner's Book pages: 28–29
Activity Book pages: 24–25

### Lesson objectives

**Listening and reading:** Listen to and read an extract from a novel about a school issue.

**Speaking:** Discuss classmates' attitudes to each other and treating each other fairly.

**Critical thinking:** Establish fair and kind ways to treat classmates through looking at the example in the novel.

**Vocabulary:** Body language verbs: *hurry; shrug; stare; scribble; shake*

**Values:** Treating classmates fairly.

**Materials:** Learner's Book, Activity Book.

### Learner's Book

 **Warm up**

- Tell learners that they are going to read about a boy who has got some problems at school. Ask them to look at the pictures on page 28 and 29 of the Learner's Book and predict what kind of problems he might have. If possible, enlarge and project the illustrations to focus learners and engage their interest. At this stage let learners speculate on why the boy (Bradley Chalkers) has problems but don't give any definitive answers until they have read the text. Write their ideas on the board for reference in the next stage.
  **Note:** Treat the subject of a difficult boy in class sympathetically from the onset, and communicate to learners that no-one deserves to be treated in this way, even if they show challenging behaviour. One of the tenets of the story is that Bradley Chalkers' problems in school are exacerbated by the unkind treatment of his classmates and teacher and could probably be improved with a more sympathetic, supportive approach.

## 1 Talk about it

- **Critical thinking:** Draw learners' attention to the way Bradley Chalkers is seated on his own in the illustration on page 28. Ask learners if they think sitting on his own helps him with his problems. Would it help if he sat with another classmate? In a group?
- Now ask learners to look at the seating arrangement in their own classroom. Answer the two questions as a class. Most classroom seating arrangements are designed to integrate learners, so point this out too.

> **Answers**
> Learners' own answers.

## 2 Read and listen 12

- Tell learners that they are now going to listen to and read a story about the boy in question, from a novel called *There's a Boy in the Girls' Bathroom* by Louis Sacher. Tell the class to listen and read the whole text quickly, looking for answers to the two gist questions in **Activity 2** and ideas already mentioned in the **warm-up stage** and **Activity 1**. Draw learners' attention to the notes on the board. Stress that, at this point, they only need look for this information and not to worry about words they do not understand.
- Start the audio and tell learners to read the text while listening.
- After reading / listening, conduct a short feedback pointing out information generated from the **warm-up stage** and **Activity 1** that also appears in the text.

> **Audioscript:** Track 12
> See Learner's Book pages 28–30.

> **Answers**
> The main character is called Bradley Chalkers.
> His problems at school: other children and teacher don't like him / are unfriendly towards him; his classmates don't want to sit next to him; the teacher expects him to do badly; he doesn't pay attention in class; he failed his language test.

## 3 Read

- In preparation for learners reading the text again (to answer the comprehension questions), pre-teach the following words, section by section: *closet* (Part 1) / *mumbled* (Part 2) / *frowned* / *awkwardly* (Part 3) / *distorted* (Part 4) / *recess* (Part 5).
- Read out the word definitions and ask learners to find the corresponding word in the text (make sure they only focus on the part where the word appears). Conduct the activity as a reading race to stretch learners and keep them engaged.
  Part 1: *closet*
  A large cupboard (US English).
  Part 2: *mumbled*
  When someone speaks very quietly and not clearly (this can be mimed).
  Part 3: *frowned* (this action can be mimed, no definition needed); *awkwardly*
  Moving slowly and with difficulty.

Part 4: *distorted*
Something that has a shape that isn't normal.
Part 5: *recess*
The time when classes stop for a short break or lunch (US English).

- Tell learners that they are going to read the story again, section by section to answer the questions after each part. They should read and then answer the questions in their notebooks.
- **Additional support and practice:** Learners could work in pairs to do the comprehension questions 1–16. Alternatively you could divide the questions up, so learners don't have to answer all of them but benefit from learning all answers in feedback later on. Put learners in A/B pairs: A answers the odd numbered questions, B, the even numbered ones, then ask them to share the answers at the end.
- After learners have written the answers for questions 1–12, put them in groups of four to check their answers together
- Allow time for this before giving feedback on the answers. Where possible, use the pictures in the book to illustrate the answers.

> **Answers**
> 1 false. He's sitting at the back of the classroom.
> 2 true
> 3 true
> 4 false. It's Jeff's first day at the school.
> 5 false. He says he's never been to the White House.
> 6 true
> 7 false. She says sorry to Jeff for giving him the seat next to Bradley.
> 8 false. They think any place near Bradley is bad.
> 9 true
> 10 true
> 11 false. He has lots of rubbish and useless things in his desk.
> 12 false. Bradley failed the language test.
> 13 false. Bradley didn't listen and cut his test paper up.
> 14 true
> 15 true
> 16 false

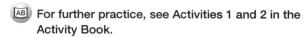 For further practice, see Activities 1 and 2 in the Activity Book.

## 4 Talk

- **Critical thinking:** Ask learners to work in pairs to answer the questions in **Activity 4**. They should discuss the questions and be prepared to give feedback to the class at the end.

> **Differentiated instruction**
> **Additional support and practice**
> - The questions in this speaking activity could be divided up, rather than have all learners tackling all questions; e.g. put learners into groups of four and give each learner a question to think about and then share with the group. Alternatively, give small groups of learners just one question to discuss.

Otherwise give small groups of learners just one question to discuss. At the end of this stage, each group would give feedback on a different question and others could listen and see if they agree or not with the answer given. Early finishers could then be given another question to discuss while others finish.

- Do a class feedback, asking volunteers or nominating learners to share their thoughts on the question themes with the class. Help learners with the language they need to express their thoughts by reformulating sentences where appropriate and highlighting useful phrases on the board. Leave the phrases on the board to help with the last stage of the lesson (**Values**).

### Extend and challenge

- Extend the discussion by asking learners how they would treat Bradley if he was in their class. How could they try to help him?

> **Answers**
> Learners' own answers.

## 5 Word study

- Focus learners' attention on the verbs highlighted in blue in the story. Ask first if learners know the meaning of any of the verbs or can demonstrate one. Then ask them to match the verbs with a definition in **Activity 5**. Tell them that if they don't know the answer, they should read the words and sentences around each verb to help them deduce the answer from the context. Don't allow learners to use dictionaries, encourage them to work at understanding the words from the context they appear in.
- Conduct a class feedback and then call out each verb and ask learners to mime it. Then ask which one is the odd-one-out and why.

> **Answers**
> a hurried / hurry
> b stared / stare
> c shook / shake
> d scribbled / scribble
> e shrugged / shrug
> *Scribble* is the odd-one-out because it is something you do with a pen / pencil; the others are all body gestures.

 **For further practice, see Activity 3 in the Activity Book.**

## 6 Pronunciation

- Focus learners on **Activity 6**. Ask them to listen to and repeat the words from the story and identify the silent letter in each word. If necessary, look at the first word together (island) and make sure learners know what a silent letter is. Pronounce the word together and ask them which letter is *not* pronounced? (s)
- After listening, put learners in teams and ask them to come up with as many other words as they can with the same silent letters. Give a short time limit

(adapted according to the ability of your learners or how long you wish to spend on the activity).

> **Audioscript:** Track 13
>
> | island | listen |
> |---|---|
> | couldn't | scissors |
> | walked | thought |

> **Answers**
> | island (s) | listen (t) |
> |---|---|
> | couldn't (l) | scissors (c) |
> | walked (l) | thought (g) |

**For further practice, see Activity 4 in the Activity Book.**

## 7 Values

- **Critical thinking:** Focus learners on the three questions and put them into pairs or small groups to discuss the answers. If you think learners might struggle to express ideas for **b** and **c**, you could put some suggestions on the board or electronic slide and elicit which they think are the best and worst:
e.g. **b** *The teacher could put Bradley in a group with other kids so that they can help him.* (✓)
*The teacher should tell Bradley off more.* (✗)
*The teacher could make sure that Bradley never sits on his own.*
*The other children should try to be kinder to Bradley.*
*The teacher could give the children a better example by treating Bradley more fairly.*
*The teacher should send Bradley to the head teacher to be punished.*
*The teacher should find out what Bradley is good at and use his skills in the class (e.g. drawing, fixing things, operating the equipment)*
*The teacher could give Bradley responsibilities in class so he feels more included.*
**c** *Bradley won't get better, he's too horrible.*
*Bradley would be friendlier because he would feel happier in class if everyone was nice to him.*
etc.

- Conduct a class feedback and accept all ideas and opinions. However, if learners are unsympathetic to Bradley's character, offer them the idea that everyone deserves a fair chance in class and however challenging Bradley's behaviour is, the way he is treated by his classmates and teacher is unfair and won't help him improve.

> **Answers**
> c Learners' own answers. Suggestions:
> They could help him by giving him a chance, including him in their groups, being kind to him and helping him with his difficulties. The teacher especially should show the children a better example by treating Bradley as an equal to his classmates, encouraging them to be friendly to him and include him more; she should help him with his problems – both academic and social and not point out his failings in front of the whole group.

For further practice, see Activity 5 in the Activity Book.

 **Wrap up**

- You could ask learners to choose three points from **Activity 7** that they feel would be the most help to Bradley in class.

## Activity Book

### 1 Read

- Learners put sentences from a summary of the story in the correct order.

> **Answers**
> a 4   b 1   c 8   d 5   e 9   f 3   g 7   h 2   i 6

### 2 Read

- Learners choose the correct answer (from a choice of two) in sentences that describe some ideas from the story.

> **Answers**
> 1 Jeff is friendly towards Bradley because he hasn't got any opinion about him.
> 2 When Jeff smiles at him, Bradley looks the other way because he doesn't know what to do.
> 3 At break time, Bradley is very surprised.

### 3 Vocabulary

- Learners complete sentences using the target verbs from the box, using the correct form of the verb.

> **Answers**
> 1 shrugged
> 2 scribbled
> 3 stared
> 4 shook
> 5 hurried

### 4 Pronunciation  [CD2 Track 31]

- Learners listen and repeat some more words from the story and identify which letters are silent in each word.

> **Answers**
> 1 wou(l)d
> 2 w(h)ich
> 3 ri(gh)t
> 4 tu(r)ned
> 5 sta(r)ed

### 5 Values

- Learners adapt six sentences to make them true (in their opinion) about their own class.

> **Answers**
> Learners' own answers.

## Lesson 6: Choose a project

Learner's Book pages: 32–33

### Lesson objectives

**Speaking:** Deliver a presentation; perform a role play; revise unit themes; discuss **Unit 2** Big question.

**Writing:** Organise and prepare notes for a presentation and role play; writing a short description of school life in another country; revise unit themes.

**Critical thinking:** Apply new skills and language acquired in **Unit 2** to project work and revision activities.

**Language focus:** Recycling language points from **Unit 2**, i.e. linking phrases; 1st conditional; modal verbs (*would, could, should*); sequencing words

**Vocabulary:** Recycling of new and reviewed vocabulary from **Unit 2**, school subjects; verbs to describe behaviour; after-school activities; verbs to describe body language

**Materials:** dice; electronic slides (if available).

### Learner's Book

**Warm up**

- Put learners in small teams and play the Dice game to revise language and themes from **Unit 2**. Write six themes from **Unit 2** on the board or slide, numbered 1–6. These can be vocabulary based (e.g. 1 *after-school activities*; 2 *food that is good for the brain*; 3 *school subjects*; 4 *behaviour*; 5 *body language*; 6 *words with a silent letter*); or theme-based (e.g. 1 *your favourite school subject*; 2 *an after-school activity you do*; 3 *a problem described in Lesson 3*; 4 *something you'd like to ask for at your school*; 5 *Bradley's story in Lesson 5*; 6 *learning tips*) or a mixture of the two.
- Give each team a dice. They need to roll the dice, and then talk about the item on the board that corresponds with the number that appears (e.g. number 3 (vocabulary) = *school subjects*). When they have finished, they pass the dice to the next person who does the same. All team members should have at least one turn.
- You can give a time limit for each turn (e.g. one minute – the learners need to talk continually for this time) or allow learners to talk for as long as they want to for each turn and give the whole activity a time limit.
- Do a practice round first to make sure learners are clear about the rules of the game.
- If you choose to make the activity theme-based, ask learners to focus on *fluency* rather than accuracy in this activity
- Circulate as learners are doing the activity and praise good speaking efforts at the end.
- Tell learners they are now going to choose from the two projects and follow the instructions below for the one they have decided on.

## 1 A presentation on school life in another country

- Put learners in small groups to do the presentation. Take them through the step-by-step instructions presented in the Learner's Book.
- Spend time helping them to choose a country to research. If they don't have a strong preference, they could choose a country that has featured recently in another school subject, or a country that they have a family connection to. Please refer to the **Teaching tip** on page 39 for more advice on how to manage the research of projects and other Learner's Book tasks.
- When learners are drafting the presentation, the topic list in the instructions will give them a structure to follow. Make sure they also follow general guidelines outlined in **Unit 1** (e.g. an introductory phrase; a device to attract the audience's attention; using sequencing phrases to give structure to the piece; appropriate ending, etc.).
- Give learners time to practise their presentation, ensure that each member has a part to say and that someone is responsible for organising the props (slides, pictures, etc.).
- When learners deliver the presentation, ask the audience to note down one example of something that is different from their school.
- Ask learners to also write a short description of school life in the country they talked about. Ask them to display the descriptions on the wall, read each other's and note down the most interesting fact from each one.

> **Answers**
> Learners' own answers – Portfolio opportunity.

###  Wrap up

- Conduct a feedback at the end of the presentations where the audience shares all the aspects of school life in other countries that they noted, that are different to life at their school.

## 2 🗨 A role play about adding something new to your school

- Put learners in pairs or small groups (depending on ability and confidence – larger groups might be better for some learners) to do this project. Ask them to spend some time discussing something that they feel their school needs.
- They now create a role play using the guidelines set out in **Lesson 3**. The functional language is the same for this project, but the theme is different (discussing something to enhance your school rather than a school problem). See guidelines in **Lesson 3** (page 48) for further guidance on setting on up a role play.
- Draw learners' attention to the language examples on page 32 of the Learner's Book, to help them with expressing their ideas for this role play activity.

- Ask learners to either perform the role plays in front of the class or in groups, as directed in **Lesson 3**. Ask listeners to note down the ideas discussed in the role plays, to share with the whole class in the wrap up stage.

> **Answers**
> Learners' own answers – Portfolio opportunity.

### 🗨 Wrap up

- Ask learners to share ideas discussed in the role plays and vote on the best one for adding something to their school.

### 🗨 Reflect on your learning

- These revision activities can be approached in different ways, according to the level and character of your class.
  - Questions 1–6 could be used as a class quiz, with learners in teams and a time limit given to write answers to each question.
  - Alternatively, you could conduct a revision session – ask learners to work in pairs and take longer to think about and write down their answers. When pairs have finished the questions, they swap with another pair and correct each other's work, with you monitoring and giving help and advice when needed.
  - You could set this task for homework / self-study.

> **Answers**
> 1 Learners' own answers.
> 2 Possible answers:
> If you eat healthy food, you'll have enough energy to study for a long time.
> If you drink plenty of water, it'll help you to concentrate better.
> You'll be too tired to do homework unless you get enough sleep.
> If you eat fish and vegetables, your brain will remember things more easily.
> You won't be able to concentrate if you eat too much white bread and sugar.
> If you get enough activity, your memory will improve.
> 3 Classmates not participating in groupwork / bullying.
> Solutions & advice - see **Unit 2, Lesson 3, Activity 4**.
> 4 Football club / a computer club / a chess club / a music club
> Learn about how to use the Internet, act, dive
> Write for the school newsletter
> 5 The boys want to start a newsletter. They write to the head teacher because they need to ask her permission to start the newsletter.
> 6 The other children were unfriendly towards Bradley; no one wanted to sit next to him and some children said unkind things to him. The new boy, Jeff Fishkin, doesn't mind sitting next to Bradley. At break time, he tries to make friends with him.

## Look what I can do!

**Aim:** To check learners have fulfilled the objectives for **Unit 2** (and to what degree).

- Present the objectives slide or poster from the introduction to **Unit 2** in **Lesson 1** and remind learners of the objectives from the start of the unit.

- Focus their attention on the '*I can ...*' statements on page 33 and read through together. You could put these on a slide or write on the board. Ask learners if they feel they can now do these tasks after completing **Unit 2**. By this point, you should have a clear idea yourself of how well your learners have completed the tasks. However, ask them to now do an initial self-assessment.
- Put learners in pairs and ask them to look through their notebooks and portfolios to find evidence of their work for each of the statements. Then they give themselves a rating as follows:
  ✓ Yes, I can – no problem!
  ? A little – I need more practice.
  ☹ No – I need a lot more practice.
- Circulate and chat to learners about their self-assessment, some might be overly modest and you can point out that their rating could be higher. If you haven't already done so, make notes about areas that learners are not confident about for future reference (see **Teaching tip**).
- Conduct a general feedback at the end and find out which tasks learners found the most interesting / useful / challenging, etc.
- **Extend and challenge:** Customise the mini-awards system idea presented in **Unit 1** for **Unit 2** (see **Unit 1** page 38).

> **Answers**
> Learners' own answers.

### ☞ Wrap up

- As a class, look at the Big question again on a slide or written on the board: *What can we learn in school besides school subjects?*
- Help learners make the connection between the question and the unit themes and tasks by first reading out the following questions and ask learners to find the corresponding unit in their Learner's Book:
  *1 Which lesson taught us how to improve our brain power?* (**Lesson 2**)
  *2 Which lesson told us the story of one boy's experience in class?* (**Lesson 5**)
  *3 Which lesson taught us about school life in other countries?* (**Lesson 1**)
  *4 Which lesson taught us the proper way to ask for something from the head teacher?* (**Lesson 4**)
  *5 In which lesson did we talk about problems at school?* (**Lesson 3**)
- Now show learners the following 'answers' to the Big question and ask them to match to a lesson in **Unit 2**. Put the following on a slide or write on the board:
  *What can we learn in school besides school subjects?*
  – *Ways to look after ourselves and be healthy and strong.*
  – *Lesson _____*
  – *What school life is like for children in other countries.*
  *Lesson _____*

- *Ways to handle problems and who can help.*
  *Lesson _____*
- *How to treat your classmates fairly.*
  *Lesson _____*
- *How to bring an idea to life or make a change.*
  *Lesson _____*
- Alternatively, call out the Big question answers and ask learners to listen (instead of reading from a slide or the board) and match to a **Unit 2** lesson.
- You may feel it more appropriate and challenging to let learners come up with their own answers to the Big question, having worked through **Unit 2**. Rather than present the suggested answers to learners for them to match with a unit, ask them to work in small groups to look through the unit in their Learner's Book and discuss their own interpretation of the Big question. Conduct a group by group feedback at the end, noting down similar ideas and highlighting different viewpoints.

> **Answers**
> (In order of answers above) Lesson 2 / 1 / 3 / 5 / 4

## Activity Book

### Revision

### 1 Vocabulary

- Learners match sentence halves to make sentences that utilise key vocabulary from **Unit 2**.

> **Answers**
> 1 f  2 d  3 a  4 e  5 b  6 c

### 2 Use of English

- Learners complete a short email by circling the correct word from a choice of two. The activity practises key grammar items in **Unit 2**.

> **Answers**
> 1 would
> 2 as well as
> 3 should
> 4 If
> 5 will
> 6 could

### 3 Over to you

- Learners complete sentences using their own ideas from **Unit 2**.

> **Answers**
> Learners' own answers.

### My global progress

- Learners think about their own responses to topics and activities in the **Unit 2** lessons and answer the questions.

**Teaching tip**

Review the learners' work and their own assessment of their progress, noting areas where learners demonstrate strength and confidence and areas where they need additional instruction and practice. Use this information to select areas for review and specific focus, as you continue to **Unit 3**.

# Review 1

Learner's Book pages: 34–35

- Review 1 offers learners the opportunity to review and recycle key language and vocabulary items from **Units 1** and **2**, presented in similar contexts to themes that appeared in these units. All items are briefly covered in activities that are similar in type to those in the Activity Book. There is a range of activity types that cover all skills areas.
- Learners can do Review 1 activities either in class or for homework. However, there are two short speaking activities, which will need to be covered in class (see below for suggestion). The Review pages can also be used to engage early finishers provided learners have already covered the relevant language points in class.
- **Speaking activities:** If learners have done the Review 1 activities at home, the speaking activities could be carried out during a Review 1 feedback session, either at the beginning or end of the class.
- **Feedback:** Answers to the activities can be elicited from learners or displayed on the board or on a slide for learners to use to correct their work. To make the correction stage more interactive, have learners swap notebooks and correct each other's work.

## 1 Listen 14

- Learners listen to an account of a first-time experience and identify what it was.

**Audioscript:** Track 14

When I grow up I want to be a pilot because I love planes. My dad says that you have to be good at Maths and Science to be a pilot. That's OK because I'm quite good at Science but I'm better at Maths.

I have been on a plane twice now and I really love flying. I'm braver than my dad though. He can't stand heights and hated it when the plane took off and landed. For me it was the opposite – I didn't mind at all! I prefer flying to any other way of travelling.

I remember the first time I saw a plane, I looked at it in amazement. I was only four years old and I thought it was a metal bird flying in the sky. And I remember the feeling of excitement the first time I went to an airport and saw the planes close up – they were so huge and powerful and I couldn't wait to get in one!

**Answers**
Dan talks about flying in a plane for the first time.

## 2 Listen 14

- Learners listen again and complete target phrases from the extract.

**Answers**
1 quite / at
2 better
3 have
4 stand
5 mind
6 prefer / to
7 amazement
8 excitement

## 3 🗩 Talk

- Learners make mini-dialogues about experiences, using prompts and practise with a partner.

**Answers**
1 Have you ever been on a rollercoaster?
(Learners' own answers.)
2 Have you ever tried Japanese food?
3 Have you ever ridden an elephant?
4 Have you ever visited another country?
5 Have you ever met someone famous?
6 Have you ever won a competition?

## 4 Vocabulary

- Learners read descriptions of various vocabulary items from **Units 1** and **2** and guess the word or phrase.

**Answers**
1 a day off
2 to admire
3 amazing
4 talented
5 to raise money
6 Art
7 to mess about
8 to hurry

## 5 Use of English

Learners choose the correct language component to complete the email, covering a range of grammar items covered in **Units 1** and **2**.

**Answers**
1 would
2 doing
3 would
4 done
5 Could
6 should
7 should
8 as well as
9 could
10 unless

## 6 📝 Write

• Learners choose one email writing task from a choice of three, covering themes from **Units 1** and **2**. All tasks require learners sort jumbled words to make three questions about the email text in **Activity 1** and **2**. They then answer the questions with a partner (if in class) or write the answers at home.

> **Answers**
> Learners' own answers.

## 7 💬 Talk

• Learners answer various questions about their own school newsletter (if applicable) and extra-curricular activities.

> **Answers**
> Learners' own answers.

# 3 Sport

**What can we learn from doing and watching different sports?**

## Unit overview

In this unit learners will:

- talk about different types of sport
- read about a paralympian
- read and summarise an article about a sports event
- read a story about a football match
- write a radio commentary.

In **Unit 3**, learners will explore the topic of sport, taking in different types of sport, sporting role models, physical activity and sporting events. The idea is to examine what these different aspects of sport can teach us in terms of life skills, as well as look at benefits in terms of physical activity. This is reflected in the Big question, which is presented in **Lesson 1**. Learners will understand that themes, tasks and projects in the unit will contribute to answering this question.

The unit begins by looking at sport at school level: which sports activities are practised and the reason for doing sport and taking part. This lesson gives learners an accessible and familiar topic with which to start the unit, as well as the opportunity to practise a range of receptive and productive language skills. Learners will then go on to look at a sporting role model and examine the attitude which has made her a success, by using appropriate language for reporting information. They will then practise listening to and giving instructions for sports exercise and look at the benefits of physical activity on the body. They will develop key writing skills through examining a reading text about a famous sports event. Finally, they will read about a football match, examining and practising descriptive language and discussing the value of team work.

Because of the nature of the topic, **Unit 3** provides learners with numerous opportunities for personalisation of themes and tasks.

The **Photocopiable activities** provide practice in: reporting statements and writing a summary (**5**) and ordering and practising commentaries for sports events (**6**).

### Language focus

Reported speech; modal verbs (advice);

**Vocabulary topics:** Types of sport and sport equipment; parts of the body; football.

### Self-assessment

- I can talk about my favourite sports.
- I can understand and talk about an article about a Paralympian.
- I can give instructions on how to do sports exercises.
- I can understand and write a summary of a sports event.
- I can understand a story about a football match.
- I can write and read out a description of a sports event.

### Teaching tips

**Approaching literature in class:** In Stage 6, learners will be exposed to a range of literature texts designed to provide rich and varied lexical input and valuable exposure to language structures in context. The longer texts are also chosen to give exposure to universal themes, which are then taken up in the **Values** section at the end of the literature lesson. However, learners may feel daunted by the length and language level of the texts, which might seem challenging. Motivate and reassure your learners by showing them that they can enjoy the extracts without understanding every word; exploit the audio by giving learners uninterrupted time to listen to the narration; dim classroom lights or close blinds to allow them to relax. All the literature texts start with a simple gist task to allow this stage to be relatively undemanding. Pay attention to the illustrations, which have been chosen to reflect key themes and illustrate important vocabulary. Spend adequate time on the warm-up activities to generate initial interest. Further guidance for managing the texts to make them accessible to learners of all levels is given in the corresponding teachers' notes.

# Lesson 1: Sport

Learner's Book pages: 36–37
Activity Book pages: 28–29

## Lesson objectives

**Listening:** Listen to comments about favourite sports and understand the reasons for taking part.

**Speaking:** Talk about sports equipment; interview a partner to find out about preferences for sports activities; conduct a survey with a larger group to find out about preferences for sports activities.

**Writing:** make notes and create a bar chart reflecting survey results.

**Critical thinking:** Develop opinions and indicate preferences for sports activities; interpret information on a bar chart.

**Vocabulary:** Types of sport; *football, judo, gymnastics, basketball, tennis, swimming, badminton, volleyball, athletics, hockey*

sports equipment; *shuttlecock, trunks, goalposts, a net, shin pads, a racquet, a hockey stick, goggles*

**Materials:** flash cards of sports activities relevant to your learners, sports equipment realia (optional); poster paper or electronic slides, coloured pens.

## Learner's Book

###  Warm up

- To introduce the Big question, start by telling the class that this unit is going to be about sport. Explain that we can learn a lot from doing and watching sport and from looking at what makes good sports people successful. So the Big question is ... *What can we learn from doing and watching different sports?*
- Introduce the unit objectives to show learners what tasks are coming up. Present the objectives on a slide or large piece of poster paper to attach to the board.
- Tell learners that you will answer the Big question and look again at the objectives at the end of the unit. Keep the objectives slide / poster to revisit at the end of the unit.
- Tell learners that you are going to start by looking at sports activities. Prepare some flashcards of sports that you know are familiar to your learners, cover the pictures and ask them to guess the word on the covered picture. As they guess, attach the pictures to the board or reveal on an electronic slide. The idea is to get learners thinking about the topic and to generate words and phrases that they already know.
- **Additional support and practice:** As well as using flashcards to introduce the topic, you could bring in some realia and elicit the names of sports from the objects; you and / or learners could mime sports you take part in and have the class guess the sport; or play *20 questions* (see **Unit 1**, **Lesson 4** for instructions).
- Focus learners on the pictures in the first page of the unit and ask if they can see any of the activities mentioned during warm-up.

## 1 🗪 Talk about it

- Put learners in pairs and ask them to talk about the three questions. If necessary, model the activity first with a pair of learners in front of the class.
- **Additional support and practice:** Structure the pair work by giving learners a letter – e.g. A / B and ask As to ask the first question to Bs (and then swap over).
- **Critical thinking:** Learners identify their own preferences from a choice of activities and extend the topic by talking about other sports that are not included in the pictures. Learners can be challenged by being asked to give reasons for doing the sports too.

> **Answers**
> Learners' own answers.

## 2 Word study

- Focus attention on the words in the box and ask learners to match them to the pictures.
- Do a quick focus on pronunciation and word stress by saying the words and tapping or clapping the stress pattern at the same time. Have the class repeat and clap after you. If learners need further practice, ask them to do the same activity again in pairs. You could extend the activity by clapping out stress patterns and ask learners to guess the word (or words – if more than one word follow the same stress patterns).

> **Answers**
> **a** athletics (Stress pattern: oOo)
> **b** gymnastics (oOo)
> **c** badminton (Ooo)
> **d** volleyball (Ooo)
> **e** hockey (Oo)
> **f** judo (Oo)

 **For further practice, see Activity 1 in the Activity Book.**

## 3 Listen 15

- Tell the class that they are going to listen to four children talking about the sports they like and the reasons why.
- Focus learners' attention on the instruction in the book and ask them to tell you what they have to do while listening to the children for the first time (listen to tell you which sports in the box the children are talking about). They need to write the words in their notebooks as they listen.
- Play the listening text; learners listen for and write the activities mentioned from **Activity 2**.
- **Additional support and practice:** Learners who need more support could write the activities first and then tick the ones they hear in the interview.
- After listening to all four speakers once, check answers with the class.

**Audioscript:** Track 15

1   I love it because you can play it anywhere – on the beach, on a playing field, in the park – you just need a ball! You don't even need a proper pitch as long as there's enough space. You can make goalposts out of anything – we use our jackets or sweatshirts ...

2   Last year I really hurt my leg playing in a match against another school. Someone hit me really hard with their stick while we were trying to get the ball. I was wearing old shinpads and they didn't protect me very well. It can get really rough on the pitch but I still love playing. I love being in a team because you work together and help each other to play a good game.

3   I really like it because you exercise all of your body and you feel really energetic afterwards. You don't need to buy much equipment – just trunks to wear in the water and goggles to protect your eyes from the chlorine in the pool.

4   I like it because you can play with one other person or in a group of four. There's a court in the sports centre near our house and my mum books it so I can play with my friends. We have to take our own racquets but we can borrow the shuttlecocks from the sports centre.

---

**Answers**
**Speaker 1** football
**Speaker 2** hockey
**Speaker 3** swimming
**Speaker 4** badminton

---

## 4 Listen

- If necessary, check learners understand the words, *pitch*, *chlorine* and *court* before listening. Write the words on the board and ask learners first if anyone knows what they mean and which speaker mentioned the words (having identified which sports are mentioned, learners may be able to guess the words even if they didn't know them before). If learners can't tell you, give them some simple definitions and ask them to tell you the corresponding word:
  *A place where you play football or hockey?* (pitch)
  *A place where you play badminton or tennis ( or basketball)?* (pitch)
  *A chemical that is used in swimming pools to keep them clean.* (chlorine)
- Focus learners' attention on the sentences a–d. Tell them that they are going to listen again to decide if the sentences are true or false. They need to correct any false sentences. Before they listen, ask them to discuss in pairs to see if they happen to know any answers at this stage; if they think they do, they can listen to check.
- Listen to check. Then work in pairs to complete the activity in notebooks.
- When you conduct feedback, play the audio again if necessary, stopping after each comment and highlighting the parts of each comment needed for the answer.

**Answers**
**a** true
**b** false. She likes being in a team because they work together and help each other to play a good game.
**c** true
**d** false. She likes it because she can play with just one other person or a group of four.

---

## 5 Word study

- Ask learners if they can remember any equipment mentioned by the four speakers. Then focus them on the pictures in **Activity 5** in the Learner's Book. In pairs, ask them to match the pictures to a word in the box.
- **Extend and challenge:** If appropriate, bring a sports bag of portable sports equipment for a specific sport into the classroom (e.g. tennis kit, racquet, ball, cap, etc.) and ask learners to guess what equipment is in the bag (take it out and show when they have guessed correctly).
- Conduct a class feedback, checking that everyone understands the meaning of the words, so that they can successfully do the next part.
- Focus again on pronunciation, following the same steps and ideas in **Activity 2**.
- Then focus learners on matching all the words with the sports mentioned in the listening task. Ask them to draw a table in their notebooks with the four sports mentioned in separate columns. Then ask them to work in pairs again to discuss the answers and complete their tables. Conduct a class feedback.

**Answers**
**a** goggles (Stress pattern: Oo) swimming;
**b** a racquet (Oo) badminton;
**c** a shuttlecock (Ooo) badminton;
**d** shin pads (Oo) hockey;
**e** hockey stick (Oo o) hockey;
**f** trunks swimming
**g** goalposts (Oo) football
**h** a net badminton

AB   **For further practice, see Activity 2 in the Activity Book.**

## 6 Talk

- Focus learners on the sports listed in the box in **Activity 5**. Ask learners to tell you which verbs go with these activities (e.g. *do* athletics and gymnastics; *go* swimming; *play* football / hockey / badminton).
- Now ask them to talk about the sports equipment in pairs, using the sports in the box as prompts. You could elicit a model structure by writing prompts or a gapped sentence on the board (e.g. *You _____ a _____ to _____ badminton*) and ask learners to tell you the missing words. Then they use the sentence as a model to make other sentences. Point out that *athletics* and *gymnastics* have no corresponding equipment listed in the box, so ask them to give you some suggestions (or input vocabulary) and write them on the board (e.g. *shorts, vest, trainers, tracksuit*). Stronger learners can diversify the language for this activity if they choose and talk about other sports and equipment. Give a time limit of about four minutes.

## 7  Talk

- **Critical thinking:** Tell learners that they are now going to interview each other using the questions in **Activity 7**. First, drill the questions to ensure learners are confident with pronunciation.

---

**Differentiated instruction**

**Additional support and practice**

- You could use the *backchaining* method to drill the questions (for instructions, see **Unit 1 Lesson 1**, **Additional support and practice**.
- Pair learners A/B and tell them to interview each other using the questions in the book. Model the procedure first by asking a confident learner a question, and encourage learners to give full, interesting answers (especially for question 2).
- Monitor and circulate as pairs are talking to help with any vocabulary or language issues.

**Extend and challenge**

- To develop learners' fluency and to discourage them from simply reading the questions directly from the book, try a *disappearing drill* (as described in **Unit 1 Lesson 1**, **Extend and challenge**).

---

**Answers**
Learners' own answers.

## 8  Write

- Now focus learners on the notes and bar chart in **Activity 8** and ask learners to identify which question was used in the survey. Draw their attention to features of the bar chart by asking questions like: *How many children did Shireen interview?* (20) *Which was the most popular answer?* (Meeting new friends), etc.

**Answers**
(Question asked) 2 What is the best thing about your favourite sport?

## 9 Write

- Tell learners that they are now going to use the example in **Activity 8** to conduct their own survey and create a bar chart to show the results. Put them in groups of four and ask them to choose a question. Alternatively, if you have a mixed ability class, you could assign groups a question (stronger learners could take question 2).
- If interviewing 20 classmates is appropriate for your learners and class size, then tell them that each group of four will interview five classmates from another group (vary this number according to your class size if necessary).

- Learners then interview their classmates, note down the answers from each interview and then come back to their original groups to combine their results. **Note:** If learners are using question 2 as their survey question, they can either use the reasons given in **Activity 8** or write their own (or a mixture of the two), according to ability and interest. When they have finished interviewing, ask them to sit with their original groups again, put their answers together and create the bar chart. Although they can create the bar chart together, each learner creates an individual chart in their own notebooks. Allow them to use coloured pens, if available.

[AB] For further practice, see Activity 6 in the Activity Book.

## Wrap up

- To finish off, ask learners to share any survey results which were different from anything mentioned in the Learner's Book, e.g. different sports, equipment and best things about your sport.

## Activity Book

### 1 Vocabulary

- Learners do a word search to find vocabulary for sports activities and answer three short questions about their own sports preferences.

**Answers**

| F | H | O | C | K | E | Y |   |   |   |   | B |
|   | O |   |   |   |   |   |   | B |   |   | A |
|   | V | O | L | L | E | Y | B | A | L | L | S |
| S | A |   | T |   |   |   |   | D |   | T | K |
| W |   | T |   | B |   |   |   | M |   | E | E |
| I | J |   | H |   | A |   |   | I |   | N | T |
| M | U |   |   | L |   | L |   | N |   | N | B |
| M | D |   |   | E |   | L | T |   | I | A |
| I | O |   |   |   |   | T |   | O |   | S | L |
| N |   |   |   |   |   |   | I | N |   |   | L |
| G | Y | M | N | A | S | T | I | C | S |   |   |
|   |   |   |   |   |   |   |   |   | S |   |   |

hockey / volleyball / gymnastics / swimming / judo / badminton / tennis / basketball / football / athletics & Learners' own answers.

### 2 Vocabulary

- Learners complete gapped sentences using words to describe sports equipment.

## 3 Read

• Learners read a series of comments about a sport and match it to one mentioned in **Activity 1**.

**Answer**
volleyball

## 4 Read

• Learners match a topic to a comment from a choice of three.

**Answers**
Basic rules 2;
Parts of the body used 3;
Location and equipment 1

## 5 ✍ Write

• Learners write a paragraph about a sport that they do or know about, using the previous activities for support.

**Answers**
Learners' own answers.

## 6 ✍ ⊞ Challenge

• Learners read survey notes and complete a bar chart with information. Then they answer questions about the information.

**Answers**
1 Swimming
2 Football
3 Basketball and badminton.

# Lesson 2: Yes I can

Learner's Book pages: 38–39
Activity Book pages: 30–31

## Lesson objectives

**Reading:** Scan a short article about a Paralympic athlete, to look for specific information.

**Speaking:** Discuss information that you found interesting or surprising in the article; share knowledge about the lesson theme, not included in the text.

**Critical thinking:** Express opinions about information in the text.

**Language focus:** Reported speech in the present (statements and questions).

**Materials:** pictures and videos clips of Paralympic athletes and events (optional for **Activities 1** and **4**); strips of paper for statements (optional: **Additional support and practice, Activity 4**).

## Learner's Book

### ⊕ Warm up

• For learners who know very little or nothing about the Paralympics, you could start the class by reading out some statements about the Paralympic Games (don't mention the name) and ask learners to guess which sporting event they are going to learn about today. Read out or write the following statements and allow them to make suggestions as you are reading / writing. You could also dictate the statements to learners (for a little extra challenge or to settle them down at the beginning of class).
  *Athletes from nearly 150 countries take part in this event.*
  *It takes place every four years.*
  *It follows the Olympic Games.*
  *Every athlete has some kind of physical disability.*
• Elicit or tell learners that today you are all going to learn about the Paralympic Games and one Paralympic athlete in particular.

### 1 Talk about it

• Focus attention on the first two questions. Elicit responses from volunteers and note down on the board the names of any Paralympic athletes that learners know from their own country. If possible, have some pictures ready to elicit these names, if you think learners might know any.
• **Critical thinking:** Learners draw on their own knowledge of the topic.

**Answers**
The Paralympic Games is a major international multi-sport event involving athletes with a range of physical disabilities, including mobility disabilities, amputations, blindness and cerebral palsy. There are Winter and Summer Paralympic Games, held every four years immediately following the Olympic Games.
Learners' own answers.

### 2 Talk

• Tell learners that they are going to read about a Paralympic athlete and focus attention on the pictures and article about Hannah Cockroft. Pre-teach the words, *wheelchair* and *medal*, if necessary by indicating these items in the pictures. Then write *break a world record* on the board and ask learners what this means, explaining that Hannah has broken a lot of world records. Use examples to illustrate the meaning if learners don't know (e.g. *Hannah has won a lot of races in her wheelchair in a faster time than anyone else doing the same sport).*

- Focus learners on the questions 1–5 and read them together. Tell learners to cover the text and discuss with their partner what the answers might be.
- Conduct a class feedback and write a range of suggestions on the board.

## 3 Read

- Now tell learners that they are going to read the article to find the answers from **Activity 2**. Emphasise that they need to *scan* the text just to find the answers to the questions.
- Before reading, look at the **Reading strategy** together, then do a concept-check question to check that learners understand the strategy. Ask them:
  *When you scan a text, do you spend a long time reading everything in detail?* (No)
  *What information are you looking for in this text?* (Only answers to the questions)
  *Do you need to spend a long time doing this?* (No)
  **Note:** Highlight to learners at this stage that scanning is a useful skill that can save time and energy when you are looking for information about something specific, e.g. when you are researching something for a project or a presentation.
- Now let learners read the text to find the answers. Give them a time limit of four to five minutes. When they have finished, ask them to compare their answers with their partner.
- Conduct a class feedback, nominating learners to answer the questions or asking volunteers. Draw attention on the board to any good guesses that were given at the beginning of this stage.

**Answers**
a  a wheelchair athlete
b  21 world records
c  2 Olympic gold medals
d  Cerebral Palsy
e  20 years old

 For further practice, see Activity 1 in the Activity Book.

## 4 Talk

- **Critical thinking:** Put learners into small groups to discuss the article and identify one or two facts that they found most surprising.

**Differentiated instruction**

### Additional support and practice

- Some learners may find it helpful to form their opinions by choosing from a selection of facts, rather than look through the text again. Give them a selection of facts from the text to consider and then select one or two that they found the most interesting or surprising. E.g.
  *Hannah would still like to go to university, despite her great success as a wheelchair athlete.*
  *She wants to compete in four more Paralympic Games.*
  *She has broken 21 world records.*

If your whole class would benefit from this approach, write these statements on the board or electronic slide. Alternatively, you could give the statements out on strips of paper to some groups and have others make their own deduction from the text.

**Additional support and practice**

- Generate further discussion by asking learners to tell you what they know about the disease cerebral palsy and what factors might have inspired Hannah Cockroft to be so successful despite her disability. It might interest learners to know that Hannah's parents always focused on what Hannah *could* do rather than what she couldn't; for example, they let her join dance classes as a very young child, even though she couldn't move in the same way as other children, focusing on the fact that she could do *some* of the moves and that she wanted to have a go. She also lives in a village in a very hilly part of the UK (near Halifax, West Yorkshire) and has said that she has always had to work hard to get up the hills in her wheelchair, so she became a fast wheelchair user!

- **Note:** Use your discretion about how far you discuss actual disabilities in class, especially if your class includes a child with a disability; also bear in mind that some learners might have family members or close friends with disabilities. Make sure the focus of the lesson is achievement and mental attitude, not disadvantages.
- Ask learners to also discuss what other sports people with disabilities do. You could show them some images (e.g. wheelchair rugby and basketball) and ask them to guess the sport. You could also show them some video clips of different Paralympic events.

**Answers**
Learners' own answers.
Sports that people with disabilities do include running / sprinting, swimming, cycling, rugby, basketball, judo, fencing and many others.

## 5 Use of English

- Focus learners back on the text and ask them to look for an example of something Hannah has said. When you hear the line, *I **hate** being told I can't do things*, write it on the board, highlighting with a different colour as per the Learner's Book example.
- Now ask learners to close their books and complete the line, *Hannah says ...* Indicate the first direct statement and see if learners can tell you how to change it to a reported statement. Elicit or input the full reported statement, highlighted as per example:
  ***Hannah says (that) she hates** being told that **she** can't do things.*
  Ask learners to tell you exactly what is different in the reported statement and elicit all of the items highlighted.
- Write the following statement on the board – *I **can't** run but **I** can wheelchair race faster than people can run.* Ask learners to change it to a reported statement.

Elicit:

*Hannah says (that) she can't run but she can wheelchair race faster than people can run.*

- Follow the same procedure with the reported questions. Elicit the question, *How do you live with your disability?*
- Write, *The interviewer wants to know ...* , on the board and ask learners to finish the sentence, 'reporting' the question. When the reported question is on the board, ask learners to tell you exactly what is different about the reported question:
*The interviewer wants to know how she lives with her disability.*
Also point out to learners that 'do' disappears from the reported question.
- Ask learners to find another question in the text. When you hear the question, *What are your plans for the future?*, write it on the board.
- Write, *She wants to know ...* , on the board and ask learners to finish the sentence, 'reporting' the question. When the reported question is completed, ask learners to tell you exactly what is different:
*She wants to know what her plans for the future are.*
Ask learners to tell you what happens to the verbs, *is* and *are* in a reported question (they move to the end of the sentence). Elicit the *subject* in the sentence (her plans) and point out that, in this case, the subject comes *before* the verb.
- Now focus learners on the question in **Activity 5** and ask them to work in pairs to choose the correct answers.

> **Answers**
> In reported 'wh' questions, the verb moves to the end of the sentence. It comes after the subject.

## 6  Use of English

- Ask learners to work in pairs to find other examples of direct speech in the text. Ask them to write the sentences in their notebooks and change to reported statements.
- Review the answers as a class. Clarify any confusions with the concept by presenting more example sentences.
- At this stage it might be worth presenting two more examples of questions for learners to change to reported questions (no others appear in the text except those used in the example above). Write the following questions on the board and ask learners to change them accordingly:
*Where do you live?* (She wants to know where **he lives**)
*What is your favourite sport?* (She wants to know what **his** favourite sport **is**).

> **Answers**
> Examples from text:
> 'You had great success at the 2012 Paralympics.'
> *The interviewer says that Hannah had great success at the 2012 Paralympics.*
> 'What are your plans for the future?'
> *The interviewer wants to know what Hannah's plans for the future are.*
> 'I want to compete in another three or four Paralympics. But I also want to go to university and be a normal person.'
> *Hannah says that she wants to compete in another three or four Paralympics. But she also wants to go to university and be a normal person.*

 For further practice, see Activity 2 in the Activity Book.

## 7 🐟 Talk and write

- Tell learners that they are now going to play the whispering game. Put them in groups of three and ask them to write down three things that they are good at. They mustn't show their sentences to anyone else in their group.
- Now do an activity demonstration in front of the class with a statement you have written about yourself. Make it a humorous false sentence and choose two confident learners ('B' and 'C') to participate. Whisper the statement to 'B' and ask him or her to whisper it to 'C' as a reported statement. 'C' then 'reports' the statement aloud; 'B' and 'C' say whether they think the statement is true or false.
- Learners then do the activity in small groups. They can write sentences according to their ability but make sure that all sentences are in the present tense (*I am really good at ... / I can ...*). You might need to check sentences with some learners before they start the whispering game.

> **Answers**
> Learners' own answers.

## 🡆 Wrap up

- Do a quick round up of the statements that learners used in the game. Ask them to tell you the funniest, most surprising, most unusual, etc. and ask them to relate the sentences using reported statements:
*Wei Xin says that he is good at ...*

## Activity Book

### 1 📝 Read

- Learners read a text about the Paralympics Games and do a comprehension activity.

**Answers**

1 A large international sports event.
2 They all have a disability.
3 Nearly 150 countries.
4 Five sports from: Wheelchair racing; racing on blades; swimming; rowing; wheelchair basketball; rugby; skiing; cycling.

## 2 Use of English

- Learners read an interview with another Paralympic athlete and practise converting statements and questions into reported sentences.

**Answers**

1 He wants to know what his attitude his sport is.
2 Jonnie says (that) he thinks about what he can do, not what he can't.
3 He wants to know what his record time is (for running the 100 metres)
4 Jonnie says (that) it's 10.9 seconds (at the 2012 London Paralympics).
5 He wants to know what Jonnie's / his target is now.
6 Jonnie says (that) his goal is to run the 100 metres in 10.6 seconds.

## 3 📝 Challenge

- Learners write questions to ask their favourite sports star. They imagine the answers and write them as reported questions and statements.

**Answers**
Learners' own answers.

# Lesson 3: Giving instructions

Learner's Book pages: 40–41

Activity Book pages: 32–33

### Lesson objectives

**Speaking:** Prepare and give instructions for sports warm-up exercises.

**Listening:** Listen to someone giving instructions and notice features of language.

**Critical thinking:** Giving advice; what you should, need to and mustn't do when doing physical exercise.

**Use of English:** Modal verbs (for advice): *need, mustn't, should*

**Vocabulary:** Parts of the body: *heart, ankle, hip, shoulder, toes, knees, hamstrings, bottom, thighs*

### Learner's Book

####  Warm up

- Ask learners to do some warm-up exercises to start the lesson and introduce the theme. Ask everyone to stand up, putting chairs under desks and moving away from the desks. Then ask everyone to stand up straight with arms at their sides and do some slow knee squats; then stand up straight again with

hands on hips and turn to each side, twisting from the waists; finally ask them to stand up straight with arms above their heads, lean forward and touch their toes. Add any more warm-up exercise that you know (that can be done safely in class) but avoid jumping jacks, running on the spot and arm rotations, as these come up later in the listening task.

**Note:** Make sure there is enough space in your classroom for learners to do this activity safely, without risk of knocking into classroom furniture or each other.

- Use the words, *muscles*, *bend* and *rotate* in your instructions in this stage to introduce / review these words in preparation for the listening task in **Activity 3**.

## 1 💬 Talk about it

- After exercising, ask everyone what type of exercises they have just done and elicit that these are warm-up exercises. Ask them which parts of their bodies were exercised and write up on the board any vocabulary that learners offer at this stage that appears in **Activity 2**. Explain that before any sport, you need to do warm-up exercises and ask learners if they know why. Ask them if they can tell you which parts of the body you should warm up and if they know any other warm-up exercises.

**Answers**
Learners' own answers.
Warm-up exercises prepare your body for longer periods of exercise by warming up the muscles beforehand. They usually last for 10–20 minutes.
You should warm up any parts of your body that you are going to use in the longer period of exercise. You can warm up with stretches or short periods of gentle exercise like running on the spot, skipping, jumping, rotating parts of the body (e.g. wrists, ankles).

## 2 📝 🔤 Word study

- Focus learners on the word list in **Activity 2**. Then ask them to stand up again and point or touch to each body part as you call out the words (e.g. *heart* – learners put their hands on the area where the heart is; *ankle* – learners touch or point to their ankles). Do the activity with them to teach any unknown words. When learners have a good grasp of the words, you could repeat the activity and make it into a game by calling the words out more quickly and in a different order. Learners have to keep up and point to the correct body part – anyone who points to the wrong part is out!

**Note:** If you feel this activity is inappropriate for any of these parts of the body, simply miss out the word(s) in this activity and use the illustration in the book to identify them later (all words are needed for the activities in this lesson).

- Now ask learners to sit down and in pairs, label the illustration in **Activity 2** by writing the names for the body parts in their notebooks.

- Use this stage to pre-teach *pump* (*What does your heart do to get the blood around your body?*) in preparation for the listening task in **Activity 3**.
- Identify any sounds in the words that may be problematic for your learners and do a pronunciation focus (e.g. vowel sounds in *heart, toes, thighs*; the /z/ sound at the end of *toes, knees, thighs*).

> **Answers**
> 1 b  2 d  3 c  4 a  5 g  6 i  7 h  8 e  9 f

 **For further practice, see Activity 1 in the Activity Book.**

## 3 Listen

- Focus learners on the illustrations in **Activity 3**. Tell them that they are going to listen to some instructions for warm-up activities. They need to listen and put the pictures in order and note down which parts of the body are mentioned.
- Before listening, ask learners to look at the pictures in pairs, and try to describe to each other what is happening in each. This will help to prepare them for the kind of vocabulary they will hear in the instructions. Alternatively, do this together as a class, if your learners need more support. You could input some language too at this stage, if needed.
- Before playing the audio, check that learners understand the task (ask them to tell you exactly what they have to do). Then ask learners to listen and do the tasks outlined above.
- **Additional support and practice:** If you feel your learners will have difficulties with the three descriptions together, you could stop the audio after each part, elicit which picture is described and the parts of the body mentioned in that part.
- When they have listened, ask them to compare their answers with their partner. Then go through the answers as a class.

> **Audioscript:** Track 16
>
> 1 First we need to get your heart pumping ready for action with some high powered jumping jacks! OK, so first stand with your feet together, then jump so your feet are apart and bring your hands up above your head, keeping your arms straight. Do 20 without stopping and finally relax!
>
> 2 You mustn't start running without warming up your leg muscles. First, run on the spot and warm up your legs and ankles. Second, place your feet wider apart to loosen up your hips too – you should warm up your hips too. At the same time bend your arms and move them backwards and forwards.
>
> 3 Now you need to warm up your upper body. Stand still and put your left arm in the air, right arm by your side. Your arms should be straight. Rotate your left arm at the shoulder forward and backwards. Do the same with your right arm. You need to do about 15 turns. Then rotate both arms together, forwards and backwards! You should rotate your shoulders quite slowly. You mustn't rotate them too fast or you'll hurt your muscles.

> **Answers**
> **Picture order:** c, a, b
> **Parts of the body mentioned:** heart, ankles, hips, shoulder

## 4 Listen

- Now ask learners to stand up again (make sure chairs are out of the way). Tell them they are now going to listen to the instructions again and do the exercises. Play the audio and pause between each activity, so learners can finish the activity (e.g. *20 jumping jacks*; *15 turns*) or do enough to get the idea.
- When they have finished ask them to tell you how they feel. Elicit and /or input interesting adjectives (e.g. *energised, energetic, exhilarated*). Ask them which parts of their bodies were exercised to recycle vocabulary from **Activity 2**, (also, can they feel their *hearts pumping*, their *muscles* stretched?, etc.).

 **For further practice, see Activities 2 and 3 in the Activity Book.**

## 5 Use of English

- Introduce examples of the target language by focusing learners' attention on the board and asking if they can tell you the first line of the exercise instructions from **Activity 4**. Elicit or write, *First we _____ to get your heart pumping*. Ask learners to tell you the missing word and elicit, *need*. Highlight *need* in a different colour or underline.
- Follow the same procedure for the next example. Write, *You _____ warm up your hips too*. As you are writing, try to elicit the words from learners as you go along. Then ask learners to tell you the missing word and elicit, *should* (and highlight).
- Follow the same procedure for the last example, *You _____ start running without warming up your leg muscles*. Elicit and highlight the missing word, *mustn't*.
- When you have the three examples on the board, read them through with learners, stressing the target modal verbs and ask some concept-check questions to check the meaning and function.
  *Which sentence means that something is not allowed?* (mustn't)
  *Which sentence means that something is a good idea?* (should)
  *When do we use need?* (when something is necessary)
  *Which verb gives the strongest message?* (mustn't)

> **Differentiated instruction**
>
> **Additional support and practice**
>
> - Give learners more examples of *need, should* and *mustn't* by using examples of rules at your school. Using familiar examples will give them a stronger grasp of the connotations of each verb.
>
> **Extend and challenge**
>
> - When you are writing sentences with target language on the board, try to elicit the words from learners as you go along. Give them clues to make them work with you to construct the sentence. For example, in the sentence, *You _____ warm up your hips too*, you could point to the class to elicit the word, *you* and point to your hips, to elicit *hips*, etc. In other sentences, use similar clues and refer

to parts of speech (*Give me a preposition! Give me an adjective that means ...*). This technique keeps learners constantly on the ball and many children will enjoy the challenge; it also prevents them getting distracted when your back is turned as you write on the board. If you are using electronic slides, you can still use the same technique if you are able to make words appear one by one.

- Now focus learners on form by drawing their attention to the modal verbs and the verbs that follow in the examples. Point them to the second example (with *should*) and ask if the modal verb changes, when you replace *you* with another pronoun (e.g. *he, I, they,* etc). Establish that it doesn't change and then ask which other modal verb behaves in the same way (*mustn't*).
- Then draw their attention to the first sentence with need and ask if this verb is the same as the other two; elicit that no, it changes when *we* is replaced with *he* or *she*.
- Ask learners to look at the verbs that follow the modal verbs and highlight them in the example sentences. Then ask learners in pairs to choose the correct words to complete the sentences about the use of verbs with *need, should* and *mustn't*.
- Check answers together as a class and clarify any confusion with more example sentences.

> **Answers**
> After *should* and *mustn't* we use the main verb. After *need*, we use *to* + main verb.

 **For further practice, see Activities 4 and 5 in the Activity Book.**

## 6 Listen 17

- Focus learners' attention on **Activity 6** and ask them to read through the gapped sentences. Tell them that they are going to listen to the last part of the audio again and complete the instructions in their notebooks (only write the missing word). Ask them what kind of words they expect to hear to fill in the gaps and elicit *need, should* or *mustn't*.
- Play the audio (last part only) and ask learners to listen for the missing verbs.
- After listening, ask them to compare their answers first with their partner. Play the audio again if necessary to check answers. Then check answers together as a class.

> **Audioscript:** Track 17
> Now you need to warm up your upper body. Stand still and put your left arm in the air, right arm by your side. Your arms should be straight. Rotate your left arm at the shoulder forwards and backwards. Do the same with your right arm. You need to do about 15 turns. Then rotate both arms together, forwards and backwards! You should rotate your shoulders quite slowly. You mustn't rotate them too fast or you'll hurt your muscles.

> **Answers**
> 1 need  2 should  3 need  4 should  5 mustn't

## Present it!

- There are several ways you could structure this activity according to the ability, fluency levels and confidence of your learners. The following is a general suggestion. Tell learners that are now going to give their partner instructions for a warm-up exercise. They are going to write the instructions first, then give them to their partner (who will do the exercise). Tell learners that they can use the pictures in the last activity for help or they can make up their own exercise.
  **Note:** This activity is intended to be fun but do emphasise that the exercise must be safe and manageable for other classmates to do (e.g. no contortions or anything that could lead to physical injury). They must also be able to do it in the space available. However, if you are able to take your class outside, this might be more fun and manageable.
- Before learners write their own instructions, hand out copies of the audioscript (or part of it) so learners can use the texts as a model. Draw their attention to the type of sentences used (sentences with modals and imperatives) and ask them to highlight them in the texts.
- Draw their attention to the use of sequencing words and phrases (*first, then, finally, now,* etc.).
- **Critical thinking:** Now ask them to write a short paragraph using their own ideas and the same language. They will use this text to instruct their partner later. Circulate and monitor as they are writing, checking the kind of activities and helping with vocabulary and grammar.
- When they have finished writing, pair them up with another learner (not the person they are sitting next to) and ask them to instruct each other and do the exercises.
- **Additional support and practice:** Some learners might benefit from a more structured approach to this activity where you construct an example together as a class and then ask them to either use this one for the activity or create another, using the example for guidance.
- **Extend and challenge:** If learners are confident and very fluent, they may only need to write some notes on their chosen exercise before instructing their partner. However, make sure you monitor and note down any errors in language or pronunciation for attention later on. If learners have written a paragraph of instructions, they could illustrate this with diagrams either in class or for homework. However, bear in mind that the priority of this activity is speaking and this extension task is purely supplementary.

> **Answers**
> Learners' own answers.

## Activity Book

### 1 Vocabulary

• Learners complete partial words and answer three questions about parts of the body.

> **Answers**
> hip thighs shoulders heart hamstrings bottom ankles knees
> **1** thighs, hamstrings, bottom, ankles, toes, knees
> **2** shoulders
> **3** heart

### 2 Listen 64 [CD2 Track 32]

• Learners listen to a set of instructions describing the Warrior pose in yoga and put pictures in order.

> **Audioscript:** Track 64
>
> 1 First you need to do some stretching activities to warm up your leg muscles. Bend down and touch your toes.
>
> 2 Next, stand with your feet together, body straight, arms by your side. Then breathe in. As you do this, jump so your feet are wide apart.
>
> 3 With your feet apart, raise your arms. They should be at the same level as your shoulders. Your shoulders should be relaxed.
>
> 4 Now turn your head to the right and look along your right arm. Now bend your right knee. Turn your right foot in the same direction as your right arm but you mustn't turn your hips. Your hips need to stay in the same position as before. Stay like this and count to ten. Take long breaths in and out. Finally, follow the instructions again for your left side.

> **Answers**
> **1** c
> **2** b
> **3** a
> **4** d

### 3 Listen 64 [CD2 Track 32]

• Learners listen again, follow the instructions and answer two questions about the exercise.

> **Answers**
> Learners' own answers.

### 4 Use of English

• Learners correct sentences by replacing an underlined modal verb with another from the box.

> **Answers**
> **1** mustn't
> **2** should
> **3** don't need
> **4** mustn't
> **5** need
> **6** should

### 5 Use of English

• Learners choose the correct verb to complete a gapped text.

> **Answers**
> **1** should
> **2** should
> **3** mustn't
> **4** needs
> **5** mustn't
> **6** should
> **7** need
> **8** need

# Lesson 4: Marathon achievement

Learner's Book pages: 42–43
Activity Book pages: 34–35

### Lesson objectives

**Speaking:** Discuss the meaning and give examples of a *challenge*.

**Reading:** Read an article about the London marathon.

**Writing:** Plan and write a summary of an article.

**Critical thinking:** Examining the meaning of a challenge and the reasons why people take part in marathons. Giving examples of personal challenges (in the positive sense) and goals.

**Vocabulary:** words from the London marathon article; *spectators, striving, charity, sponsor*

**Materials:** a video clip and or images of a marathon event (if possible). Copies of **Photocopiable activity 5**.

## Learner's Book

###  Warm up

• Before learners open their books, show them a short video clip of a marathon event. This could be one that has taken place in their country or abroad. Elicit what it is and what they know about it (where it is; approximately how many runners / spectators; how many kilometres; why people take part). Note answers down on the board for reference later. Alternatively you could show them a picture from a newspaper or magazine or use the photos in the Learner's Book to introduce the theme.

### 1 Talk about it

• Focus learners on any questions that they haven't answered in the warm-up stage and ask them to talk briefly in pairs.
• During feedback, ask in particular if anyone knows anyone who has taken part in a marathon. Ask if they know why they did it, how far they ran, how they felt. If you have taken part in a marathon, tell learners to guess how far you ran, where / why you did it, etc. and show them some pictures if possible. **Critical thinking:** if marathons don't take place in the country where you work, discuss with learners the reasons why (climate, practicalities, etc.).

## 2 Read

- Focus learners on the pictures and article in **Activity 2**. Read the task questions together. Tell them that they are going to read the article and look for the answers to the questions.
- Ask them to read the article and give a time limit of about five minutes.
- After reading, ask learners to briefly discuss the questions in pairs and then elicit the answers.
- **Extend and challenge:** As well as the set questions, ask learners if the text mentioned any of the information that they offered in the warm-up stage (recorded on the board).

**Answers**
Over 35 000 people take part.
The route is 42 kilometres long.
Reasons to take part are: to break world records; enjoying a challenge; to raise money for charity.

## 3 Word study

- Focus learners on the words in blue in the article and ask first if anyone knows what they mean. Then read through the definitions and ask learners to match with a word in blue in the text.
- When you go through the answers, do a little pronunciation work on word stress and any problematic sounds.

**Answers**
a sponsor (stress pattern: Oo)
b striving (Oo)
c charity (Ooo)
d spectators (oOo)

## 4  Read

- Focus learners on **Activity 4** and ask them to work in pairs. They are going to read the article again and make notes in their notebooks under the headings. The headings are designed to help learners narrow down the information in the article and identify the main points, in preparation for writing a full summary in the final lesson stage. Point out to them that this activity (and **Activity 5** following) will help them write their own summaries of the article later on.
- Go through the answers as a class and record on the board or on a slide for learners to refer to in the final lesson stage.
- **Additional support and practice:** To give learners extra support with managing the information in the text, put the key points on card or strips of paper (see below, e.g. /42 km route/) and ask learners to match to the headings in **Activity 4**. Make one set per group of three or four. For example, key points as follows: *in spring / every year* (When the marathon takes place)

**Answers**
When the marathon takes place: *in spring every year.*
What it is: *a sports event with thousands of runners who run a 42 km route; over a million people watch.*
Who takes part: *men and women; all ages and nationalities; athletes in wheelchairs, on foot; serious athletes and ordinary people.*
Reasons for taking part: *break world records; enjoy a challenge; raise money for charity.*

**[AB] For further practice, see Activities 1, 2 and 3 in the Activity Book.**

## 5 Read

- Focus learners on the sentences in **Activity 5** and tell them that these sentences will make a very short summary of the article. This should give them an idea of how concise a summary can be. Ask them to work in pairs again to put the sentences in the same order as the points appear in the article.
- When they have finished, go through the answers together as a class.
- At this point ask learners why they think summary writing is important. Explain that it is very useful when you need to find the main points in a lot of information. This can help you when you are studying for exams, writing a report or researching for a piece of work or project.

**Answers**
1 c  2 e  3 b  4 a  5 d

## 6 Talk

- **Critical thinking:** Round up the class with a discussion about what it means to 'enjoy a challenge'. Stimulate the discussion with some pictures of people rock-climbing, parachuting, etc. and ask learners why they think people like to do these things. If you have ever done anything like this for a 'challenge' you could share the story with learners here. Ask learners what challenges they enjoy and if they have ever done anything like a marathon or sponsored event for charity. Have they ever dressed up like the people in the pictures?

**Answers**
*Enjoy a challenge* – to like doing something that makes you work hard and achieve a goal.

## Write

- Ask learners to look at the **Writing tip** and read through the four points together as a class. Tell them that the tips will help them in the summary writing activity they are going to do.
- Now ask learners to use the sentences in **Activity 5** (in the correct order) as a framework to develop the summary and make it into a cohesive paragraph of 75 – 80 words. Tell them to use the notes from **Activity 4**, (all the main points are contained there) and add some simple linking devices, such as '*and*'

and 'because'. Refer them back to the answers for **Activity 4** on the board or slide.

- Learners could work in pairs to construct the summary, but each learner must write their own summary in their notebooks.
- When they have finished, write the summary in the answer box on the board or have it prepared on a slide, so learners can compare it with their own texts.

> **Answers**
> **Sample answer:**
> The London marathon is a sports event that takes place every year in London in Spring. Over 35 000 people run along a 42 kilometre route through the city, watched by over one million people. The runners are all nationalities, ages and abilities. There are athletes in wheelchairs, on foot; serious athletes and ordinary people. Most people do the marathon to raise money for charity and because they enjoy a challenge, others do it to break world records.
> (77 words)

 For further practice, see Activity 4 in the Activity Book.

###  Wrap up

- Dictate about eight to ten examples of challenges and ask learners to copy them down. Make them a mixture of serious and humorous examples, e.g. *climbing a mountain, doing a parachute jump, tidying my bedroom,* etc. Ask learners to discuss in small groups, finally choosing their top three challenges to share with the class.

## Activity Book

**Note:** Activity book activities give targeted practice in all the points on the **Writing tip** in the Learner's Book.

### 1 Read

- Learners read an article about a school Fun Run and answer a question.

> **Answer**
> over $20 000

### 2 📝 Write

- Learners read the article again and match underlined sentences with headings, to give practice in identifying main points and making notes.

> **Answers**
> a 2    b 1    c 5 and 6    d 3    e 4

### 3 Write

- Learners match the sentences from the article to a word with a similar meaning.

> **Answers**
> 1 costumes    2 the park    3 pets    4 families

### 4 Challenge

- Learners write a summary of the Fun Run article in 65–75 words.

> **Answers**
> Learners' own answers.
> **Sample summary:**
> Every year in June, our school does a Fun Run for charity in our local park. Hundreds of people take part and more people watch and cheer.
> Pupils, teachers, families and pets take part! Some people dress up in fancy dress costumes.
> We ask our family and friends to sponsor us to raise money for charity and we get fit too. Our school Fun Run has raised over $20 000 for charity.
> (72 words)

### 5 🔢 Calculations

- Learners answer questions from the information in the text, which require them to do calculations.

> **Answers**
> 1  3000 spectators    2  $30

For further practice in reported statements and questions and summary writing, see **Photocopiable activity 5**.

## Lesson 5: Football crazy

Learner's Book pages: 44–45
Activity Book pages: 36–37

### Lesson objectives

**Listening and reading:** Listen to and read an extract from a novel about football.

**Speaking:** Discuss experiences of live sports events; discuss responsibilities and benefits of team work.

**Intonation:** Understand meaning from intonation and word stress; practise reading with emphasis to express emotions and actions.

**Writing:** Describe a sports event.

**Critical thinking:** Identify situations where learners work in teams and responsibilities involved; consider the benefits of working in a team.

**Vocabulary:** Football: *strikers, defenders,* (goal) *keeper, midfield, goal* (area); descriptive words: *struggled, bounced, blasted, awesome, fired, strike, exploded*

**Values:** Teamwork

**Materials:** audio of sports events commentary or visuals of sports events relevant to learners' interests. Copies of **Photocopiable activity 6**.

## Learner's Book

### 🖝 Warm up

- If possible, introduce this lesson by playing three or four extracts of sports commentary that would be of interest to your learners (e.g. video clips without the visuals) and see if they can guess the sports event (either a specific match or race or the type of sport). Alternatively, you could show learners a range of images from international, national or local sports events (or a mixture) and ask them to identify the event.

## 1 💬 Talk about it

- **Critical thinking:** Focus learners on the three questions in **Activity 1** and ask them to discuss in pairs. Point out that the questions cover any kind of sports events from national to local, so learners can discuss any event from a national football game to school sports day or a local match of any sport. Ask them to describe the event and how they felt.
- Conduct a class feedback, allowing learners time to share any interesting experiences with the class. Use this stage to input or review relevant vocabulary to describe sports events (e.g. *score a goal, cheer,* etc) and keep useful words or phrases on the board or slide for reference in later stages.

> **Answers**
> Learners' own answers.

## 2 Read 18

- Tell learners that they are now going to listen to and read an extract from a novel about football (*Off Side* by Tom Palmer). First focus their attention on the **Listening strategy** and explain that, as they listen, they need to pay special attention to the way the narrator reads the story and the expression in his/her voice. Ask them how this can help them understand the story better and elicit or input the following ideas: *The expression in the narrator's voice can tell us a lot by letting us know if a part of the story is exciting, happy, funny, frightening or sad, etc. Narrators change the pace of their voices or emphasise short sentences, when something dramatic is about to happen; they lower their voices to indicate something bad is about to happen; they also emphasis important words to help us keep track of the story. The expression in the narrator's voice can help us understand the sense of the story, even if we don't understand all the words.*
- Focus learners on **Activity 2** and tell them they are going to listen to the first part of the story. Ask them to look at the pictures and introduce Danny and his dad. Ask them to tell you where they are (at a football match). Then read the rubric for **Activity 2** so they are clear about the story context and the initial gist questions. Stress that, at this point, they only need to listen for this information and not to worry about words they do not understand.
- Start the audio and tell learners to read the text while listening.
- When they have answered the questions, ask them to compare their answers with their partner. Then conduct a short feedback.

> **Audioscript:** Track 18
> **Part 1**
>
> Danny and his dad came to every City home game. And Danny acted as commentator because, when he was younger, his dad had been blinded in an accident. He'd had to stop work, stop playing football with Danny, stop almost everything.
>
> Danny remembered worrying if his dad would give up going to the football too. But on the day of the first game, after he was out of hospital, dad had stood up.
>
> 'Danny?'
>
> 'Yeah.'
>
> 'Come on, son. City are at home. What are you waiting for?'
>
> Since then Danny had become skilled at describing live football, telling his dad just enough so that he could follow the game ...

> **Answers**
> Danny helps his dad by telling him what's happening in the game / acting as commentator. He does this because his father is blind.

## 3 Read 18

- Ask learners to read and listen to the first part again and this time, answer the questions at the end of the extract, following the same procedure as for **Activity 2**. These questions help to establish the context of the story.

> **Answers**
> a Danny's football team are called City.
> b They watch the team in their home city (near where they live).

## 4 Read 18

- Tell learners that they are going to read and listen to the rest of the story and then read again, to answer the questions after each part in their notebooks. Explain that this time the story moves to a description of a live football match, which Danny and his dad are watching in the stadium.
- Play the audio all the way through first to let learners enjoy the whole story; then ask them to read the story part by part and answer the questions.
  **Note:** The extract is quite challenging, in terms of vocabulary especially, but the questions have been graded to give learners a manageable comprehension task. The intention is to build confidence in handling a challenging text with graded tasks, and by exposing learners to expressive narration, from which they can get a strong sense of the story themes and ideas, without the need to understand every word. Therefore, try to refrain from having learners look up every unfamiliar word in dictionaries and encourage them to deduce meaning from context. Further work will be done on handling some of the more challenging vocabulary in a later stage and in the Activity Book.
- After learners have written the answers for questions c–i, put them in groups of four to check their answers together.

- Allow time for this before giving feedback on the answers. Where possible, use the pictures in the book to illustrate the answers.
- **Extend and challenge:** After reading, ask learners for their responses to the story and narration, by using the questions in **Activity 2** the Activity Book.

---

**Audioscript:** Track 18

**Part 2**

... The second half was fantastic. City poured players forward. Their twin strike force looked lethal. Sam Roberts, England's leading scorer and new sensation, Ghanaian international Anthony Owusu. Danny struggled to keep up his commentary just as much as the United defenders struggled to keep up with City's strikers.

'Owusu is playing deep,' Danny told his dad. 'Roberts further up.'

And as he spoke, City's midfield dynamo launched a high cross into the United area. The ball ricocheted off a defender to Owusu, who controlled it on his knee and volleyed it with amazing power. At first the ball seemed to be going way over, but then it began to dip into a powerful arc. Half a second later it was crashing in off the crossbar and bouncing about in the goal.

**Part 3**

One-nil. An awesome strike.

Danny and his dad leapt into each other's arms as the crowd exploded. First with the loudest cheer of the season, then with the name of the scorer. Over and over again.

*Ow-usu! Ow-usu! Ow-usu!*

When the fans had gone quiet enough for anyone to talk, Dad spoke.

'What happened?'

This always amused Danny. His dad would be leaping around, punching the air, screaming at the top of his voice one minute, then calmly asking to know why he's been jumping around in the first place.

'Owusu ...' Danny said breathlessly.

'I gathered that.'

'... he just blasted it in!'

'Yeah?'

**Part 4**

Danny knew his dad needed more. So he decided to give it to him: like a proper reporter on the radio. He breathed in and began.

'City's amazing Ghanaian international has scored the goal of the season. Picking the ball up on the edge of the area, he took it on his knee, then fired an unstoppable volley past the paralysed United keeper. That's Owusu's twentieth goal of the season. And just goes to show that he deserved the African Player of the Year award he received only two weeks ago'.

---

Answers

c 1   d 2   e 1   f 2   g 2   h 2   i 3

---

 **For further practice, see Activities 1 and 2 in the Activity Book.**

## 5 Word study

- Focus learners on the diagram in **Activity 5** and ask them to label it in pairs. Then go through the answers as a class.
- **Additional support and practice:** Read out the definitions in **Activity 4** in the Activity Book and ask learners to listen and label the diagram. You could just give them the definition and ask them to tell you the word and then label or give them the word and definition and ask them just to label.

---

Answers
1 goalkeeper
2 goal area
3 defenders
4 midfield
5 strikers

---

 **For further practice, see Activity 4 in the Activity Book.**

## 6 Word study

- Focus learners on the story again and draw their attention to the words in blue (*descriptive words*) by asking them to tell you how many they can see (there are 7 – *awesome strike* counts as two).
- Tell them that you are going to give them some words with similar meaning and they need to match them to the words in blue.
- Before they do the activity, show the class an example of how to deduce something by context using the word, *exploded* (Part 3). Ask learners what football fans do when their team score a goal (*go crazy, cheer very loudly, shout a lot,* etc.); then ask them to find a word in the text to describe 'very loud cheers' (*exploded*). Give a very short time limit to encourage them to skim the text for gist, rather than pour over every word. When they have found the answer, ask what information around the word (the *context*) helped them to deduce its meaning (*a fantastic goal just scored, the score, Danny and his dad hugging*).
- Now put the following definitions on the board or a slide: very good, kick very hard, a hard kick or hit, run very fast, go up and down, find something difficult. Ask learners to work in pairs to match them to the words in blue. Set this activity up with an element of competition and give a time limit. Emphasise that they are not allowed to use dictionaries and must try to deduce the meanings from the context.
- Then go through the answers as a class. Explain to learners that if they look up some of these words in the dictionary, they might not find the meaning given here (e.g. *blasted, exploded, fired*). This is because when writers write in a very descriptive way, they often use words in a different way to the meaning in the dictionary.
- **Extend and challenge:** Instead of giving the learners written definitions for the words in blue, read the definitions aloud and ask them to scan the text quickly to find the corresponding word.

## 7 Word study

- Now ask learners to do **Activity 7** as a consolidation activity. This text will also help them in the writing stage, so it is a good idea to ask them now to write out the whole text in their notebooks, (with the underlined words replaced with the more descriptive words), so they have a model text.
- To check answers, you could read out the text, stop at an underlined word and let learners tell you the word that should replace it. Try reading the text with expression, in preparation for the next stage.

**Answers**
a  blasted
b  struggled
c  fired
d  awesome
e  strike
f  keeper
g  bounced
h  exploded

 For further practice, see Activity 3 in the Activity Book.

## 8 Intonation 19

- Focus learners on **Activity 8** and ask them if they noticed how the narrator emphasised certain words when reading the story. Then tell them that they are now going to listen to the last part of the story again and repeat the sentences. They need to note down which words were emphasised.
- Play the audio, pausing after each sentence or clause to allow learners to repeat and note down the emphasised words. Make the activity fun and active by exaggerating the stress on the words and ask learners to do the same. At the end let them compare with a partner.
- During feedback, note the emphasised words on the board, so learners can check spelling. Then play the extract again so learners hear it as a continuous commentary. This text (like the text in the previous stage) will serve as a model in **Activity 9**.

**Audioscript:** Track 19
'City's amazing Ghanaian international has scored the goal of the season. Picking the ball up on the edge of the area, he took it on his knee, then fired an unstoppable volley past the paralysed United keeper. That's Owusu's twentieth goal of the season.

**Answers**
**Key words emphasised:** amazing goal season fired
unstoppable past paralysed twentieth

## 9  Write

- Explain to learners that they are now going to write their own short sports commentaries. If possible, show them some short video clips of exciting sports events for inspiration (e.g. a famous goal or Usain Bolt's gold medal winning sprint in the 100m at the London 2012 Olympics) and to listen to the commentary (for the passion and excitement rather than the language, which may be too colloquial).
- Ask learners to work in pairs or small groups for this activity. Tell them to choose a sports event that they feel passionate about and to imagine they are watching it live and have to communicate what's happening and the exciting atmosphere. You could ask them to write for someone who can't see it (like Danny's father in the story) or a TV audience.
- Ask learners to think of a dramatic opening line and focus them on the two examples from **Activity 7** and **8** as models. This line could describe the lead up to a dramatic climax (e.g. **Activity 7** text) or something amazing that has just happened and the events leading up to it (e.g. **Activity 8** intonation text). Tell them to use descriptive words from the texts and other ones that they know. Circulate and monitor and help out with vocabulary and grammar.
- **Additional support and practice:** Ask learners to work in groups and give them opening lines to start them off, e.g. *The fastest man in the world is blasting down the track … . Brazil's best striker has just scored again!*
- When they have finished writing, ask them to practise reading the commentaries in their groups and identify words for emphasis. Ask them to practise again, this time with the emphasised words and then pair them up with a new partner to read out and listen to each other's commentaries.

**Answers**
Learners' own answers.

## 10 Values

- **Critical thinking:** Turn learners' attention now to the topic of teamwork. First elicit from the class what kind of teams they are involved in at school and outside. Put their answers on the board to emphasise the variety of teams they work in. Then focus them on the questions in **Activity 10** and ask them to discuss in pairs. Alternatively, you could ask them to work in small groups, divide the questions up and give a different question to each group (according to interests and/or ability).
- Conduct a class feedback and allow learners to share their thoughts on aspects of the questions.

**Answers**
Learners' own answers.

 For further practice, see Activity 5 in the Activity Book.

## Wrap up

- Ask learners to read out the funniest or most dramatic sports commentaries in front of the class. Listeners have to guess which sport or sports event the commentary is about.

## Activity Book

### 1 Read

- Learners consider sentences about the story and decide if they are true or false. They correct the false ones.

> **Answers**
> 1 true
> 2 false. Danny's dad is blind.
> 3 true
> 4 true
> 5 false. Owusu and Roberts are strikers.
> 6 false. Anthony Owusu scores a goal.
> 7 false. The *City* fans cheer very loudly.
> 8 true

### 2 Over to you

- Learners answer questions giving personal opinions about the story and how listening to a story being narrated can make a difference to understanding.

> **Answers**
> 1 Learners' own answers.
> 2 Learners' own answers.
> Listening to a story can make a difference to comprehension because the listener can pick up clues about story themes from the narrator's voice. The way the narrator expresses the sentences through pace, emphasis and intonation all give valuable clues without the listener having to understand every word that is read.

### 3 Vocabulary

- Learners find further descriptive words in the story and match to a definition.

> **Answers**
> a lethal
> b ricocheted
> c unstoppable volley
> d paralysed
> e midfield dynamo
> f twin strike force

### 4 Vocabulary

- Learners read descriptions of different parts of a football team and match to a word.

> **Answers**
> 1 defenders    2 midfield    3 strikers    4 (goal) keeper

### 5 Values

- Learners write a short description of a school team that they belong to.

> **Answers**
> Learners' own answers.

 For further practice in creating and practising sports commentaries, see **Photocopiable activity 6**.

## Lesson 6: Choose a project

Learner's Book pages: 48–49

### Lesson objectives

**Speaking:** Deliver and record a sports commentary; discuss **Unit 3** Big question.

**Writing:** Plan and write an article about a sports star or event; plan and write a descriptive commentary about a sports event; revise unit themes.

**Critical thinking:** Apply new skills and language acquired in **Unit 3** to project work and revision activities.

**Language focus:** Recycling language points from **Unit 3**, i.e. reported speech; modal verbs (advice).

**Vocabulary:** Recycling of new and reviewed vocabulary from **Unit 3**, i.e. types of sport and sport equipment; parts of the body; football; descriptive words

**Materials:** paper; poster paper; coloured pens; audio recording equipment (optional) (for project work); poster or electronic slides (for **Wrap up**).

## Learner's Book

### Warm up

- Do a '*Find someone who*' activity to revise language and themes from **Unit 3**. Give learners the following sentences on a worksheet or ask them to copy them down in their notebooks;
  *Find someone who ...*
  1 *plays for a school team*
  2 *has been to a big sports event*
  3 *does judo*
  4 *has seen a famous sports star*
  5 *can advise you about warm up exercises*
  6 *can name two Paralympic athletes*
  7 *can tell you eight 'football words'*
  8 *is good at gymnastics.*
- If learners are not already familiar with this activity, explain that they have to find someone in the class who has done any of these things by asking their classmates direct questions. If a classmate answers *yes* to a question, write their name next to it. Then move on and ask other classmates the remaining questions. The objective is to find someone for each of the questions.

- First ask learners how to make a question for each piece of information. Give them a few minutes to construct the questions with a partner if necessary, or just elicit each question verbally if your learners are confident speakers. For example: *Find someone who plays for a school team* ... (Direct question) *Do you play for any school teams?*
- When you have checked that they have formed the questions correctly, do a little pronunciation practice and drilling on any problem sounds or longer questions. Model the activity first in front of the class, if necessary, to make sure learners understand the task.
- **Extend and challenge**: If classmates respond *yes* to the questions, learners could follow up with *Wh*-questions, e.g. *Do you play in any school teams?* Yes, I do. → *Which team do you play in?*
- Then ask learners to stand up, mingle and ask each other the questions. Give them a time limit.
- When they have finished, do a quick feedback to find out who replied positively to each question.
  **Note:** You could adapt some of these questions to make them more directly relevant to your class.
- Tell learners they are now going to choose from the two projects and follow the instructions below for the one they have decided on.

## 1 Write an article about a sports star or sports event

- Take learners through the step by step instructions presented in the Learner's Book. Spend time helping them to generate ideas for their chosen theme by having them look at pictures or video clips and asking them questions about their favourite sports people and sporting events they might have been to or seen on TV.
- When learners are drafting the questions in stage 2, monitor and help with structuring the questions correctly and generating suitable vocabulary.
- When learners are researching the answers to their questions in stage 3, use the **Teaching tip** in **Unit 2** (Unit overview) to focus their search. If learners can't find the answers to their questions, tell them that they can invent them from the knowledge that they already have about the subject.
- When learners are planning their article, refer them to the texts in **Lessons 2** and **4** as models. If they are writing about a sports person, they could start the article with an interesting quote, in a similar way to the article in **Lesson 2**.
- When they write a summary, refer them to the **Writing tip** and tasks in **Lesson 4** for guidance.
- After they have completed stage 6, ask learners to display the posters on the classroom walls and walk around reading the articles and noting down at least two interesting or surprising facts that caught their attention.

 **Wrap up**

- Conduct a feedback at the end where learners share points they found interesting from each other's articles.

## 2 Make a commentary of a sporting event

- Take learners through the step by step instructions presented in the Learner's Book. If learners select a real event for their commentaries, give them the opportunity to watch it first (e.g. on YouTube) so that they can make notes. Their notes need to focus on: *Who? Where? What happened?*
- Ask them to write their descriptions in stage 2 in small groups (one text per group). Refer them to the descriptive words and examples in **Lesson 5** as models, as well as the example sentences in the project 2 rubric. Circulate and monitor, helping with language and writing style. Make sure all learners are participating in each group, e.g. writing; focusing on vocabulary, checking grammar, etc. Learners can write the commentaries just using present tenses, if they choose.
- When learners have finished their drafts, give them time to practise reading the commentaries aloud and identifying words for emphasis. Again, monitor and circulate, helping with pronunciation and encouraging exaggerated, passionate delivery in the manner of sports commentators. Make the activity fun and active and ask learners to listen to and comment on each group members' delivery.
- Ask each group to choose one group member to make an audio recording. The idea of this is to mimic as far as possible a radio or TV commentary. If learners have described a real event, you could even try to synchronise the recordings with a video clip of the event. If these facilities are not available, learners could read out their commentaries in front of the class. If learners listen to the commentaries without any visuals, ask them to guess the sports events being described.

 **Wrap up**

- Ask learners to vote on the most exciting recording, best expression, etc. However, make sure that you praise *all* class efforts and ask learners to applaud after each commentary.

## Reflect on your learning

- These revision activities can be approached in different ways, according to the level and character of your class.
  - Questions 1–7 could be used as a class quiz, with learners in teams and a time limit given to write answers to each question.
  - Alternatively, you could conduct a revision session – ask learners to work in pairs and take longer to think about and write down their answers. When pairs have finished the questions, they swap with another pair and correct each other's work, with you monitoring and giving help and advice when needed.
  - You could set this task for homework / self-study.

> **Answers**
> **1** Suggestions:
> You wear these when you play hockey (shin pads).
> You wear these to protect your eyes (goggles).
> You use this to play badminton (racquet).
> You hit this with a racquet when you play badminton (shuttlecock).
> You hit the ball with this when you play hockey (hockey stick).
> You kick the ball into this when you score a goal in football (goalposts).
> You hit the shuttlecock over this when you play badminton. (net).
> **2** Learners' own answers.
> **3** Hannah says that she wants to compete in another three or four Paralympics.
> Hannah says that she wants to go to university.
> The interviewer wants to know what her plans for the future are.
> **4** Learners' own answers.
> **5** Possible answers:
> To raise money for charity.
> To break world records.
> To enjoy a challenge.
> **6** Danny tells his dad what's happening in the football match. He needs to help him because he is blind.
> **7** Learners' own answers.

## Look what I can do!

**Aim:** To check learners have fulfilled the objectives for Unit 3 (and to what degree).

- Present the objectives slide or poster from the introduction to **Unit 3** (in **Lesson 1**) and remind learners of the objectives from the start of the unit.
- Focus their attention on the 'can do' statements and read through together. You could put these on a slide or write on the board. Ask learners if they feel they can now do these tasks after completing **Unit 3**. By this point, you should have a clear idea yourself of how well your learners have completed the tasks. However, ask them to now do an initial self-assessment.
- **Critical thinking:** Put learners in pairs and ask them to look through their notebooks and portfolios to find evidence of their work for each of the statements. Then they give themselves a rating as follows:
  ✓ Yes, I can – no problem!
  ? A little – I need more practice.
  ☺ No – I need a lot more practice.

- Circulate and chat to learners about their self-assessment (some might be overly modest and you can point out that their rating could be higher). If you haven't already done so, make notes about areas that learners are not confident about for future reference (see **Teaching tip**).
- Conduct a general feedback at the end and find out which tasks learners found the most interesting / useful / challenging, etc.
- **Extend and challenge:** Customise the mini-awards system idea presented in **Unit 1** for Unit 3 (see **Unit 1** page 38).

> **Answers**
> Learners' own answers.

## ☞ Wrap up

- As a class, look at the Big question again on a slide or written on the board: *What can we learn from doing and watching different sports?*
- Elicit initial responses, or put learners in small groups to look through **Unit 3** and discuss the Big question in relation to the unit themes. However, learners may need guiding to help them make the connection between the question and the unit themes and tasks. If so, write these 'answers' to the Big question on the board (or put on a slide).
  **Big question 'answers':** We can learn ...
  1 ... how people overcome difficulties and achieve their goals.
  2 ... how sport can make us feel healthier and have good friendships.
  3 ... how people do other good things through sport.
  4 ... how to describe a sports event in an interesting way.
  5 ... how to do activities that make our bodies fitter and stronger.
- **Critical thinking:** Ask learners to look through their Learner's Book and match an answer to a lesson. Then ask them to find an example for each answer from the lesson in question.
- **Extend and challenge:** Most of the answers given to the Big question could be turned into further class discussion, if this hasn't been done in previous lessons, e.g. **Lesson 2:** Hannah Cockroft's example of turning her disability into something positive through sport.

## Activity Book

### 1 Revision

* Learners complete a crossword covering key grammar and vocabulary from **Lessons 1–6** in **Unit 3**.

**Answers**
**Across: 3** warm   **5** need   **6** muscles   **8** team
              **9** do   **10** stick   **11** goal   **12** race
**Down: 1** swimming   **2** knee   **4** inside   **6** medals   **7** strike

### My global progress

* Learners think about their own responses to topics and activities in the units and answer the questions.

**Answers**
Learners' own answers.

### Teaching tip

Review the learners' work and their own assessment of their progress, noting areas where learners demonstrate strength and confidence and areas where they need additional instruction and practice. Use this information to select areas for review and specific focus, as you continue to **Unit 4**.

# 4 The big screen

## Unit overview

In this unit learners will:
- talk about different types of film
- read about the history of films
- listen to and discuss a film review
- create scenes from a film
- read and understand a film storyline.

In **Unit 4**, learners will explore the topic of films; covering different types of film, film history, expressing opinions about films and how film scenes are put together. Learners are presented with the Big question in **Lesson 1** and will understand that tasks and projects in the unit will contribute to answering the question. The unit begins by developing the language needed to describe different types of contemporary films and, within this, practising communication and listening skills. Learners then go on to explore the history of films and language often used to describe events on a timeline. In **Lesson 3**, they will then practise explaining different parts of a film and expressing opinions through the communication skills focus. In **Lesson 4**, they will practise writing skills by creating a storyboard showing different parts of film scene, using dialogue and description. Finally, they will read an extract from a novel of a well-known film and continue work from the previous unit in understanding vocabulary from context.

Like other units, the **Unit 4** topic gives learners numerous opportunities to develop all skills through lesson themes that draw on their own interests and creativity.

The **Photocopiable activities** provide practice in: using relative clauses to describe a film (**7**) and reviewing film-related vocabulary (**8**).

### Language focus

Adverbs (with adjectives); past simple passive tense; relative clauses.

**Vocabulary topics:** Types of films; strong adjectives; cinema history; understanding words from context.

### Self-assessment
- I can talk about different types of film.
- I can understand a timeline showing the history of cinema.
- I can discuss a film review.
- I can create a storyboard to show a film scene.
- I can understand a story that has been made into a film.

### Teaching tips

**Deducing vocabulary from context:** Draw learners' attention to the idea of approaching unfamiliar vocabulary in a reading text by first looking at the context in which it is set, rather than automatically using a bilingual dictionary. The first step is to work at deducing meaning from the words and sentences around the word. Learners should also consider the theme of a whole paragraph and also look at any visual images and headings around the text.

The idea is to give learners skills that will encourage them to be autonomous and confident readers. Over-reliance on dictionaries can hinder learners especially when tackling descriptive vocabulary, as definitions do not always match with the meaning in the text. Therefore, encouraging them in this approach at this stage will prepare them for challenges with more complex reading texts in later years. Further guidance and practice is given on how to identify words from context in this unit.

# Lesson 1: The big screen

Learner's Book pages: 50–51
Activity Book pages: 40–41

## Lesson objectives

**Listening:** Listen to movie trailers to identify the film type.

**Speaking:** Describe a film you have seen using descriptive adjectives and adverbs.

**Critical thinking:** Indicate preferences for film types and describe impressions of films you have seen.

**Language focus:** Adverbs (with adjectives)

**Vocabulary:** Types of films; *animation, comedy, horror, science-fiction, adventure, drama, action, historical*

Strong adjectives: *hilarious, amazing, terrifying, heart-breaking, thrilling, gorgeous*

**Materials:** poster paper or electronic slides; two or three trailers from popular current children's movies (optional – see **Warm up**).

## Learner's Book

###  Warm up

- If you have the facilities, you could introduce the unit by playing two or three short trailers of current popular films (without showing the opening shots and title) and ask learners to quickly guess the films. Then, introduce the Big question, by telling the class that this unit is going to be about films. Explain that they are going to look at several different sides to films and movie-making – recent films and films in the past and also look at how scenes are put together. So the Big question is ... *What goes into making a film?*
- Write the question on the board or (for an electronic presentation, create a slide with interesting graphics). Tell learners that you are all going to do tasks and projects in the unit that will answer this question.
- Introduce the unit objectives to show learners what tasks are coming up. Present the objectives on a slide or large piece of poster paper to attach to the board.
- Tell learners that you will answer the Big question and look again at the objectives at the end of the unit. Keep the objectives slide / poster to revisit at the end of the unit.
- Tell learners that you are going to start by looking at types of films. Choose a film that falls into a distinct film category and play a quick game of *20 questions*, where learners ask yes / no questions to guess the name of the film (see **Unit 1 Lesson 4 Warm-up stage**).
- When learners have guessed the name of the film, ask them if they can tell you what type of film it is. then elicit other words for film types and write their suggestions on the board for reference in the next stage.

## 1  Talk about it

- Put learners in pairs, focus them on **Activity 1** and ask them to talk about the questions.
- Do a quick feedback around the class, asking learners to tell you what type of films their partner likes. Then do a class vote on where they prefer to watch films.
- **Critical thinking:** Learners identify their own preferences for different types of films and places to watch them. Learners can be challenged by being asked to give reasons too.

> **Answers**
> Learners' own answers.

## 2 Word study

- Focus attention on the words in the box and ask learners to match them to the pictures. Then ask around the class which of these types of films learners have seen recently. Use this stage to focus on word stress and pronunciation, if necessary.

> **Answers**
> **a** adventure (stress pattern: oOo)
> **b** horror (Oo)
> **c** historical (oOoo)
> **d** animation (ooOo)
> **e** drama (Oo)
> **f** comedy (Ooo)
> **g** science-fiction (Oo-Oo)
> **h** action (Oo)

**[AB]** For further practice, see Activities 1 and 2 in the Activity Book.

## 3 Listen 20

- Tell the class that they are going to listen to some movie trailers and match to film type in **Activity 2**. Play each trailer, pause and ask learners to tell you the type of film.
- Play the trailers again and ask learners if they can tell you a little about the story from what they've heard.
- **Additional support and practice:** If you need to structure the second part a little more, prompt learners with the following questions:
  **Trailer 1** *Are Horace and Boris nice or naughty?* (naughty) *Are they friends or enemies?* (enemies) *Why is their dad going to take them for a weekend away?* (To make them friendlier towards each other). *Do you think it will be a success?* (No)
  **2** *What is the heroine's name?* (Torah) *What must she do?* (Go on a journey to protect the secret of her country). *Do you think it will be a safe or dangerous journey?* (dangerous).
  **3** *Who is going to frighten everyone in this movie?* (Suzi – an evil old cat); *What do you think she will do?* (Learners' own answers)
  **4** *Where are the heroes?* (Lost in space in their spaceship) *Are they safe?* (No, something is attacking them) *What do you think is going to attack them?* (A monster? An alien?)

**Audioscript:** Track 20

**1** Get ready to laugh 'til you scream. Terrible twins, Horace and Boris are back and they're crazier than ever! Dad thinks a fun-filled weekend in the great outdoors will encourage the brothers to 'bond'. How wrong can he be?!

**2** An adventure too big for one land ...

**Boy:** Torah – don't leave us ...

**Torah:** But I have to ... I am defender of the Secret Scroll ... I must do all I can to save it ...

She knew what she had to do to protect the secret of her land ... but would she survive the journey into the unknown ...?

**3** **Mum:** Don't be sad ... Suzi was an old cat and she had a good life ... and besides, the ones we love never really leave us ...

**Little boy:** I sure hope she doesn't leave me ...

Be careful what you wish for, little boy! Suzi is back ... and she has some unfinished business ... Not everyone was sweet to Suzi during her long life ... now it's payback time!

**4** Lost in an unknown galaxy, 3 billion light years from home ...

**Zigon:** The mutant force is upon us, Captain ... we must release the ultra rays ...

**Captain:** Not yet, Zigon, if we release the rays, we risk destroying ourselves as well as the mutant force ...

**Zigon:** But Captain, there is nothing else ...

**Captain:** Never say never, Zigon, I have a plan ...

---

**Answers**
**1** Comedy **2** Adventure **3** Horror **4** Science-fiction

---

## 4  Talk

- Ask learners which movie they would like to see after hearing the trailers. They can either answer this as a class or in pairs. Learners can be challenged by being asked to give reasons too.

---

**Answers**
Learners' own answers.

---

## 5 [AB] Word study

- Focus learners on the sentences, 1–5, in **Activity 5** and check understanding of the words, *special effects, scenes, accident, character* and *mission* by giving learners the following definitions and asking them to match to these words. You could challenge them more by reading out the definitions and ask them to find the words in the text. Definitions:
A part of a film (*scene*); when someone hurts themselves badly (*accident*); someone in the film's story (*character*); a special journey to achieve a goal (*mission*)
**Note:** Illustrate special effects with an example rather than a definition, e.g. when you see characters travelling in space in a film, it is done with *special effects* because they can't film scenes in real space.
- Use sentence 1 to illustrate the activity. Ask learners to tell you the word in blue (*terrifying*) and match it to an adjective, a – g (a. *very frightening*). Draw

---

their attention to the adverb, *very*, and explain that *terrifying* has a similar meaning to *frightening* but is a *stronger* adjective.

- Ask learners to do the same with sentences, 2–5. When they have matched the adjectives in blue with adjectives, b–g, ask them to match a sentence with a film type.
- When you conduct feedback, do a pronunciation focus (word stress and difficult sounds) of the strong adjectives, to prepare learners for the speaking activity (6) at the end.
- **Extend and challenge:** After the feedback and pronunciation stages, review the strong adjectives again by clapping (or tapping) the stress pattern and ask learners to tell you the corresponding adjective.

---

**Answers**
**1** a & e (horror)
**2** c (comedy)
**3** g (science-fiction)
**4** b (drama)
**5** d & f (adventure)
**Word stress:** terrifying (Oooo); evil (Oo); hilarious (oOoo); amazing (oOo); heart-breaking (O-oo); thrilling (Oo); gorgeous (Oo)

---

[AB] **For further practice, see Activity 3 in the Activity Book.**

---

## Use of English

- Ask learners to close their books and write the following sentences on the board (or slide); ask learners to see if they can remember the missing words and that these words make the adjectives even stronger. Elicit or input the adverbs, *absolutely* and *really*.
- The film was _____ hilarious, we couldn't stop laughing ... (*absolutely*)
- The story is _____ thrilling – I didn't want the film to end. (*really*)
- Next, delete the adverbs and replace with *very*. Ask learners if this is correct and then explain that you can't use *very* with strong adjectives.
- Ask learners to open their books again and focus on the last two lines of the **Use of English** box in **Lesson 1**. Read the explanation and example sentence.
- Ask learners which adverbs they could use to emphasise the meaning of the adjectives more. Elicit or input *very* or *really* (illustrate on the board if necessary, by writing the sentence and erasing *quite* and *a bit*).
- Now ask learners to look at the sentences from **Activity 5** again with a partner and find all the adverbs and adjectives.

---

**Answers**
**1** really evil
**2** absolutely hilarious
**3** absolutely amazing; quite slow; a bit boring
**4** a bit silly; not very believable
**5** really thrilling; really beautiful

---

For further practice, see Activity 4 in the Activity Book.

## 6  Talk

- **Critical thinking:** Tell learners that they are now going to use the adverbs and adjectives to describe films they know. Model the activity with a confident learner using the example (about *Ice Age 4*).
- **Additional support and practice:** Ask learners to close their books and focus on the board. Then elicit the example dialogue (about *Ice Age 4*) using learners' own suggestions for the film example (or a similar dialogue). Elicit the questions by asking learners, *Give me a question about the type of film ... What type of ...?*, etc.
  When your example dialogue is complete (just two or three questions), try the disappearing drill technique (see **Unit 1**, **Lesson 1**) to give learners extra confidence in the speaking stage.
- Ask learners to practise the dialogues in pairs. Monitor and circulate, helping with any language issues and noting good use of the descriptive language for the feedback stage.
- Round the activity off by asking learners as a class to tell you which films they discussed. Nominate learners who were using the descriptive language well to share their conversations with the class.

## ⮕ Wrap up

- To finish off, ask learners which films they are planning to see in the near future and why.

## Activity Book

### 1 Vocabulary

- Learners complete short descriptions of film types using target vocabulary in the box.

> **Answer**
> 1 Adventure
> 2 Historical
> 3 Horror
> 4 Science-fiction
> 5 action
> 6 Comedy
> 7 Drama
> 8 animation

### 2 ✏ Write

- Learners write about the last film they saw and the types of film they like.

> **Answers**
> Learners' own answers.

### 3 Vocabulary

- Learners find seven adjective pairs (adjective / strong adjective) in a word snake and write in the correct column in a table.

> **Answers**
>
> | Adjectives | Strong adjectives |
> | --- | --- |
> | funny | hilarious |
> | beautiful | gorgeous |
> | sad | heart-breaking |
> | surprising | amazing |
> | bad | evil |
> | frightening | terrifying |
> | exciting | thrilling |

### 4 Use of English

- Learners complete sentences with the correct adverb.

> **Answers**
> 1 really  2 very  3 very  4 quite  5 absolutely  6 really

### 5 ✏ Challenge

- Learners give their opinions of a range of pictures by choosing adjectives and adverbs to describe them.

> **Answers**
> Learners' own answers.

## Lesson 2: The first films

Learner's Book pages: 52–53
Activity Book pages: 42–43

### Lesson objectives

**Listening:** Identify specific information in a radio interview about the history of cinema.

**Language focus:** Past simple passive tense
**Vocabulary:** Cinema history: *a film projector, make up, audience, popcorn, a cinema screen, a pianist*

**Materials:** video clips or images of silent movies (optional for **Warm up**). Copies of **Photocopiable activity 7**.

### Learner's Book

### ⮕ Warm up

- If possible, introduce the topic of cinema history and the first movies by showing the class a brief clip of a silent movie (e.g. Charlie Chaplin or something with a comedy theme). Ask learners when they think the movie was made and then brainstorm how it is different from movies today. Write learners' ideas on the board, and draw their attention to items which will help with the vocabulary in **Activity 2** (e.g. heavy makeup, effect of the projector, the background music from the pianist).
- Alternatively, you could show learners some stills pictures of silent movies or use the pictures in the Learner's Book to generate interest at this stage.

## 1 💬 Talk about it

- Focus attention on the two questions about films made in learners' own country. Either discuss as a class or ask learners to discuss in pairs, if you think they will have some knowledge of this topic. If the country in question does not have a film industry, ask learners if they know which countries in the region do and if they know the names of any films produced there.
- **Critical thinking:** Learners activate their own knowledge of a topic.

**Answers**
Learners' own answers.

## 2 Word study

- Focus learners on the images in the Learner's Book and ask them to match to a word in the box. Refer them to any items that came up during the warm-up stage and help with other words as appropriate.
- During feedback, do some work on pronunciation and word stress, so learners will recognise the words more easily in **Activity 3**.
  **Note:** Make sure learners say the article when giving the words (e.g. *a* pianist). This is especially important for learners who don't use articles in their first language, or where the article use is different from English.

**Answers**
a  make-up (stress pattern: Oo)
b  popcorn (Oo)
c  an audience (Ooo)
d  a cinema screen (Ooo o)
e  a pianist (Ooo)
f  a film projector (O ooo)

## 3 📝 Listen 21

- Tell learners that they are now going to listen to an interview with a movie expert. Ask them to look at the **Activity 3** rubric and tell you what the expert is going to talk about (a short history of cinema) and what they need to do while they listen (write the order that the words in **Activity 2** appear in the interview).
- Play the audio and ask learners to write the words in **Activity 2** as they hear them.
- **Additional support and practice:** If you think your learners will struggle to listen and write the words, ask them to write the words first in their notebooks and number them as they hear them in the interview.
- Conduct feedback.

**Answers**
Order: cinema screen / film projector / audience / pianist / make-up / popcorn

## 4 Listen 21

- After listening for the first time, ask learners if they noticed any dates. If they did, ask them if they can remember any information around those dates (if they can't remember at this point, it isn't a problem). Now

focus their attention on the **Listening strategy** and point out that when they listen to any listening extract, they should try to notice any dates, because dates often guide the listener to important information.
- Focus learners on the timeline in **Activity 4**. Read through the information that is already there and draw their attention to the gaps. Emphasise the dates (years) and point out that the missing information is either a date, or information around a date.
- Before learners listen, ask them to read out the years to you to ensure that they understand how to say the years in English (e.g. 1891 – eighteen ninety-one) and will be able to recognise them in the interview.
- Now tell them to listen and complete the gaps.

### Differentiated instruction

**Additional support and practice**

- If necessary, stop the audio after each answer to the interviewer's questions, to give learners a chance to complete the gaps.
- At the end of the interview, ask them to compare their answers with their partner. Play the audio again for them to check answers, before conducting feedback.

**Extend and challenge**

- Ask learners to respond to the interview by telling you which information surprised them the most and which facts they already knew. Ask them if they know any more facts about cinema history.

**Audioscript:** Track 21

**Interviewer:** Think about it ... we watch films every day of our lives – movies, music videos, YouTube, advertisements ... . And films are everywhere ... on your laptop, tablet, phone, cinema screen and TV. But how did it all start? Let's ask our movie expert, Professor Chang. Professor Chang, tell us! Where did it all start?

**Prof. Chang:** Well, in 1891, the first film projector was invented by the Edison company. It showed moving pictures on a tiny screen in the machine, but only one person at a time could look at it! Can you believe that? Then in 1895, the first moving pictures were shown to an audience, who even paid to see them!

**Interviewer:** Really! And where did it go from there?

**Prof. Chang:** OK, from 1907 people watched silent films in cinemas. And the music was played by a pianist in the cinema. The actors didn't speak, so they had to use their faces – and their facial expressions – to show what was happening in the story. So they wore lots of make-up to draw attention to their eyes especially.

**Interviewer:** And these early films were all made in black and white, weren't they?

**Prof. Chang:** Yes, that's right. And it cost just five cents to watch them at a movie theatre. Oh, and did you know that popcorn was first sold in cinemas in 1912?

**Interviewer:** Really? Now what about other important events in film history?

**Prof. Chang:** Well, the first film with sound was released in 1927 and these films were called 'talkies', for obvious reasons! And Mickey Mouse made his first appearance in a film in 1928. 1928 is officially the year of Mickey's birthday! And finally, in 1935, the first movie was filmed in colour ... the modern age cinema had arrived!

**Answers**
a the first film projector
b 1895
c silent films
d popcorn
e 1927
f Mickey Mouse
g colour

 **For further practice, see Activity 1 in the Activity Book.**

## 5 Use of English

- Introduce the past simple passive by asking learners, *When was the first film projector invented?* Elicit the sentence and write on the board (or slide): *The first film projector was invented in 1891.*
- Erase the words, *was invented* and elicit the words again from learners. This time highlight the words in a different colour.
- Now repeat the process to elicit another example sentence. Ask, *When were the first moving pictures shown to an audience?* Elicit: *The first moving pictures were shown in 1895.*
- Now focus learners on both example sentences and ask some concept-check questions to establish meaning and function. Ask:
  *Are the sentences in the present or past tense?* (past)
  *In these sentences, what is the action?* (invented / shown)
  *Do we know who did the action?* (No) *Do you think that is important in these sentences?* (It isn't)
- Tell learners that we use this passive structure to talk about events in the past; we want to focus on the event, not the person who did it. But when we want to mention who did the action, we use *by*: *The first film projector was invented in 1891 **by** the Edison company.*
- Now ask learners how we form the passive structure and indicate the highlighted parts of the example sentences. Make sure they notice that *was* can change to *were* and that the past form of the verb is the same form that is used in the present perfect (the past participle).
- Focus learners on **Activity 5** in the Learner's Book and ask them to complete the rule for forming the past simple passive in pairs.
- Erase the example sentence, *The first moving pictures were shown in 1895*, as it is the first question in **Activity 6**.

**Answers**
were

## 6 Use of English

- Learners should now do **Activity 6** to practise making sentences using the target structure. First do question 1 together as a class to make sure they understand the task. Then ask learners to do the rest of the sentences, 2–5, and then compare their answers with their partner.

- Go through the answers together as a class. Clarify any confusion with the concept by presenting more example sentences and asking the concept-check questions again.

**Answers**
1 were shown
2 was played by
3 were made
4 were called
5 was filmed

 **For further practice, see Activities 5 and 6 in the Activity Book.**

## 7  Pronunciation 22

- First ask learners to practise saying the years in pairs. Then ask them to copy the pairs of years (a / b) for each part of the task (1–4) in their notebooks. Then they listen to the audio and circle the year that they hear.
- **Extend and challenge:** Ask learners to close their books, then listen to the audio and write down the year that they hear. Give further practice in saying years and personalise the activity by asking learners what years their parents and grandparents were born (if you feel this is appropriate). Alternatively, you could ask them to tell you the years when significant events in their country's history happened (this could also be an opportunity for a cross-curricular tie-in).

**Audioscript: Track 22**
1 1891    2 1907    3 1995    4 1812

**Answers**
1 1891    2 1907    3 1995    4 1812

**For further practice, see Activities 2, 3 and 4 in the Activity Book.**

## 8 Pronunciation

- Start by asking learners how much it costs to go to the cinema now. Is there any difference between the prices of cinema tickets? Which are the cheapest? Most expensive?
- Focus them on the cinema ticket images in the Learner's Book and ask them the year of the tickets. Then ask how much it cost to go to the cinema in these years and what type of currency the tickets are in (US dollars).
- Give learners the current exchange rate between their national currency and US dollars. Do an example together in the class (e.g. something costing $5 / 50 cents) to make sure learners understand how to convert the dollar amount into their own currency using multiplication or division. Then ask learners to work in pairs and calculate the costs of the cinema tickets in their own currency.

**Answers**

It cost 30 cents (US) to go to the cinema in 1907.

Learners' own answers.

##  Wrap up

- Wrap up with a quick quiz, using the information in this lesson, to see how much learners can remember about the history of cinema. Formulate your questions in the past simple passive, e.g. *When was the first movie in colour made?*

## Activity Book

### 1 Listen and Strategy check 65 [CD2 Track 33]

- Learners listen to a short history of animation and practise the listening strategy by matching information to years on a timeline.

**Audioscript:** Track 65

In 2001, the film *Shrek* was the first winner of the Academy Award for the Best Animated Feature. The story of a green ogre, whose princess turns into a beast like him, is one of the most popular animation films of all time. With its clever storyline and fantastic computer-generated visual effects, it has made almost $500 million in cinema sales.

Animated films have come a long way since the first ones were made in the early 1900s. At this time, hundreds of drawings were needed to produce just one minute of film. Then in 1913, animators discovered clever ways to make the process quicker. In 1928, the first film starring Mickey Mouse was made by Walt Disney and a legend was born. It was also the first time that sound was added to cartoon drawings. In 1937, the first full-length animated film was produced by Walt Disney too. It was called *Snow White and the Seven Dwarves*. Animated films became popular in the 1940s and 1950s, when classic Disney films such as *Bambi, Peter Pan* and the *Lady and the Tramp* were watched by millions of people in cinemas. Then during the 1990s, there was another revolution. Computers were used for the first time to make animated films. In 1995, *Toy Story* was released – the first full-length animated film on computer.

**Answers**

Read the information first and make guesses about years or dates. ✓

When you listen again recheck the dates. ✓

**1** b    **2** f    **3** d    **4** e    **5** g    **6** c    **7** a

### 2 Pronunciation

- Learners answer a question about how to express decades.

**Answers**

**b** 1940–1949

### 3 Listen 66 [CD2 Track 34]

- Learners listen and write the decade they hear; then listen again and repeat the phrase.

**Audioscript:** Track 66

**a** In the early 1900s

**b** In the 1950s

**c** During the 1990s

**d** The 1920s

**Answers**

**a** 1900s    **b** 1950s    **c** 1990s    **d** 1920s

### 4 Pronunciation 67 [CD2 Track 35]

- Learners practise how to say years after the year 2000, by listening and writing the year they hear. Then they listen again and repeat the years.

**Audioscript:** Track 67

**1a** *two thousand and one*

**1b** *two thousand and four*

**1c** *two thousand and eight*

**2a** *twenty ten*

**2b** *twenty fourteen*

**2c** *twenty twelve*

**Answers**

**1 a** 2001    **b** 2004    **c** 2008

**2 a** 2010    **b** 2014    **c** 2012

### 5 Use of English

- Learners correct errors in past simple passive sentences.

**Answers**

**1** was made

**2** were shown

**3** was called

**4** weren't used

**5** was (the first cartoon) created?

### 6 Use of English

- Learners complete sentences using the past simple passive structure.

**Answers**

**1** were produced

**2** was created

**3** weren't made

**4** were needed

**5** was released

### 7 Challenge

- Learners write six sentences about things they have or haven't experienced using the present perfect.

**Answers**

Learners' own answers.

**For further practice in using relative clauses and creating a film review, see Photocopiable activity 7.**

# Lesson 3: What makes a good film?

Learner's Book pages: 54–55

Activity Book pages: 44–45

## Lesson objectives

**Speaking:** Describe and recommend a film that you have seen.

**Listening:** Listen to a conversation describing and recommending a film.

**Writing:** Summarise a conversation.

**Critical thinking:** Describe and give a personal opinion about a film

**Language focus:** Relative clauses with relative pronouns, *that, who, where, when*.

**Materials:** visual images of recent children's films (optional for **Warm up**). Copies of **Photocopiable activity 8**.

## Learner's Book

###  Warm up

- Put a selection of images on the board of well-known children's films (e.g. stills, movie advertisements / posters, characters, etc) that your learners might have seen. Ask them to tell you the films the images are from and which ones they have seen. If images are not available, you could just write the names of films on the board and ask learners which ones they have seen.
- Now ask learners which films they liked and didn't like and why. Use this stage to find out how much learners can describe different aspects of films and express their opinions.

### 1 Talk about it

- **Critical thinking:** Focus learners on **Activity 1** and read the two questions together. Then ask learners individually to think of a film they liked and write down three good things about it; then think of a film they didn't like and write three negative points about it.
- Now ask learners to compare their notes with their partner. Then ask them the questions as a class. As learners share their answers, use this stage to elicit or input any useful vocabulary for **Activity 2** (e.g. *plot, actors, characters, setting, special effects*).

> **Answers**
> Learner's own answers.

### 2 Listen 23

- Tell learners that they are going to listen to two girls, Ana and Sofia talking about the film, *The Rise of the Guardians*. Ask if anyone has seen the film and what they thought about it.

- Draw their attention to the words in the word cloud and read through them as a class, checking that learners understand what the words mean. Tell them that they are going to listen to the audio and write down which of these things the girls talk about. Stress that this is all they have to do in the first listening and not to worry if they don't understand all of the conversation.
- Play the audio and ask learners to write down what the girls talk about.
- **Additional support and practice:** If you think your learners will struggle to write the things the girls talk about as they listen, ask them to write them first in their notebooks and circle them as they hear them in the conversation.
- When you've finished playing the conversation, give learners a little time to finish writing down any points and compare their answers with their partner. Then conduct feedback with the whole class. If necessary, play the audio again and stop after the girls mention the points in **Activity 2**.

---

**Audioscript:** Track 23

**Ana:** Have you seen any good films recently?

**Sofia:** Yes, last week I went to see *Rise of the Guardians*, with my mum and little brother.

**Ana:** Oh, yeah? I don't think I've heard of that. What kind of film is it?

**Sofia:** It's an adventure story, all in animation. The special effects are amazing. The characters are so life-like that they look like real people.

**Ana:** Really? And what's it about?

**Sofia:** It's about a group of superheroes, who have amazing abilities. All the superheroes are characters from children's stories.

**Ana:** Like who?

**Sofia:** The Easter Bunny, the Tooth Fairy and one character is like Santa Claus. These superheroes have to protect all the children in the world from an evil spirit called Pitch. Pitch wants to frighten the children and steal all the things that they believe in.

**Ana:** Eh? I don't understand! What do you mean?

**Sofia:** Well, he wants to steal things that children believe are true. So, he tries to make children believe that the superheroes don't exist. If children don't believe in the superheroes, the superheroes can't protect them.

**Ana:** Strange! It sounds quite interesting though. Where is it set?

**Sofia:** It's set in lots of imaginary places but there is a good scene where one of the heroes goes to Antarctica.

**Ana:** Would you recommend it? My dad and I are going to the cinema this Saturday.

**Sofia:** Yes, I think so. I liked the ending when the superheroes win and the bad guy is beaten. But I wouldn't recommend it for young kids. My little brother got really bored because he didn't understand the plot. It's a good story, but quite complicated. You have to concentrate quite hard to follow what's going on.

---

> **Answers**
> plot / good and bad points / type of film / setting / characters/
> special effects

## 3 Listen 23

- Focus learners on question 3 and read the question together. Ask learners to read through the summary before listening to see if they can guess any words at this point. Then ask them to listen for any points that they couldn't guess and to check any that they guessed.
- When they have listened to the conversation again, give them enough time to read through the summary again, write down the correct words and check with their partner. Then conduct a feedback with the whole class.

> **Answers**
> **a** adventure
> **b** stories
> **c** evil
> **d** frighten
> **e** steal
> **f** set
> **g** recommend
> **h** but not
> **i** difficult

## 4 Use of English

- Focus learners on **Activity 4** and ask them to sort the words in 1–5 to make the five questions that Ana asked. Do the first one together as a class. Give them a few minutes to sort the words and check with a partner. If you want to quicken the pace a little after the listening, ask learners to work in pairs to unjumble the questions and make it into a class race.
- Elicit the correct completed questions and write them on the board for learners to check their answers against.
- Now ask learners to match the questions with a description, a–e. Do the first one together as a class. Then ask learners to match and compare their answers with their partner.

> **Answers**
> **1** Have you seen any good films recently? b
> **2** What kind of film is it? e
> **3** What is it about? c
> **4** Would you recommend it? d
> **5** Where is it set? a

 **For further practice, see Activities 1 and 2 in the Activity Book.**

## 5 Use of English

- At this point tell learners that they are going to describe films they've seen recently to each other, but first you are going to look at ways of making the sentences they use longer and more interesting.

- Ask learners to close their books and put them in A/B pairs, (sitting side by side, one learner is 'A', the other 'B') for a pair work dictation activity. Tell them that they are going to dictate sentences from the girls' conversation in **Activity 2** to each other and give them the following handouts (for students A and B):
  **Student A:**
  1 The characters are so life-like _____
  2 _____, **who** have amazing abilities.
  3 There is a good scene _____
  4 _____ **when** the superheroes win.
  **Student B:**
  1 _____ **that** they look like real people.
  2 It's about a group of superheroes, _____
  3 _____ **where** one of the superheroes goes to Antarctica.
  4 I liked the ending _____.
  **Note:** The intention of this activity, using the four relative clause sentences in the **Use of English** box, is to focus them on the two distinct parts of the sentences with the relative pronouns.
- Ask learners to dictate the missing parts of each other's sentences to each other (make sure that they sit so that they can't see each other's handouts, so have to listen carefully to hear the missing parts of their sentences). Student A reads out the first part of sentence 1 while student B listens and writes, then student B finishes the sentence while student A listens and writes. Both learners should finish with a completed sentence with a relative clause. Repeat the procedure for the three other sentences. If they haven't done this activity before, model first with a confident pair of learners, so others understand what to do.
- **Additional support and practice:** Instead of the pair work dictation, you could do a running dictation (if this is manageable in your classroom) if you feel learners might benefit from a more active task at this point in the lesson. Put learners in A/B pairs, fix the four sentences separately around the classroom on strips of paper and have student A dictate the sentences to student B (see **Unit 2**, **Lesson 2** for full instructions). Alternatively, you could split the four sentences and ask learners to match the sentence halves. The sentence halves could be written on the board or a slide and learners could match and write the complete sentences in their notebooks.
- When learners have completed the sentences, ask them how many parts there are to each sentence. Focus them on the two parts of the sentence (before and after the relative pronoun) and ask them to underline the part that contains the relative pronoun, e.g.
  *The characters are so life-like that <u>they look like real people</u>.*
  Explain that this part of the sentence is called a *relative clause* (clause = *part*). It tells us which person, thing, place or time someone is talking about.

- Now ask learners to circle the relative pronouns in their sentences. Write *people / things / places / the time something happened*, on the board. Ask them to match to the relative pronouns.
- Now focus them on **Activity 5** in the Learner's Book to consolidate their understanding. When you go through the answers, ask learners to tell you (or point out to them) which part of the sentence the relative pronoun refers to, e.g. (see in bold below):
  The characters are so **life-like that** they look like real people.
  It's about a group of **superheroes, who** have amazing abilities.
  There is a good **scene where** one of the heroes goes to Antarctica.
  I liked the **ending when** the superheroes win.
- At this stage, learners would benefit from seeing the sentences in the context of the dialogue. Either hand out copies of the audioscript and ask learners to find the target sentences and highlight them; or play the audio again and ask learners to call out '*Stop!*' when they hear one of the sentences. Then ask them to repeat it (and then continue the audio). Alternatively, you could give learners a sentence (or two) each and ask them to listen specifically for their sentence/s in the audio, holding it up when they hear it (this ensures that all learners are actively listening).

**Answers**
who / that
that
where
when

 For further practice, see Activities 4 and 5 in the Activity Book.

## 6 Use of English

- Focus learners on **Activity 6** and ask them to think of a film that they like. Tell them that they are going to write information about the film to complete the sentences.
- Give them an example first, by completing the sentences yourself on the board, using a film that you like. Then ask them to do the same with their own film. Monitor and circulate, helping with structure and vocabulary where needed. Early finishers can write a second set of sentences about another film.
- When they have finished ask them to compare their sentences with a partner. Choose one or two good examples to show the whole class.

**Answers**
Learners' own answers.

### Present it!

- In this stage, learners prepare to have a similar conversation to **Activity 2** with a partner. First, they need to answer the questions in **Activity 4** again about their own choice of film. Write these questions on the board or have them prepared on a slide, so learners can refer to them easily. Give them some time to answer the questions in their notebooks. Learners work individually, adding to the sentences they formed in **Activity 6** to form rounded answers to the questions.
- Before learners interview each other, model the activity first with a confident learner, with you asking the first two questions (*Have you seen any good films recently? / What kind of film is it?*). Encourage the learner in the demonstration to give full answers (rather than just one word), like Sofia's replies in the model conversation in **Activity 2**.
- Drill the five questions before setting up the conversations, so learners are confident in their delivery. Use the backchaining technique and whispering drills for variety (see **Lessons 1** and **2**) if needed.
- Give learners a letter, A or B and tell them that they are now going to ask and answer questions about films they like. As they listen, they need to write short notes about their partner's answers with a view to sharing this with the class in the final stage of the activity. If necessary, model this note-making task in front of the class by asking a learner a question and noting down the main points of his/her answers on the board.
- Now ask learners to ask and answer each other's questions and write notes. Encourage them as far as possible to speak without reading directly from their written answers to the questions. Circulate and monitor, noting down any repeated errors. However, it is not recommended that accuracy is the emphasis of this activity, rather fluency and quality of ideas.
- When pairs have finished their conversations, ask them to look at their notes and prepare a short summary to tell the class about their conversation with their partner. Ask learners to practise the summaries with their partners by reading the text and then turning it over and telling their partner. The partner listens and checks that the information is correct.
- At the end, nominate some confident learners to tell the class about their conversation with their partner. If necessary, show them the example sentence at the end of the activity in the Learner's Book to start them off (*At the weekend, Diego ...*).

**Answers**
Learner's own answers.

**Wrap up**

- **Critical thinking:** Ask learners if there are any films they would now like to see, after talking to their partners and listening to other classmate's summaries. Ask them to explain the reason why too.

Answers
Learners' own answers

## Activity Book

### 1 Read

- Learners match answer to questions to form a dialogue about the film, *Life of Pi*.

Answers
1 b    2 d    3 e    4 a    5 c

### 2 Read

- Learners read the answers again and answer questions about *plot*, *setting* and *characters*.

Answers
1 e    2 India    3 A boy called Pi; a tiger.

### 3 Use of English

- Learners underline five examples of relative clauses in the text in **Activity 1**.

Answers
c Yes, I would. I liked the scenes where the boy faces the tiger, and then makes friends with him. My dad didn't like the film though! He says he prefers films that have more realistic plots!
e It's about a boy called Pi, who has an incredible adventure at sea. It starts in India, where his family own a zoo. But they have to sell the zoo and all the animals. They decide to sail to Canada, where they can sell the animals and build a new life.

### 4 Use of English

- Learners choose the correct relative pronoun to complete sentences about films.

Answers
1 when
2 that
3 where
4 that
5 when
6 who
7 where
8 who

### 5 Challenge

- Learners complete sentences about the film, *Epic*, to form relative clauses.

Answers
1 Epic is an adventure story that looks amazing.
2 It's about a young girl who goes on a special journey.
3 She is transported to a forest where there is a fight between good and evil.

4 There are a group of villains who want to destroy the forest.
5 One of the nicest scenes is when she meets the other characters for the first time.
6 It is a film that I would recommend to my friends.

To review film-related vocabulary, see **Photocopiable activity 8.**

## Lesson 4: Creating film scenes

Learner's Book pages: 56–57
Activity Book pages: 46–47

### Lesson objectives

**Speaking:** Suggest sound effects and special effects to add to film scenes.

**Reading:** Read the scene descriptions on a storyboard and choose a film title.

**Writing:** Create a film storyboard and storyline.

**Critical thinking:** Imagining scenes following on from scenes depicted in the Learner's Book; suggesting sound and special effects to add to film scenes; creating their film scenes from their own ideas.

**Vocabulary:** Ways of speaking: *snigger, insist, sigh, whisper, ask*

**Materials:** a video clip of a comedy film familiar to learners (optional); poster paper, coloured pens.

### Learner's Book

#### Warm up

- Before learners open their books, describe a scene from a film that you know learners are familiar with. If possible, choose an action-packed scene that they can easily visualise.
- Describe it in as much detail as you can, using sequencing words like first and next, so learners get a sense of continuity. Ask learners to guess the film title.

#### 1 Talk about it

- **Critical thinking:** Focus learners on the two questions in **Activity 1**. You can either do the questions as a class or ask them to discuss in pairs. If learners struggle with the second question, ask them how they get ideas for their own stories that they write in class (refer to a specific class activity if possible) and point out that film makers might get their ideas in the same way.
- During feedback, stretch learners by asking them why particular film plots appeal to them.

Answers
Learners' own answers.

## 2 Read

- Draw learners' attention to the storyboard illustration in the Learner's Book and explain that film makers plan out their ideas for film scenes by using storyboards.
- Ask them to look at the illustrations and point out that they are not in the correct order of the story. Tell them to look at the illustrations to get a *sense* of the story and then discuss, in pairs, the best title for the film. They can either choose one of the titles, a–c, or invent their own.
- During feedback, invite suggestions for alternative titles; then have a class vote on the best one.

> **Answers**
> Learners' own answer or any answer a–c, (although c is the only title that picks up on the trick Boris plays on his brother).

## 3 Read

- Focus learners on the sentences, a–f, in **Activity 3**. First read the sentences aloud to learners, with expression and emphasis, as if reading part of a story. Make sure that your vocal tone clearly reflects the verbs *sighed* and *sniggered*, as these are vocabulary items that will come up later in the lesson.
- Ask learners to read the sentences again and match to the illustrations. When they have finished, ask them to compare their answers with their partner before feedback as a class.
- **Additional support and practice:** To give learners extra support with matching the sentences to the pictures, ask them to first identify one or two key words in the sentences and then look for those items in the pictures. They will need to double check as some items appear in several illustrations.
  **Key words:** Horis / Boris / fighting / Dad / camping / campsite / tent / cheerful.

> **Answers**
> a 2   b 5   c 4   d 6   e 1   f 3

## 4  Talk

- To introduce this activity, if possible, play learners a short video clip of a comedy film (preferably a cartoon or animation) with some humorous and exaggerated sound / special effects. This is a good opportunity to introduce onomatopoeia. Explain what onomatopoeia is, and, if possible, identify some examples from the clip. Ask learners if they can think of any examples. While they are watching, ask them to tell you what is happening so the connection between the action and the sound / special effect is made very clear. Afterwards do a quick round up of what the class noticed about the sound / special effects and any background music, etc.
- **Critical thinking:** Now ask learners to look at the illustrations with their partner and discuss what sound and special effects could be added. Encourage them to use functional language for suggestions.

**Note:** Learners will no doubt struggle with vocabulary associated with sound effects in particular. Rather than input a lot of obscure and low-frequency vocabulary, ask learners to simply make the sound instead.
They can have fun doing this (if you don't mind the classroom becoming a little noisy!).

- Conduct a quick class feedback. Ask for volunteers to make the sound effects they discussed in the previous stage.

> **Answers**
> Learners' own answers.
> Ideas for sound / special effects:
> Scene 1 / the ants' nest – menacing music gets louder. Scene 2 / fighting – comedy sound effects for punches and thuds. Scene 3 - Setting up camp - light-hearted music and country sounds, snow white and the seven dwarfs type of music. Scene 4 / car journey – sound of car driving along with menacing music, signalling trouble ahead. Scene 5 / Dad's idea – light bulb appears above his head. Scene 6 / At the campsite – country sounds (e.g. birds tweeting, crickets chirping, bees buzzing) but with menacing music playing faintly in background.

**AB** For further practice, see Activity 2 in the Activity Book.

## 5 Punctuation

- Ask learners to close their books and write the examples in the **Writing tip** on the board *without* punctuation. Read the lines to learners, emphasising *sniggered* and *sighed*.
- Now ask for volunteers to come to the board and add each item of punctuation to the sentences, ie. First the speech marks; then the commas and finally the exclamation mark. Have a different learner add each different item in a different colour.
- Then ask learners to open their Learner's Book again and read the **Writing tip** together, focusing in particular on the last two sentences (*Use speech marks … use a comma*), which explain the basic rules for usage when writing.
- Ask learners when they think exclamation marks are used; what information does an exclamation mark give? Elicit or tell them that exclamation marks show emotions and feelings, especially if someone is shocked, surprised or upset; speaks loudly or shouts; or says something funny.
- Focus learners on **Activity 5**. First, look at the reporting verbs and elicit the meanings. Ask learners which verb means, *say a question* (ask), and illustrate the others by saying something in the manner of the verb and asking learners to say the verb. Then ask learners to read the direct speech for the next four scenes and replace the verb, *said*, with a reporting verb.
- Next, ask learners to focus on the punctuation. Again, they can do this in pairs, writing and punctuating the sentences in their notebooks.
- As learners are doing the activity, write the sentences on the board ready for the feedback stage. When learners are ready, invite volunteers or nominate learners to come to the board and punctuate the sentences. Others check their sentences against these examples.

- **Extend and challenge:** Early finishers could draw scenes 7–10 and write scene 11 (dialogue and sentence). If learners really enjoy the story, they could write and draw more add-on scenes.

> **Answers**
> **Scene 7:** 'So that's why he wants me to sleep there ... Well, I've got other ideas!' <u>whispered</u> Horis
> **Scene 8:** 'No, Boris, I insist! I can't possibly take that place. You must sleep there!' <u>insisted</u> Horis. 'No Horis, really, I couldn't ... YOU must sleep there!' <u>insisted</u> Boris.
> **Scene 9:** '... Tell you what, boys ... I'll take that place.' <u>sighed</u> Dad.
> **Scene 10:** 'Hee hee ... serves him right!' <u>sniggered</u> Horis.

 **For further practice, see Activities 1, 3 and 4 in the Activity Book.**

## 📝 Write

- In this final activity, learners create their own storyboard in small groups. They can use one of the trailers in **Lesson 1** for ideas or think of their own. Tell learners that they need to create four to six film scenes (vary the number to allow learners to work at their own pace; stronger / faster workers can aim for six scenes).
- Ask learners to start by brainstorming ideas in groups. If learners choose one of the trailers in **Lesson 1**, play the audio again and spend time with each group helping them to brainstorm ideas for their chosen film.
- Learners should aim to synchronise the different parts of this activity and roles can be selected to suit ability and preference, e.g. one draws while the others construct dialogue and sentence. Stress that perfect artwork is not essential – simple drawings and stick figures are fine.
- Ask learners to draft out the written parts first. Circulate and help with grammar, vocabulary and punctuation. Encourage learners to use reporting verbs.
- Tell learners to think of a title for their film and make a note, but not to write it on the poster. At a later stage, learners will think of titles for each other's work; this will then be compared to the creators' idea.
- When writing drafts have been checked and corrected, ask learners to transfer them to a large poster to be integrated with the art work. Dialogue can go into speech bubbles, or be written in a space under the picture (this would preserve the reporting verb). Sentences go in a space below the picture.
- Allow learners to embellish the posters with sound effects (you could input colloquial words to describe sounds, e.g. *Ha ha; bang!,* etc.) or give assistance with describing special effects.
- **Critical thinking:** When posters are ready, ask learners to display them on their classroom wall. Ask them to walk around, read each other's storyboards and think of a title for each one. If you think this is too demanding, focus individuals or groups on just one specific storyboard to create a title for.
  **Note:** There is a lot of work in this stage and depending on curriculum and time available, it could be extended over two lessons.

- **Extend and challenge:** If you have the facilities and time in the curriculum, learners could direct and film one or two scenes from their storyboard in their groups. Pre-teach instructions such as *Action!* and *Cut!* first.

> **Answers**
> **Portfolio opportunity:** Learners' own ideas.

## 👉 Wrap up

- **Critical thinking:** When learners have looked at all the storyboards, ask them to give their ideas for titles to the storyboard creators. Learners compare the titles and choose the best one for their storyboard. The class could also vote on funniest storyboard, best art work, etc.

## Activity Book

### 1 Vocabulary

- Learners complete dialogues with a reporting verb from the box.

> **Answers**
> 1 whispered
> 2 insisted
> 3 sniggered
> 4 asked
> 5 sighed

### 2 Read

- Learners read the storyboard and put the pictures in the correct order.

> **Answers**
> a 3    b 4    c 2    d 1 (Picture order: d / c / a / b)

### 3 Punctuation

- Learners add speech marks, exclamation marks and commas to pieces of dialogue; then they match the dialogue to the pictures and text in **Activity 1**.

> **Answers**
> 1 'You are joking!' exclaimed Lily, 'I'm not going out there at this time of night!'
> 'Well, I'll go on my own then!' replied Lara, 'I want to find out what it is.' Picture b
> 2 'Hey, Lara! Are you awake too? I can't sleep,' whispered Lily. 'Me neither. I've been awake for hours,' replied Lara. Picture d
> 3 'It's some kind of light. But where's it coming from?' wondered Lara.
> 'Let's go and have a look.' Picture a
> 4 'Lara, come and have a look at this! What do you think it is?' Picture c

### 4 📝 Challenge

- Learners write sentences and dialogues for the next two scenes of the story in **Activities 2** and **3**.

> **Answers**
> Learners' own answers.

# Lesson 5: Spectacular special effects

Learner's Book pages: 58–59
Activity Book pages: 48–49

## Lesson objectives

**Listening and reading:** Listen to and read an extract from the novel, *Jurassic Park*, that has been made into a film (this extract comes from a *Jurassic Park* intermediate level reader).

**Speaking:** Discuss themes that are inferred in the text; make predictions about the next scene of the book; speculate on why the book was made into a film and what kind of books make good films; discuss aspects of personal safety by looking at the example in the text; give examples of how to look after yourself when outside home.

**Critical thinking:** Make deductions from inferences made in the text; make predictions based on information in the text; speculate on why some stories make good films; consider aspects of personal safety by looking at the example in the text and how to look after yourself when outside home.

**Vocabulary:** Guessing meaning from context using words from the text; *shade, emerged, hind, palm, weight, scrambled.*
**Values:** Looking after yourself.

**Materials:** video or picture images from films with good special effects, e.g. *Lord of the Rings, Avatar, Jurassic Park* (optional); poster and coloured pens (optional for **Values** extension activity).

## Learner's Book

### 👉 Warm up

- Tell learners that they are going to read about a story that has been made into a film. Fix or project some images of films with good special effects (or show some short video clips) and ask what the films have in common. Elicit or tell learners that the films all have good *special effects.*
- Alternatively, you could think of a film with good special effects (apart from *Jurassic Park*) and ask learners to guess through the *20 questions* game (see **Unit 1**, **Lesson 4**, warm-up stage for instructions). This would be a good opportunity to recycle vocabulary and themes from previous lessons with questions like *Is it a science-fiction film? Is the plot scary? Is it set in ...?*, etc. At the end of the game, establish that the film in question has good *special effects.*
- Once learners make the link between the film/s in question and special effects, see if they can identify some specific special effects in preparation for the next stage (e.g. make up, scenery, movement of characters, crowd scenes, etc.)

### 1 🗨 Talk about it

- **Critical thinking:** Draw learners' attention to the questions in **Activity 1** and ask learners as a class to respond. Find out which films learners have seen with good special effects and ask them how they think special effects are created.

> **Answers**
> Learners' own answers.
> **How special effects are created in films:** traditionally, special effects can be *photographic*, using techniques with cameras to produce special visual effects; they can be *mechanical*, using props, scenery, models and special machines that produce weather extremes or pyrotechnics (effects with fire); special effects can also be produced using *make up* (to change an actor's physical appearance) and *set design* (e.g. using special materials to build constructions that will easily collapse). However, since the early 1990s, computer generated imagery (CGI) has played a major part in creating special effects; many of the effects previously produced photographically or mechanically are now produced with CGI, resulting in cheaper and safer ways to create special effects in film.

### 2 Talk

- Ask learners if they have ever seen any of the *Jurassic Park* films and what they are about. If possible, show learners some stills images from the films to generate interest, or focus them on the picture in the Learner's Book (but ask them to cover the text until the next stage).
- Tell them that the first *Jurassic Park* film was important in cinema history and ask them to try and guess why. Write their ideas on the board but don't say at this point if they are correct or not.

> **Answers**
> Learners' own answers.
> **The *Jurassic Park* films are about** a group of scientists who visit an amusement park, which is inhabited by cloned dinosaurs. The dinosaurs are supposed to be confined in a controlled environment but sabotage sets them free, putting the scientists and other people on the island in great danger. They attempt to escape the island.

### 3 Read

- Go through learners' ideas on the board and then ask them to read the paragraph to find out why *Jurassic Park* is important in cinema history, and if their predictions were correct. Tell them to read and then discuss the answer with their partner. Then elicit the answer from the class.
- After feedback, if possible, it would be good to show learners a video clip from *Jurassic Park 1* and point out some of the CGI in question.

> **Answers**
> **Why the first *Jurassic Park* film was important in cinema history:** It is generally regarded as being the first film to make major advances on digital film making, in the use of CGI. Afterwards many other films followed its lead in creating special effects primarily using CGI.

 For further practice, see Activities 1 and 2 in the Activity Book.

## 4 Read and listen 24

- Tell learners that they are now going to listen to and read part of the novel, *Jurassic Park*. Read the **Activity 4** rubric to set the context for the extract and give learners the gist question, *What strange meeting does Tina have near the beach?* Tell the class to listen and read the whole text quickly, only looking for the answer to this question. Stress that, at this point, they only need look for this information and not to worry about words they do not understand.
- Start the audio and tell learners to read the text while listening.
- After reading / listening, let them discuss the answer to the gist question with a partner and then conduct a short feedback with the class.

**Audioscript:** Track 24
See Learner's Book pages 59–60.

### Answers
Tina meets a strange creature that appears to be / she thinks is an unusual lizard.

## 5 Read

- Tell learners that they are going to read the story again, part by part to answer the questions after each part. Draw their attention to the glossary at the end of the first two sections.
  **Note:** There will probably be other unknown words but, at this point, try not to pre-teach any more vocabulary because there will be an opportunity later on to discuss more unknown words and how to work out their meaning from context.
- They should read and then answer the questions in their notebooks.
- **Additional support and practice:** After learners have written the answers for questions a–i, put them in groups of four to check their answers together.
- Allow time for this before giving feedback on the answers. Where possible, use the pictures in the book to illustrate the answers.

### Answers
a Tina and her parents were at the beach.
b No. Tina was near the sea.
c Bird tracks
d A lizard came out of the jungle
e It stood on two legs.
f No, she thought it was cute.
g No, it came towards her (without fear).
h The lizard was about the same size as a chicken.
i It jumped on her hand and then moved up her arm towards her face.

[AB] For further practice, see Activities 3 and 4 in the Activity Book.

## 6 🗩 Talk

- **Critical thinking:** Read questions 1–3 together; then ask learners to work in small groups to discuss and be prepared to give feedback to the class afterwards.
- After feedback, focus learners on questions 4–6 and follow the same procedure.

- **Additional support and practice:** (Questions 4–6): These questions could be divided up, rather than have all learners tackling all questions; e.g. put learners into groups of three and give each child a question to think about and then share with the group. Or give just one question per group. At the end of this stage, each group would give feedback on a different question and others could listen and see if they agree or not with the answer given. Early finishers could then be given another question to discuss while others finish.
- Do a class feedback, asking volunteers or nominating learners to share their thoughts with the class. Help learners with the language they need to express their thoughts by reformulating sentences where appropriate and highlighting useful phrases on the board.

### Answers
**1–3** Learners' own answers.
Suggestions for answers:
**4** Ideas: it is very dramatic and has a lot of exciting action scenes; the plot is original and contains a lot of drama, action and suspense (will people on the islands manage to escape the dinosaurs?); it is very exciting to look at, e.g. beautiful, dramatic tropical island landscapes; huge, fierce dinosaurs...
**5** Famous examples are: the Harry Potter books; *Life of Pi; The Lion, the Witch and the Wardrobe; Diary of a Wimpey Kid;* Disney classics: *Adventures of Pinocchio; Bambi, Life in the Woods; Snow White and the Seven Dwarves* etc. There are many other examples.
**6** The kind of books that make good films for children are stories with a simple plot structure (not too many twists and turns); a varied dramatic element – lots of 'highs and lows'; a 'problem' and the quest for a solution; a variety of sympathetic characters and villains; interesting and varied settings; stories containing a moral element or 'life lesson'.

## 7 Word study

- To introduce the **Reading strategy**, write the following sentences on the board (or slide) and ask learners to tell you which ideas they feel are the most helpful if they don't understand a word in a reading text:
  1 Don't read the sentence, just the word, and try to guess it.
  2 Read the whole sentence to get an idea of the word's meaning and then guess the word.
  3 Always check the words in a dictionary.
  **Note:** These sentences appear in the Activity Book, **Unit 4, Lesson 5, Strategy check**.
- Elicit learners' responses and then explain that strategy 2 is the most helpful because, if you look at the words and phrases around the unfamiliar word, they will usually give you clues and it is easier to guess the meaning. Tell them that it is also helpful to look at pictures around the text, the theme of the paragraph and any headings or titles. (See the **Teaching tip** in the unit overview for more information.)
  **Note:** Strategy 1 is not helpful at all because the word will be impossible to guess, as there are no clues. Strategy 3 is not helpful because, if you always rely on dictionaries, the pace of your reading becomes very slow. Also, dictionary definitions can be

confusing (especially bilingual dictionaries) because the meaning given is often different from the context in which the word is being used, and this is confusing.

- Focus learners' attention on the verbs highlighted in blue in the story. Tell them that they have to read the sentence before and after each word and look for clues in the meanings of other words. Then they choose the correct definition or synonym from the options given in **Activity 7**.

- Do the first one as an example. Find *shade* in the text and ask learners to tell you which words / phrases can help them understand the meaning (e.g. *move out of the sun, palm trees*). Then ask learners to do questions 2–6 in pairs.
  **Note:** Don't allow learners to use dictionaries, encourage them to work at understanding the words from the context they appear in; if they ask you for help, point to the words/phrases around the word in question to help them see that the clues are there in the text.

- Conduct a class feedback. If learners mention any other unknown words from the text, ask them to identify the word in the text and deduce its meaning in the same way.

> **Answers**
> 1 a　2 a　3 b　4 a　5 b　6 a

 **For further practice, see Activity 6 in the Activity Book.**

## 8 Pronunciation 25

- Focus learners on **Activity 8**. Ask them to listen to and repeat the words from the story, paying special attention to the 'th' sound. Is it a hard sound? Or soft? Demonstrate the sounds first and ask learners to listen and repeat. Then play the audio once and ask learners to listen and repeat the words. Establish which have a hard and soft 'th' sound.

- After listening, put learners in small teams and ask them to come up with as many other words as they can with words containing 'th'. Give a short time limit. Then ask learners to read the words in their groups and establish whether the 'th' is hard or soft.

> **Audioscript:** Track 25
> 1 threw
> 2 breath
> 3 the
> 4 thick
> 5 thought
> 6 then

> **Answers**
> **Hard sound:** 3 the 6 then
> **Soft sound:** 1 threw 2 breath 4 thick 5 thought

## 9  Values

- **Critical thinking:** Focus learners on the first two questions and put them into pairs or small groups to discuss the answers. Also ask them to discuss what they would have done in Tina's situation.

- Conduct a class feedback. Then focus learners on question 3 and ask them to think of at least three points for each example. Elicit an example for each category first, e.g.
  *When you are in a place with lots of traffic, you should always use a pedestrian crossing.*
  *If you are in the countryside, you mustn't go near any wild animals.*

- **Extend and challenge:** Extend this activity by having learners create a safety leaflet or poster, relevant to their environment, on children can look after themselves in the city or countryside.

> **Answers**
> Learners' own answers.
> General suggestions:
> Always let an adult you trust know where you are or where you're going.
> Don't talk to people you don't know.
> Remember your home phone number.
> Know what number to call if there is an emergency.

##  Wrap up

- Round up the class by asking learners to discuss what they would have done in Tina's situation.

## Activity Book

### 1 Read

- Learners complete a gapped summary of the *Jurassic Park* film story using words in the box.

> **Answers**
> 1 science fiction
> 2 scientists
> 3 island
> 4 dinosaurs
> 5 controlled
> 6 escape
> 7 breaks
> 8 dinosaurs
> 9 escape

### 2 Read

- Learners answer a multiple-choice question about the film, *Jurassic Park*.

> **Answers**
> b It showed computer generated special effects that were new at the time.

### 3 Read

- Learners read the *Jurassic Park* extract again and put pictures from the story in the correct order.

## 4 Read

- Learners answer multiple-choice questions about the text.

## 5 📝 Write

- Learners answer a question about a theme from the text and give reasons for their answer.

## 6 Word study

- Learners identify a strategy (from a choice of three) that will help them deduce unknown words from context.
- They read sentences from the story and underline words / phrases that help to clarify the meaning of target words highlighted in the sentence.

# Lesson 6: Choose a project

Learner's Book pages: 62–63

## Lesson objectives

**Speaking:** Deliver a presentation reviewing a film or presenting a timeline about a historical event; revise unit themes; discuss **Unit 4** Big question.

**Writing:** Organise and prepare notes for a film review presentation; create a historical timeline; revise unit themes.

**Critical thinking:** Evaluate a film; draw on own knowledge and research to create a timeline; apply new skills and language acquired in **Unit 4** to project work and revision activities.

**Language focus:** Recycling language points from **Unit 4**, i.e. Adverbs (with adjectives); past simple passive tense; relative clauses.

**Vocabulary:** Recycling of new and reviewed vocabulary from **Unit 4**, i.e. Types of films; strong adjectives; cinema history; understanding words from context

**Materials:** paper; poster paper or electronic slides; poster paper, pictures, coloured pens (for Project 2).

## Learner's Book

### 👉 Warm up

- Put learners in small teams and play the Dice game to revise language and themes from **Unit 4** (see **Unit 2**, **Lesson 6**, warm-up activity for instructions). Your themes from **Unit 4** could be:
  1 *Types of film*; 2 *Facts about cinema history*; 3 *Things that happened in the Jurassic Park story*; 4 *Adjectives to describe films*; 5 *Words for parts of films*; 6 *Describe a film you like*.
- Give each team a dice. If learners have never done this activity before, go through the procedure described in **Unit 2** (see above). If they have done the activity before, ask them to tell you what the rules are. Remember, all team members should have at least one turn.
- Do a practice round first to make sure learners are clear about the rules of the game.
- For the theme-based questions (i.e. 2, 3, 6), ask learners to focus on *fluency* rather than accuracy in this activity.
- Circulate as learners are doing the activity and praise good speaking efforts at the end.
- Tell learners they are now going to choose from the two projects and follow the instructions below for the one they have decided on.

### 1 A film review presentation

- Put learners in small groups and take them through the step by step instructions presented in the Learner's Book. Spend time helping groups to generate ideas for their chosen film. Ask them questions based on the headings outlined in stage 2. When they are outlining the plot, help them to summarise to ensure this stage doesn't become too long.
- When learners are drafting the presentation, make sure they follow the headings in stage 2 to help them structure the piece; encourage them to use sequencing phrases.
- Give learners time to practise their presentation, ensure that each member has a part to say and that someone is responsible for organising the props (slides, pictures, video clips, etc.).
- When learners deliver the presentation, ask the audience to note down the adjectives used to describe the film and why the presenters chose the adjectives.

**Wrap up**

- After the presentations, do a summary of all the films that were reviewed and the overall opinion about each one.

## 2 Create a timeline about film or TV history

- Put learners in small groups and take them through the step by step instructions presented in the Learner's Book. As they will need to look for information about their chosen topic, refer to the **Teaching tip** on page 39 for advice on how to manage this research. If possible, have each group choose a different topic (including some of their own choice) so that all the mini-presentations are different in the final stage.
- When they are at the drafting stage, ask them to create a first draft and check this for accuracy in grammar and word choice.
- When they have produced a satisfactory draft, ask them to make a poster showing the timeline clearly. Encourage them to make the poster clear and eye-catching because it will be used in the mini-presentation later.
- When they have finished the poster, give them time, as a group, to practise delivering a mini-presentation to the class, to explain the timeline. The presentation will just be a few minutes, describing each key point on the timeline and a little bit of information around it. However, draw their attention to some key phrases to structure the mini-talk, e.g. *We're going to talk about … Our timeline starts in the 1920s when … And finally, our timeline ends in … when …*
  Make sure they are clear about how to say the key dates too.
- Ask learners to present their timelines to the class. Their classmates listen and note down something they didn't know before from each presentation.

 **Wrap up**

- Ask learners to share their notes about new information they learned from each other's mini-presentations.

## Reflect on your learning

- These revision activities can be approached in different ways, according to the level and character of your class.
  - Questions 1–8 could be used as a class quiz, with learners in teams and a time limit given to write answers to each question.
  - Alternatively, you could conduct a revision session. Ask learners to work in pairs and take longer to think about and write down their answers. When pairs have finished the questions, they swap with

another pair and correct each other's work, with you monitoring and giving help and advice when needed.
- You could set this task for homework / self-study.

## Look what I can do!

**Aim:** To check learners have fulfilled the objectives for **Unit 4** (and to what degree).

- Present the objectives slide or poster from the introduction to **Unit 4** in **Lesson 1** and remind learners of the objectives from the start of the unit.
- Focus their attention on the 'I can …' statements on page 63 and read through together. You could put these on a slide or write on the board. Ask learners if they feel they can now do these tasks after completing **Unit 4**. By this point, you should have a clear idea yourself of how well your learners have completed the tasks. However, ask them now to do an initial self-assessment.
- Put learners in pairs and ask them to look through their notebooks and portfolios to find evidence of their work for each of the statements. Then they give themselves a rating as follows:
  ✓ Yes, I can – no problem!
  ? A little – I need more practice.
  ☹ No – I need a lot more practice.
- Circulate and chat to learners about their self-assessment (some might be overly modest and you can point out that their rating could be higher). If you haven't already done so, make notes about areas that learners are not confident about for future reference (see **Teaching tip**).
- Conduct a general feedback at the end and find out which tasks learners found the most interesting / useful / challenging etc.
- **Extend and challenge:** A mini-awards system: Customise the idea presented in **Unit 1** for **Unit 4** (see **Unit 1** page 38).

## 📖 Wrap up

As a class, look at the Big question again on a slide or written on the board: *What goes into making a film?*

- Put learners in small groups and ask them to brainstorm all the parts of films again, e.g. *the plot, characters, setting, storyboard, costumes, actors,* etc
- During feedback, elicit the key parts of a film onto the board. Then ask learners to answer the Big question by thinking of and matching a verb to a part, e.g. (*What goes into making a film?*) *write a plot, choose the actors, draw a storyboard,* etc. They can work in groups again to do this.
- Then ask learners to think about what the *audience* does when they see a film. Elicit these points from the class together, e.g. *watch a film, talk about it, review it, enjoy it, laugh at it, write about it, recommend it,* etc. Write their ideas on the board.
- Now ask learners what they have done in this unit. Elicit phrases that represent activities from the lesson, e.g. *talk about films, review films, write about films, draw a storyboard,* etc. Help learners to see that the activities they have covered represent something from each camp – both the film makers and the audience.

## Activity Book

### Revision

### 1 Multiple-choice quiz

- Learners complete sentences 1–12 by choosing the correct answer, a–c. Sentences cover key grammar and vocabulary from **Lessons 1–6** in **Unit 4**.

> **Answers**
> 1 b 2 a 3 b 4 c 5 a 6 b 7 c 8 c 9 b 10 c 11 b

### 2 My global progress

- Learners think about their own responses to topics and activities in the units and answer the questions.

> **Answers**
> Learners' own answers.

### Teaching tip

Review the learners' work and their own assessment of their progress, noting areas where learners demonstrate strength and confidence and areas where they need additional instruction and practice. Use this information to select areas for review and specific focus, as you continue to **Unit 5**.

# Review 2

Learner's Book pages: 64–65

- Review 2 offers learners the opportunity to review and recycle key language and vocabulary items from **Units 3** and **4**, presented in similar contexts to themes that appeared in these units. All items are briefly covered in activities that are similar in type to those in the Activity Book. There is a range of activity types that cover all skills areas.
- Learners can do Review 2 activities either in class or for homework. However, there is a short speaking activity, which will need to be covered in class (see below for suggestion). The Review pages can also be used to engage early finishers provided learners have already covered the relevant language points in class.
- **Speaking activities:** If learners have done the Review 2 activities at home, the speaking activity could be carried out during a Review 2 feedback session, either at the beginning or end of the class.
- **Feedback:** Answers to the activities can be elicited from learners or displayed on the board or on a slide for learners to use to correct their work. To make the correction stage more interactive, ask learners to swap notebooks and correct each other's work.

## 1 Listen 26

- Learners listen to an interview about sports habits and preferences and put the activities in the pictures in order.

> **Audioscript:** Track 26
>
> Our reporters are out and about talking to kids like you! They want to know what your favourite sports are and what you do to keep fit ...
>
> **Interviewer:** Hello Lana, what do you do to keep fit?
>
> **Lana:** Well, I'm into most sports. I like basketball and at the weekend I like to go to the park and play football with my my favourite sport is athletics – I love running!
>
> **I:** That's great! What do you like about running?
>
> **L:** It makes me feel healthy and energetic and I like being outside in the fresh air. And I really love being in an athletics team with other kids. We meet up every week and we have a lot of fun. I make new friends too.
>
> **I:** Do you have any tips for other children who want to start running?
>
> **L:** Yes, you should always warm up properly before running. You mustn't start running without doing warm-up exercises, otherwise you could hurt yourself.
>
> **I:** Why's that?
>
> **L:** Because your muscles need to be warm to work well before you can start exercising properly.
>
> **I:** What kind of exercises should you do?
>
> **L:** Running on the spot is good, so is skipping and jumping jacks. You should also stretch your hamstrings and thigh muscles too ...

> **Answers**
> **Picture** c / d / a / b

## 2 Listen 26

- Learners listen a second time and decide if statements about the interview are true or false. They correct the false sentences.

**Answers**

1 false. Lana's favourite sport is athletics / running.
2 false. It makes her feel healthy and energetic.
3 false. They meet up every week.
4 false. She says that you should do warm-up activities before running.
5 false. She says that your muscles need to be warm.
6 false. She says that you should stretch your hamstrings and thigh muscles.

## 3 💬 Talk

- Learners ask a partner the interviewer's questions and write his/her answers as reported statements.

**Answers**
Learner's own answers.

## 4 Vocabulary

- Learners read descriptions of various vocabulary items from **Unit 4** and guess the word.

**Answers**

1 make-up
2 a projector
3 the plot
4 hilarious
5 thrilling
6 horror
7 the audience
8 costumes

## 5 Use of English

- Learners choose the correct language component to complete the film review, covering a range of grammar items from **Unit 4**.

**Answers**

1 that
2 that
3 absolutely
4 when
5 really
6 very
7 a bit
8 where
9 made
10 was

## 6 📝 Read

- Learners read the review again and extract information.

**Answers**

**Type of film:** Science fiction.
**Setting:** Outer space (in another galaxy).
**Plot:** It's about a lost spaceship that encounters an evil mutant monster (that lives on another planet).
**Good points:** The special effects.
**Bad points:** The film is very long and a bit boring in parts.
**Fun fact:** When the film was shown in cinemas for the first time in the 1950s, people ran out screaming!

## 7 📝 Write

- Learners write an email to a friend about a film that they have seen recently, mentioning type of film, plot and setting and the good and bad points about the film.

**Answers**
Learner's own answers.

## 8 💬 Talk

- Learners discuss the two stories in **Units 3** and **4** and decide which one they prefer and explain their choice.

# 5 Inventions

## Unit overview

In this unit learners will:

- talk about important gadgets and equipment
- read about a famous inventor
- present and listen to new ideas for inventions
- write about a revolutionary invention
- read a story about a young inventor.

In **Unit 5**, learners will explore the world of inventions, considering gadgets and equipment that have changed our lives, as well as experience a light-hearted look at the process of creating new inventions. The Big question centres around predominant themes of the unit and learners will understand that tasks and projects in the unit will help them to answer the question at the end.

The unit begins by looking at everyday gadgets and equipment and what they mean to us. This accessible opening topic offers learners an ideal opportunity to practise productive and receptive skills through discussion of a familiar and popular subject. In the next lesson, learners examine the beginnings of an essential modern day invention and learn the language to describe what life was like before. Learners then go on to plan and deliver an oral presentation to describe an invention that they have 'created', using appropriate language to predict its use in the future. They then write an essay about an important invention, giving opinions and reasons; looking at grammatical and functional language included in this type of writing. Finally learners read a story about the challenges of a young inventor and discuss the issue of self-belief. The **Photocopiable activities** provide practice in: talking about past habits as a young child (**9**) and using second conditional forms to ask and answer questions about imaginary situations (**10**).

### Language focus

*Used to* for past habits; future simple forms (for future predictions); second conditional (imaginary situations).

**Vocabulary topics:** Gadgets and equipment; phrases for stating preferences and comparing; phrases for giving opinions and reasons; adverbs.

### Self-assessment

- I can talk about and compare useful gadgets and pieces of equipment.
- I can read and discuss information about a famous inventor.
- I can deliver a presentation about a new idea for an invention.
- I can understand and ask questions about my classmates' ideas.
- I can write a short essay giving my opinion about something.
- I can read and understand a story about a young inventor.

### Teaching tips

**Know your audience:** When learners are preparing a text for a speaking activity (e.g. a presentation) or a writing task, ask them to consider who the audience or reader is going to be, e.g. classmates, the teacher, or older or younger students. This will help them to focus the task in terms of organisation, content and choice of language. An awareness of this point at this stage will prepare them better for tasks that present themselves at secondary level, when task types become more varied and complex and issues of register and appropriacy are more prevalent. Further practice is given on this point in this unit.

# Lesson 1: Inventions

Learner's Book pages: 66–67

Activity Book pages: 52–53

## Lesson objectives

**Listening:** Listen to a conversation comparing favourite gadgets; listen for information and functional language.

**Speaking:** Compare and contrast different gadgets and equipment.

**Critical thinking:** Compare, contrast and indicate preferences for different gadgets and equipment.

**Vocabulary:** Gadgets and equipment; *a zip, a tablet computer, a compass, a bicycle, a laptop, a mobile phone*

**Comparing and contrasting:** *It's got to be my ... because .../ it's more useful than .../ it depends on ...*

**Materials:** poster paper or electronic slides.

## Learner's Book

###  Warm up

- To introduce the Big question, start by telling the class that this unit is going to be about inventions. Explain that you are going to look at how important and popular inventions, past and present, have changed our lives, and create your own invention. So the Big question is ... *How have important inventions changed our lives?*
- Write the question on the board (for an electronic presentation, create a slide with interesting graphics). Tell learners that you are all going to do tasks and projects in the unit that will answer this question.
- Introduce the unit objectives to show learners what tasks are coming up. Present the objectives on a slide or large piece of poster paper to attach to the board.
- Tell learners that you will answer the Big question and look again at the objectives at the end of the unit. Keep the objectives slide / poster to revisit at the end of the unit.
- Tell learners that you are going to start by looking at gadgets and equipment. Ask learners to give you some examples of a *gadget – a small electronic piece of equipment*; let learners make suggestions and if possible, show them some examples (e.g. a mobile, a pocket calculator, etc.). Then put them in small groups and give each a different room of a house or school; ask them to think of any words they know for gadgets that you might find in those places.
- Conduct a quick feedback, eliciting one or two ideas from each group. This activity will help to activate prior knowledge and define what a *gadget* actually is.

### 1 🗩 Talk about it

Put learners in pairs and ask them to talk about the three questions. Circulate and help with any unknown vocabulary. Then nominate a few learners or ask for volunteers to share their thoughts. Alternatively, you could ask learners to report back what their partner talked about.

- **Critical thinking:** Learners identify their own preferences for gadgets, giving reasons why.

> **Answers**
> Learners' own answers.

### 2 🗩 Word study

- Focus learners' attention on the pictures and go through the names of each item. Then put learners in teams and read out the quiz questions, giving points for correct answers. Then ask learners to read the quiz questions again and match to the pictures for consolidation.

> **Answers**
> **1** a laptop   **2** a zip   **3** a bicycle   **4** a compass
> **5** a mobile phone   **6** a tablet

[AB] **For further practice, see Activities 1, 2 and 3 in the Activity Book.**

### 3 📝 Listen 27

- Tell the class that they are going to listen to a conversation between two friends talking about their favourite gadgets. Elicit from learners which gadgets they think the children might talk about.
- Focus learners' attention on the instruction in the book and ask them to tell you what they have to do while listening to the interview for the first time (answer the questions, 1 and 2 in their notebooks). Then tell them to note down the gadgets mentioned *while* listening and the advantages and disadvantages of each one, *after* listening.
- Play the audio. After listening, ask learners to make notes and then compare their answers with their partner. If necessary, play the audio again to either check answers or focus specifically of question 2.

> **Audioscript:** Track 27
>
> **Ben:** What is your favourite gadget? What couldn't you live without?
>
> **Lucia:** It's got to be my mobile phone – I can't live without it. I can use it to talk to my friends, send texts, as a camera, a calculator, a stopwatch and a calendar! If I could choose one thing, it would be my phone ... . What about you?
>
> **Ben:** Hmmm. I do like my phone too, but the most important gadget for me is my laptop. I can use it to surf the Internet, send emails, play games and do my homework.
>
> **Lucia:** But you can send emails and surf the Net on a phone too ... and it's smaller. I think it's more useful than a laptop
>
> **Ben:** That's true, but it depends on the type of phone ... and you can't use your phone to write things like essays ...
>
> **Lucia:** Yes – I suppose they are both useful for different reasons.

**Answers**
1 A mobile phone and a laptop.
2 Advantages of a mobile phone: It is small and has multiple uses – it can be used to talk to friends, send texts, as a camera, a calculator, a stopwatch and a calendar.
Disadvantages: the facilities on a phone depend on the type of phone – not all phones have the same functions – and phones can't be used as a word processor.
Advantages of a laptop: Multiple uses - surf the Internet, send emails, play games and do homework.
Disadvantages: bigger than a mobile phone and many of the functions on a laptop can be done on a phone too (depending on the type).

## 4 Listen 27

- Focus learners' attention on the phrases a-e, from the conversation. These phrases are used to express preferences and compare the gadgets. Tell them that they are going to listen again to complete the phrases. Before they listen, ask them to predict what words might be missing.
- Listen to check. Then complete the sentences in notebooks after listening.
- When you check the answers, do some pronunciation work on connected speech, in preparation for the speaking activity in **Activity 6**. E.g.
  *It's got to be my mobile phone… The most important gadget … It depends on …*
- **Extend and challenge:** The points made in the conversation could be expanded into a mini-debate. Ask learners if they agree with the points made by Lucia and Ben. If not, why not? What other advantages and disadvantages are there to laptops and mobile phones?

**Answers**
a It's got to be my **mobile phone** – I **can't** live without it! (Lucia)
b I can use it **to talk** to my friends (Lucia)
c The **most** important gadget for me is a **laptop**. (Ben)
d I think it's **more** useful than a **laptop**. (Lucia)
e That's **true**, but it depends **on** the type of phone … (Ben)

 For further practice, see Activity 4 in the Activity Book.

## 5 Write

- **Critical thinking:** Ask learners to work individually on this task and to start by thinking carefully about gadgets they use and which is the most important. Give them a few minutes to do this. Circulate and help with vocabulary where needed.
  **Note:** This little writing exercise is designed to allow learners time to articulate ideas and practise using the functional language from **Activity 4**, in preparation for the pyramid speaking activity in **Activity 6**.
- Ask learners to complete the sentences in **Activity 5** and then compare their ideas with their partner.

**Answers**
Learners' own answers.

## 6 Talk

- First, ask learners to work in pairs and think of a third item to add to the two they have already described in **Activity 5**. If learners have written about the same gadget in **Activity 5**, tell them to think of another, so they have three different choices. They need to note down reasons why the gadgets are important. Circulate and help, inputting relevant vocabulary where needed.
- Alternatively, you could make this discussion more varied (and more focused within groups) by giving pairs a specific area to consider, e.g. inventions in transport / household appliances / communication, etc. In this case, spend time with each group brainstorming relevant vocabulary.
- **Critical thinking:** When learners have discussed three items in pairs, team pairs up to become a group of four. Then ask them to discuss their ideas and together decide on the three most important items for their group. They need to compare and contrast their ideas and preferences, using the functional language from **Activity 4**, and negotiate three definitive items together. (If you have given learners specific areas to look at, make sure pairs are teamed up with another pair who have discussed the same area).
  A: *The most important gadget for me is a … because …*
  B: *That's true but …*
- Tell learners to make notes about the reasons for their choices, in preparation for the last stage.
- Now bring the class together and listen to each group presenting their ideas to the class and giving reasons. Write the different gadgets / inventions on the board.
- At the end, decide together as a class, through comparing and negotiating, which three gadgets / inventions are the most important.

**Answers**
Learners' own answers.

## Wrap up

- **Critical thinking:** Ask learners to look around their classroom and think of gadgets and inventions that are needed and why.

## Activity Book

### 1 Vocabulary

- Learners match words to pictures of gadgets.

**Answers**
a a memory stick;
b a tablet;
c a camera;
d a mini-DVD player;
e an MP3 player

### 2 Vocabulary

- Learners use words from **Activity 1** to complete sentences about electronic gadgets.

## 3 📝 Read

- Learners answer questions about the information in the sentences in **Activity 2**.

Answers
1 Speaker 2
2 Speaker 1
3 The touch screen
4 Some headphones.

## 4 📝 Write

- Learners complete sentences about gadgets that they and their family use (using target functional language comparing and expressing preferences).

Answers
Learners' own answers.

## 5 Listen 68 [CD2 Track 36]

- Learners listen to someone talking about her class survey (about gadgets). They identify the question asked in the survey from a choice of three.

**Audioscript:** Track 68

We asked 30 students in our class about their favourite electronic gadgets. We wanted to know the reason *why* our classmates liked their gadgets so much, so we asked them to choose the most important reason from a list. You can see the results here on this pie chart.

For a lot of us – 40% – the most important reason for using our favourite gadgets is to download apps and play games, so we use our favourite gadgets mainly for entertainment. But for 35%, the most important reason is to communicate with each other through calling, messaging, and sometimes Facetime and Skype. Then, for 15% of us, the reasons are more practical – to store information. And that includes saving files of school work, saving useful websites as favourites, and also saving photos and videos. And finally, for 10% of us, the most important reason is to be creative – so that includes taking photos, making videos, as well as using some drawing apps ...

Answers
b What is the most important reason for using your favourite gadget?

## 6 🔁 Listen 68 [CD2 Track 36]

- Learners listen again and label a pie chart from the information in the survey and written notes in the activity.

Answers
40% column = 3 (For entertainment)
35% column = 1 (Communicate with each other)
15% column = 2 (Store information)
10% column = 4 (Be creative)

# Lesson 2: Great minds

Learner's Book pages: 68–69
Activity Book pages: 54–55

## Lesson objectives

**Reading:** Find specific information in a text about Thomas Edison, inventor of the modern light bulb. Use your own knowledge to increase your understanding of a text.

**Speaking:** Talk about what people did before modern inventions; how the electric light bulb has changed since Edison's version and how it might change in the future.

**Critical thinking:** Use your own knowledge to make assumptions and predictions.

**Language focus:** *Used to* to describe past habits.

**Materials:** Images of old-fashioned and modern day inventions (optional). Copies of **Photocopiable activity 9**.

## Learner's Book

### 🖙 Warm up

- Ask learners to keep their books closed and tell them that you are thinking of a very important invention and they have to guess what it is. Then introduce the lesson topic by playing *20 questions* (see **Unit 1**, **Lesson 4** for instructions) to elicit *light bulb*.
- Now put learners into small groups and give them one minute to write down all the places where you see electric light. After a minute, stop the class and ask them to count how many places they have listed. The group with the longest list reads it out and the others tick the places that are the same on their lists. If other groups have mentioned different places on their list they can add them to the first list. The idea is to build a picture of just how essential and prevalent electric light is in our world today.

## 1 🗨 Talk about it

- Focus attention on the question in **Activity 1**. Either elicit responses from learners as a class or ask them to discuss briefly in pairs and then conduct a class feedback. Write their ideas on the board (to illustrate the reading strategy in the next stage).
- **Critical thinking:** Learners use their own knowledge to make assumptions.

Answers
In the past, before the use of electricity, people used candles, fire, oil lamps and gas lamps for light.

## 2 🖼 Read

- Before learners look at the task for the reading text in **Activity 2**, draw their attention to the reading strategy by asking them why you always ask them to talk about reading topics before reading. Listen to their suggestions and then tell them that if they talk about a topic first, this will give them clues about the information that might be in the text; they can then look for their ideas in the text as they read.

- Point out their ideas on the board from **Activity 1** and explain that these ideas will help them understand the text better when they read it. Tell them that they are going to read about a famous inventor called Thomas Edison. Ask them to check if these ideas are mentioned when they read and also to identify what Edison's most famous invention was.

- Ask learners to read the text to find the answers to the two gist questions in **Activity 2**, mentioned above.

> **Answers**
> Learners' own answers.
> Edison's most famous invention was the modern electric light bulb.

## 3 Read

- Focus learners on the statements in **Activity 3** and read them together. Tell them to read the text again to find out if the statements are true or false. They should work through the statements on their own, then check with a partner.

- **Additional support and practice:** For extra support, learners could work through the statements 1–6 in pairs or you could divide the statements between pairs – one does 1,3 and 5; the other, 2,4 and 6.

- When learners have finished, go through the answers together as a class, highlighting any information which learners deduced already in the pre-reading stage (e.g. statements 1 and 2).

> **Answers**
> 1 true
> 2 false. Gas lamps were used to light the streets.
> 3 false. Edison's modern light bulb was cheap and long lasting.
> 4 false. Edison improved the first electric light bulbs and made them cheaper and more practical.
> 5 true
> 6 false. He created 1,093 other inventions in his lifetime.

 **For further practice, see Activity 1 in the Activity Book.**

## 4  Talk

- Put learners in pairs or small groups to discuss the questions in **Activity 4**. Ask them to think of at least two ways that electric light bulbs have changed since Edison's time. If you have some kind of reward system operating in your classroom, offer some kind of 'reward' for the most imaginative answer to the second question about ways to improve electric lighting further.

> **Answers**
> Since Edison's lifetime, electric light bulbs have become much more energy efficient and now run on less energy and last a lot longer. It is also possible to buy lots of different sizes and designs of electric light bulb.
> Learners' own answers.

## 5 [AB] Use of English

- Write three examples from the **Use of English** box on the board, leaving a space for the *used to* forms:
  *People _____ light their homes with candles ...*
  *They didn't _____ have electric light in their homes.*
  *What did people _____ do before electric light?*

- Elicit the missing components from learners.

- Ask learners some concept-check questions to establish when the *used to* form is used. E.g. *Are these sentences about the past or the present time*? (past) *Are they talking about actions or situations that happened only once?* (No). *How often did the actions / situations happen in the past?* (All the time). Then explain to learners that these actions and situations were habits in the past – i.e. they happened all the time – and this is when we use the form, *used to*.

- Highlight the form in the affirmative, negative and question forms. Change the pronoun (e.g. replace *they* with *you* and *he* and elicit that the form remains the same in all cases, even if the pronoun is changed. Then focus learners on the verb form that comes after *used to* (base infinitive) so they can see how the whole structure is formed.

- Focus learners on **Activity 5** and ask them to choose the correct option.

- Review the answer as a class. Clarify any confusion with the concept by presenting more example sentences and asking the concept-check questions again.

> **Answers**
> In a question or negative sentence we use *use to*.

[AB] **For further practice, see Activities 3, 4 and 5 in the Activity Book.**

## 6 Talk

- Focus learners on the pictures in the Learner's Book and ask them to describe what they see. Then write, *People used to ...* on the board, point to one of the pictures and ask learners to finish the sentence, (e.g. *People used to use phones with a dial*). Elicit another sentence with the negative form (e.g. *Phones didn't use to have push buttons*). Highlight the different components (*used to* + verb) in different colours or underline. Then ask the class to make another full sentence about one of the other pictures. If possible, show learners more images of similar items to stimulate more language (e.g. an old-fashioned bicycle with large front wheel, a credit card, old-fashioned pram, etc.).

- Do some pronunciation practice with the example sentences, using the backchaining technique and whispering drills. Use a disappearing drill to build fluency and confidence (see **Unit 1, Lesson 1** and **2** for more details of all techniques).

- Now ask learners to make more sentences in pairs, using the target structure and the images for inspiration.

## Differentiated instruction

**Additional support and practice**

- To scaffold the activity a little more and build confidence, learners can write sentences first, then turn over their notebooks and remember as many as possible by looking at the pictures for guidance. You could also check the written sentences, then quickly write one or two key words as prompts and ask learners to say the sentences using the key words as guidance.
- Finish off the activity by hearing some example sentences from around the class. .

**Extend and challenge**

- Ask learners to imagine the sentences people will say with *used to* in 100 or 200 years time, talking about the way we live now, e.g. *people didn't use to have flying cars! People used to only live on Earth …*

**Answers**
Learners' own answers.
Suggestions:
People used to have a dial on their phones.
People used to make calls on bigger phones.
20 years ago, mobile phones used to be much bigger and heavier.
Light bulbs used to be more expensive.
There didn't use to be so many different light bulb shapes and sizes.
Light bulbs didn't use to last as long as they do now.
Before the Internet, people used to read more books.
Before the Internet, it was more difficult to find information quickly.
Before the Internet, people didn't use to use their computers to find out information.

## Wrap up

- Ask learners to tell the class about things that they used to do five years ago that they don't do now.

## Activity Book

### 1 Read

- Learners do a multiple-choice exercise to support their understanding of the reading strategy. Then they read a text about the history of the mobile phone and match a picture to a section of the text.

**Answers**
Talk about the reading topics first. ✓
a 4   b 6   c 3   d 2   e 5   f 1

### 2 Use of English

- Learners identify four sentences with *used to* in the text and underline them.

**Answers**
… used to have a separate mouth and ear piece.
People used to call someone using a round dial.
… the battery used to run out after 20 minutes!
They used to weigh nearly a kilo …

### 3 Use of English

- Learners match sentence halves to make true sentences about mobile phones.

**Answers**
1 f   2 e   3 d   4 b   5 c   6 a

### 4 Use of English

- Learners complete sentences about televisions with the correct form of used to and a verb from the box.

**Answers**
1 Televisions didn't use to have so many channels.
2 People used to watch TV in black and white only.
3 People didn't use to change TV channels with a remote control.
4 Did your grandparents used to own a TV when they were young?
5 Before TVs, people used to listen to the radio to hear the news.

### 5  Challenge

- Learners answer questions about themselves using *used to*.

**Answers**
Learners' own answers.

- For further practice in talking about past habits (using forms of *used to*), see **Photocopiable activity 9**.

## Lesson 3: Bright ideas

Learner's Book pages: 70–71
Activity Book pages: 56–57

### Lesson objectives

**Speaking:** Prepare and deliver a presentation about an idea for an invention.

**Listening:** Listen to a presentation about an invention idea and notice features of content and organisation.

**Critical thinking:** Create and describe an idea for an invention. Describe how the invention could solve an existing problem.

**Language focus:** Future simple tense (to describe future predictions).

**Materials:** pictures of unusual inventions (for warm-up); poster paper, coloured pens.

## Learner's Book

### Warm up

- Put pictures on the board of two or three unusual inventions (e.g. a Sinclair C5, Segway, etc). Ask learners to comment on the inventions, i.e. What use do they have? Would they use one? Do they think the inventions have been successful? Why? Why not?
**Note:** You could search *Inventions in transportation* on the Internet for pictures.

# 1 💬 Talk about it

- **Critical thinking:** Focus learners on **Activity 1** and ask them to start thinking of their own ideas for new inventions. These ideas can be as realistic or as outlandish as they like. Ask learners to work in pairs and choose one of the categories listed in **Activity 1**. **Note:** This stage is just a brainstorming session, designed to generate interest in the topic and lay some groundwork for the final presentation stage of the lesson.
- Conduct a quick feedback, asking learners to share some initial ideas at this stage.

> **Answers**
> Learners' own answers.

# 2 Listen 28

- Tell learners that they are now going to listen to someone (Kim) presenting her idea for an invention. Before they listen, draw their attention to the **Speaking tip** and reiterate the points outlined in the strategy (see also **Teaching tip** in the **Unit 5** Overview).
- Tell learners to listen to Part 1 of the presentation. They need to listen to find out who Kim is presenting her idea to and why.

> **Audioscript:** Track 28
>
> **Teacher:** OK, Kim, are you ready? Remember you are presenting your idea to a group of judges in a competition – they have a lot of money to give to the best invention idea. If you win this money, you'll be able to make your invention and sell it. Convince them that it is a fantastic idea and deserves the prize! Now off you go ...

> **Answers**
> Kim is presenting her idea to a group of judges in a competition. If she wins the competition, she'll win a prize of a lot of money. The prize money will enable her to make her invention idea and sell it.

# 3 Listen 29

- Now focus learners' attention on pictures in the Learner's Book. Ask them to describe each picture, either together as a class or in pairs. Tell them that they are now going to listen to the second part of Kim's presentation, where she describes her invention idea. While they listen, they need to decide which picture best matches Kim's idea.
- After listening, give learners a minute or so to discuss with their partner which picture she describes. Then conduct feedback.

> **Audioscript:** Track 29
>
> OK. Good morning everyone. My name's Kim and today I'm going to describe an idea for a fantastic invention. Here is a picture of my idea. These are Super Jet Boots. This invention will change the way people travel because it is much faster and safer than a car and much cheaper than a plane. As you can see, Super Jet Boots let you fly through the air because they have powerful jets on the bottom of the boot.

> You control these jets with buttons on the side of the boot. You just put them on, press the buttons ... and go! And the jets lift you high into the air. Super Jet Boots are a fast and easy way to travel and will solve the traffic problems in our city because people won't need to travel by car any more. Also, with Super Jet Boots people won't have so many traffic accidents. There is plenty of space in the air for people to travel, so people won't crash into each other – and they'll be able to travel as fast as they like.
>
> To sum up, Super Jet Boots are a fast and safe way to travel because you can fly through the air instead of on the road. They are also environmentally friendly. If people travel by Super Jet Boots, they won't need to use their cars. Now that's the end of my presentation. Thank you for listening. Does anyone have any questions?

> **Answer**
> Picture c

# 4 Listen 29

- Tell learners they are now going to listen to Part 2 again and answer the questions in **Activity 4**. Focus their attention on the two questions and read them together. For the second question, explain that Kim organises the information in her presentation in a way which makes it easy for the audience to follow. Elicit how Kim starts the presentation (by introducing herself and telling the audience the purpose of her talk) and anything else learners might have noticed about the order of the information. Then tell them to listen to check and / or answer the questions.
- **Additional support and practice:** To help learners identify how the speaker organises the information in the presentation, give them these headings and ask them to order as they listen.
  A summary of the idea (Order: 4)
  A description of the idea. (1)
  Why people need this invention (3)
  How you use the invention. (2)
- Before learners listen, check they understand the meaning of *jet*, *buttons*, *crash* and *environmentally friendly*. Point to the pictures to pre-teach *jet* and *buttons*; mime *crash* by knocking your fists together to imitate the action of two cars crashing into each other and give them an example for *environmentally friendly* (e.g. trams are *environmentally friendly* because they don't burn any fossil fuels like petrol, that pollutes the air).
- After listening, give learners a few minutes to discuss answers with their partner; then conduct a class feedback. If necessary play the audio again, stopping after each part that answers questions 1 and 2.

> **Answers**
> 1 She shows her audience a picture of her idea.
> 2 Organisation of information: 1 A description of the idea. 2 How you use the invention. 3 Why people need this invention. 4 A summary of the idea.

## 5 Listen 30

- Now listen to the last part, and ask learners to complete the audience's questions. Read through the questions first, then play the last part. If necessary, you could stop the audio after each question to give learners time to complete the questions.

**Audioscript:** Track 30

**Judge 1:** Yes, thanks, Kim for your interesting idea. But I've got a question. How do you keep your balance on the Super Jet Boots?

**Kim:** Oh that's not a problem! The jet will be so powerful that you can stand up straight!

**Judge 2:** And where will you put the jet fuel to give the boots power?

**Kim:** Er ... , I think it'll go in the bottom of the boots, in the soles.

**Teacher:** OK. Thanks Kim. Very interesting ... . But there are lots of good ideas in this competition. Which idea will the judges choose? We'll have to wait and see ...

**Answers**
1 How do you keep your balance on the Super Jet Boots?
2 Where do you put the jet fuel to give the boots power?

## 6 🗩 Talk

- **Critical thinking:** Ask learners to discuss the two questions in pairs. Did they like Kim's idea? Why? Why not? Ask them to write at least two questions that they would ask her if they had attended her presentation.
- During feedback, elicit examples of questions and make a note on the board or on a slide. These notes will be useful as reference in the final stage of the lesson where learners ask each other questions about their own presentations. Highlight a couple of questions and ask learners to imagine how Kim would respond. Again, this is good practice for the final stage when learners will need to think on their feet and spontaneously answer questions from the audience after their own presentations.

**Answers**
Learners' own answers.

## 7 🔲 Use of English

- Write the three examples from the **Use of English** box on the board, leaving a space for *will* / *won't* + verb. Ask learners if they remember the sentences from the presentation.
  *This invention _____ the way people travel ...* (*will change*)
  *People _____ into each other ...* (*won't crash*)
  *Which idea _____ the judges _____?* (*will* / *choose*)
- Elicit the missing components from learners.
- Ask learners some concept-check questions to establish when the future simple tense is used in this context. E.g. *Are these sentences about the present or future time?* (future) Does the speaker think these

things will definitely happen or are very likely to happen? (Very likely to happen – she thinks there is a very strong possibility – she is making a *prediction*.)
- Highlight the form in the affirmative, negative and question forms. Write another example (e.g. *He will move house next year*) and change the pronoun (e.g. replace with *you* and *we* and elicit that the form remains the same in all cases, even if the pronoun is changed). Then focus learners on the verb form that comes after *will* / *won't* (base infinitive), so they can see how the whole structure is formed.
- **Extend and challenge:** If you feel learners would benefit from something more active at this point in the lesson, you could introduce the target language focus by having them do a running dictation (for instructions, see **Unit 2**, **Lesson 2**). The items to dictate and copy would be the three example sentences from the **Use of English** box. As well as energising learners, this activity ensures that they notice every component of the target language through the actions of memorising, dictating, listening and copying. When learners have copied the sentences, ask them to highlight the key components (i.e. *will*/*won't* + verb); then follow the rest of the steps in **Activity 7**, starting with the concept questions.
- Focus learners on **Activity 7** and ask them to choose the correct option.
- Review the answer as a class. Clarify any confusion with the concept by presenting more example sentences and asking the concept-check questions again.
- Do some pronunciation practice with the example sentences. If you feel learners need extra reinforcement, use the backchaining technique and whispering drills; use a disappearing drill to build fluency and confidence (see **Unit 1**, **Lessons 1** and **2** for more details of all techniques).

**Answers**
1 When you use different pronouns (*I, you, he, she, it, we, they*) the form of *will* and *won't* stays the same.
2 We use the infinitive form after *will*/*won't*.

## 8 Use of English

- Ask learners to do **Activity 8** to consolidate their understanding of the target language. They can either do the activity individually and then compare answers with their partner, or do the activity together in pairs.

**Answers**
1 Will I save money? – Yes you will.
2 Super Jet Boots will solve the traffic problems in our city.
3 You won't have to travel by car any more.
4 You won't have / see so many traffic accidents.
5 The jet will be so powerful that you can stand up straight.
6 You will be able to travel as fast as you like.

 For further practice, see Activity 1 in the Activity Book.

## Present it!

- Tell learners that they are now going to prepare their own presentations about their own ideas for inventions. In preparation, first, go through key points from Kim's presentation that they can draw on: 1) organising the presentation in sections using the headings from the answers to Activity 4 part 2; 2) using a picture to engage the audience's attention at the beginning; 3) using the future simple form to make predictions about how their invention will be used.
- Put learners into pairs or groups of three to prepare and deliver their presentations. Together they choose one of their ideas from **Activity 1** (or think of a new one) and make notes under the headings from **Activity 4**. Tell them to think about who their audience is going to be, to make the purpose of the presentation clear at the beginning, and to add sequencing phrases, e.g. *Today we're going to talk about ...*
- Ask them to draw a large, clear picture to illustrate their idea on poster paper.
- Ask learners to write out their presentation from their notes and produce one text per group, either in class time or at home. Check the scripts for grammar, vocabulary and organisation; however, the emphasis is on organisation and quality of ideas rather than perfectly accurate scripts.
- Give learners the opportunity to practise their presentations together. Each member of the group should deliver a part of the presentation. Monitor the groups, making sure you spend some time with each, helping with any pronunciation difficulties. Check that everyone has a part to present and that someone is responsible for displaying the illustration of the idea.
- **Critical thinking:** Before learners present to the class, think about how you want to organise the question session: you could leave it open for any learner to be a 'judge' and ask a question after each presentation, or you could give specific learners the duty (different learners for each presentation so the duty is more evenly distributed) in a *Dragon's Den* type of activity. Other learners can note which ideas they particularly like and why, in preparation for the vote at the end.
- Ask learners to deliver their presentations in pairs or groups of three in front of the class. Introduce each group first and generate a supportive atmosphere by having learners applaud each group before and after each presentation. When each group finishes, make a positive comment about their presentation before handing over to the 'judges' to ask questions.
- **Additional support and practice:** Use of notes in delivery: stronger learners may be able to deliver without looking too closely at their notes; others may need to read from their notes at this stage. Use your discretion with regard to how much you allow this, taking into account ability and confidence

levels in your class. Ultimately in later years, learners need to be able to deliver oral presentations without reading word for word from notes. Ideally, we should encourage them to get into this habit as soon as possible but learners will probably need the support of reading from their notes in these early stages.
- **Extend and challenge:** As learners are delivering their presentations, note down main errors; either give to each group a note of the errors to correct themselves, or write up on the board at the end for a class error correction session (without stating which group or individual made the errors). **Note:** This would come after plenty of positive feedback regarding the presentations. Positive feedback must always come first and be emphasised.

> **Answers**
> Learners' own answers – Portfolio opportunity.

## Wrap up

- **Critical thinking:** At the end, have a vote on the best invention idea. Alternatively, you could have several categories – most realistic idea / craziest idea / best art work, etc.

## Activity Book

### 1 Use of English

- Learners complete a text outlining a presentation with *will* / *won't* and a verb from the box.

> **Answers**
> 1 will change
> 2 will improve
> 3 will be
> 4 won't have to
> 5 will make
> 6 won't get
> 7 will like
> 8 will do

### 2 Read

- Learners read the presentation text again and match the sections A – E to a heading.

> **Answers**
> 1 Why people need this invention. D
> 2 Introduction. A
> 3 How you use the invention. C
> 4 A summary of the idea. E
> 5 Description of the idea. B

### 3 Write

- Learners sort words to make five 'audience' questions about the ideas in the presentation text.

## 4 Over to you

- Learners write two more questions to ask the presenter of the presentation in **Activity 1**.

**Answers**
Learners' own answers.

## 5  Challenge

- Learners write about a new invention for their school, using future predictions.

**Answers**
Learners' own answers.

# Lesson 4: Changing the world

Learner's Book pages: 72–73
Activity Book pages: 58–59

### Lesson objectives

**Reading:** Read an essay giving an opinion about a life-changing invention; identify the reasons given for the opinion.

**Writing:** Plan and write an essay giving an opinion about an important invention.

**Speaking:** Talk about imaginary situations in the context of what we would do without modern inventions.

**Critical thinking:** Asserting an opinion about which inventions are important and supporting it with reasons.

**Language focus:** Second conditional to describe imaginary situations.

**Vocabulary:** Functional language for giving opinions and reasons.

**Materials:** pictures of important inventions past and present (optional for **Warm up**). Copies of **Photocopiable activity 10**.

## Learner's Book

### Warm up

- Before learners open their books, take in some pictures of famous inventions, past and present and ask learners to guess what they are. Hold the pictures so that the class can't see the images and ask them to call out suggestions. When you hear a correct suggestion, put the corresponding picture on the board in preparation for the next stage.
  **Note:** Choose diverse images, e.g. *a wheel, a television, rope, a satellite, a microchip, a match stick*, to make

learners think about the origins of world-changing inventions.

- If pictures are difficult to obtain, present the above items in a letter dictation. Dictate the words letter by letter in a continuous stream (without breaking between words), which learners listen to and copy down. Then ask them to find six important inventions in the letter line, e.g.
  w-h-e-e-l-t-e-l-e-v-i-s-i-o-n-r-o-p-e = wheel/television/rope.

## 1 ⤬ Talk about it

- **Critical thinking:** Focus learners on the questions in **Activity 1** and put them into small groups to discuss and make a list. They can look at the pictures or their word list and discuss those inventions and / or think of others. Ask them to identify two which they feel are the most important and why.
- Conduct a class feedback, taking suggestions for the most important inventions and the reasons. Help learners articulate their thoughts at this stage by inputting useful phrases and reformulating any awkward expression.
  **Note:** Do not focus heavily on accuracy here, the emphasis is on fluency and generating ideas; any error correction should be gentle and with a view to inputting useful phrases for the writing stage later on.

**Answers**
Learners' own answers.

## 2 Read

- Tell learners that they are going to read an essay about a very important invention. Focus them on the pictures of wheels in the Learner's Book and ask what they think the essay is going to be about. Then read the last question in the **Activity 2** rubric (*What two things couldn't people do without this invention?*) and ask learners to look for this information as they read.
- After reading, give learners a couple of minutes to discuss answers to the question with a partner, then elicit the answers.

**Answers**
The invention Hassan discusses is the wheel.
According to Hassan, people wouldn't be able to travel anywhere quickly or easily and they wouldn't be able to work quickly or efficiently.

## 3 Read

- Focus learners on the **Writing tip** and explain that when we give opinions in our written work, we should always explain the *reason* for that opinion. Tell them that in the next task, they are going to read the essay again and find the reasons for the two main points Hassan (the writer) makes. Read questions **a** and **b** together and then tell learners to read the text again and find the answers.

- When they have finished reading, ask them to compare answers in pairs, then go through the answers as a class.
- **Extend and challenge:** Ask learners if they agree with the points Hassan makes and if they can think of any more to add.

> **Answers**
> **a** It is important for people to travel so that they can know about other places. If they couldn't travel, their world would be very small or limited.
> **b** We need wheels to carry things and for parts for machines in factories and farms.

## 4 Word study

- Ask learners to go back to the text and look at the phrases in blue. Read through the phrases as a class and then ask learners to work in pairs to match the phrases with a function. Ask them to record the phrases in a table in their notebooks (to have a record and also for a later stage in the lesson).
- When you go through the answers, refer back to the text and focus learners on how the phrases are used in context, within the essay.

> **Answers**
> **a** In my opinion / I think that ...
> **b** because / this means that / for these reasons ...
> **c** such as / for example ...

 For further practice, see Activity 1 in the Activity Book.

## 5 Use of English

- Elicit the two examples of the 2nd conditional from the essay by writing the first part of the sentences on the board, and ask learners to find and read out the rest of the sentence from the text, e.g.
  *If we didn't have ... (...the wheel, people would have to carry heavy things).*
  *If we had to travel long ... (... distances without the wheel, it would be very difficult).*
- Highlight the components of the 2nd conditional in different colours or in bold as per the **Use of English** box.
- Ask learners some concept-check questions to establish the use of the 2nd conditional in this context. E.g.(referring to the first example) *In our world today, do we have the wheel?* (Yes!) *So is this sentence talking about a real situation?* (No, it's not real – it's talking about an imaginary situation).
- Highlight the affirmative and negative forms of the structure. Ask learners how many parts there are to each sentence (two) and highlight the structure in each part (*If* + past simple, *would* + verb). Swap the clauses around (e.g. *It would be very difficult if we had to travel long distances without the wheel*) and ask learners if this is correct (yes). Change the pronoun (e.g. replace *we* with *you* and *she*) and elicit that the form remains the same in all cases, even if the pronoun is changed.

- Erase the 2nd conditional components in each sentence and ask learners to tell you the missing words. Then erase part of the sentences and elicit again, then erase more, and so on (in the style of a disappearing drill – see **Unit 1, Lesson 1**) until learners can tell you the whole sentences from memory.
- Now focus learners on **Activity 5** and ask them to find other examples of 2nd conditional sentences in the essay. Ask them to find the sentences and compare with their partner.
- Go through the examples from the text as a class. Clarify any confusion with the 2nd conditional concept by presenting more example sentences and asking the concept-check questions again.

> **Answers**
> **Paragraph 1:** It would also be difficult to see other cities and countries.
> This means that we wouldn't know about other places and our world would be very small.
> **Paragraph 2:** If we didn't have the wheel, people wouldn't be able to work easily and efficiently.
> Note: The sentence, *Without the wheel, people could not travel anywhere very easily or quickly* (Paragraph 1) is also a 2nd conditional structure. However, at this stage it is probably better to focus just on examples with *would*. If learners notice this sentence and ask, explain that *could* can be used in place of *would* and, in this sentence, it means *would not be able to*.

 For further practice, see Activities 2 and 3 in the Activity Book.

## 6 Talk

- Tell learners that they are now going to practise making 2nd conditional sentences. Focus them on the topics in **Activity 6** and elicit one or two examples on the board, e.g.
  *If we didn't have email, we would send more letters.*
  *We would read more books if we didn't have television.*
- Repeat the disappearing drill procedure from **Activity 5** to help learners remember the form. When they are confident, put them in pairs and ask them to think of five sentences about the topics (vary this number with stronger learners).
- **Additional support and practice:** To scaffold the activity a little more and build confidence, learners can write sentences first, then turn over their notebooks and remember as many as possible. You could also check the written sentences, then quickly write one or two key words as prompts and ask learners to say the sentences using the key words as guidance.

> **Answers**
> Learners' own answers.

##  Write

- **Critical thinking:** Tell learners they are going to write their own opinion essay about an important invention and draw their attention to the instructions for the final writing task in the Learner's Book. They need to explain why the invention is so important and give reasons and examples to support their opinion, using the functional language from the essay and highlighted in **Activity 4**.

- Learners will probably need some time to research their chosen inventions. This can be done outside of class. In this case set this and the writing of the first draft for homework (see the **Teaching tip** in **Unit 2** overview for guidelines on how to manage and support research). You could then allow time in the next class for learners to polish up their drafts while you circulate and offer assistance. They then write a final draft.

- After writing their essays ask learners to discuss what they wrote about in small groups. Either take away the essays or ask them to cover the text so they can't read directly from it. Ask them to have their table of useful phrases for giving opinions (from **Activity 4**) in front of them and, as they talk, tick off the phrases they use in the course of their discussions. For example, *In my opinion ... this is because ... such as ...*

> **Answers**
> Learners' own answers – Portfolio opportunity.

##  Wrap up

- When you have corrected the essays, hand out to learners to read each other's work (one per learner). Ask them to make a note of the invention topic and one reason why the writer thinks it is important. If learners are reading an essay on the same topic that they wrote about (this is quite likely), ask them to find a different reason to the ones they gave in their own essay.

## Activity Book

### 1  Read

- Learners put missing sentences in the correct place to complete an essay about the importance of television.

> **Answers**
> 1 b   2 f   3 c   4 a   5 d   6 e

### 2 Use of English

- Learners complete gapped 2nd conditional sentences with the correct form of verbs in brackets given at the end of each sentence.

> **Answers**
> 1 had / would buy
> 2 won / would celebrate
> 3 would visit / went
> 4 could / would / live
> 5 moved / wouldn't want
> 6 met / would / ask

### 3 Write

- Learners form sentences about a range of gadgets, using the 2nd conditional.

> **Answers**
> Learners' own answers.

### 4 Challenge

- Learners choose one of the gadgets in **Activity 3** and write about why they think it is important, using the essay given in **Activity 1** as a model.

> **Answers**
> Learners' own answers.

For further practice in using 2nd conditional forms to talk about imaginary situations, see **Photocopiable activity 10**.

## Lesson 5: Believe in yourself

Learner's Book pages: 74–75
Activity Book pages: 60–61

### Lesson objectives

**Listening and reading:** Listen to and read an extract from a short story about a young inventor. Answer questions about story content and themes; detect viewpoints from information in the text.

**Speaking:** Discuss story themes, especially reactions to unusual ideas and the importance of believing in yourself.

**Critical thinking:** Respond to different ideas and examine the idea of believing in yourself and your own capabilities.

**Vocabulary:** Adverbs; *carefully, securely, quickly, roughly, gently*

**Values:** Believing in yourself.

**Materials:** Learner's Book, Activity Book.

## Learner's Book

### Warm up

- Tell learners that they are going to read about a young inventor who creates an unusual and interesting invention. First, ask learners how they think the process of inventing something starts (i.e. with an idea) and then establish the creative process of trial and error that goes on in the inventing process, e.g.
  1 Idea → 2 Do an experiment / make a model → 3 Try it out → 4 Do inventors get it right first time? No! → 5 Try again ..., etc.
- Ask learners if they think inventors should give up at stage 4 – hopefully they will agree that they shouldn't!
- If you have a short interesting anecdote about having a crazy idea, especially one that turned into something good, then share it with learners here. This could be about yourself or someone you know, and would give them a good example for **Activity 1**.

### 1 Talk about it

- Focus learners on the questions in **Activity 1**. Have them discuss these in pairs first, then share as a class.

## 2 Read and listen 31

- Tell learners that they are now going to read and listen to the story about the young inventor, from a short story called *Start Small, Think Big*. Ask them to describe the illustration on page 74 and then read the question in **Activity 2**. Then tell the class to listen and read the first part of the text, looking for the answer to the gist question. Stress that, at this point, they only need look for this information and not to worry about words they do not understand.
- Start the audio and tell learners to read the first part of the text while listening.
- After reading / listening, check the answer with the class.

**Answers**
Garth's 'crazy idea' was an invention for an 'umbrella hat' – an umbrella shade positioned on a hat.

**Audioscript:** Track 31

**Part 1**
Garth stood outside his house grinning from ear to ear. He was thrilled at the rainy, windy October afternoon. This was perfect weather for testing his fabulous new invention – his Umbrella Hat – for the very first time. He **carefully** placed the hat on his head, fastened the strap **securely** under his chin and started walking purposefully along the street. He was so excited about his new invention and could hardly wait to try it out. Did it keep the rain off? Did the wind get underneath the hat and blow it askew? After a few minutes, he happily realised that his invention worked wonderfully in these testing conditions. He even passed a man wrestling with an umbrella, a bag of shopping and a yapping dog on a lead. The man stared open-mouthed as Garth calmly walked past. He just knew the man was full of admiration at this amazing new device that kept you dry and left your hands free. Soon everyone would want to own one!

## 3 Read 31

- In preparation for learners reading the text again (to answer the comprehension questions), pre-teach the following words, paragraph by paragraph: *grinning / askew / wrestling* (Part 1); *sneering / tossed / jibes* (Part 2); *humiliated / tears / peering* (Part 3); *brightening* (Part 4); *ignorant / voucher* (Part 5). (Pre-teach any other words at your own discretion).
- Pre-teach using a combination of word definitions, synonyms, antonyms, showing examples with realia, mimes / gestures etc. Give learners clues in whatever form is most accessible to them and ask them to find the corresponding word in the text (make sure they only focus on the section where the word appears). Conduct the activity as a reading race by reading out the definitions, miming, showing realia, etc., to stretch learners and keep them engaged. Suggestions for clues:
  **Part 1:** *grinning:* mime a grinning action; *askew:* show learners an example of something that has been knocked *askew* or give them a definition, e.g. when something is knocked off-balance or out of

its normal arrangement (eg. a hat, a piece of hair); *wrestling:* – mime a struggling action, as if trying to take control of something.
  **Part 2:** *sneered:* mime a sneering expression and / or give a definition: looking at something with an expression that indicates that you think it is stupid and want to make this obvious in a negative way; *tossed:* – mime this action with an object by throwing it over your shoulder in a careless way; *jibes:* (definition): cruel words or remarks.
  **Part 3:** *humiliated:* (definition) when something makes you feel stupid; *tears:* mime the action of crying and indicate tears running down your face; *peering:* mime the action of looking at something closely and quizzically.
  **Part 4:** *brightening:* (definition) when your mood changes from sad to happy.
  **Part 5:** *ignorant:* (synonym, definition) stupid, having no knowledge of something (in a way that could affect other people negatively); *voucher* (definition or show an example): a ticket that can be exchanged for something for sale in a shop.
- Tell learners that they are going to read the story again, part by part to answer the questions after each part. They should read and then answer the questions in their notebooks. For additional support, see **Differentiated instruction, Additional support and practice**.
- After learners have written the answers for questions 1–14, put them in groups of four to check their answers together.
- Allow time for this before giving feedback on the answers. Where possible, use the pictures in the book to illustrate the answers.

**Answers**
1 Garth was excited about his invention; he believed that it was something that was very useful and lots of people would want to own one.
2 The problem of staying dry in wet weather and having both hands free so you could carry other things.
3 He went outside on a rainy and windy day to see if the invention protected him from the weather.
4 The Barker Boys were *hostile* towards Garth (unfriendly and aggressive).
5 He pulled it off his head and threw it on the ground.
6 They laughed at it in a cruel way. Todd Barker said cruel things about the invention and insulted Garth.
7 He thought it looked stupid ('dumb') and that no one would want to wear it.
8 Garth felt very upset and shaken ('trembling'). The boys had made him feel stupid ('humiliated').
9 He saw a lady standing behind him, looking at him as if she was worried about him ('peering at him with concern').
10 She was very interested in it and thought it was a wonderful idea.
11 Garth's mood changed and he felt much happier ('brightening').
12 The lady's advice was that he shouldn't let stupid boys (like the Barker Boys) make him feel bad; that he should continue to invent things because one day he would make something really good.
13 She wanted to organise a competition to find the best young inventor in the town, to encourage children with creative ideas.
14 He felt much better and more enthusiastic (the implication is that the lady's interest made him believe in himself again). He started to think of lots of new ideas for inventions.

**Audioscript:** Track 31

**Part 1** Garth stood outside his house grinning from ear to ear. He was thrilled at the rainy, windy October afternoon. This was perfect weather for testing his fabulous new invention – his Umbrella Hat – for the very first time. He **carefully** placed the hat on his head, fastened the strap **securely** under his chin and started walking purposefully along the street. He was so excited about his new invention and could hardly wait to try it out. Did it keep the rain off? Did the wind get underneath the hat and blow it askew? After a few minutes, he happily realised that his invention worked wonderfully in these testing conditions. He even passed a man wrestling with an umbrella, a bag of shopping and a yapping dog on a lead. The man stared open-mouthed as Garth calmly walked past. He just knew the man was full of admiration at this amazing new device that kept you dry and left your hands free. Soon everyone would want to own one!

**Part 2** Then his heart sank. Striding towards him on the other side of the road were the Barker Boys, three nasty neighbourhood brothers. Garth turned **quickly** to run back home, but it was too late. The three boys were soon standing around him, sneering with cruel delight. Todd, the biggest one, grabbed his Umbrella Hat and **roughly** pulled it off his head. "What's THIS?" he spat. "It's an Umbrella Hat," Garth squeaked, "You wear it when it rains and ..." But the boys weren't listening. Instead they were doubled over, howling with laughter. "It looks dumb! Do you *really* think anyone would wear that stupid thing?" Todd sneered, "You're just a freak, Garth, living in a freak's dream world ..." He tossed the hat over his shoulder and the three boys ran off shrieking with laughter. The mocking jibes rang in Garth's ears long after they were out of sight.

**Part 3** Trembling and humiliated, Garth picked up his battered invention from the ground. He could feel hot tears prickling his eyes. Maybe the repugnant Todd Barker was right ... in reality, who would ever want to wear his invention? He was just fooling himself...
Suddenly he looked up and saw a smart lady in a suit peering at him with concern.
"I was just leaving my house when I saw you and those boys. Are you okay?"

**Part 4** Then she saw the Umbrella Hat in Garth's hand. It was broken now, limp and grubby.
"Er ... what's that?"
"It's my Umbrella Hat. I made it myself ..." sighed Garth wearily, waiting for the lady to start laughing like the Barker Boys. But she **gently** took the hat out of his hands, held it up and inspected it with interest.
"What a wonderful idea! Did you think of it yourself?"
"Yes!" said Garth, suddenly brightening. Then, to his delight, the lady started to ask him lots of questions about the Umbrella Hat and how he had put it together.

**Part 5** Finally she exclaimed, "What a fine creative mind you have, Garth! If you can invent something so clever now, whatever will you be able to do when you're a grown-up? Don't ever let stupid ignorant boys like that put you down! Keep inventing and one day you will create something really marvellous!"
"And you've given me a fabulous idea," she continued, "I own a gadget shop – Gadgets4U – and I'd like to run a competition to find the best young gadget inventor in our town. We must encourage wonderful creative minds like yours, Garth! I will display the three best inventions in my shop and as prizes, the inventors will each get a big fat voucher to spend on gadgets. I would really like you to enter my competition, Garth – I'm sure you'll have every chance of winning a prize."

Garth gasped in amazement. Gadgets4U was one of his favourite places in the whole world and the thought of having one of *his* inventions displayed in that wonderful place was too exciting for words. He hugged the lady and ran home to invent something fantastic for her competition. He suddenly felt much better and could already feel lots of new ideas bubbling up, waiting to spring into life!

 **For further practice see Activity 1 in the Activity Book.**

## 4  Talk

- **Critical thinking:** Ask learners to work in pairs to answer the questions in **Activity 4**. They should discuss the questions and be prepared to give feedback to the class at the end. For additional support with managing the questions, see **Additional support and practice**.
- Do a class feedback, asking volunteers or nominating learners to share their thoughts on the question themes with the class. Help learners with the language they need to express their thoughts by reformulating sentences where appropriate and highlighting useful phrases on the board. Leave the phrases on the board to help with the last stage of the lesson (**Values**). To extend some points generated by these questions, see **Differentiated instruction, Extend and challenge**.

**Answers**
Learners' own answers.
Suggestions:
**2** The lady's attitude was completely the opposite: she thought the invention was very interesting and a very good idea, coming from such a young boy. She could see Garth's potential (what he might be able to do in the future) by looking at his invention.
**3** She told Garth not to let negative people (ie. like the Barker Boys), who did not know anything about inventions, make him feel stupid and small. She also made the point that Garth should keep inventing because one day he might create something really great.
**4** He felt better because the lady had a positive, encouraging attitude and showed that she believed in him and other children like him. Her comments and her idea to organise the competition showed this. Garth was also encouraged by the competition: the chance to win a prize and show his work in the lady's gadget shop – a place he already knew and loved very much.

 **For further practice see Activity 2 in the Activity Book.**

## 5  Word study

- Focus learners' attention on the adverbs highlighted in blue in the story. Ask first if learners know the meaning of any of the adverbs or can demonstrate one. Then have them choose the correct adverb to complete the sentences in **Activity 5**. Tell them that if they don't know the answer, they should read the words and sentences around each adverb to help them deduce the answer from the context. Don't allow learners to use dictionaries, encourage them to work at understanding the words from the context they appear in.

- Conduct a class feedback and then call out the adverbs, *gently*, *carefully* and *quickly* and ask learners to mime them (with gestures and miming actions). Use definitions to elicit *securely* and *roughly* (e.g. *when you do something to make you safer* / *to do something in a way that might hurt someone or knock them over*).
- For an extension task to draw learners' attention to more adverbs in the text, see **Extend and challenge**.

> **Answers**
> Meaning:
> *gently*: softly and quietly, without force
> *carefully*: taking care and paying attention;
> *quickly*: with speed, fast;
> *securely*: when you do something to make you safer;
> *roughly*: to do something in a way that might hurt someone or knock them over.
> **1** securely;  **2** gently;  **3** carefully;  **4** roughly;  **5** quickly

 **For further practice see Activities 3 and 4 in the Activity Book.**

## 6  Pronunciation 🔊32

- Focus learners on **Activity 6**. Ask them to listen to and repeat the words from the story and identify the difference in the pronunciation of the 'a' sound in each group of words.

> **Answers**
> a) All contain a long 'a' sound /eɪ/.
> b) All contain a short 'a' sound /æ/.

> **Audioscript:** Track 32
> **a**  day facing spray make way
> **b**  hand can began sadder have

 **For further practice see Activity 5 in the Activity Book.**

## 7 💬 Values

- **Critical thinking:** Focus learners on the **Values** heading and ask learners what they think it means. If they are not sure, or find it difficult to explain, tell them that it means that *you believe that you can do things that are important to you, rather than taking the word of another person, who might tell you that you can't do something or that your ideas are silly* (like in Garth's case).Then focus learners on the three statements and read them together, and put them into pairs or small groups to discuss which one/s they agree with.
- Conduct a class feedback, asking learners which statement they feel is the most positive and helpful. Accept all ideas and opinions.
- Next, focus learners on the situations in question 2. Ask them to share (in the same pairs / small groups) the thoughts and feelings that go through their minds when they are in one of these situations. Are there any situations where they have no problems believing

in themselves? Or are there situations here where they should try to believe in themselves more? Can they think of other situations when it is important to believe in yourself?
- Conduct a class feedback, encouraging learners to share thoughts and opinions.
  **Note:** This activity represents a nice opportunity to empathise and find commonalities in challenging situations.
- To extend some points generated by these questions, see **Differentiated instruction, Extend and challenge**.

> **Answers**
> Learners' own answers.

 **For further practice see Activity 6 in the Activity Book.**

## Wrap up
- Ask learners what they think will happen next in the story.

> **Differentiated instruction**
>
> **Additional support and practice**
> - **Activity 3:** Learners could work in pairs to do the comprehension questions 1–14. Alternatively you could divide the questions up, so learners don't have to answer all of them but benefit from learning all answers in feedback later on. Put learners in A/B pairs: A answers the odd numbered questions, B, the even numbered ones, then have them share the answers at the end.
> - **Activity 4:** The questions in this speaking activity could be divided up, rather than have all learners tackling all questions; e.g. put learners into groups of 4 and give each child a question to think about and then share with the group. Or give small groups of learners just one question to discuss. At the end of this stage, each group would give feedback on a different question and others could listen and see if they agree or not with the answer given. Early finishers could then be given another question to discuss while others finish.
>
> **Extend and challenge**
> - **Activity 4:** The discussion could be expanded by looking at ways that Garth could deal with the actions and comments of the Barker Boys.
> - **Activity 5:** After examining the adverbs highlighted in **Activity 5**, stretch learners by having them look through the text to find more examples of adverbs. Conduct the activity as a reading race by putting them into five groups and have each group look through the whole story together (or give each group a specific section to look at). Give learners a time limit to find as many examples as possible and, give points for each new example.
>   **Answers:** *purposefully, happily, calmly* (section 1); *wearily, suddenly* (section 4); *finally* (section 5).

- **Activity 6:** the **Values** exercise could be expanded to discuss other ways of handling and overcoming difficult situations. You could also ask learners who they feel is the most supportive amongst the people around them (e.g. parents, siblings, friends, teachers) and what they do to give support.

## Activity Book

### 1 Read

- Learners read the extract again from the novel and put sentences about the story in the correct order.

| Answers | | | | |
|---|---|---|---|---|
| **a** 3 | **b** 1 | **c** 4 | **d** 9 | **e** 10 |
| **f** 7 | **g** 2 | **h** 8 | **i** 6 | **j** 5 |

**Order:** b / g / a / c / j / i / f / h / d / e

### 2 Read

- Learners choose the correct answer (from a choice of two) in sentences that describe some ideas and themes from the story.

**Answers**
**1** a   **2** b   **3** b   **4** a

### 3 Word study

- Learners change adjectives into adverbs, then complete sentences about the story with the correct adverb.

**Answers**
**2** securely
**3** quickly
**4** roughly
**5** gently

### 4 Word study

- Learners underline the verbs that the adverbs describe, in the sentences in **Activity 3**.

**Answers**
**1** put
**2** fastened
**3** turned
**4** pulled
**5** took

### 5 Pronunciation 69 [CD2 Track 37]

- Learners listen and repeat sentences, matching the sentences that have the same 'a' sound.

**Answers**
**1** / 4;   **2** / 3.

---

**Audioscript:** Track 69

**Narrator:** Activity Book, Lesson 5 Activity 5

**Narrator:** 1

*Face* the *day* in a positive *way*!

**Narrator:** 2

Don't be *sad* and *mad*, be *happy* and *glad*!

**Narrator:** 3

*That man has sat* on his *hat*!

**Narrator:** 4

You *may* be *crazy* but you're not *lazy*!

### 6 Values

- Learners read attitudes associated with the idea of believing in yourself and tick the ones that are the most helpful.

**Answers**
**1** If other kids can do it, so can I! ✓
**2** If I can't do it, everyone will laugh at me.
**3** If I don't try, I won't know if I can do it. ✓
**4** If I fail, I'll feel really bad!
**5** If I know I've tried my best, I'll feel OK. ✓

## Lesson 6: Choose a project

Learner's Book pages: 78

### Lesson objectives

**Speaking:** Deliver a presentation about the history of an invention; discuss how inventions will change in the future; revise unit themes; discuss **Unit 5** Big question.

**Writing:** Organise and prepare notes for a presentation; prepare and write a quiz about inventions; revise unit themes.

**Critical thinking:** Select information to include in the presentation or quiz; ask questions about classmates' presentations; make predictions about how inventions might change in the future; apply new skills and language acquired in **Unit 5** to project work and revision activities.

**Language focus:** Recycling language points from **Unit 5:** *used to* to describe past habits; future simple forms (for predictions); second conditional (for imaginary situations).

**Vocabulary:** Recycling of new and reviewed vocabulary from **Unit 5:** gadgets and equipment; phrases for stating preferences and comparing; phrases for giving opinions and reasons; adverbs

**Materials:** Learner's Book, Activity Book; electronic slides (if available).

## Learner's Book

###  Warm up

- Put learners in small teams and play the *Stop the bus!* game to revise some language and themes from **Unit 5** and to help generate ideas for Project 2 (the quiz). Follow the instructions for the game in **Unit 1**, **Lesson 6** (Project / review lesson). Topics can be as follows: an invention, gadget or piece of equipment in the following categories:
  *Transport / communication / safety or medicine / comfort or convenience*
  E.g. Letter 'T'
  Train / telephone / traffic lights / tablet
- Do a practice round first to make sure learners are clear about the rules of the game.
- After each round, record points on the board and declare an overall winner at the end. Remember to congratulate *all* teams on their efforts too.
- Tell learners they are now going to choose from the two projects and follow the instructions below for the one they have decided on.

## Portfolio opportunity

### 1 A presentation about the history of an invention

- Put learners in small groups to do the presentation. Take them through the step-by-step instructions presented in the Learner's Book.
- Spend time helping them to choose which invention to research. They can also think of another invention if they wish. Draw their attention to the content areas listed in stage 2 to help focus their research and organise their notes. (Please refer to the **Teaching Tip** in **Unit 2** overview for more advice on how to manage the research of projects). They can also add other headings if they wish.
- When learners are drafting the presentation, monitor and make sure they are using sequencing phrases to guide the audience through the presentation. Also check that they have considered who their audience is going to be.
- Allow time for preparing visuals for the presentation, e.g. slides and pictures of the chosen invention.
- Give learners time to practise their presentation, ensure that each member has a part to say and that someone is responsible for organising the props (slides, pictures, etc).
- Before learners deliver their presentations, nominate specific learners to ask a question at the end (different children for each presentation so the duty is more evenly distributed). Alternatively, you could ask *all* learners to write a question during each presentation and then randomly choose specific ones to ask their question afterwards (this ensures that everyone has a listening task during each presentation).
- **Critical thinking:** After listening to all the presentations, put learners in groups and give them one invention that has been discussed. Ask them to discuss how they predict this invention will change in the future and write down two or three sentences using future forms.
- Share ideas during feedback.

### Wrap up

- Consider the ideas shared in the last Project 1 stage and vote on the predictions that are most and least likely to actually happen.

## Portfolio opportunity

### 2 A quiz about inventions

- Learners can do this project in pairs or small groups. Take them through the step-by-step instructions presented in the Learner's Book. For a mixed ability class, see **Differentiated instruction, Additional support and practice**. See also the **Teaching tip** in the **Unit 2** overview for advice on managing the research stage.
- Have learners write a rough draft first and check it for grammar, vocabulary and spelling etc. Then have them write the quiz in a presentable form and decorate with pictures.
- Finally, they hand their quiz to another group to complete.

### Wrap up

- When learners have finished doing each other's quizzes, hand them back to the original groups for marking. Finally, compare scores across the class.

## Reflect on your learning

Learner's Book page: 79
Activity Book page: 62

### Learner's Book

### Reflect on your learning

- These revision activities can be approached in different ways, according to the level and character of your class.
  - Questions 1–7 could be used as a class quiz, with learners in teams and a time limit given to write answers to each question.
  - Alternatively, you could conduct a revision session – have learners work in pairs and take longer to think about and write down their answers. When pairs have finished the questions, they swap with another pair and correct each others, with you monitoring and giving help and advice when needed.
  - You could set this task for homework / self-study.

**Answers**

1 a zip / a tablet / a compass / a bicycle / a laptop / a mobile phone.

**Answers**

1 a zip / a tablet / a compass / a bicycle / a laptop / a mobile phone.
2 The modern light bulb. Before, people used to use candles, gas lamps and oil lamps.
3 Suggestions:
   *People used to only make calls on a landline.*
   *Telephones used to be much bigger.*
   *Telephones used to have a dial.*
   *People didn't use to carry their phones in their bags.*
   *People didn't use to be able to contact each other so quickly.*
5 Suggestions:
   *Without the wheel, people could not travel quickly or efficiently.*
   *Planes, cars, trains and bicycles wouldn't exist.*
   *People wouldn't have so much knowledge or information about other places.*
   *We wouldn't be able to work because we need wheels to travel and carry things. Machines depend on wheels to make them work, especially machines in factories and on farms.*
6 Learners' own answers.
7 Garth invented (his own version of) an Umbrella Hat. The Barker Boys sneered and laughed at his invention and Todd Barker threw it on the ground. But the lady who owned the shop was impressed by the invention; she thought it was a wonderful idea and showed that Garth had a fine creative mind.

## Look what I can do!

**Aim:** To check learners have fulfilled the objectives for **Unit 5** (and to what degree).

- Present the objectives slide or poster from the introduction to **Unit 5** (in **Lesson 1**) and remind learners of the objectives from the start of the unit.
- Focus their attention on the 'can do' statements and read through together. You could put these on a slide or write on the board. Ask learners if they feel they can now do these tasks after completing **Unit 5**. By this point, you should have a clear idea yourself of how well your learners have completed the tasks. However, ask them to now do an initial self-assessment.
- Put learners in pairs and ask them to look through their notebooks and portfolios to find evidence of their work for each of the statements. Then they give themselves a rating as follows:
   ✓ Yes, I can – no problem!
   ? A little – I need more practice.
   X / ☹ No – I need a lot more practice.
- Circulate and chat to learners about their self-assessment (some might be overly modest and you can point out that their rating could be higher). Make notes about areas that learners are not confident about (if you haven't already done so) for future reference (see **Teaching Tip**).
- Conduct a general feedback at the end and find out which tasks learners found the most interesting / useful / challenging, etc.
- For an extension task, see **Differentiated instruction, Extend and challenge**.

**Answers**
Learners' own answers.

##  Wrap up

As a class, look at the Big question again on a slide or written on the board: *How have important inventions changed our lives?*

- First, have learners look through their Learner's Book and identify five important inventions from the lessons and the work they have done over the unit.
- **Critical thinking:** Then ask them to look at the following list of possible responses to the Big question (on the board or a slide). Tell them to compare their five inventions to the points and put a tick next to the ones that apply. E.g.
   Television
   *By helping us to communicate with each other more easily.* ✓
   *By helping us to get lots of information quickly.* ✓
   *By helping us to get somewhere more quickly.*
   *By giving us entertainment.* ✓
   *By making our lives easier and more comfortable.*
- Now ask learners to add any other points to the list that could answer the Big question, and check their five inventions against those points. (Or give this task to early finishers).
- **Critical thinking:** For an approach to stretch stronger learners in answering the Big question, see **Extend and challenge**.

**Answers**
Learners' own answers.

## Activity Book

### Unit 5 Revision

#### 1 Vocabulary

- Learners sort letters to make words for gadgets and equipment; then use the words to complete short descriptions.

**Answers**
zips   mobile phones   compass   bicycles   laptops
1 bicycles
2 compass
3 zips
4 mobile phones
5 laptops

## 2 Use of English

- Learners use grammatical components to complete sentences. The exercise practises key grammar items in **Unit 5**.

| Answers |
| --- |
| **1** will |
| **2** used to |
| **3** would |
| **4** didn't use to |
| **5** would |
| **6** won't |
| **7** used to |

## 3 Over to you

- Learners complete sentence halves using their own ideas, using key language items from **Unit 5**.

| Answers |
| --- |
| Learners' own answers. |

## My global progress

- Learners think about their own responses to topics and activities in the **Unit 5** lessons and answer the questions.

| Answers |
| --- |
| Learners' own answers. |

### Differentiated instruction

**Additional support and practice**

- **Project 2:** You could vary the number of questions learners write for the quiz according to ability, and also restrict themes (e.g. transport and communication only); e.g. stronger learners could write two or three questions for each category; other learners – one question for each category or four each for *transport* and *communication* topics (total: 8 questions).

**Extend and challenge**

- **Look what I can do!**
  A mini-awards system: Customise the idea presented in **Unit 1** for **Unit 5** (see **Unit 1** page 38).
- **Wrap up:** You may feel it more appropriate and challenging to let learners come up with their own answers to the Big question, having worked through **Unit 5**. Rather than present the suggested responses, have them work in small groups to look through the unit in their Learner's Book and discuss their own interpretation of the Big question. Conduct a group by group feedback at the end, noting down similar ideas and highlighting different viewpoints.

**Teaching Tip**

Review the learners' work and their own assessment of their progress, noting areas where learners demonstrate strength and confidence and areas where they need additional instruction and practice. Use this information to select areas for review and specific focus, as you continue to **Unit 6**.

# 6 Explorers

**Big question** What have been the effects of explorations and expeditions?

## Unit overview

In this unit learners will:
- talk and read about famous expeditions in the past
- listen to an account of a historical exploration
- present and listen to plans for our own expeditions
- write an explorer's diary extract
- read a story about a young explorer.

In **Unit 6**, learners examine the notion of exploration and look in particular at the reasons why expeditions have been made in the past and present time, and what we can learn from this. The Big question encapsulates these ideas and gives learners the opportunity to examine this theme, in the context of unit tasks and activities, at the end of the unit.

The unit begins with an overview of different kinds of exploration that have taken place over the last 1000 years; this focus builds on learners' practical skills in reading, speaking and developing vocabulary, and their ability to find reasons for making expeditions at different historical times. Next, they listen to a more detailed account of a historical expedition, drawing out useful language items and looking at the impact of the event from a historical perspective. Presentation and speaking skills are developed further in this unit when learners present ideas and plans for their own imagined expedition. This theme is continued in the writing focus in **Lesson 4**, where learners write a diary or blog entry for their expedition, looking at lexical and topical components that enhance this type of text. Finally, they will read a fictional story about a young explorer and discuss the value of welcoming someone from another place or culture into your community.

The **Photocopiable activities** provide practice in: forming questions using the question word + noun structure (**11**) and describing expeditions from given prompts (**12**).

### Language focus

Question forms (*Question word + noun*); linking expressions (showing time); cardinal and ordinal numbers; *-ed* and *-ing* adjectives

**Vocabulary topics:** Expeditions; voyages and exploration; equipment.

### Self-assessment
- I can talk and read about historical expeditions.
- I can read and discuss information about explorations in the past.
- I can deliver a presentation about a plan for an expedition.
- I can understand and discuss my classmates' presentations.
- I can write a diary or blog entry about events that happened during an expedition.
- I can read and understand a story about a young explorer.

### Teaching tips

Recycle and review vocabulary from Stage 6 with vocabulary cards. These cards are quick and easy to produce and can be used for a range of purposes in the classroom. As you work through Stage 6, record all items of vocabulary on small cards (one item per card), so you develop a bank of cards that reflect all themes and lexical sets. When recording lexis, record 'chunks' or groups of words where possible (e.g. *discover an island*), as vocabulary chunks are often more useful and meaningful to learners than isolated items, and reflect themes more clearly (leading to more effective memorisation by association). Also include an article or quantifier where appropriate (e.g. a gadget, some equipment) to increase learners' awareness of usage. You could also include an example sentence and information about word form and pronunciation too.

Vocabulary cards can be used for a multitude of activities, which will all revise and recycle useful lexis. Learners can categorise them, build sentences, create stories, listen to definitions and match. They can be used during warm-up and wrap-up stages; to engage early finishers and you can even ask learners to make the cards themselves at the end of a lesson or unit. A warm-up activity using vocabulary cards is included in the final lesson of this unit.

# Lesson 1: Explorers

Learner's Book pages: 80–81
Activity Book pages: 64–65

## Lesson objectives

**Reading:** Identify main themes and specific information in short descriptions of explorations on a historical timeline.

**Speaking:** Discuss reasons for making expeditions in the past, present and future.

**Critical thinking:** Deduce reasons for making expeditions in the past; speculate about possible reasons for future expeditions.

**Vocabulary:** Expeditions; *sail, discover, mission, voyage, route*

**Materials:** poster paper or IWB slides; visuals linking unit topic with studies in other subject areas or links with a recent news story (optional see **Warm up**); pictures of historical explorers and expeditions (optional); a map of the world.

## Learner's Book

 **Warm up**

- To introduce the Big question, start by telling the class that this unit is going to be about explorers and expeditions from one part of the world to another. Explain that we can learn a lot from looking at what has happened when people make explorations of this kind and the reasons for doing it. So the Big question is ... *What have been the effects of explorations and expeditions?*
- Write the question on the board (for an electronic presentation, create a slide with interesting graphics). Tell learners that you are all going to do tasks and projects in the unit that will answer this question.
- Introduce the unit objectives to show learners what tasks are coming up. Present the objectives on a slide or large piece of poster paper to attach to the board. Tell learners that you will answer the Big question and look again at the objectives at the end of the unit. Keep the objectives slide / poster to revisit at the end of the unit.
- Before learners look at the first lesson in **Unit 6**, you could introduce the unit by drawing parallels between this topic and any similar topics your learners have been covering recently in other subject areas. Alternatively, you could draw on any recent news events that your learners would be familiar with and make links. If you do this, try to have some visuals on display or a magazine / newspaper article to generate interest and help them make the link.

## 1 Talk about it

- Put learners in pairs and ask them to talk about the three questions. If possible, have some visuals depicting historical explorers and expeditions that your learners might be familiar with, to stimulate the discussion. You could structure the discussion more by having learners focus on the visuals and identify the three points mentioned in the questions – name of explorer / where they went / what they discovered.
- Conduct a quick feedback to get an idea of how much knowledge learners already have of this topic area.
- **Critical thinking:** Learners activate their own knowledge of the topic.

> **Answers**
> Learners' own answers.

## 2 Read

- Read the four headlines together and then ask learners to look at the timeline and match a headline to a text. Tell them to read the texts quickly (give them a time limit to emphasise this) and look for key words to help them to match. Point out the dates too.
- **Additional support and practice:** Draw learners' attention to specific words in the headlines that can be linked to ideas and synonyms in the texts on the timeline, e.g.
  Headline 1: *Risky / beginning* → (links to) *dangerous / source of the River Nile* (Text C)
  Headline 2: *Cosmic / lady* → *space / woman* (Text D)
  Headline 3: *Ancient / huge land* → *1001 / North America* (Text A)
  Headline 4: *ocean* → *sea* (Text B)
  When they have matched the components, ask them to check answers with a partner before feedback.
- When you go through the answers, ask learners which key words helped them match the texts with the headlines. Also, clarify where these explorers came from, and where they travelled to (using the map), if learners are unfamiliar with the countries mentioned.

> **Answers**
> **1** Text C   **2** Text D   **3** Text A   **4** Text B

## 3 Read

- Draw learners' attention to the dates given with each text. Ask them to work out the number of years between the first and the latest expedition. Set this up as a race to see who can be the first to work out the answer.

> **Answers**
> 962 years

## 4 Read

- Focus learners' attention on the sentences describing reasons for the expeditions (a – d). Read them together and ask them to read the texts again and match each one with a reason.
- **Extend and challenge:** Instead of having learners match the texts with the reasons given in **Activity 4**, ask them to read the texts and find the reasons for the expeditions (cover the 'answers' in **Activity 4**), then

write in their own words. Afterwards, they can check their answers with the reasons stated in **Activity 4**.

- When they have matched the components, ask them to check answers with a partner before feedback.

> **Answers**
> 1 Text D    2 Text C    3 Text A    4 Text B

 **For further practice, see Activities 1 and 2 in the Activity Book.**

## 5 Word study

- Focus learners on the words in blue in the texts. For this task, you could either conduct a reading race, reading out the definitions and ask learners to call out the corresponding word in the text, or ask learners to read and match a word to a definition in their notebooks.

> **Answers**
> a sail   b discover   c a mission   d a voyage   e a route

 **For further practice, see Activity 3 in the Activity Book.**

## 6  Talk

- Ask learners to work in pairs or small groups. First, do a quick recap on historical reasons for making expeditions. Encourage learners to add any other examples that they might know to the ones given in the book.
- **Critical thinking:** Now ask learners to discuss reasons that people might have for making expeditions in the *future*. Ask them first what they think are the biggest problems in the world today and make a note of ideas that could be linked with the question of future expeditions, e.g.
  *World population is getting bigger and bigger → build houses on other planets or in places where there is a lot of space.*
  *Environmental problems / climate change → expeditions to find solutions.*
  *Fighting diseases → expeditions to find new medicines.*
  You could also focus on expeditions made for fun or personal challenge, e.g. to break a world record, go somewhere where no-one has been before; travel to a place in a way that no-one has travelled before, etc.
- Ask learners to write at least three ideas for expeditions in the future. Depending on the character of your class, these ideas can be serious or humorous.
- Conduct a class feedback listening to different pairs / groups' ideas. Identify any common themes in learners' ideas.

> **Answers**
> Learners' own answers.

##  Wrap up

- To finish off, ask learners to predict which expedition idea is most likely to happen in the next five years.

## Activity Book

### 1 Read

- Learners read texts on a timeline about prominent female astronauts and match a heading to a text.

> **Answers**
> a 3    b 4    c 1    d 2

### 2 Read

- Learners answer questions about the reasons for the missions described in the texts.

> **Answers**
> a 3    b 1    c 2    d 4    e 3    f 2

### 3 Vocabulary

- Learners complete a short gapped text about a modern day explorer with words from the box.

> **Answers**
> 1 mission
> 2 to discover
> 3 sailed
> 4 route
> 5 voyage

# Lesson 2: Exploration exploits

Learner's Book pages: 82–83
Activity Book pages: 66–67

## Lesson objectives

**Listening:** Identify specific information in a listening text about the historical exploration of the Americas.

**Speaking:** Discuss positive and negative aspects of a historical event.

**Writing:** Write a quiz about another historical expedition using own researched information.

**Critical thinking:** Make deductions about positive and negative elements; draw on own knowledge of historical events; select information from research.

**Language focus:** Question forms (question word + noun).

**Vocabulary:** Voyages and exploration: *continent, valuable, era, increase, destroy, empire*

**Materials:** Learner's Book, Activity Book. Copies of **Photocopiable activity 11**.

## Learner's Book

##  Warm up

- Play the game, *Hot Seat*, to revise vocabulary from the last lesson, as this will be useful in this lesson too. Ask a confident learner to come and sit at the front of the classroom with his / her back to the board (in the *Hot Seat*). Explain to the class that you are going to write a word from the last lesson on the board and they have to explain it to their classmate in the *Hot Seat* – but they mustn't say the actual word or give a translation. They can use any other method to give clues about the word (e.g. give definitions, an example sentence with the word missing, do mimes, gestures, say the part of speech, etc). Their classmate has to listen and guess the word. To add an element of competition you could ask learners to work in teams and award points for clues given that lead to the learner in the *Hot Seat* guessing the correct answer. **Note:** This game works best when two or more teams can compete against each other (and have two or more learners in *Hot Seats*). However, this can be difficult to set up with a large class. You could put learners into teams, with one team member in the *Hot Seat*, but you would need to be able to trust them not to whisper the word to their team member when you weren't looking!

• If learners haven't played this game before, play one practice round to make sure learners understand the rules.

• Use the game to revise other words from the audioscript in preparation for the listening task later on.

## 1 💬 Talk about it

• **Critical thinking:** Ask learners to do a recap, in pairs or small groups, of the historical explorers that they have talked about so far and their reasons for making their journeys. Encourage them to add other reasons for expeditions that they might know about.

• Conduct a class feedback, noting down reasons on the board, so learners build up an idea of the breadth of reasons that have inspired historical expeditions. If you feel it is appropriate for your class, include controversial reasons too, e.g. colonisation, etc. (**Note:** This is alluded to in the listening extract and learners are asked to discuss positive and negative points about the exploration of the Americas in **Activity 5**).

> **Answers**
> Suggestions for other reasons: to make new discoveries about animals and plants; to explore ancient building sites; to carry out research into natural phenomena e.g. extreme weather, climate change, geographical changes etc. Controversial reasons (e.g. colonisation) as appropriate.

## 2 📝 💬 Talk

• Before learners listen, draw their attention to the listening strategy and talk them through it using the explanation above. Ask them why it is useful to talk about a topic before listening; listen to their ideas and point out that discussion will show them what they already know and this can help when they listen. Also

the words they use might appear in the listening text and this will help them understand it better.

• Now focus learners on the map illustration and ask them to talk about what they can see in pairs. If they already have some knowledge of the exploration of the Americas, encourage them to apply their knowledge to the map; if not, ask them to simply describe what they can see in the illustration and speculate what the ship and the highlighted areas might indicate.

• As learners are talking, ask them to write down words to describe the illustration and any associated ideas, in a list in their notebooks.

## 3 Listen 🔊33 [CD2 Track 1]

• Tell learners that they are now going to listen to an account of the European exploration of the Americas. Ask them to listen for any ideas that they talked about in **Activity 2** and tick any words that they hear from their word list. **Note:** There may be some unfamiliar words in the extract. It is advised that you check these between first and second listening when learners have a sense of the context and may be able to guess the meanings.

• After listening, ask learners to confer with a partner about any words or ideas they might have heard from their notes. Then do a brief class feedback.

> **Audioscript:** Track 33
> **Part 1**
>
> For thousands of years people lived in the Americas long before the first Europeans arrived. In 1200 CE, the Incas settled in the city of Cuzco, which is now in Peru. And in 1325 CE, the Aztecs settled in what is now Mexico City, and built a large, beautiful and powerful city.
>
> So who were the first Europeans to arrive in the Americas? Everyone knows it was Christopher Columbus, right? No, actually that's wrong! The first Europeans to arrive here were the Vikings from Northern Europe, over 400 years before Columbus. The difference was that they didn't stay!
>
> But Columbus did stay ... It all started when he set sail on 3 August 1492. He had three ships: the Niña, the Pinta and the Santa Maria. They were wooden ships with sails. There were about 90 men in the ships. Food for the voyage was kept in the ship's hold – cheese, wine, water and live chickens.
>
> The voyage took longer than Columbus thought. There was no land, just ocean. The men got scared. They were running out of food and water. After 36 days, a sailor on the Pinta saw an island. On 12 October 1492 the explorers went ashore. Columbus called the island San Salvador. It was in the Bahamas.
>
> Columbus soon realised that there were many things in this huge continent that would be useful and valuable in his country. After his first voyage, he took back gold and exotic birds and plants. His voyages started an era of European exploration that would last 400 years.

> **Answers**
> Learners' own answers.

## 4 Listen 🄴 [CD2 Track 2]

- Before listening again, check learners understanding of the following words and phrases: *settled, ship's hold, went ashore, running out of food and water, gold* and *exotic birds*. Write them on the board and ask first if anyone knows what they mean, giving little clues. If learners don't know, read definitions and ask them to match to a word or phrase, e.g.
  *A yellow metal that costs a lot of money* (gold); *when you have made a new home somewhere* (settled); *birds that are unusual and colourful* (exotic birds); *when you arrive at the beach from the sea* (went ashore); *when there are no more supplies of something* (running out of ...).
- Talk a little in general about what information learners have understood after the first listening. Next, ask them if they noticed the names of any places. If they did, put their suggestions on the board (just the place names). Tell learners that they are going to listen for a second time and this time they need to pay special attention to places. Focus their attention on the task for **Activity 4**, pointing out that this time, they need to make connections between these headings and places mentioned; also point out that the listening extract includes a second part.
- **Additional support and practice:** This activity could be scaffolded a little more by writing all place names on the board (rather than only ones elicited from learners) and ask learners to listen specifically for links between those place names and the three details, a–c.
- After listening, ask learners to work in pairs to match the headings with points a–c, on the map. Then check answers as a class.

**Audioscript:** Track 34
**Part 2**

The Europeans found gold and silver in the Americas, and they also discovered plants such as potatoes and corn, that no-one had heard of in Europe. Over many years, they increased their power by taking control of different parts of this enormous continent.

Most of the indigenous people, including the Aztecs and the Incas, were not happy with the Europeans. They disagreed with them and tried to fight them.

But some of the Aztecs were unhappy with their rulers and, in 1521 CE, they joined with the Spanish explorers and attacked the Aztec capital. Together, they were quickly able to destroy the Aztec Empire. The Spanish brought other people from their country to live in the new land and build businesses and in 1533 CE the Spanish army destroyed both the Aztec and the Inca empires, which had been in the Americas for thousands of years. It was a time of great discovery for some but with a price to pay in other ways...

The Incan people stayed in the region. Today, many people from Inca families still live in Chile, Bolivia, Peru, and Ecuador. These people still speak Quechua, the official Incan language, and keep their traditions.

---

**Answers**
a Aztec empire
b Columbus' landing point
c Inca empire

---

## 5 🗩 Talk

- First, focus on the information in the listening extract and elicit some general information such as, how long the European exploration of the Americas lasted (400 years); which people already lived in the Americas when the Europeans arrived (Aztecs and Incas). Then ask what good things the exploration of the Americas brought for the Europeans (see answers) and if this was good for the Aztec and Inca peoples too (see answers).
- **Additional support and practice:** If you feel your learners might struggle to identify good and bad points without specifically listening for them, play the extract a third time and make this the listening task. For extra support, write good and bad points (listed together, not in separate categories) about the exploration (see **Activity 5** answers) on the board, ask learners to copy into notebooks and tick as they hear them mentioned in the extract. Then ask them to divide into good and bad points.
- **Critical thinking:** Next, put learners in small groups and ask them to talk about good and bad points about the exploration of the Americas. Having drawn out relevant points in the previous stage, activate learners' critical thinking skills by leaving them to decide amongst themselves which categories the points should go into.
- If your learners have prior knowledge of this topic, ask them to add more points to the lists from their own knowledge.
- When you conduct feedback, write good / bad points columns on the board and list learners' answers. If any groups disagree over the categorisation of a point, listen to each side of the argument and ask for a class consensus before recording.

---

**Answers**
Suggestions:
Good points (for European explorers): The Europeans discovered useful and valuable things such as gold, silver, corn, potatoes and exotic birds.
Bad points: Most of the indigenous people (e.g. Aztecs and Incas) were against / did not want the European invasion of their land. Europeans took control of different parts of the continent. There was disagreement and fighting. Eventually, the Spanish army destroyed the Aztec and Inca empires.

---

## 6 Word study

- Ask learners to work in pairs to choose the correct meaning for the selected words from the listening text. If you feel it would benefit your learners to see the words again in context, hand out copies of the audioscript and ask them to highlight the words first and then choose the meaning. Avoid the use of dictionaries to encourage learners to deduce the answer from the context.

- When you go through the answers, do some pronunciation work on the words, concentrating on difficult sounds and syllable stress.

> **Answers**
> 1 b   2 b   3 a   4 a   5 a   6 a
> continent (Ooo) valuable (Ooo) era (Oo) increase (v) (oO) destroy (oO) empire (Oo)

 **For further practice, see Activity 4 in the Activity Book.**

## 7  Use of English

- Introduce the question forms (question word + noun) by writing the partial question (from the **Use of English** box) on the board (or slide) and eliciting the question word from learners, e.g.
  _____ *ships did Columbus have? (How many)*
- Erase the words, *How many* and elicit the words again from learners. This time highlight the words in a different colour.
- Now repeat the process to elicit the other example from the box:
  _____ *food did Columbus take? (What)*
  (Erase and elicit again, highlighting in a different colour).
- Now focus learners on both example questions and underline the nouns in each (*ships, food*). Ask them what kind of words these are and elicit that they are *nouns*. Point out the structure to learners – that in these questions the *question word* is followed by a *noun*.
- Ask learners to do **Activity 7** in pairs. They have to think of a suitable question word to complete the questions about Columbus' first voyage to the Americas, then match to an answer.
  **Note:** Learners may be confused about the difference between *what* and *which*. An accessible explanation might be: *which* is used to refer to a specific set of items, a 'closed' choice or a few possibilities, (e.g. *Which islands ... ?* – there are only a few possibilities in this case; *What islands ... ?* would open up the possibilities far too wide to be the correct answer here); whereas *what* is more general and open and implies a far wider choice of possibilities.

> **Answers**
> 1 How many  d
> 2 Which  e
> 3 What  f
> 4 How many  c
> 5 Which  b
> 6 Which  a

 **For further practice, see Activities 2 and 3 in the Activity Book.**

## 8 Write

- **Critical thinking:** Learners can do this project in pairs or small groups. Focus their attention on the quiz

in **Activity 7** as a model and tell them that they are going to write a similar quiz about another historical expedition. Give them some examples that are relevant to their country or culture or to other subject areas at school. Ask them to conduct their research in groups and then write six questions about their topic (vary this number according to the ability and motivation of your learners). Refer to the **Teaching tip** in the **Unit 2** overview for advice on managing the research stage.
- Point out to learners that they can use any question types for their quizzes, so as not to restrict creativity.
- Ask learners to write a rough draft first and check it for grammar, vocabulary and spelling, etc. Then ask them to write the quiz in a presentable form and decorate with pictures.
- Finally, they hand their quiz to another group to complete.
- When groups have finished completing each other's quizzes, they hand back to the quiz writers for marking. Do a quick comparison of quiz scores at the end of the lesson.

> **Answers**
> Learners' own answers.

## Wrap up

- Wrap up with another quick quiz, using the information from the listening extract, to see how much learners can remember about the exploration of the Americas. Recycle some of the vocabulary in the **Word study** (**Activity 6**) in your questions, e.g.
  *How long did the **era** of exploration last?*
  *Which **empire** existed in the land that is now Peru?*

## Activity Book

## 1 Read

- Learners read a text about the 14th century Moroccan explorer, Ibn Battuta. They complete sentences about the text by choosing the correct option from a choice of two.

> **Answers**
> 1 b   2 b   3 a   4 b   5 b

## 2 Use of English

- Learners sort words to make questions about the text in **Activity 1**, using the target structure.

> **Answers**
> 1 What transport did Ibn Battuta use?
> 2 How many years did he travel for?
> 3 Which continents did he travel in?
> 4 How many kilometres did he travel?
> 5 Which country was he born in?

## 3 Use of English

- Learners write more questions about expeditions, using question words and prompts.

**Answers**
1 Which countries did the explorers visit?
2 What dangers did they face?
3 How many days did they travel for?
4 What things did they find?
5 What food did they eat?
6 Which people did they meet?
7 What information did they learn?

## 4 Vocabulary

- Learners complete sentences with a word from the box.

**Answers**
1 continent
2 valuable
3 era
4 increased
5 empire
6 destroyed

**For further practice in forming questions (using the question word+noun structure), see Photocopiable activity 11.**

# Lesson 3: Intrepid explorers

Learner's Book pages: 84–85
Activity Book pages: 68–69

## Lesson objectives

**Speaking:** Prepare and deliver a presentation about a plan for an expedition.

**Listening:** Listen to a presentation about an expedition plan; identify reasons for the expedition, the planned route and target vocabulary.

**Critical thinking:** Create and describe a plan for an expedition, identifying reasons for the trip and equipment needed.

**Language focus:** Linking expressions; *while, until, as soon as.*

**Vocabulary focus:** Equipment; *a laptop, a compass, waterproof clothing, light cotton clothing, maps, insect repellent, a first aid kit, tents, a video camera*

**Materials:** images representing an expedition idea (optional for **Warm up**); a map of the world (optional); poster paper, coloured pens.

## Learner's Book

###  Warm up

- Introduce the lesson focus by telling learners briefly about an expedition you (the teacher) would like to go on. If possible, show them some images and ask them to guess what type of expedition, which country / region and the reasons why. Ask them what equipment you would need to take and if there are any dangers that you should look out for.

## 1 🗨 Talk about it

- **Critical thinking:** Focus learners on **Activity 1** and read the three questions together. Do an initial brainstorm with the class to share their first thoughts about an expedition they would like to go on. If possible, have a map displayed (on the board or projected) and highlight the places learners mention. Then ask them to discuss the questions in pairs, and mention that they are going to plan a presentation later in the class on this topic, so this activity will help generate some ideas (although they will have longer to develop their ideas later on). **Note:** The expedition ideas can be as realistic or as outlandish as they like.
- Conduct a quick feedback, asking learners to share some initial ideas at this stage.

**Answers**
Learners' own answers.

## 2 Listen 35 [CD2 Track 3]

- Tell learners that they are now going to listen to three boys (Ben, Ravi, James) presenting their plan for an expedition. Before they listen, draw their attention to the map illustration and photos in the Learner's Book and ask some questions to ascertain where the boys plan to go. Then ask learners to discuss briefly in pairs what they think the boys want to find out from the trip and why.
- Tell learners to listen to Part 1 of the presentation and see if their ideas are mentioned. They need to listen to find out what the boys want to find out from the trip and why.
- When you conduct feedback, draw learners' attention to the photo of the jaguar and use it to elicit the answers to the first question. Also make sure learners know the meaning of *habitat* (the place where the animal lives).

**Audioscript:** Track 35
**Part 1**

**Ben:** Hi, I'm Ben and this is Ravi and James. We're here to present our expedition plan. We're going to make an expedition to the centre of the Amazon jungle, to find out about wild jaguars. We're going to find out more about how they live and their habitats so that we can understand them better and protect their environment.

**Answers**
The boys plan to make an expedition to the centre of the Amazon jungle, to find out about wild jaguars and their habitats, so they can understand them better and protect their environment.

## 3 Listen 36 [CD2 Track 4]

- Now focus learners' again attention on the map illustration in the Learner's Book. Go through the names on the map that are mentioned in the audio (*Iquitos, Peru, Amazon river, Leticia*) and practise saying them with learners, so they are familiar with the sounds before they listen.

- This time, they need to listen to follow the route on the map. They also need to listen for a presentation feature that makes the presentation more interesting and easier for the audience to follow.
- After listening, give learners a minute or so to discuss with their partner the route described and the feature which makes the presentation more interesting. Then conduct feedback.
- During this stage, also check learners understand *local guide* (a person who comes from the area and knows it very well), *paw prints* (the marks or tracks an animal makes with its 'feet'), *nocturnal* (here adjective means that an animal is active at night).
- **Extend and challenge:** You could draw learners' attention to more information from this section (and build a more detailed picture of the planned expedition) by asking questions as follows:
  *Who will help the boys find their way in the jungle?* (A local guide)
  *How will they know they have found the jaguars' habitat?* (They'll look for paw prints)
  *How will they record the animals' movements?* (With a video camera that records at night).

---

**Audioscript:** Track 36
**Part 2**

**Ravi:** If you look our map, you can see where our expedition will start – in the town of Iquitos in Peru. From here we're going to travel down the Amazon river to Leticia – here. We'll camp and spend the night here. We've never been to the jungle before, so we'll take compasses and maps with us to show us the way. We'll also have a local guide with us so we don't get lost.

From Leticia, we'll trek deeper into the jungle until we come to the jaguars' habitat. We'll look for their paw prints so we know we're in the right place. Then we'll set up our video cameras to record them at night because they are nocturnal animals. The cameras will record while we're sleeping.

---

**Answers**
Route: Iquitos, Leticia, into the jungle
The boys make their presentation more interesting by using a map and pictures to explain the route of their expedition and planned activities. The visual image helps the audience to follow the presentation.

---

## 4 Listen 37 [CD2 Track 5]

- Tell learners they are now going to listen to the final part of the presentation. Read through the two questions in the rubric together. Emphasise the words, *during* and *after*, so learners are clear about the focus of this task.
- After listening, give learners a few minutes to discuss answers with their partner; then conduct a class feedback.
- During this stage, also check learners understand *mosquitoes* (flying insects that can give you an itchy bite and sometimes carry dangerous diseases like malaria) and *poisonous tree frog* (use the photo to illustrate).

---

**Audioscript:** Track 37
**Part 3**

**James:** The cameras have sensors that tell them when a big animal is nearby. As soon as the jaguars appear, the video will start working. We'll check the video equipment every day.

There are lots of dangerous insects and reptiles in the Amazon, such as mosquitoes, snakes and poisonous tree frogs. We'll take light clothes that cover our arms and legs and wear lots of insect repellent. When we're sleeping, we'll have tight zips on our tents to keep out any dangerous creatures.

When we get home, we're going to use our videos to make a TV documentary about jaguars in the Amazon.

---

**Answers**
**During the expedition:** they will use video equipment to film the jaguars and check it every day; they'll take light clothes and insect repellent; they'll sleep in the jungle.
**After:** they'll make a TV documentary about jaguars in the Amazon.

---

## 5 Word study 38 [CD2 Track 6]

- Now listen to the whole presentation again, and ask learners to listen specifically for the equipment that the boys mention and why they need it. They need to write down the equipment that they hear and then discuss why it is needed after the audio has finished.
- **Additional support and practice:** Learners who need more support could write the equipment words first and then tick the ones they hear in the presentation. If necessary, you could also stop the audio after mention of equipment and the reason it is needed, to either elicit the answer or give learners time to make notes.
- After listening, give learners a few minutes to discuss answers with their partner; then conduct a class feedback.
- Do some pronunciation work (e.g. syllable stress, connected speech, difficult sounds) on selected words in preparation for later tasks and learners' own presentations.

---

**Answers**
Maps: (reason) to find their way in the jungle.
A compass: to find their way in the jungle.
A video camera: to film jaguars.
Light cotton clothing: to protect against insects and poisonous reptiles.
Insect repellent: to protect against insect bites.
Tents: to sleep in and protect against dangerous creatures.
laptop (Oo) compass (Oo) waterproof clothing (Ooo / Oo) cotton clothing (Oo / Oo) insect repellent (Oo / oOo) video camera (Ooo / Ooo)

---

 For further practice, see Activities 1, 2, 3 and 4 in the Activity Book.

## 6 Use of English

- Write the three examples from the **Use of English** box on the board, leaving a space for the linking expression. Ask learners if they remember the sentences from the presentation.
  1 *The cameras will record _____ we're sleeping.* (while)
  2 *We'll trek deeper into the jungle _____ we come to the jaguars' habitat.* (until)
  3 *_____ the jaguars appear, the video will start working.* (as soon as)

- First tell learners that the missing words give us information about the *time* something happened. Ask learners if they can tell you the missing words; if not, write the three linking expressions on the board and ask them which ones go where (or just input the linkers if learners don't know).

- **Extend and challenge:** If you feel learners would benefit from something more active at this point in the lesson, you could introduce the target language focus by having them do a running dictation (for instructions, see **Unit 2**, **Lesson 2**). The items to dictate and copy would be the three example sentences from the **Use of English** box. As well as energising learners, this activity ensures that they notice every component of the target language through the actions of memorising, dictating, listening and copying. When learners have copied the sentences, ask them to highlight the key components (the linking expressions, *while, until, as soon as*); then follow the rest of the steps in **Activity 6**, starting with the concept-check questions.

- Ask learners some concept-check questions to establish when each type of linker is used.

- For number 1 (*while*), ask how many actions are taking place (2); then draw a timeline to indicate that two actions are happening at the same time but over a length of time, e.g.
  *We are sleeping*
  9 pm → → → → → → → 6 am
  _____ →
  9 am → → → → → → → 6 am
  *The cameras are recording.*

- For number 2 (*until*), ask how many actions are mentioned (2); then ask, *do they happen at the same time?* (no). *Which action comes first?* (we trek into the jungle). *Which action happens after that?* (we come to the jaguars' habitat). *Are we still trekking?* (No)

- For number 3 (*as soon as*), ask again how many actions take place (2); then draw a time line to show two actions happening at the same point in time, e.g.
  The jaguars appear ——————————— →
                                          →
  The video starts working

- Focus learners on **Activity 6** and answer the questions.

- Review the answer as a class. Clarify any confusion with the concept by presenting more example sentences and asking the concept-check questions again.

**Answers**
1 until    2 while    3 as soon as    4 a noun

 For further practice, see Activities 5 and 6 in the Activity Book.

## 7 🗩 Talk

- First focus learners on the **Speaking tip**. Write a few example sentences from the presentation as follows (without contractions) and ask learners if this is how we *say* the sentences (no). Ask them how the sentences need to change to sound more natural when we are *speaking* and elicit which words can be contracted.

  | | |
  |---|---|
  | *I am Ben and this is Ravi ...* | (I'm Ben ...) |
  | *We are going to make an expedition to ...* | (We're going ...) |
  | *We will camp and spend the night here ...* | (We'll camp ...) |

- Drill the contractions and then focus learners on **Activity 7**. Ask them to look at the section from the presentation and read it aloud with a partner, making the necessary contractions, adding in linkers and words for equipment (by looking at the illustrations).

- **Additional support and practice:** To scaffold this activity more, ask learners to rewrite the section first, adding contractions, linkers and the equipment words. Then ask them to cover their written piece and say the section aloud to a partner (having clarified the necessary additions in the writing stage, rather than 'thinking on their feet').

- When you go through the answers, read out the text with some mistakes and ask learners to put up their hands (or call out) when they hear an error.

**Answers**
While we're walking I'll wear light cotton clothing. I'll check the compass every ten minutes until we arrive. As soon as I get to the jungle, I'll put on insect repellent and we'll put up the tent.

 For further practice, see Activity 1 in the Activity Book.

### Present it!

- Tell learners that they are now going to prepare their own presentations about their expedition plans, in groups of three. Go through the step-by-step instructions outlined in the Learner's Book and draw their attention to the highlighted words in bold. These give the structure of the presentation, as represented in the model. First give them time to think of an idea and remind them of their discussions at the beginning of the lesson.

- Ask them to draw a large, clear map, on poster paper, to illustrate their expedition route and decorate it with pictures relevant to the presentation.

- Ask learners to write out their presentation from their notes and produce one text per group, either in class time or at home. Check the scripts for grammar, vocabulary and organisation; however, the emphasis is on organisation and quality of ideas rather than perfectly accurate scripts.

- Give learners the opportunity to practise their presentations together. Each member of the group should deliver a part of the presentation. Monitor the groups, making sure you spend some time with each, helping with any pronunciation difficulties. Draw their attention to the use of contractions when they are speaking. Check that everyone has a part to present and that someone is responsible for displaying the map illustration.
- **Critical thinking:** Before learners present to the class, give listeners a task by asking them to note down *where* the expedition will take place and one reason *why* the speakers want to make the expedition. Tell them they can also ask any questions if they like.
- Ask learners to deliver their presentations in pairs or groups of three in front of the class. Introduce each group first and generate a supportive atmosphere by having learners applaud each group before and after each presentation. When each group finishes, make a positive comment about their presentation before welcoming the next group.
- **Additional support and practice:** Use of notes in delivery: stronger learners may be able to deliver without looking too closely at their notes; others may need to read from their notes at this stage. Use your discretion with regard to how much you allow this, taking into account ability and confidence levels in your class. Ultimately in later years, learners need to be able to deliver oral presentations without reading word for word from notes. Ideally, we should encourage them to get into this habit as soon as possible but learners will probably need the support of reading from their notes in these early stages.
- **Extend and challenge:** As learners are delivering their presentations, note down main errors; either give to each group a note of the errors to correct themselves, or write up on the board at the end for a class error correction session (without stating which group or individual made the errors). **Note:** This would come after plenty of positive feedback regarding the presentations. Positive feedback must always come first and be emphasised.
- After listening to all the presentations, vote on which expedition idea is the most *useful*, the most *unusual* and the most *dangerous*.

> **Answers**
> Learner's own answers.

👉 **Wrap up**

- **Critical thinking:** After listening to all the presentations, have a vote on one expedition you would all like to go on as a class.

## Activity Book

### 1 Read

- Learners read a text describing an expedition plan and put the paragraphs in the correct order.

> **Answers**
> **Paragraph order:** b/ a/ c

### 2 Read

- Learners find words in the text to label photographs.

> **Answers**
> **a** a shipwreck    **b** a wetsuit    **c** an oxygen tank

### 3 Read

- Learners read incomplete sentences about the text and circle the ending that is *not* correct (from a choice of three).

> **Answers**
> **1** c    **2** b    **3** a    **4** a

### 4 Vocabulary

- Learners underline ten examples of equipment in the text in **Activity 1**.

> **Answers**
> a compass, sea maps, wet suits, oxygen tanks, underwater cameras, laptop, light clothing, waterproof clothing, first aid kit, video

### 5 Use of English

- Learners circle the correct linking expression to complete the sentences.

> **Answers**
> **1** until
> **2** while
> **3** As soon as
> **4** as soon as
> **5** until

### 6 Use of English

- Learners complete a gapped paragraph with the correct linking expression.

> **Answers**
> **1** until
> **2** until
> **3** While
> **4** As soon as
> **5** while
> **6** as soon as

# Lesson 4: Keeping track

Learner's Book pages: 86–87
Activity Book pages: 70–71

## Lesson objectives

**Reading:** Read a diary of an expedition; identify specific information and make deductions from inferences.

**Writing:** Plan and write a diary entry about an expedition.

**Critical thinking:** Make decisions about order of paragraphs by looking at in-text references; make deductions about feelings expressed in the text from inferences.

**Language focus:** Cardinal and ordinal numbers.

**Vocabulary:** Text-specific words and phrases; *guarding a nest, young* (noun), *deadly, spotted, rolled, jaw, unharmed*

**Materials:** images of travel diaries and blogs (**Warm up**).

## Learner's Book

###  Warm up

- Before learners open their books, show them an example of a diary or a blog and talk about what is contained within this type of text. If possible, show images that are as visually appealing as possible, e.g. a diary with photos and scrapbook items attached (see *Google images*: search term – *travel diary*); or a blog entry with photos. Choose examples that learners will engage with and relate to, e.g. a diary or blog from a school trip.
- Alternatively, if you personally have written a travel diary or blog, you could show learners this example.

### 1 🗩 Talk about it

- Read the two questions in **Activity 1** together; then ask learners to discuss in pairs. If learners have ever contributed to a class blog about a school trip, or other school event, then talk about that too and, if possible, have a look at the blog and what is contained in it.
- During feedback, write suggestions for the second question (*What information ... ?*) on the board, for comparison later with the diary text in **Activity 2**.

> **Answers**
> Learners' own answers.

### 2 Read

- Tell learners that they are now going to read a diary entry about an expedition to the Senegal River, in West Africa. If possible, show them the route of the river on a map. Ask them to look at the photos in the Learner's Book and elicit ideas about the purpose of the trip.

- Now ask them quickly to glance at the text and tell you what they notice about the paragraph order (it is mixed up). Ask them what they need to do in the next task (put the paragraphs in the correct order). Next, draw their attention to the **Writing tip** about time references and dates. Tell them that these references help the reader to follow more easily the sequence of events described in a blog or diary entry.
- Now ask them to read through the texts, put the paragraphs in the correct order and note down the time references. Tell learners not to worry about unknown words at this point – these will be dealt with in the next stage.
- **Additional support and practice:** To clarify the ordering process, give small groups of learners copies of the diary entry cut up into paragraphs for them to order. Physically ordering paragraphs in this way can make it easier to deduce which paragraph goes where.
- When they have finished, tell them to check the order with a partner. Then go through the answers with the class. Ask them what other factors, besides the time references, helped them work out the paragraph order (e.g. the number of crocodiles mentioned, phrases such as *Further up the river ...*).

> **Answers**
> Paragraph order: b / d / a / c
> Time references: *Up at 4.30 am / At about 11 am / at 6.30 pm*

### 3 Read

- Before learners read the text again, read through the questions, a–c, together and then ask them to look for the answers in the text. After they have read, they can work in pairs to write the answers in their notebooks. Point out that this time they should read the text in the correct order.
- **Critical thinking:** When you go through the answers for (c), ask learners what clues there are in the text to indicate that Nadia felt these emotions. Listen to their suggestions and, if necessary, draw their attention to the following features:
  Phrases such as: *SO worth it, What a sight to see!, We saw the most amazing thing!*; use of exclamation marks (shows something that the writer finds surprising or exciting; capitalisation for emphasis (e.g. *SO*).
- **Extend and challenge:** Ask learners to respond to the text by asking questions; e.g. How would they feel if they saw a crocodile carrying eggs in this way? Do they think it is surprising or not? Would they like to visit West Africa and do an expedition like this? What else would they expect to see on the Senegal River? Questions could be put to the whole class together or discussed in small groups. If applicable, ask learners if there are any similarities in content and organisation between Nadia's diary and examples they looked at in the warm-up stage.

**Answers**
a At the Senegal River
b She is there to study Nile crocodiles. Nadia and her team are recording the nesting habits of the crocodiles so they can reduce the number of crocodile attacks on local people. Nile crocodiles often attack when they think their nests are in danger.
c happy, excited, interested

## 4 Word study

- Focus learners on the words in blue in the diary text. Ask first if anyone knows what the words mean and elicit meanings from the pictures where possible. Where learners don't know the meaning, either ask them to look up the words in their dictionaries or read out the definitions in a reading race, and ask them to find the words in the text:
- **Note:** This activity could be carried out between **Activities 2** and **3** (first and second readings) if learners need the vocabulary support at that point. However, if it is carried out at this stage, learners will have had more time to deduce any unfamiliar words from context.

**Answers**
spotted: to recognise or catch sight of something
nest: the place where crocodiles lay their eggs
unharmed: not hurt
rolled: to turn something over and over
guarding: to protect something
jaw: the bone that supports your teeth and mouth
deadly: very dangerous
young: baby animals

## 5 Use of English

- Focus learners on the text again and ask them to find all the examples of numbers mentioned. Tell them to look for cardinal numbers too, e.g. *first, second*. As learners suggest the words, write them into two columns on the board: Cardinal /Ordinal
- Draw learners attention to the **Use of English** box in the Learner's Book and explain that cardinal numbers tell us the *amount* of something; ordinal numbers tell us the *order*.
- Now ask them to do **Activity 5**, using ordinal and cardinal numbers. If necessary, do question 1 together. Ask them to do the rest individually and then compare their answers with their partner.

**Answers**
1 How long was the first Nile crocodile? It was about 4 metres long.
2 How many crocs did they find up the river? They found three more crocs.
3 What did they see the second time? They saw another croc crack open an egg.
4 How many eggs did the crocs lay between them? They laid about 100 eggs.

 For further practice, see Activities 4, 5 and 6 in the Activity Book.

## 6  Calculate

- Focus learners on Nadia's notes in **Activity 6**. They can do this calculation activity individually or in pairs. Make it into a race to see who can calculate the answer the fastest. If necessary, remind learners how to do the calculation (add all the measurements together and divide by the number of measurements listed, i.e. $4 + 3 + 3.5 + 3.5 + 4.5 + 2.5 = 21 \quad 21 \div 6 = 3.5$).

**Answers**
3.5 metres

## 7 Calculate

- Follow the same procedure for the calculation in **Activity 7**. If necessary, remind learners how to do the calculation (divide area size, 1500 metres, by number of crocs, 6, i.e. $\mathbf{1500 \div 6 = 250}$ ).

**Answers**
If there are six crocodile nests in a 1500 metre area, there is an average of one nest per **250** metres.

## Write

- **Critical thinking:** Tell learners they are going to write their own diary entries, using their expedition plans from **Lesson 3**. Draw their attention to the second bulleted point about content to include and refer them to the sections in the model text that express these points. Also remind them of the **Writing tip** about time references to help organise the sequence of events being described.
- Put learners into the same presentation groups as for **Lesson 3** and ask them to work together to decide on a suitable part of their expedition idea to record in the diary. Spend time helping learners with this by focusing them on what they aimed to find out on their trips, when this happened and the result. This part might prove the most suitable section to record. They then work together to produce a first draft of their diary entry, with each learner recording the draft in their notebooks
- Encourage learners to use suitable language and tenses (past simple and continuous) by showing them the example from the Learner's Book, completed to reflect one of your groups' ideas.
  *At about 10 am we went to ... While we were ... we saw ...*
- Monitor the writing stage, helping learners with grammar and vocabulary as needed. When you are satisfied with first drafts, ask learners to produce a second draft.

**Answers**
Learners' own answers – Portfolio opportunity.

 For further practice, see Activity 7 in the Activity Book.

**Wrap up**

- When you have corrected the diary entries, hand out to learners to read each other's work (one per group). Ask them to make a note of *where* the writers are, *why* they are there and *how they feel* about what they have seen and done.

## Activity Book

### 1 📝 Read

- Learners complete a blog about a visit to a wildlife park by reading an information leaflet showing times of daily activities.

> **Answers**
> **1** 11.00    **2** 12.30    **3** 2.15    **4** 3.00

### 2 Read

- Learners read the text again and complete information about numbers in a gapped text (an extract from the information leaflet).

> **Answers**
> **1** 2.5 metres
> **2** three tonnes
> **3** (over) 1.5 metres
> **4** four months old

### 3 Use of English

- Learners circle ordinal numbers and underline cardinal numbers in the text in **Activity 1**.

> **Answers**
> **Cardinal numbers:** Paragraph 1 – 9.30 am; two; three; four; 11.00
> Paragraph 2 – 12.30; 2.15; 2.5 (metres); three (tonnes)
> Paragraph 3 – 3.00; 1.5 (metres)
> **Ordinal numbers:** Paragraph 1 – first; Paragraph 3 – second

### 4 Use of English

- Learners choose an ordinal or cardinal number to complete sentences. A number prompt is given at the end of each sentence and learners have to decide which form is needed to complete the sentences.

> **Answers**
> **1** fifth / five
> **2** Two / second
> **3** four / fourth
> **4** third / three
> **5** first / one

### 5 Pronunciation 🔊 **70** [CD2 Track 38]

- Learners listen and repeat cardinal numbers expressing time and measurement. They have to note which number is pronounced differently to the others.

> **Audioscript:** Track 70
> **1** two fifteen pm    **2** six forty-five pm
> **3** nine thirty am    **4** two point five metres

> **Answers**
> Number 4 (the measurement) is pronounced differently.

### 6 Pronunciation 🔊 **71** [CD2 Track 39]

- Learners listen and circle the numbers they hear from a choice of ordinal and cardinal numbers.

> **Answers**
> **1** fourth    **2** third    **3** five    **4** sixth

### 7 📝 Challenge

- Learners write a blog or diary entry about what they did last weekend, using time references and dates to organise their work.

> **Answers**
> Learners' own answers.

## Lesson 5: Big adventures

Learner's Book pages: 88–89
Activity Book pages: 72–73

### Lesson objectives

**Listening and reading:** Listen to and read an extract from a novel about a young explorer. Answer questions about story content and themes.

**Speaking:** Discuss story themes about welcoming visitors.

**Critical thinking:** Make comparisons between situations described in the story and your own experience. **Photocopiable activity 12**.

**Language focus:** Participle adjectives with *-ed* and *-ing*.

**Vocabulary:** Descriptive language; *translated, tore off, chewed, popped, scoop up, circular, heaps*

**Values:** Making visitors welcome.

**Materials:** realia (travel objects: see **Warm up**); photographic images of Ethiopia (optional for **Wrap up**). Copies of **Photocopiable activity 12**.

### Learner's Book

### 📝 Warm up

- Put the following objects (if available) in a bag. Add more if available.
  *a compass   a map   a camera   insect repellent*
  *sunglasses   a sunhat   sun screen*
  *items from a first aid kit*
- Take the bag around the classroom and let learners feel it and try and guess the objects. As they guess, take the objects out. Then cover them and see how many learners can remember. When learners have guessed all the objects, ask them what they have in common (items you take on an expedition or journey). Hopefully learners will remember some of the objects from the previous lessons in this unit.

- Now tell learners that they are going to read about a young explorer who is on a very exciting journey. This part of the story is about his experience as a guest in another country.

## 1  Talk about it

- Focus learners on the questions in **Activity 1**. Ask them to discuss these in pairs first, then share as a class.

**Answers**
Learners' own answers.

## 2 Read and listen 39 [CD2 Track 7]

- Tell learners that they are now going to read and listen to the story about the young explorer, from a novel called *The Boy Who Biked the World* by Alastair Humphreys. Ask them to describe the illustration on page 88 and then read the three questions in **Activity 2**. Then tell the class to listen and read the first part of the text, looking for answers to the three gist questions. Stress that, at this point, they only need look for this information and not to worry about words they do not understand.
- Start the audio and tell learners to read the first part of the text while listening.
- After reading / listening, go through the answers with the class.

**Audioscript:** Track 39
See Learner's Book page 88.

**Answers**
Tom is in Ethiopia, in East Africa.
He travelled to Ethiopia by bike.
Learners' own answers. (The implication in the text is that this is Tom's first meeting with Abai – *"Why don't you come and meet my family?"* (Abai) *"And I would love to see your house."* (Tom) *They were very surprised when they saw Tom.* (Abai's family) *He was a very unusual visitor. Abai told Tom he was very welcome in their home.*)

## 3 Read 40 [CD2 Track 8]

- Ask learners to look carefully at the illustrations and describe them (this will help them to guess any unknown words in the next extract from context).
- Tell learners that they are going to read the story again, part by part to answer the questions after each part. They should read and then answer the questions in their notebooks.
- **Additional support and practice:** Learners could work in pairs to do the comprehension questions 1–10. Alternatively you could divide the questions up, so learners don't have to answer all of them but benefit from learning all answers in feedback later on. Put learners in A/B pairs: A answers the odd numbered questions, B, the even numbered ones, then ask them to share the answers at the end.
- After learners have written the answers for questions 1–10, put them in groups of four to check their answers together.

- Allow time for this before giving feedback on the answers. Where possible, use the pictures in the book to illustrate the answers.

**Audioscript:** Track 40
See Learner's Book page 89–90.

**Answers**
1 The family asked Tom questions about his expedition.
2 Abai and his dad helped the family to communicate with Tom by translating from Amharic to English and vice versa.
3 A very big piece of *injera*, a type of bread, lots of stews and cooked vegetables.
4 Abai helped Tom by showing him how to eat the food using pieces of the *injera* bread to pick it up.
5 Yes, Tom liked the food very much. He described the flavour as *spicy*.
6 They ate from the same huge piece of *injera* bread (all taking a piece of the bread and using it to pick up the food).
7 They asked questions to find out about each other's countries.
8 She was surprised that people in England didn't eat *injera* bread.
9 Tom learned that the Ethiopian calendar is seven years behind the rest of the world and that it is a different year there. He also learned that telling the time is different in Ethiopia.
10 He felt much happier because Abai's family had been kind to him and welcomed him into their home.

[AB] **For further practice, see Activity 1 in the Activity Book.**

## 4 Talk

- **Critical thinking:** Ask learners to work in pairs to answer the questions in **Activity 4**.
- Do a class feedback, eliciting as many points as possible for question 1 and eliciting several responses to question 2, so comparisons can be made with different family's habits and customs. Ask learners to compare their family's food and eating habits with the customs described in the extract.

**Answers**
1 Abai and his family make Tom feel welcome by enthusiastically welcoming him into their home, even though they are shocked to see a 'very unusual visitor'.
They invite him to sit down and share their food with them at the table, especially all eating from the same piece of *injera* bread.
Abai shows Tom how to eat dinner with the bread in the Ethiopian way.
He and his father translate so the family and Tom can communicate.
The family are interested in Tom's expedition and ask him lots of questions.
They allow him to stay the night and then wave him off in the morning until he is out of sight.
2 Learners' own answers.

## 5 Word study

- Focus learners' attention on the words highlighted in blue in the story. Ask first if learners know the meaning of any of the words or can demonstrate one.

- Now ask them to look at the words closely and work out the meaning by looking at the illustrations and the words and phrases around the word in question. Don't allow learners to use dictionaries, encourage them to work at understanding the words from the context they appear in.
- Conduct a class feedback, encouraging learners to mime as many of the words as possible or make gestures (e.g. *tore off, scoop up, popped, chewed, circular, heaps*).

> **Answers**
> tore off – break something off quickly
> scoop up – pick up quickly
> popped – to put something quickly into your mouth (in this context)
> chewed – to break up food in your mouth
> circular – a round shape
> heaps – lots of something (implies a mound, items stacked or piled up)
> translated – to change words and sentences from one language to another

## 6 Word study

- Ask learners to do **Activity 6** individually and then check with a partner, before going through the answers as a class.
- To go through the answers you could read the text and then give a mixture of right and wrong answers. Learners have to stop you when they hear a wrong answer and correct it.

> **Answers**
> **a** circular
> **b** translated
> **c** heaps
> **d** tore off
> **e** scoop up
> **f** popped
> **g** chewed

 For further practice, see Activity 2 in the Activity Book.

## 7 Use of English

- Ask learners to guess something that you (the teacher) are interested in. When you get a suitable reply, write gapped sentences on the board and elicit the form of the missing participle adjective, e.g.
  I am _____ in photography. (interest**ed**)
  For me, photography is very _____ (interest**ing**)
- Ask learners which form describes 'my *reaction*' ( *–ed* form, e.g. interest**ed**); then explain that the *–ing* forms describe the *cause* of the reaction.
- Give learners some more examples, so they can notice the pattern by understanding the meaning (this is preferable than just having them try and understand the concept). Draw their attention to the examples from the text, outlined in the **Use of English** box in the Learner's Book; also give them some more personal examples that they can easily relate to.
- Now ask learners to practise making decisions about which form to use in **Activity 7**. They can do the

activity in pairs or ask them to work on their own, then compare answers with their partner. Draw their attention to the first example sentence to show them that the base word in brackets needs to be changed to a participle adjective; which one depends on the meaning of the sentence.

- You could go through the answers in the same way as suggested in **Activity 6**. Learners would then have to listen carefully to hear the form of the adjective and decide if it was correct or not.

> **Answers**
> **1** [Ex] interesting
> **2** fascinating
> **3** exciting
> **4** amazed
> **5** tired
> **6** tiring

 For further practice, see Activities 3 and 4 in the Activity Book.

## 8 Pronunciation 41 [CD2 Track 9]

- Focus learners on **Activity 8**. Ask them to listen to and repeat the words from the story.
- Ask them which two letters make the *ch* sound in the last two words.

> **Audioscript:** Track 41
> See Learner's Book page 91.

> **Answers**
> tu

## 9 Values

- **Critical thinking:** Focus learners on the **Values** heading and read through all of the questions together. Then put learners into small groups to discuss the questions. They need to talk about the questions, drawing on their personal experiences and be prepared to share their answers with the class afterwards.
- Alternatively, you could give each group just one question to focus on, and ask them to listen to other groups' responses to the other questions during feedback.

> **Answers**
> Learners' own answers.

##  Wrap up

- Ask learners how they would like to travel, if they took a trip around another country. Which country would they visit? What kind of transport would they use?
- Alternatively, you could show learners some photographic images of Ethiopia, especially the landscape and hilly terrain (and the kind of house Abai's family lived in or Ethiopian food, if possible) and find out what they know about the country.

## Activity Book

### 1 Read

- Learners read the extract again from the novel and decide if statements about the story are true or false. They correct the false sentences.

> **Answers**
> 1 false. Tom was very pleased when Abai invited him to his house.
> 2 true
> 3 false. There was plenty of food for Tom as well as all the family.
> 4 false. Only Abai and his dad could speak English.
> 5 false. Abai's Mum served the food with a type of bread called *injera*.
> 6 true
> 7 true
> 8 false. Tom said 'thank you' for the food in Amharic, the national language of Ethiopia.
> 9 true
> 10 false. Tom learned that the Ethiopian calendar is seven years behind the rest of the world's calendar.
> 11 false. He also learned that, according to Ethiopian time, the day begins when the sun rises (in early morning).
> 12 true

### 2 Word study

- Learners complete sentences with the correct word from the box.

> **Answers**
> 1 chew
> 2 tore off
> 3 heaps
> 4 circular
> 5 translated

### 3 Use of English

- Learners choose the correct participle adjectives (from a choice of two) to complete the summary of the story.

> **Answers**
> 1 tired
> 2 surprised
> 3 pleased
> 4 fascinated
> 5 exciting
> 6 interested
> 7 surprised
> 8 amazing
> 9 tiring
> 10 excited

### 4 Challenge

- Learners use participle adjectives in the box to write sentences about themselves and their experiences.

> **Answers**
> Learners' own answers.

**For further practice in talking about expeditions, see Photocopiable activity 12.**

## Lesson 6: Choose a project

Learner's Book pages: 92

### Lesson objectives

**Writing:** Organise and write a diary or blog entry imagining a day in a modern day expedition; (or) prepare notes for a presentation about a historical explorer or expedition; revise unit themes.

**Speaking:** Deliver a presentation about a historical explorer or expedition; revise unit themes; discuss **Unit 6** Big question.

**Critical thinking:** Imagine the events of a day in a modern day expedition; research information about and explain the effect of an historical expedition; a film; apply new skills and language acquired in **Unit 6** to project work and revision activities.

**Language focus:** Recycling language points from **Unit 6**, i.e. Question forms (Question word + noun); linking expressions (showing time); cardinal and ordinal numbers; participle adjectives.

**Vocabulary:** Recycling of new and reviewed vocabulary from **Unit 6**, i.e. Expeditions; voyages and exploration; equipment; descriptive language from the story, *The Boy Who Biked the World* (**Lesson 5**)

**Materials:** paper; poster paper or electronic slides; poster paper, pictures, coloured pens (for Project 2); sets of vocabulary cards (**Warm up**).

## Learner's Book

### ☞ Warm up

- Put learners in small teams and give each team a set of vocabulary cards with words and collocations from **Unit 6** (including some ordinal numbers). Each card contains one word / collocation. (**See Teaching tip, Unit 6** overview for more information about vocabulary cards).
- First ask learners to sort the cards into categories, e.g. expeditions / exploration of the Americas / equipment / words from the story in **Lesson 5** / ordinal numbers. Then ask them if they can see any further categories in the words, e.g. words about the sea / verbs / people / animals, etc.
- Then call out some definitions and ask learners to find the corresponding word or expression and hold it up. Award points for the first team to hold up the correct word. E.g.
  *Find me a word which means to find something new.* → discover
  *Which word means a baby animal?* → young → *Is it a noun or a verb here?* → *A noun!*
- You can do further work with the cards if time permits, e.g. Ask learners to turn them over, pick one up at random and make a sentence; or pick three up together and make a sentence / s containing all three.
- Tell learners they are now going to choose from the two projects and follow the instructions below for the one they have decided on.

## 1 Write a blog or diary entry about a modern-day expedition

- Put learners in small groups and take them through the step-by-step instructions presented in the Learner's Book. As they will need to look for information about their chosen topic, refer to the **Teaching Tip** on page 39 for advice on how to manage this research. Draw their attention to the instruction in stage 2 to help focus and organise their research.
- If learners need some support when they reach the stage of imagining a typical day during the expedition, tell them to imagine themselves in the environment of the expedition first (e.g. in the jungle, on a ship, in the Antarctic, etc), then visualise the experience using all senses, e.g. *What can they see? Hear? Smell? Is there any food? What does it taste like? If they reach out, what can they touch?* Then focus them on emotions – *how does the experiences make them feel? Are they happy, enthusiastic, excited? Worried, tired? A mixture of emotions … ?,* etc.
- When they are at the drafting stage, ask them to create a first draft and check this for accuracy in grammar and word choice. Make sure the draft answers the two questions outlined in stage 4.
- When they have produced a satisfactory draft, ask them to copy it onto clean paper for display; they can decorate it with sketches or pictures if time permits.
- Next, either display the texts on the classroom wall and ask learners to walk around and read, or pass the texts around from group to group, so each text is read by each group. As learners read the texts, they need to answer the questions, (a) and (b) in stage 4 about each one.

> **Answers**
> Learners' own answers – Portfolio opportunity.

###  Wrap up

- When learners have read all the entries and answered the questions, vote as a class on which diary / blog entry describes the most exciting day.

## 2 Do a presentation about a historical explorer or expedition

- Put learners in small groups to do the presentation. Take them through the step-by-step instructions presented in the Learner's Book.
- Spend time helping them to choose which expedition or explorer to research. Draw their attention to the topic areas listed in stage 2 to help focus their research and organise their notes. (Please refer to the **Teaching tip** in **Unit 2** overview for more advice on how to manage the research of projects).
- When learners are drafting the presentation, monitor and make sure they are using sequencing phrases to guide the audience through the presentation.

- Allow time for preparing visuals for the presentation, e.g. slides and pictures that are relevant to the chosen expedition or explorer.
- Give learners time to practise their presentation, ensure that each member has a part to say and that someone is responsible for organising the props (slides, pictures, etc.).
- When learners are listening to each other's presentations, tell them to write answers to the following questions: *Where did the expedition go? Why did the explorers make the expedition?*

> **Answers**
> Learners' own answers – Portfolio opportunity.

###  Wrap up

- **Critical thinking:** After listening to all the presentations, put learners in groups to consider all the expeditions and decide which one was a) the most important; b) the most interesting; c) the most dangerous. Then have a vote to decide as a class on one example for each category.

### Reflect on your learning

- These revision activities can be approached in different ways, according to the level and character of your class.
  - Questions 1–7 could be used as a class quiz, with learners in teams and a time limit given to write answers to each question.
  - Alternatively, you could conduct a revision session. Ask learners to work in pairs and take longer to think about and write down their answers. When pairs have finished the questions, they swap with another pair and correct each other's, with you monitoring and giving help and advice when needed.
  - You could set this task for homework / self-study.

> **Answers**
> 1 Lief Ericson went to North America (now Canada) to look for farm land. Vasco da Gama went to India to bring goods back to sell in Europe / establish a trade route between Europe and India. Richard Burton and John Speke went to Africa to discover the source of the River Nile. Valentina Tereshkova went into space to find more information about the earth's atmosphere.
> 2 The first European explorers found gold, silver, exotic birds, potatoes and corn in the Americas.
> 3 Learners' own answers.
> 4 Ben and his friends wanted to find out about the habitat and lifestyle of the jaguar in the Amazon jungle, to better protect the animals' environment.
> Equipment: maps, a compass, light clothing, video cameras, tents, insect repellent.
> 5 Nadia was studying Nile crocodiles. She describes how they carry their young to the water and gently crack open the eggs containing baby crocodiles with their teeth.
> 6 Abai and his family welcomed Tom by inviting him to have dinner with them and stay in their home overnight.
> 7 The family shared a huge piece of *injera* bread (traditional Ethiopian bread) and used it to scoop up the other food – stews and cooked vegetables. The food was spicy and tasted very good.

## Look what I can do!

**Aim:** To check learners have fulfilled the objectives for **Unit 6** (and to what degree).

- Present the objectives slide or poster from the introduction to **Unit 6** (in **Lesson 1**) and remind learners of the objectives from the start of the unit.
- Focus their attention on the '*I can ...*' statements and read through together. You could put these on a slide or write on the board. Ask learners if they feel they can now do these tasks after completing **Unit 6**. By this point, you should have a clear idea yourself of how well your learners have completed the tasks. However, ask them now to do an initial self-assessment.
- Put learners in pairs and ask them to look through their notebooks and portfolios to find evidence of their work for each of the statements. Then they give themselves a rating as follows:
  ✓ Yes, I can – no problem!
  ? A little – I need more practice.
  ☹ No – I need a lot more practice.
- Circulate and chat to learners about their self-assessment (some might be overly modest and you can point out that their rating could be higher). If you haven't already done so, make notes about areas that learners are not confident about for future reference (see **Teaching tip**).
- Conduct a general feedback at the end and find out which tasks learners found the most interesting / useful / challenging, etc.
- **Extend and challenge:** A mini-awards system: Customise the idea presented in **Unit 1** for **Unit 6** (see **Unit 1** page 38).

> **Answers**
> Learners' own answers.

### ☞ Wrap up

- As a class, look at the Big question again on a slide or written on the board: *What have been the effects of explorations and expeditions?*
- Put learners in small groups to discuss the question and give them a time limit to come up with six examples of *effects* or impacts of explorations and expeditions (e.g. discover important scientific information, discover a new place, etc). Learners can also list examples from the Activity Book. Elicit an example first from the whole class.
- You could turn this into a game and award points to the first group who come up with six effects, based on what they have studied in **Unit 6**.
- Elicit their answers onto the board and now ask learners to match an *effect* with an *explorer*. They can look back through **Unit 6** if they wish. Again, award points to the first team to match correctly.
- **Additional support and practise:** If you feel learners will need support coming up with answers to the Big question, you could write the effects on the board (or slide) and ask learners to work in small groups to

look through **Unit 6** and match to an explorer. Award points to the first group to match all points. E.g. *Important scientific information was discovered* → *Valentina Tereshkova.*
*An important place was found* → *Richard Burton and John Speke / Lief Ericson.*
(See **Wrap up** answers for other suggestions).

> **Answers**
> Example answers:
> Important scientific information was discovered (Valentina Tereshkova).
> An important place was found (Richard Burton and John Speke; Lief Ericson).
> A route was found to transport things to sell (Vasco da Gama).
> New kinds of food were discovered (Columbus).
> Valuable things were discovered (Columbus)
>  + controversial effects (e.g. colonisation); learners' own ideas from own reading about modern-day inventions; examples from the Activity book (e.g. female astronauts; Ibn Battuta).

## 1 Revision

- Learners complete a crossword covering key grammar and vocabulary from **Lessons 1 – 6** in **Unit 6**.

> **Answers**
> **Across**
>  1  while
>  4  mission
>  5  as
>  6  shining
>  8  valuable
> 10  first
> 11  destroy
> **Down**
>  1  which
>  2  era
>  3  discover
>  7  tiny
>  9  aid

## My global progress

- Learners think about their own responses to topics and activities in the units and answer the questions.

> **Answers**
> Learners' own answers.

### Teaching tip

Review the learners' work and their own assessment of their progress, noting areas where learners demonstrate strength and confidence and areas where they need additional instruction and practice. Use this information to select areas for review and specific focus, as you continue to **Unit 7**.

## Review 3

Learner's Book pages: 94–95

- Review 3 offers learners the opportunity to review and recycle key language and vocabulary items from **Units 5** and **6**, presented in similar contexts to themes that appeared in these units. All items are briefly covered in activities that are similar in type to those in the Activity Book. There is a range of activity types that cover all skills areas.

- Learners can do Review 3 activities either in class or for homework. However, there is a short speaking activity, which will need to be covered in class (see below for suggestion). The Review pages can also be used to occupy early finishers, provided learners have already covered the relevant language points in class.
- **Speaking activities:** If learners have done the Review 3 activities at home, the speaking activity could be carried out during a Review 3 feedback session, either at the beginning or end of the class.
- **Feedback:** Answers to the activities can be elicited from learners or displayed on the board or on a slide for learners to use to correct their work. To make the correction stage more interactive, ask learners to swap notebooks and correct each other's work.

## 1 Vocabulary

- Learners name items in a series of pictures and divide into gadgets and equipment. They then add three more words to each list.

> **Answers**
> **Gadgets:** a tablet (picture d); a mobile phone (pic. c)
> **Equipment:** rollerblades (pic b); a (mountain) bike (pic. a)
> + Learners' own answers.

## 2 Listen 42 [CD2 Track 10]

Learners listen to someone talking about something he likes and identify his favourite item from the pictures.

> **Audioscript:** Track 42
> **Part 1**
>
> My favourite thing is my bike. If I had to choose just one thing, it would be my bike! I ride it to school and at weekends when I'm with my friends. I think bikes are more useful than cars for short distances because they're really cheap and they keep you fit too.
>
> My friend Mikey prefers rollerblades. He thinks they are better than bikes because they're faster. But I think bikes are better than rollerblades because you can ride them in more places. I ride my bike up and down hills and on grass, as well as on the road. You can't do that with rollerblades! I used to have some rollerblades when I was younger. I didn't like them much because I used to fall over all the time!
>
> When I grow up I'll probably learn to drive but I think I'll always prefer my bike to any other kind of transport.

> **Answers**
> Ollie's favourite item is his bike.

## 3 Listen 42 [CD2 Track 10]

- Learners listen to the listening extract again and answer comprehension questions.

> **Answers**
> 1 Ollie compares a bike with a car.
> 2 He thinks a bike is better because bikes are cheap, they keep you fit and are easier to park.
> 3 He rides it to school.
> 4 He used to fall over.
> 5 He'll learn to drive.

## 4 Talk

- Learners complete sentences about themselves, then compare their responses with a partner's.

> **Answers**
> Learners' own answers.

## 5 Read

- Learners read and complete the journal with words from the box.

> **Answers**
> 1 as soon as
> 2 voyage
> 3 sailing
> 4 waterproof clothing
> 5 second
> 6 video recorders
> 7 while
> 8 discover
> 9 destroying
> 10 valuable
> 11 increased
> 12 two

## 6 Use of English

- Learners write questions to match given answers about the information in the journal text in **Activity 8**.

> **Answers**
> 1 Which animals are they studying?
> 2 What equipment do they have on the boat?
> 3 What clothing are they wearing?
> 4 How many dolphins have they seen so far?
> 5 How many days will the voyage take?

## 7 Punctuation

- Learners rewrite sentences using contractions. Then they tell their partner which ones are true for them and correct any sentences that are false.

> **Answers**
> 1 Next weekend we're going to visit my grandparents.
> 2 I've been at this school for five years.
> 3 When I'm older, I'll probably learn to drive.
> 4 At the moment I'm studying for an exam.
> 5 Next month we're going on a school trip.

## 8 Talk

- Learners compare the stories in **Units 5** and **6**. They discuss with a partner which ones they liked best and why.

> **Answers**
> Learners' own answers.

# 7 Jobs and work

**How do people get to do the jobs they do? Why do they do their jobs?**

## Unit overview

In this unit learners will:

- talk about why people do the jobs they do
- read about people who love their jobs
- present ideas for designing a work uniform
- write a job advertisement
- read and talk about a poem about jobs.

In **Unit 7**, learners will explore the notion of jobs and work: how people choose the work they do, qualities and skills needed to do certain jobs, and positive attitudes to work. Learners are presented with the Big question in **Lesson 1** and will understand that tasks and projects in the unit will contribute to answering this question. The unit begins by focusing on how people get to do the jobs they do, giving learners the opportunity to draw on their own knowledge of the work of their family members and to consider how they might choose a profession in the future. Here they practise language describing skills and interests through a listening text and communicative tasks that encourage discussion and comparison. They will then read about work in a specific area (the media) and look at personal qualities needed to do this type of work, as well as carry out an interview about a job, using the reading text as a model. In **Lesson 3**, they are given a design task which will exercise skills in problem solving as well as creativity, leading to an oral presentation about a work uniform. In **Lesson 4**, they will write a short humorous job advertisement and also gain an introduction to the idea of how people find a job. Finally, they will read a poem about different kinds of jobs and examine the message within regarding positive attitudes towards the notion of work.

The **Photocopiable activities** provide practice in speaking and writing through a task which requires learners to work together to create their own business (**13**) and reviewing job-related vocabulary (**14**).

### Language focus

Prepositions after adjectives; present continuous forms (actions happening now); *could* (expressing possibility)

**Vocabulary topics:** Compound nouns; adjectives describing personal qualities; features on clothing; suffixes.

### Self-assessment

- I can talk about why people do the jobs they have.
- I can read and discuss information about someone who loves her job.
- I can present ideas for designing a work uniform.
- I can understand and discuss my classmates' presentations.
- I can write an advertisement for a job.
- I can read and talk about a poem about jobs.

### Teaching tips

**Error correction:** Decide before an activity or task if you want the focus to be *accuracy* or *fluency* and make this clear to learners too. Fluency activities that require learners to speak for longer turns (e.g. presentations, short discussions) may be restricted if you focus too much on grammatical accuracy and try to correct learners while they are speaking. Encourage learners to develop their fluency and personal confidence by allowing them to speak without interruption and then conducting an anonymous error correction focus at the end of the activity, highlighting major or repeated errors. Suggestions are made on how to conduct this in **Unit 1, Lesson 3 (Extend and challenge)** and repeated throughout for all units, with particular reference to **Lesson 3** speaking activities.

Errors that arise in question and answer exchanges with the teacher can often be managed well by using *reformulation*, i.e. you (the teacher) repeat back a corrected version of something a learner has said, without explicitly referring to the error. This technique mimics the way children learn their first language when communicating with adults around them.

# Lesson 1: Jobs and work

Learner's Book pages: 96–97

Activity Book pages: 76–77

## Lesson objectives

**Listening:** Listen to four people's accounts of how they came to do the jobs they do; match to a picture by listening for key words.

**Speaking:** Talk about which job sounds the most interesting; discuss skills and interests that you have which might lead to a job in the future.

**Critical thinking:** Express opinions about different jobs; make assumptions about future jobs based on own skills and interests.

**Language focus:** Prepositions after adjectives (expressing skills, capabilities and interests); *crazy about, (work) hard at, good with, interested in, fascinated by.*

**Vocabulary:** Compound nouns; *car mechanic, marine biologist, science teacher, police officer, conservation group, TV documentary, work experience, voluntary work, university degree*

**Materials:** poster paper or IWB slides; images representing different jobs.

## Learner's Book

###  Warm up

- To introduce the Big question, start by telling the class that this unit is going to be about jobs and work. Explain that we are going to talk about how people get their jobs and qualities and skills needed, as well as different kinds of job and what they involve. So the Big question is ... *How do people get to do the jobs they do? Why do they do their jobs?*
- Write the question on the board (for an electronic presentation, create a slide with interesting graphics). Tell learners that you are all going to do tasks and projects in the unit that will answer this question.
- Introduce the unit objectives to show learners what tasks are coming up. Present the objectives on a slide or large piece of poster paper to attach to the board.
- Tell learners that you will answer the Big question and look again at the objectives at the end of the unit. Keep the objectives slide / poster to revisit at the end of the unit.
- Tell learners that you are going to start by looking at how different people got their jobs. Introduce the topic by showing learners a selection of images that represent well-known jobs or ones specific to the country / culture in which you work, e.g. a keypad for a PC, a car mechanic's tool, a doctor's stethoscope, a nurse's thermometer, a police officer's hat, etc. Ask learners to look at the image and guess the job. Vary the images according to your learners' level of vocabulary, i.e. have a selection of obvious and more obscure images to meet all levels of ability in

the class. Try to make one image relevant to a job with which you have a personal connection (e.g. a family member's job), to make a link with discussion questions in **Activity 1**.
- Learners could then do the same activity in pairs, drawing an image from a job for their partner to guess. Then focus them on the first page of the unit and ask if they can see any of the jobs they talked about in the pictures.

### 1 💬 Talk about it

- Read the questions in **Activity 1** together first. Then put learners in pairs and ask them to talk about the questions.
- Afterwards, conduct a short feedback so learners can share their ideas as a whole class. Pick up especially on any similar ideas expressed to those in the listening text. Elicit any unusual jobs that learners have talked as this is an area which may particularly captivate learners' interest.
- **Critical thinking:** Learners relate the topic to their own experience (providing a familiar point of reference at this stage) and express opinions about jobs that are familiar to them through the experience of family members.

> **Answers**
> Learners' own answers.

### 2 Vocabulary

- Focus attention on the words in the box. Read through them together and ask learners to match them to the pictures.
- When learners have correctly matched, do some pronunciation work on difficult sounds, word stress and connected speech to prepare learners for the listening task.
- **Critical thinking:** Talk about each job: prepare learners for the listening task content by eliciting their ideas about what each job involves and skills and interests needed to do the jobs well.

> **Answers**
> **a** car mechanic (O ooo)
> **b** marine biologist (Oo oOoo)
> **c** vet
> **d** science teacher (Oo oo)
> **e** police officer (Oo ooo)

### 3 Listen 43 [CD2 Track 11]

- Tell the class that they are going to listen to four people describing how they got their jobs. Ask them to listen and write down the job described. Pause the audio after each speaker to allow them time to write the word. Then ask them to check their answers as a partner, before going through the answers as a class.
- **Extend and challenge:** To elicit more details about the information in the listening texts, ask learners these questions (either orally, after each extract, or write on the board / put on a slide):

*1 Which job needed good grades in maths and science?*
(Vet) *What subjects did Speaker 1 need to be good at?*
(maths and science)
*2 What subject did Speaker 2 like a lot at school?*
(science)
*3 Why does Speaker 2 say that 'teaching runs in my family'?* (because two of his family members have been / are teachers too)
*4 What was Speaker 3 interested in when he was a young boy?* (cars and motorbikes) *What did he do when he was fourteen years old?* (started to help his dad with his car)
*5 What did Speaker 4 see at school when he was fourteen?* (a TV documentary about pollution in the sea) *How did this help him to choose his job later on?* (he wanted to do something to help improve the situation)

---

**Audioscript:** Track 43

**1:** I've been crazy about animals ever since I was a little girl. When I was about twelve, I met a friend of my parents, who worked with animals. She said that it wasn't enough just to love animals, I had to work really hard at maths and science at school and then go to university and study for a long time. So that's what I did! It helped that I was good at maths and science anyway. So, it's no surprise to anyone that I'm a vet!

**2:** How did I get to do my job? Well, I was always really keen on science at school and I wanted to help kids understand science and enjoy it like I did. I think I'm quite good with kids in general, I understand the way they think and learn, so teaching is a perfect job for me. Oh, and my uncle was a maths teacher and one of my cousins is an English teacher, so teaching runs in our family. Oh, what do I do? I'm a science teacher in a city high school.

**3:** I've always loved cars and motorbikes. When I was little, I used to watch my dad working on his car. I became really interested in engines and I started to help my dad with his car when I was about fourteen. A friend of my dad's owned a garage and when I left school, I did work experience at his garage and I learnt how to be a car mechanic. Now I have my own garage, and my two nephews work for me.

**4:** I was always fascinated by the ocean because we live by the sea. Then something happened when I was about fourteen, which kind of changed my life. We watched a TV documentary at school about how bad the pollution in the sea was and it got me thinking … what can I do to help? So, when I was sixteen, I did some voluntary work for a conservation group with one of my friends, then later I did a university degree in marine biology – studying wildlife and plants that live in the sea. Now I work for an organisation that finds out how our oceans are changing and what we can do to protect marine wildlife.

---

**Answers**
**Speaker 1** vet
**2** science teacher
**3** car mechanic
**4** marine biologist

## 4 Talk

- **Critical thinking:** When learners have finished listening, elicit again the jobs that were described and ask them to talk in pairs about which one they think sounds the most interesting and why. Then ask learners to share their thoughts with the whole class.

---

Alternatively, you could just ask this question to the whole class, then ask each learner to choose a job from the four described and do a class vote on the most interesting.

**Answers**
Learners' own answers.

## 5 Word study

- To introduce the concept of compound nouns, put a selection of nouns on the board and ask learners first of all to tell you what kind of words they are (nouns): e.g.
  *tree / science teacher / job / motorbike / palm tree / marine wildlife*
- Ask learners which nouns have just one part and which have two parts (one part= *tree / job*; two parts = *science teacher, motorbike, palm tree, marine wildlife*). Explain that nouns with two parts like these are called *compound nouns*. Circle the examples on the board; then focus attention on the **Use of English** box and go through the explanation.
- Focus learners on **Activity 5**. Point out that these words all make up compound nouns from the listening text and ask them to match the different parts. When they have matched, they should check with their partner.
- Alternatively, you could ask learners to match the parts in a more active mingling activity. Make two or three sets (depending on class number, e.g. three sets for a class of 30) of the compound noun parts on pieces of card or paper (one word per piece). Give each learner one piece of paper / card and tell them to walk around and find the person with a word which forms a compound noun from the listening task.

**Answers**
**1** d  **2** a  **3** e  **4** b  **5** c

 For further practice, see Activity 5 in the Activity Book.

## 6 Word study

- Focus learners on the compound nouns in **Activity 6** and read out the words. Ask the class if anyone knows what these words mean. Give learners a chance to activate their own knowledge first (some might have siblings or family members studying for university degrees, for example) and then, if necessary, explain what the words mean, drawing on real life examples and the examples given in the listening extracts (e.g. Speakers 3 and 4).
- **Critical thinking:** Next ask learners to discuss briefly in pairs how these things might help someone get a job. Then invite learners to share their thoughts as a class. At this stage, support their understanding by giving them authentic examples from your own experience or that of people you know.

## 7 Listen 43 [CD2 Track 11]

- Before listening again, ask learners what they can remember about what the four speakers in **Activity 3** talked about, asking in particular about what interests and skills the speakers had that led to their choices of job.
- Focus learners on the sentences in **Activity 7**. Tell them that you are going to play the extracts again and stop after each one; they have to listen for the sentence and complete the gaps.
- **Additional support and practice:** Instead of pausing after each speaker, you could pause immediately after the focus sentence has been read, ask learners to repeat the line and then complete the gaps. For extra challenge, ask learners to shout, *Stop!* after they hear the target sentence, then pause the audio.
- When you go through the answers, give learners an extra challenge by reading some sentences correctly and some incorrectly; they have to listen carefully in order to decide if the sentence is correct or not and correct any incorrect sentences, e.g.
  Teacher: *I've been **interested about** animals since I was a little girl.*
  Learners: No! *I've been **crazy** about animals since …*
- Ask learners to tell you again which person said each sentence.
- Now focus learners on the structure of the target phrases in the sentences. Ask them to find the *adjectives* in each sentence (crazy / hard / good / interested / fascinated) and then tell you what kind of words follow (prepositions and nouns: about animals / at maths / with kids / in engines / by the ocean). Then focus their attention on the **Use of English** box in the Learner's Book and read the explanation and two example sentences.

**Answers**
1 I've been crazy about animals since I was a little girl. (Vet)
2 I had to work really hard at maths and science (Vet)
3 I think I'm quite good with kids in general. (Science teacher)
4 I became really interested in engines. (Car mechanic)
5 I was always fascinated by the ocean. (Marine biologist)

 For further practice, see Activity 3 in the Activity Book.

## 8 Talk

- First ask learners to write answers in their notebooks to the following questions to get them accustomed to using the phrases in **Activity 7** and applying them to their own experience:
  1 Write three things that you are *good at* (e.g. school subjects, hobbies, personal qualities).
  2 Now write three things that you are *interested in*.
  3 Now write something that you are really *fascinated by* (e.g. a place, topic, person, gadget).
  4 Now write something that you have to work *hard at* to get a good result.
- **Critical thinking:** Tell learners to compare their responses to their partners. Then ask them to discuss with their partner how the interest and talents that they've noted down might lead to a job in the future.
- Demonstrate the task with the whole class first. Ask a confident learner to tell you about a job he/she is interested in and why; then either write the learner's response on the board as an example, or elicit a sentence as follows:
  *I'd like to be a pilot because I'm very interested in planes. I'm also good at science and I know a lot about …*
- Ask learners to practise making similar statements in pairs. Monitor and circulate, helping out with vocabulary and encouraging the use of the target phrases.
- Conduct feedback by asking volunteers or nominating learners to share their thoughts and ideas with the class.

**Answers**
Learners' own answers.

 For further practice, see Activity 6 in the Activity Book.

##  Wrap up

- To finish off, nominate learners to tell the class about ideas (about jobs) that they had in common with their partner and ones that were very different.

## Activity Book

### 1 Read

- Learners read a text about unusual jobs and complete statements about the information in the texts by choosing the correct answers.

**Answers**
1 b    2 a    3 b    4 a    5 b

### 2 Use of English

- Learners underline four examples of *adjectives + prepositions + nouns* in the text in **Activity 1**.

**Answers**
**Text about Lisa**
fascinated by chocolate
knowledgeable about food
good with people
**Text about Tom**
good at Maths

## 3 Use of English

- Learners choose the correct preposition to complete phrases using the target language; then complete the phrases to make true sentences about themselves.

**Answers**
**1** on **2** by **3** at **4** about **5** in **6** about **7** at **8** with
Learners' own answers.

## 4 Word study

- Learners look at highlighted noun phrases in the text and decide which two are compound nouns.

**Answers**
water slides / theme parks

## 5 Word study

- Learners make five compound nouns from jumbled words in a word cloud; then identify the odd-one-out.

**Answers**
car mechanic marine biologist police officer science teacher TV documentary
Odd-one-out: TV documentary (the other compound nouns describe jobs)

## 6 Challenge

- Learners write a paragraph about a type of job that interests them, including the skills they think they need to do the job well.

**Answers**
Learners' own answers.

# Lesson 2: The joy is in the job

Learner's Book pages: 98–99
Activity Book pages: 78–79

## Lesson objectives

**Reading:** Read about someone who loves her job; practise skimming techniques to understand the sense and main points of the text.

**Speaking:** Talk about personal qualities that are important to certain jobs; interview someone you know about their job.

**Writing:** Write about the job of someone you know using their answers from the interview.

**Critical thinking:** Speculate what personal qualities are needed for different types of job.

**Vocabulary:** Media jobs: *camera operator, reporter, director, presenter, weather forecaster*; Personal qualities: *fascinating, enthusiastic, confident, friendly, calm, knowledgeable*

**Materials:** video clip of a relevant children's TV programme (optional for **Warm up**); a ball (suitable for classroom use) (optional).

## Learner's Book

###  Warm up

- You could introduce the topic by playing *20 questions* (for instructions, see **Unit 1**, **Lesson 4**, **Warm up**), choosing a media job that your learners will probably know already (to make a link with discussion questions in **Activity 1**).
- Learners could then do the same activity in pairs. Then focus them on the first page of the unit and ask if they can see any of the jobs they talked about in the pictures.
- Alternatively, you could show learners a clip from one of their favourite TV programmes and elicit what sort of jobs people do in front of the camera and behind the scenes, to make this TV programme. Use this activity to introduce and build on vocabulary that appears in **Activity 2**.

### 1 Talk about it

- Focus attention on the first two questions. If you haven't already done the video clip activity suggested in the warm-up stage, you could do it now as a lead-in to learners discussing the questions in pairs. Alternatively, ask learners to suggest popular TV programmes and talk together about the sort of jobs people do to create them (e.g. actors, writers, TV presenters, camera operators, make-up artist). Again this activity could be used to introduce and build on vocabulary that appears in **Activity 2**.
- **Additional support and practice:** If you think learners might struggle to think of relevant words themselves, you could give them a list of TV jobs and ask them to compare against a favourite TV programme/s, identifying ones that might apply. Either write the jobs on the board or, for an extra challenge (and to focus attention at the beginning of the class), dictate the words and ask learners to copy down; then work in pairs to decide if they are relevant to the programme/s in question.
- **Critical thinking:** making deductions and assumptions about TV jobs.

**Answers**
Learners' own answers.

## 2  Word study

- Focus learners on the media jobs listed in the box and read each one together. Ask them what the jobs have in common (all connected with TV) and elicit or tell them that they are *media* jobs – types of jobs that communicate information to the public (i.e. you and me).
- Some of these jobs may have been mentioned in **Activity 1**. Ask learners to look up any unknown words in their dictionaries, or read out definitions and ask learners to match to a word. You could put learners in teams and make this into a competition, adding a few more words and definitions to stretch learners further.

> **Answers**
> camera operator: someone who controls the camera that films people and scenes for TV.
> reporter: someone who researches important news for TV programmes and presents it to camera.
> presenter: someone who introduces a TV programme and guides the viewers through the contents of the programme.
> director: someone who tells the actors and TV presenters what to do and how to deliver their lines during the filming of a programme.
> weather forecaster: someone who presents information about the weather to TV audiences.

[AB] **For further practice, see Activity 2 in the Activity Book.**

## 3 Read

- Focus attention on the texts. Tell learners that they are going to read about someone who loves her job. Ask them to look at the picture and predict what kind of job the woman does from the ones mentioned in **Activity 2**. Learners could be stretched by asking them *why* they think she does a particular job. Let learners speculate – don't give them the answer yet.
- Now ask them to read the text quickly and identify the job that the woman is talking about. Give them a time limit of about two minutes to emphasise that they only have to read to gain a general sense of the text and that they are not reading for details. This is in preparation for the focus on skimming techniques in the next stage.
- Ask them to check their answer with each other after reading, before establishing the answer with the class.
- At this stage, check learners are clear about vocabulary items, *chat show, off air* and *on camera*. Ask them to find the items in the text by asking questions, e.g. *What kind of TV programme does the presenter present?* (a chat show); *find an expression which means when the programme isn't on TV and we can't see it* (off air), and *when the TV presenter is talking to the camera* (on camera).

> **Answers**
> She is a (TV) presenter.

## 4 Read

- Focus learners on **Activity 4** and ask them to read the text again to match the questions to paragraphs 1–3. Read each question together first, then draw learners' attention to the numbered paragraphs in the text. Give them a time limit of about four minutes to read the text again and match. Ask them to work individually then compare their answers with their partner.
- Check answers and ask learners which words in the text helped them match to the questions (e.g. Paragraph 1: *introduce the show ... interview children*; Paragraph 2: *love my job because ...*; Paragraph 3: *enthusiastic ... confident*)
- Next take learners through the reading strategy outlined above. First ask them why they think you gave them a strict time limit in which to do the tasks in **Activity 3** and **4**. Elicit or point out that this was to ensure that they just focused on the main points and didn't have time to worry about unknown phrases and words. This means that they will be able to read more quickly and understand more than they realise, if they are not continually focusing on unknown words. Point out that it is still possible to understand the sense of the text, even if they can't understand every word. If they have done **Activity 3** and **4** successfully, they should begin to see how the strategy works.
- Explain to learners that this technique is called *skimming*.

> **Answers**
> a 2    b 3    c 1

## 5 Word study

- Draw learners' attention back to the TV presenter in the picture. Ask if they can remember some of the qualities she mentioned in the text. Elicit ideas, then focus learners on the adjectives in blue in the text and ask how many they can see (6 adjectives).
- Read the words together and ask learners to repeat the adjectives after you, focusing on pronunciation and syllable stress (in preparation for the feedback stage and speaking task later).
- Next focus their attention on **Activity 5**. Ask: *Do these adjectives mean the same as the ones in blue?* Elicit: *No, they are antonyms or opposites.* Now tell learners to match the adjectives in blue with their opposite in **Activity 5**.
- Allow learners to do this activity in pairs so they can share their knowledge of the adjectives both in the text and **Activity 5**. Tell them to do the ones that they know first, then focus on the others (rather than doing the activity in the order, 1–6). Discourage the use of dictionaries, instead monitor and circulate, helping with vocabulary as needed. Give examples and definitions, so learners gain extra language practice in listening and speaking through their interaction with you during this task. Encourage learners to deduce meanings from the context in the text.
- Go through the answers as a class, focusing again on pronunciation.
- **Extend and challenge:** Having established the answers, you could do a quick active consolidation game, especially if learners need an energy lift.
  - Ask the class to stand up and choose a confident learner to start. Throw a ball and say an adjective from **Activity 5** (e.g. *shy*) – the learner has to catch the ball and say the opposite adjective (*confident*). He / she then throws the ball to another learner, saying another adjective from **Activity 5**. The learner catches it and says the opposite.
  - Play the game around the class. If learners have received the ball and can't say the opposite adjective, they have to sit down. If they say it correctly, they keep standing.
  - You can carry on the game by repeating the same pattern or extend by having learners say one of the adjectives in blue and the recipient has to say the opposite adjective from **Activity 5** (e.g. *enthusiastic → uninterested*). The winner is the last learner standing.

**Answers**
1 unfriendly (Ooo) – friendly (Oo)
2 uninterested (Oooo) – enthusiastic (ooooOo)
3 nervous (Oo) – calm
4 shy – confident (Ooo)
5 ignorant (Ooo) – knowledgeable (Oooo)
6 boring (Oo) – fascinating (Oooo)

## 6 Word study

- Focus learners on **Activity 6** and ask them to find other words in the text that describe personal qualities. Tell them to work individually first, then compare with their partner.
- **Critical thinking:** Then ask learners to work together to think of other words and phrases to describe personal qualities that they think might be relevant for this job or other similar jobs in the media. (There is an opportunity to extend into other job categories in the next activity). Conduct a class feedback, recording good suggestions on the board. Then ask learners to record all words and phrases in their vocabulary notebooks to build a word bank under the title: *Personal qualities*.

**Answers**
**Other words in the text to describe personal qualities:**
talented fun interesting have lots of energy be good with children
+ Learners' own answers.

 For further practice, see Activity 1 in the Activity Book.

## 7 🗨 Talk

- Focus attention on the pictures and ask learners to work in pairs. Tell them to choose two pictures that interest them and give them a minute or two to think of personal qualities that might be needed for those jobs. Then put them in pairs and ask them to tell their partner about the qualities they need to do those jobs. Do an example together first as a class, eliciting key words and phrases by gapping an example sentence as follows:
  *To be a doctor, I think you need to be _____(good at science) and _____ (knowledgeable about) ...*
- Allow early finishers to choose other jobs to talk about, or extend the activity so all learners choose another job and discuss it in the same way. You could put learners into groups, give each a different type of job or a category (e.g. *jobs caring for people; working with animals; working with children,* etc.) and ask them to brainstorm job titles and qualities needed.
- For feedback: you could ask learners to read out a sentence about a job and have other learners guess what it is, e.g. *For this job you need to be good at art and knowledgeable about flowers and plants* (a florist).

**Answers**
**Example answers:**
Florist – *interested in flowers; friendly & good with people (for selling).*

Actor – *confident; interested in people; have lots of energy; talented; enthusiastic.*

Doctor – *good at science; knowledgeable about parts of the body and medicines; good with people; confident, friendly, calm.*

Architect – *good at drawing, maths and science; knowledgeable about buildings and how they are used.*

## 8  Write

- Explain to learners that they are now going to do their own interview using the questions in **Activity 4**. This activity can be given for homework, with learners interviewing a family member or friend. Alternatively, you could arrange for a colleague from your school (or outside, if this is possible) to come into the class and be interviewed by the learners (e.g. the head teacher, another teacher who teaches a popular subject).
- Learners should ask the questions and write notes about the responses in their notebooks.
- Learners then write up their notes in the form of a description of the person's job, what they do and the qualities they need to do their job. Focus them on the text in **Activity 3** as a model but point out that the pronoun will change from 'I' to 'he' or 'she', e.g.
  *My aunt is a dentist.* She *looks at people's teeth and finds out if they are healthy or not …*
  *To do* her *job,* she *needs to be knowledgeable about … and good with …*
- Point out that they can use the correct order of the questions as a structure for their description, e.g. What the person does in their job / Why they like it (or not!) / What qualities are needed.

> **Answers**
> Learners' own answers – Portfolio opportunity.

**AB** For further practice, see Activities 3 and 4 in the Activity Book.

##  Wrap up

- When learners have written the descriptions, ask them to read each other's and note down the qualities mentioned. Then find out as a class which qualities were mentioned most often. This information could be used as a useful 'life lesson' – general qualities that are needed to do jobs well (regardless of the actual job).

## Activity Book

### 1 Vocabulary

- Learners complete gapped sentences with the correct adjective.

> **Answers**
> 1 knowledgeable
> 2 fascinating
> 3 confident
> 4 enthusiastic
> 5 friendly
> 6 calm

### 2 Vocabulary

- Learners read a definition and write the corresponding word, focusing on spelling.

> **Answers**
> 1 presenter
> 2 director
> 3 camera operator
> 4 presenter
> 5 weather forecaster

### 3 Read and Strategy check

- Learners do a multiple-choice exercise to support their understanding of the reading strategy (skimming). Then they read a text (a dialogue) about a news reporter (with missing sentences) and put four sentences in the correct place within the text.

> **Answers**
> Read quickly first to get the general sense of the whole text. ✓
> Then read the text more slowly to understand the main topic of each paragraph. ✓
> 1 b   2 d   3 c   4 a

### 4  Challenge

- Learners read the text again and write a short description of the job using headings.

> **Answers**
> **Job title:** news reporter for a local TV channel.
> **What he does:** he goes to the news scene, finds out what's happening and writes a short report. Then he stands in front of a film camera and tells the report to TV viewers at home.
> **Why he likes it:** news stories are always changing and often there is happy news to report. He enjoys telling viewers about the good things people do in their communities.
> **What qualities are needed to do the job. Why?** He needs to be knowledgeable about what's happening in his local area, so that he can choose the most interesting and important stories to report. He also needs to be confident in front of the camera and behind it too because he has to interview lots of different people to find out information. He needs to stay calm in case there are any problems.

## Lesson 3: Designing a uniform

Learner's Book pages: 100–101
Activity Book pages: 80–81

> ### Lesson objectives
>
> **Speaking:** Prepare and deliver a presentation about an idea for a uniform design for work or school.
>
> **Listening:** Listen to a presentation about an idea for a work uniform design and notice features of content.
>
> **Critical thinking:** Create and describe an idea for a uniform design. Describe how the design addresses practical issues.

**Vocabulary focus:** Features on clothing; *stripe, inside pocket, sleeve, logo, waterproof material, zip, zipped pocket, light, belt with pockets, alarm*

**Materials:** pictures of work uniforms for different types of job + one picture of a non-uniform job (for **Warm up**); poster or A3 paper, coloured pens.

## Learner's Book

### 👆 Warm up

- Put pictures on the board of several uniformed jobs (e.g. ones listed in **Activity 1** and/or ones that are specific to the country or culture in which you work). Include a picture of a non-uniformed job (e.g. an office worker, teacher, florist, etc.).
- Elicit the names of the jobs from learners and then ask which one is the odd-one-out and why. Elicit that the non-uniformed job is different because the other jobs all have *uniforms*.

### 1 💬 Talk about it

- Ask learners as a class if anyone they know wears a uniform to work. Talk generally about different uniforms and input / highlight vocabulary that will be useful for later stages. Talk about the kind of clothes people wear to work that are not part of a uniform.
- Next put learners in small groups and ask them to talk about what people wear for the jobs listed in **Activity 1**. You could focus the task more by asking them to pick three specific ones to talk about or allocate specific jobs to each group.
- Conduct a quick feedback, asking learners to share some initial ideas at this stage. Again, input / highlight vocabulary that will be useful for later stages.

**Answers**
Learners' own answers.

### 2 💬 Talk

- Ask learners first if they know of any other jobs (not mentioned in **Activity 1**) in their country which have a uniform. Then focus on one job in particular (e.g. a firefighter) and put a representative image on the board. Elicit a key duty in that job and ask learners how the uniform helps the person do that aspect of the job.
- **Critical thinking:** Ask learners to talk in pairs about other aspects of the uniform in question that help the person do the job. Then ask them if they can think of any other things that designers have to think about when they design any work uniform. Stimulate learners' thought processes by giving prompts to answer this question, e.g.

*Would a postwoman wear shoes with a heel?* (No!) *Why not?* (Because she has to walk a lot.) *Would a fire fighter wear a t-shirt?* (No! Because he has to protect his arms.)

- Elicit learners' ideas and build up a list on the board. This will assist learners in **Activity 3** and the problem solving exercise later in the lesson (when they design a work uniform).

**Answers**
**Designing a work uniform: considerations (example answers)**
The climate and weather in the country where they work ...
What the person has to do in their job, e.g. do they have to move a lot or move quickly? Will they have to do lots of walking, running, climbing, carrying, lifting, cleaning?
Are there any safety or security issues with the job?
People's different shapes, sizes and ages.
Whether men or women or both will wear the uniform.
If the uniform needs to have distinctive colours or logos so it will be easily recognised by people in a shop, street, from a distance, at night time, etc.
The times that the person will be working, e.g. when it is dark.
The cost of the uniform.
+ Learners' own answers.

### 3 Listen 🔊44 [CD2 Track 12]

- **Critical thinking:** Tell learners that they are now going to listen to someone (Lucia) presenting her idea for a work uniform. Before they listen, draw their attention to the illustration and ask which job they think the design is for. Encourage them to use modals of probability in their answers and to give reasons, e.g. *It could / might be a uniform for a ... because ... It can't be ... because ...*
- Ask learners to describe the illustration. If they mention words that will later come up in the listening task, write them on the board, to help learners with the listening task and **Activity 4** (**Word study**).
- Now tell learners that they are going to listen to the whole presentation. They need to listen to find out which job the uniform design is for. Draw their attention to points made in **Activity 2** (regarding what designers think about when they are designing uniforms) and tell them that Lucia will mention some similar points. They need to listen and identify which similar points Lucia makes.
  **Note:** Stress to learners that they are only listening for the information outlined above and not to worry about words or parts of the presentation that they don't understand.
- When you conduct feedback, establish which job Lucia's design is for and ask learners to identify other ideas mentioned from the list on the board from **Activity 2**. Tick them clearly so learners can reference them easily in the next two activities.

**Audioscript:** Track 44

**Part 1**

Good morning everyone, I'd like to present to you my idea for a new design for a postman or post woman's uniform. I noticed that the postmen in my neighbourhood need a new uniform because the clothes they wear now look uncomfortable and a bit boring.

If you look at the picture here, my new uniform is like a tracksuit, dark blue with a green and white stripe across here and down the sleeves. The top is a jacket with a zip and inside pockets, to keep money and other small things. The post office logo is on the right at the top and underneath is a blue t-shirt. As you can see, the trousers are quite wide. They are made of waterproof material from the ankle to the knee, so, if it rains a lot, the bottom of the trousers don't get wet. There are zips at the bottom and zipped pockets on the side. The postmen or women will wear trainers because they have to walk a lot and trainers are comfortable. This uniform is practical because it makes it easy for them to do their job.

**Part 2**

There is a special cap and if you look closely, you can see a light at the front. The postman or woman can switch this on if they are delivering letters very early in the morning when it is still dark. And here you can see a special belt, which has pockets to carry a mobile phone, keys and an alarm – in case the postman gets attacked by a dog – the alarm scares the dog away! The postman needs pockets and the belt to carry things, so that his hands are free to deliver the letters. He also has a pocket on the belt to carry an i-pod – so he can listen to music while he works.

As you can see, my uniform design will suit people who are all shapes and sizes – big or slim, tall or small – because the clothes are loose-fitting and stretchy. I hope all postmen and women will feel comfortable and smart in my design!

**Answers**

Lucia is presenting an idea for a postman/woman's uniform. Possible ideas from Activity 2 that are mentioned are:
*Climate and weather.*
*What the person has to do in their job – in this case, lots of walking, carrying things.*
*Working hours – especially when there is little or no natural daylight.*
*People of all shapes and sizes will wear the uniform.*
*Safety and security issues (e.g. the need for an alarm and a head light)*

---

## Speaking tip

Point out to learners the importance of pictures and diagrams in presentations. These devices help the audience to follow the presentation and provide a focus for their attention, which can help learners feel less self-conscious as they get used to the task of speaking in front of a group. Visual images provide a framework on which to 'hook' the presentation, as the presenter can organise the presentation around the pictures and diagrams.

## 4 Word study

- Focus learners again on the illustration and ask them to work in pairs to identify the different features on the clothing.

---

- Go through the answers as a class, then ask learners to find as many of these features as they can on their own clothes and on any clothing that might be nearby (e.g. jackets or PE kit).
- Focus learners on the **Speaking tip**, and explain the points outlined above. Tell them to look at Lucia's illustration when they listen to her presentation again in the next two activities and notice how she refers to her picture in her presentation.

**Answers**

a stripe
b inside pocket
c sleeve
d logo
e waterproof material
f zip
g zipped pocket
h light
i belt with pockets
j alarm

 For further practice, see Activities 1, 2 and 3 in the Activity Book.

## 5 Listen 44 [CD2 Track 12]

- Now focus learners' attention on **Activity 5**. Read through the questions and ask learners to listen for the answers. Tell them that they are only going to listen to the first part of the presentation and they need only listen for the answers to the questions (i.e. they don't have to understand the entire text).
- Play the extract.
- **Additional support and practice:** If learners need extra support in identifying the answers to the questions, pause the audio directly after the relevant bits and elicit the answers straight away (rather than play the entire extract all the way through).
- After listening, give learners a minute or so to discuss the answers with their partner. Then conduct feedback.

**Audioscript:** Track 44
(see Activity 3 page 145)

**Answers**

1 She thinks that the clothes they wear now look uncomfortable and a bit boring.
2 Inside pockets are useful to keep money and other small things.
 Waterproof material protects the bottom of the trousers from getting wet, if it rains a lot.
 Training shoes: postmen/women have to walk a lot and trainers are comfortable

## 6 Listen 44 [CD2 Track 12]

- Tell learners they are now going to listen to just Part 2. Follow the same procedure as outlined in **Activity 5**. Make sure learners understand the meaning of *tracksuit* (show them an example, e.g. PE kit or the illustration in **Activity 3**) and *style* (a design that looks similar).

- If necessary play the audio for Parts 1 and 2 again, stopping after each part that answers the questions in **Activities 5** and **6**.

> **Answers**
> a  A cap with a light: this will help the postman / woman to see if they are delivering post when it is dark.
>   A belt with pockets: to carry a mobile phone, keys, an alarm and an i-pod
>   An alarm: this will protect against attacks by dogs.
> b  Lucia thinks that a tracksuit style uniform will suit all people and be comfortable to wear, whatever their shape or size.

## 7 Listen 44 [CD2 Track 12]

- Focus learners on **Activity 7** and ask them how many phrases they can see (5). Tell them to read the rubric and tell you why Lucia used these phrases in her presentation (to draw her classmates' attention to her picture).
- To elicit the words to complete the phrases, play the whole presentation again and ask learners to either call out, *Stop!* or put their hands up when they hear a target phrase. Then stop the audio to allow them time to write the phrase in their notebooks. (To save time, you could ask them to copy the sentence parts in their notebooks before listening, leaving a gap to complete the rest when they listen).
- **Additional support and practice:** Instead of listening for and copying the sentences directly from the audio, write the missing sentence parts on the board and ask learners to match and complete the parts in 1–5 first. Then they listen to check, calling out, *Stop!* or putting their hand up when they hear a target sentence.
- Point out to learners how these phrases link with the **Speaking tip** (outlined in **Activity 4**).

> **Answers**
> 1  If you look at the picture here, my new uniform is like a tracksuit,
> 2  This is the post office logo
> 3  As you can see, the trousers are quite wide.
> 4  If you look closely, you can see a light at the front.
> 5  And here you can see a special belt, which has pockets to carry a mobile phone.

 **For further practice, see Activities 4, 5 and 6 in the Activity Book.**

## 8 Talk

- **Critical thinking:** Ask learners to discuss the three questions in pairs. Did they like Lucia's idea? Why? Why not? How similar or different is it to the uniform postmen/women wear in their country? Which of Lucia's ideas would they change to better suit their country?

- Make time for a class feedback to share ideas as this will help stimulate ideas for learners' own presentations in the next stage.

> **Answers**
> Learners' own answers.

## Present it!

- **Critical thinking:** Tell learners that they are now going to prepare their own presentations about their own ideas for work uniforms. Take them through the step-by-step instructions outlined in the Learner's Book. Learners could also design sports strips or alternative school uniforms, if you feel it would be more suitable for your class. Designs can also be humorous or fantastical, if preferred (but learners need to be able to explain their design decisions, however outlandish).
- Go through key points from Lucia's presentation that they can draw on: 1) her illustration of her design idea; 2) her use of vocabulary to describe special clothing features, labelled on her picture; 3) her use of specific phrases to direct her audience's attention to the illustration as she speaks; 4) the way her design reflects solutions to problems she sees with the current postmen's / women's uniform.
- Put learners into pairs or groups of three to prepare and deliver their presentations. Ask them to discuss work uniforms (or school uniforms or sports strips) that are worn in their country and decide which ones they would like to change. Make sure they are clear about the reasons *why* they would like to make changes and that their new design should reflect solutions to problems they see in the original designs.
- Ask them to draw a large, clear picture to illustrate their idea on poster paper (stress that it doesn't have to be a perfect picture).
- Ask learners to make a first draft of their presentation, using Lucia's as a model as follows:
  - 1 Purpose of presentation: what the new design is for and why the current design needs changing.
  - 2 Explanation of each new feature and the reason why it has been included (using the illustration to guide the explanation).
  - 3 An overall comment about the design as a whole.
- Tell them to think about who their audience is going to be, to make the purpose of the presentation clear at the beginning, and to add sequencing phrases (all points from previous presentation tasks). E.g.
  *Today we're going to present to you our idea for ...*
- They should produce one text per group, either in class time or at home. Check the scripts for grammar, vocabulary and organisation; however, the emphasis is on organisation and quality of ideas rather than perfectly accurate scripts.

- Give learners the opportunity to practise their presentations together. Each member of the group should deliver a part of the presentation. Monitor the groups, making sure you spend some time with each, helping with any pronunciation difficulties. Check that everyone has a part to present and that someone is responsible for displaying the illustration of the idea.
- Ask learners to deliver their presentations in pairs or groups of three in front of the class. Introduce each group first and generate a supportive atmosphere by having learners applaud each group before and after each presentation. When each group finishes, make a positive comment about their presentation; invite questions from the audience if there is time.
- **Additional support and practice:** Use of notes in delivery: stronger learners may be able to deliver without looking too closely at their notes; others may need to read from their notes at this stage. Use your discretion with regard to how much you allow this, taking into account ability and confidence levels in your class. Ultimately in later years, learners need to be able to deliver oral presentations without reading word for word from notes. Ideally, we should encourage them to get into this habit as soon as possible but learners will probably need the support of reading from their notes in these early stages.
- **Extend and challenge:** As learners are delivering their presentations, note down main errors; either give to each group a note of the errors to correct themselves, or write up on the board at the end for a class error correction session (without stating which group or individual made the errors).
- **Note:** This would come after plenty of positive feedback regarding the presentations. Positive feedback must always come first and be emphasised.

> **Answers**
> Learners' own answers.

AB **For further practice, see Activity 7 in the Activity Book.**

## Wrap up
- **Critical thinking:** At the end, have a vote on the best design idea. Alternatively, you could have several categories – most realistic idea / craziest idea / best art work, etc.

## Activity Book

### 1 Vocabulary
- Learners label the illustration from the Learner's Book with target vocabulary describing clothing features.

> **Answers**
> 1 stripe   2 sleeve   3 logo   4 zip   5 pocket   6 belt
> 7 inside pocket   8 belt with pocket   9 wide-legged design
> 10 trainers   11 waterproof material

### 2 Vocabulary
- Learners match sentence halves (a – e) describing features on the illustration with the picture (labelled 7–11).

> **Answers**
> 7 a   8 e   9 d   10 c   11 b

### 3 Vocabulary
- Learners match sentence halves (1–5) to sentence halves (a–e) in **Activity 2**, to make complete sentences describing the clothing features and the reason for their inclusion in the design.

> **Answers**
> 1 c   2 a   3 e   4 b   5 d

### 4 Listen 72 [CD2 Track 40]
- Learners listen to Part 1 of a two-part text of a girl talking about her school sports kit and match the description with a picture.

> **Audioscript:** Track 72
> **Part 1**
> If you look at this picture here, you can see the sports kit that we wear at school for cross-country runs. As you can see, it has dark blue tracksuit trousers with a white stripe down the side and a dark blue t-shirt with short sleeves. The t-shirt has the school logo here on the top right hand side. We also carry a small backpack to carry water and some snacks to eat, when we run long distances. When the weather is colder, we wear a dark blue tracksuit top with a zip at the front. The logo is in the same place as the t-shirt and it has a white stripe down each sleeve, to match the tracksuit trousers.

> **Answers**
> Picture b

### 5 Listen 72 [CD2 Track 40]
- Learners listen to Part 1 again and correct the underlined word in a list of statements about the description in **Activity 4**.

> **Answers**
> 1 running   2 dark blue   3 stripe   4 right   5 backpack   6 zip

### 6 Listen 73 [CD2 Track 41]
- Learners listen to Part 2 and cross out the incorrect word in a list of statements about the listening text.

> **Audioscript:** Track 73
> **Part 2**
> There are some things I'd like to change about this sports kit. Firstly, the colour is very dark and I think we need a brighter stripe on the t-shirt and top – maybe a high visibility stripe. Then people in cars could see us more clearly when we are running near roads or when there isn't much sunlight. Secondly, the school logo is quite small and you can't see it very clearly. It would be better if it was at the top of the sleeve, near the shoulder. Thirdly, the backpack needs a side pocket for the water bottle. At the moment, the bottle has to go inside the backpack and you can feel it moving around when you are running.

## 7 📝 Challenge

- Learners design a sports kit for their favourite sport. They have to draw their design, then write a description about the different features. Alternatively, they can change the design of a sports kit they currently use. Prompts are given to help structure the description.

# Lesson 4: Looking for a job

Learner's Book pages: 102–103

Activity Book pages: 82–83

## Lesson objectives

**Reading:** Read three unusual job advertisements and notice features of content, style and use of language.

**Writing:** Write an advertisement for an unusual job.

**Critical thinking:** Using own knowledge to think of ways people can get a job; matching abilities and interests to suitable jobs; create an advertisement for an unusual job.

**Language focus:** Present continuous tense to describe actions happening now.

**Materials:** job advertisements from magazines, newspapers, the Internet (authentic or invented) (for **Warm up**). Copies of **Photocopiable activity 13**.

## Learner's Book

###  Warm up

- Put learners in small groups and distribute some simple job advertisements (e.g. classifieds) from newspapers, magazines, online, etc. (authentic or invented). Elicit the text type (job advertisements) and the type of jobs they are advertising. Elicit more details as appropriate, depending on time available and learner ability.
- Alternatively, you could project the advertisements and ask learners to answer the same questions by looking at the images on the screen.
- Explain to learners that you are all going to look at more job advertisements in the lesson today.

### 1 💬 Talk about it

- **Critical thinking:** Focus learners on the questions in **Activity 1** and ask them if they know any more ways people can get a job besides through an advertisement. They can answer this question in pairs, or as a class.

### 2 Read

- Focus learners on the advertisements in **Activity 2**. Read the job titles in the box together. Then give learners a time limit of about two minutes to read the advertisements and match to a job title.
- When they've finished, ask them to compare their answers with their partner before going through the answers as a class.
- **Extend and challenge:** Ask these questions to ask learners to analyse the texts further and extract more information. You could conduct the activity as a reading race, putting learners in teams to find the answers and win points, or put the questions on a slide and ask them to write the answers.
  1 *What do you have to be knowledgeable about to get the astronaut job?* (planets)
  2 *For which job do you have to be really interested in science?* (the inventor)
  3 *Where will the interviews be for the astronaut job?* (in the satellite station)
  4 *What qualities do you need for the zookeeper job?* (be interested in all animals, be brave)
  5 *Which type of transport should you be able to fly for the astronaut's job?* (a rocket)
  6 *Which job is looking for someone to be the boss of a team?* (zookeeper – 'lead the team')
  7 *Where can you find more information about the inventor job?* (on the website)
  8 *Where will the interview be for the inventor job?* (in the time machine)
- Focus learners on the information contained in the advertisements – what kind of person the interviewers want to apply for the job (e.g. *an enthusiastic astronaut ... genius-level inventor ... friendly zookeeper ...*); qualities and abilities needed (e.g. *Must know a lot about planets; must be fascinated by science ...*); where to get more information (e.g. *please visit our website...*); where interviews take place (e.g. *interviews will be held in the lion enclosure*).

### 3 Read

- **Critical thinking:** Focus learners on the statements (1–4) in **Activity 3**. Read them together and then ask learners to read the text again and decide which of the candidates are suitable for any of the jobs. Check

learners understand *candidates* (someone who applies for a job), *biology* (study of living things), *natural science* (study of nature), *astronomy* (study of planets and stars in space).
- Ask learners to do the task individually, then check answers with their partner. Then go through the answers as a class.
- **Extend and challenge:** Ask learners which job they would like to apply for and why. Ask them how their chosen job links in with skills and interests they already have.

> **Answers**
> **1** Priya inventor
> **2** Finn zookeeper
> **3** Zainab astronaut

 **For further practice, see Activities 1 and 2 in the Activity Book.**

## 4  Use of English

- Focus learners on the target language by writing the following sentences on the board (or slide) and ask learners to read the text to find the missing words:
  *We _____ for enthusiastic and dedicated astronauts ...* (are looking)
  *We _____ genius-level inventors ...* (are recruiting)
- Ask learners to identify the action in the sentence (are looking / are recruiting). Ask them if it is a regular action or something happening at the moment (at the moment). Ask them if the interviewers have found the people for the job and establish that no, they are still looking – so the action is ongoing / continuous.
- Focus learners on the form and ask how we make the sentence (with *be* + verb + *-ing*).
- Focus learners on the question in **Activity 4** and ask them to complete it in pairs.

> **Answers**
> The form of the verb, *to be*, changes according to the pronoun.
> I **am** looking ... He/she **is** looking ...

 **For further practice, see Activities 3 and 4 in the Activity Book.**

## 5  Use of English

- First, draw learners' attention to the **Writing tip** by writing some full versions of sentences from the advertisements on the board, e.g.
  *You must know a lot about planets.*
  *Experience is needed ...*
  *You must be fascinated by science.*
- Ask them if these sentences are the same as those that appear in the advertisements. If they don't notice immediately, ask them to find the sentences in the text and tell you how they are different.
- Ask learners why they think shortened sentences are used in advertisements. Elicit or explain that advertisements need to communicate a lot of information in as few words as possible. Advertisers

usually have to pay for every word they use and this means they have to miss out some words.
- Mention to learners now that they are going to write their own advertisement and they will need to use shortened sentences to make it look like a real one. First, focus them on the advertisement text in **Activity 5** and explain that the text has two problems: 1) some of the sentences are too long and 2) there are mistakes in the grammar in some of the sentences. Ask them to correct the text and then check with their partner.
- To go through the answers, read the text aloud with errors and ask learners to either call out, *Stop!* and then tell you the correction, or put their hands up when they hear an error.

> **Answers**
> Are you good with a spade? We <u>are</u> looking for a talented gardener.
> - ~~You~~ Must be crazy about flowers and plants.
> - ~~You~~ Must be calm and not afraid of bugs and insects.
> - Experience ~~is~~ needed.
> - We are interview<u>ing</u> now. Call us on 6978 5454

 **For further practice, see Activities 3 and 4 in the Activity Book.**

##  Write

- **Critical thinking:** To help learners generate ideas for writing their own job advertisements, put them into small groups and ask them to brainstorm ideas using the following categories:
  *Unusual jobs*
  *A job you would like to do*
  *A job you would like someone to do for you*
  *A job you would like someone to do in your school*
- Learners need to think of two ideas to form into job advertisements, using the examples in **Activity 2** as models. Depending on their level, your learners can either create the advertisements individually (and then have a partner proofread it), or create the advertisements together in pairs, (and hand to another pair to proofread).
- Draw their attention to the order of the advertisement text, as explained in **Activity 2**: *kind of person / qualities and abilities needed / where to get more information / where interviews take place.*
- Circulate and monitor, helping especially with vocabulary (as this will be very specific according to learners' individual ideas).
- When learners have completed a first draft, ask them to swap with a partner (or another pair, if learners are collaborating on this task) and proofread each other's work, checking grammar (use of present continuous), spelling and use of shortened sentences where possible.
- When learners are ready to draft their final versions, ask them to draw a picture or decorate their texts.

- When final drafts are completed, ask learners to display them on the classroom wall. Ask learners to walk around and read each other's job advertisements, then choose one job that they would like to do.

> **Answers**
> Learners' own answers.

 **For further practice, see Activity 5 in the Activity Book.**

 **Wrap up**

- **Critical thinking:** When learners have read each other's advertisements, ask them to share with the class which job they would like to do and why.

## Activity Book

### 1 Read

- Learners read the first lines of three advertisements and match to a picture.

> **Answers**
> 1 c    2 a    3 b

### 2 Read

- Learners match lines from the rest of the advertisements to the correct jobs in **Activity 1** and write the correct sentence numbers.

> **Answers**
> **a** 1, 5, 11, 8
> **b** 3, 9, 12, 7
> **c** 2, 6, 10, 4

### 3 Use of English

- Learners complete sentences using the correct form of the present continuous with verbs in the box.

> **Answers**
> 1 is studying
> 2 am sending
> 3 are selling
> 4 are not sitting / aren't sitting
> 5 are / speaking
> 6 not watching

### 4 Use of English

- Learners complete sentences about themselves using the present continuous.

> **Answers**
> Learners' own answers.

## 5 Challenge

- Learners complete a job advertisement with their own ideas.

> **Answers**
> Learners' own answers.

**For a collaborative activity related to creating a business (practising adjective + preposition structures), see Photocopiable activity 13.**

# Lesson 5: Achieving a goal

Learner's Book pages: 104–105
Activity Book pages: 84–85

### Lesson objectives

**Listening and reading:** Listen to and read a poem about jobs and work. Answer questions about poem content and themes.

**Speaking:** Discuss poem themes about job types and attitudes to work.

**Writing:** Write some rhyming lines using the poem as a model.

**Critical thinking:** Discuss the kind of job you'd like to have and why; discuss attitudes towards work and jobs; consider the steps needed to achieve a goal.

**Language focus:** *Could* for possibility.
**Vocabulary:** Suffixes: jobs with *-er, -or, -ist* endings
**Values:** Working hard and setting goals.

**Materials:** vocabulary cards; pictures of jobs (optional), poster paper and pens (optional). Copies of **Photocopiable activity 14.**

### Learner's Book

 **Warm up**

- Make sets of vocabulary cards (see **Unit 6** overview, **Teaching tip**), one for each small group of learners, with the following words:
  *a doctor   a nurse   a builder   a dentist   a singer an actor   an artist   a hairdresser   a plasterer   a fire fighter   a police officer   a teacher   a car mechanic*
- Put learners into small groups and give each a set of cards. Ask them to turn over the cards so they can't see the words. Then ask one learner in each group to pick up a card, read it, but not show it to the other team mates.
- Ask the learners with the cards to act or mime the job on the card. Do a demonstration with the class beforehand if necessary. The other learners in the group have to guess the job. If they guess correctly, they keep the card. The winner in each group is the learner who has collected the most cards by guessing correctly.

- At the end of the miming activity, ask learners to put all the cards together on their tables, face up so they can see the names of the jobs. Now ask them to categorise the jobs as follows:
Artistic jobs (e.g. creative, entertainment) / practical jobs (e.g. manual jobs) / jobs helping other people (e.g. caring professions, public service, or medical).

**Answers**
Artistic: a singer, an actor, an artist, a hairdresser.
Practical: a builder, a plasterer, a car mechanic.
Helping people: a doctor, a nurse, a dentist, a fire fighter, a police officer, a teacher.

## 1  Talk about it

- Focus learners on the questions in **Activity 1**. Ask them to discuss these in pairs or small groups with reference to the jobs on cards in front of them. Then share as a class.
- Ask learners to think of more jobs to add to the categories.

**Answers**
Learners' own answers.

## 2 Read 45 [CD2 Track 13]

- Tell learners that they are now going to read and listen to a poem about jobs called *You can be anything* by Teri Hopkins. Ask them to describe the illustrations on pages 108 and 109, then read the question in **Activity 2**. Then tell the class to listen, looking for answers to the question. Stress that, at this point, they only need look for this information and not to worry about words they do not understand.
- Start the audio and tell learners to read the poem while listening.
- After reading / listening, go through the answers with the class and ask them to match the jobs in the poem to the illustrations.

**Audioscript:** Track 45
**See Learner's Book pages 104–105.**

**Answers**
Poem mentions *doctor, builder, dentist, singer, actor, hairdresser, plasterer, fire fighter, police officer, scientist by title.*
It also mentions *blacksmith* by description (verse 1, line 6).

## 3 Talk 45 [CD2 Track 13]

- **Critical thinking:** Put learners in small groups and ask them to focus on the last illustration of the boy and the girl (considering different jobs and 'dreaming') on page 105. Ask them what jobs the children are dreaming about. Then ask them what they think the children could do to help them get the jobs they want when they are older.
- Tell learners that they are going to read and listen to the poem again. Afterwards, focus them on the questions in **Activity 3**. Read through the questions together and then ask them to discuss in their groups.

Point out that they should be prepared to share their thoughts with the class afterwards.
- **Additional support and practice:** You could divide the questions up, giving some groups questions 1 and 2 and others, 3 and 4 (so learners don't have to answer all but benefit from hearing feedback on all answers later on). Questions 1 and 2 are arguably a little more straightforward than 3 and 4, so you could divide the questions up according to learners' abilities and levels of language.

**Answers**
1 The poem mentions ten jobs by title (*doctor, builder, dentist, singer, actor, hairdresser, plasterer, fire fighter, police officer, scientist by title*. It also mentions *blacksmith* by description (verse 1, line 6). Total: 11 jobs.
   There are some similarities in terms of loose categories such as artistic, manual and helping people (see warm-up stage and Activity 1). However, most jobs are quite diverse in nature.
2 The writer might be making the point that potentially there are many different jobs open to us all and that the possibilities are endless.
3 The writer advises that your job should make you feel happy and if you feel happy in your work you will always be successful; that you should make an effort and have ambitious goals.
4 Learners' own answers.

[AB] **For further practice, see Activity 1 in the Activity Book.**

## 4 Word study

- Ask learners to copy the table in **Activity 4** in their notebooks. Then focus them on the endings, *-er, -or, -ist,* and explain that these endings (*suffixes*) are very common in words that describe the person doing a job.
- Now ask learners to look for ten words for jobs in the poem, look at the word endings and write them in the correct column in their notebooks. When they've finished, they should try and add five more jobs to the list, using the other **Unit 7** lessons to help them, if necessary.
- **Extend and challenge:** You could do a quick 'job quiz' to practise listening skills and test learners' understanding of definitions. Give then definitions of the jobs in **Activity 4** and ask them to respond with the job title, e.g.
*Who does experiments to find out about important things?* (a scientist)
*Who performs on a stage or in a film?* (an actor)
Then ask learners if they know anyone who does any of the jobs in the poem.

**Answers**

| -er | -or | -ist |
|---|---|---|
| builder | doctor | dentist |
| singer | actor | scientist |
| hairdresser | | |
| plasterer | | |
| fire fighter | | |
| police officer | | |

Learners' own answers, e.g. florist, news reporter, weather forecaster, TV presenter, director, camera operator,

For further practice, see Activities 2 and 3 in the Activity Book.

## 5 Pronunciation 46 [CD2 Track 14]

- Focus learners on **Activity 5**. Ask them to listen to the second verse of the poem again. What rhyming sounds can they hear at the end of each line?

> **Answers**
> **1** try / sky
> **2** day / may
> **3** hair / dare
> **4** walls / halls

## 6 Pronunciation 47 [CD2 Track 15]

- Ask learners to repeat the rhyming words and sounds in **Activity 5**. Then put them in pairs and ask them to match the words and sounds to the words in **Activity 6**.

> **Audioscript and answers**
> my (try / sky )
> way (day / may)
> share (hair / dare)
> falls (walls / halls)

 For further practice, see Activities 4, 5 and 6 in the Activity Book.

## 7 Use of English

- Read the two lines of the poem from the **Use of English** box. Ask learners to find other lines with *could* in the poem and elicit six or seven examples around the class. This will stress how frequently the structure appears in the poem, (emphasising the poem theme of possibility).
- Focus learners on the three definitions for *could* in **Activity 7**. Ask learners which one they think is the correct definition for the use of *could* in the poem. If learners have any problems with choosing the correct definition, remind them of the points mentioned in **Activity 3**, question 2, about the poem's message: many types of job exist in the world and there are many *possibilities*.

> **Answers**
> **3** It is *possible* that you will be a doctor or a dentist.

 For further practice, see Activities 7 and 8 in the Activity Book.

## 8  Write

- Focus learners on the pictures and elicit the jobs in the illustrations (Picture 1: artist; 2: footballer).
- Ask them to try and complete the sentences under the pictures using the structure in the poem. First brainstorm words to describe what an artist does (e.g. *looks at things, draws, paints,* etc.) and what a footballer does (e.g. *kicks the ball, scores goals, tackles, dribbles the ball,* etc.). Then ask learners to work in pairs to make two rhyming sentences, using any of the words on the board.

- Next, ask learners to use their own ideas and vocabulary to make two more sentences. Distribute some photos of different jobs to give them ideas. Tell them to try and make the sentences rhyme if possible but allow non-rhyming sentences if you think this would be more manageable for them.
- **Additional support and practice:** As an alternative to having learners construct their own rhyming sentences, put the following sentences on the board in a mixed up arrangement and ask learners to match rhyming pairs.
  *You could be a florist who sells beautiful flowers. / You could be an architect who designs buildings and towers. You could be a police officer who protects the law./ You could be a dentist caring for teeth that are sore. You could be a reporter who tells us the news. / You could be anything you like but you must choose!*
- During feedback, ask learners to read out sentences they have invented for the class.

> **Answers**
> You could be an artist who paints / looks and draws
> You could be a footballer who kicks and scores
> Learners' own answers.

## 9 🗨 Values

- Focus learners on the **Values** heading and read through the first question together. If possible, give learners an example of something you (the teacher) have worked hard to achieve and how you felt afterwards
- Then put learners into pairs to discuss the questions. They need to talk about the questions, drawing on their personal experiences.
- Conduct a short feedback; ask learners to volunteer answers.
- Focus learners on Liam's notes in question 2 and ask the class what they think Liam wants to achieve. Give them a short time to read and take in the text.
- Ask the class question 3 and elicit what actions Liam is going to take to achieve his goal. If they are slow to respond, ask the following questions to focus them on the target points:
  *How often is Liam going to practise? When? How long?* (every day, half an hour after school and Saturday mornings)
  *Who is he going to tell about his goals?* (Dad and Jake)
  *When is the United match?* (28th Aug) *Who's he going to watch?* (the strikers)
  *When are the trials for the* under-12s school team? (10th and 11th September)
- Now ask learners to write down a goal that they want to achieve. Give them a short time to think about it. If they are stuck for ideas, focus them on the topic areas in question 1.
- Then ask them to work in pairs again, tell each other their goals and help each other to write a list of actions that will help them achieve their goal (using Liam's notes as a model).
- At the end, ask confident learners to share their ideas with the class.

- Alternatively choose a 'class goal'. This could be something that you (the teacher) would like your class to aim for. Ask learners to work in small groups and write down action points on poster paper for achieving the class goal. Then put on the wall and vote on the best plan. Make a class commitment to follow that plan.

> **Answers**
> 1 Learners' own answers.
> 2 Liam wants to be a striker in the school football team.
> 3 Liam is going to: practise every day, half an hour after school and Saturday mornings (he says *when* he is going to practice and for *how long*); let people close to him know what he wants to achieve so that they are better able to help him; watch a football match on a specified date with the particular aim of watching how the strikers play (to pick up tips); put his name down for the trials for the new school team; attend the trials on the 10th and 11th September.
> 4 Learners' own answers.

 **Wrap up**

- If learners discuss individual plans and goals in **Activity 9**, ask confident learners to share their ideas with the class.

## Activity Book

### 1 Read

- Learners read the poem, *You can be anything* by Teri Hopkins again, and tick the sentences that express the advice in the poem.

> **Answers**
> **1 3 4 5 6 8**

### 2 Word study

- Learners complete the words for jobs with the correct suffix. Then they identify the jobs that appear in the poem.

> **Answers**
> scientist florist fire fighter
> teacher police officer dentist
> builder hairdresser artist doctor
> singer actor plasterer
> **Jobs in poem:** scientist, fire fighter, police officer, dentist, builder, hairdresser, doctor, singer, actor, plasterer

### 3 Word study

- Learners match a word in **Activity 2** to a picture.

> **Answers**
> **a** doctor **b** a builder **c** a dentist **d** scientist

### 4 Pronunciation 74 [CD2 Track 42]

- Learners listen and repeat rhyming sounds from the poem and identify the rhyming sound.

> **Answers**
> 1 try / sky          2 day / may
> 3 hair / dare        4 balls / halls

### 5 Pronunciation 74 [CD2 Track 42]

- Learners match sounds in other words to the rhyming sounds in **Activity 4**.

> **Answers**
> **a** calls (4 balls / halls)
> **b** lie (1 try / sky)
> **c** pay (2 day / may)
> **d** care (3 hair / dare)

### 6 Pronunciation

- Learners write a word that rhymes with each word pair in **Activity 4**.

> **Answers**
> Learners' own answers.

### 7 Use of English

- Learners complete gapped sentences with *could* or *couldn't* and a verb from the box.

> **Answers**
> 1 could work
> 2 could learn
> 3 could watch
> 4 could finish
> 5 could be
> 6 couldn't travel

### 8 Use of English

- Learners complete sentences with *could* or *couldn't* to make them true for them.

> **Answers**
> Learners' own answers.

 To review job-related vocabulary, see **Photocopiable activity 14**.

## Lesson 6: Choose a project

Learner's Book pages: 108–109

> ### Lesson objectives
>
> **Speaking:** Deliver a presentation about a job you would like to have; revise unit themes; discuss **Unit 7** Big question.
>
> **Writing:** Organise and prepare notes for a presentation; prepare and write a quiz about different jobs; revise unit themes.
>
> **Critical thinking:** Select information to include in the presentation or quiz; consider a job you would like to have and the reasons why; make assumptions about qualities needed to do certain jobs; apply new skills and language acquired in **Unit 7** to project work and revision activities.

**Language focus:** Recycling language points from **Unit 7:** prepositions after adjectives; present continuous forms (actions happening now); *could* (expressing possibility).

**Vocabulary:** Compound nouns; adjectives describing personal qualities; features on clothing; suffixes

**Materials:** electronic slides (if available).

## Learner's Book

### Warm up

- Put learners in small teams and play the *Name 3* game to revise some language and themes from **Unit 7** and encourage learners to use 'chunks' of language. This game will also help generate ideas for both projects.
- Tell learners that you have a list of three items in front of you that they have to guess to win points for their team. Focus them on items or language you wish to review or focus on, e.g.
  - Three things a TV presenter does: *speaks in front of a camera / interviews people / finds out information:* (note focus on 'chunks' of language – verb/noun phrases, as well as revision of unit themes)
  - Three qualities a doctor needs: *knowledgeable about medicine / kind / good at science:* (note focus on adjective + preposition phrases).
- For a variation on this game to challenge higher levels, see **Extend and challenge**. For a simpler version of the game, see **Additional support and practice**.
- Read out the question. Learners need to brainstorm words and phrase and when they have three, raise their hand. Three answers that correspond with teacher's own answers gets the team three points; if the team gives less than three answers, then the other teams have a chance to win the points.
  **Note:** Only allow learners to win the points if they give three identical or similar answers to the teacher's – this makes them think more carefully about *all* their answers and ensures they generate more language.
- Do a practice round first to make sure learners are clear about the rules of the game.
- After each round, record points on the board and declare an overall winner at the end. Remember to congratulate *all* teams on their efforts too.

---

**Differentiated instruction**

**Additional support and practice**

- You could allow learners to write any three items to answer the question, i.e. their answers don't have to match the teacher's – they can gain points for just three good answers.

**Extend and challenge**

- Three items can be extended to five or more for some or all the questions.
- Tell learners they are now going to choose from the two projects and follow the instructions below for the one they have decided on.

---

## 1 A quiz about different jobs

- Learners can do this project in pairs or small groups. Take them through the step-by-step instructions presented in the Learner's Book. See also the **Teaching tip** in the **Unit 2** overview for advice on managing the research stage.
- **Additional support and practice:** You could vary the number of questions learners write for the quiz according to ability, and also restrict themes (e.g. *building* and *medicine* only); e.g. stronger learners could write two or three questions for each category; other learners – one question for each category or five each for *building* and *medicine* topics (total: 10 questions).
- Ask learners to write a rough draft first and check it for grammar, vocabulary and spelling. Then ask them to write the quiz in a presentable form and decorate with pictures.
- Finally, they hand their quiz to another group to complete.

---

**Answers**
Learners' own answers.

---

### Wrap up

- When learners have finished doing each other's quizzes, hand them back to the original groups for marking. Finally, compare scores across the class.

## 2  Do a presentation about a job you would like to have

- Depending on the language and confidence levels of your learners (and class time available) they could do this task either individually or in pairs or small groups. Although the presentation theme is a personal one, learners could still work together and choose a job that interests both or all of them.
- Take them through the step-by-step instructions presented in the Learner's Book.
- **Critical thinking:** Spend time talking to them about the type of job they wish to focus on. Draw their attention to the content areas outlined in stage 2 to help focus their research and organise their notes. Also refer them to the text in **Lesson 2**, for useful background in describing a job.
  **Note:** The choice of job could be quite serious or humorous or outlandish, depending on the personalities of your learners. Allow them to interpret the theme in any way that engages them or feels comfortable.
- With regard to researching the job in question, refer to the **Teaching tip** in **Unit 2** overview for more advice on how to manage the research of any project theme. Learners could also interview someone who actually does the job that interests them, if this could be arranged (using the questions in **Lesson 2**). If learners make a choice of job that is difficult to research, they could imagine and invent answers for the different sections outlined in stage 2.

- When learners are drafting the presentation, monitor and make sure they are using sequencing phrases to guide the audience through the presentation.
- Allow time for preparing visuals for the presentation, e.g. slides and pictures relevant to the job in question.
- Give learners time to practise their presentation, ensure that each member has a part to say and that someone is responsible for organising the props (slides, pictures, etc.). If learners are delivering a presentation on their own, team them up in pairs, so they can practise and listen to each other's.
- **Critical thinking:** While learners deliver their presentations, ask the audience to make a note of the job described with a view to voting on the most interesting or most unusual one at the end.

**Answers**
Learners' own answers.

 **Wrap up**
- Ask learners to categorise the jobs they heard about first (e.g. jobs with animals / jobs with food / jobs with technology / jobs on TV, etc.). Then hear their views on which jobs they found the most interesting. Finally have a class vote on the most interesting or the most unusual jobs (or any other categories you feel are appropriate).

 **Reflect on your learning**
- These revision activities can be approached in different ways, according to the level and character of your class.
  - Questions 1–6 could be used as a class quiz, with learners in teams and a time limit given to write answers to each question.
  - Alternatively, you could conduct a revision session. Ask learners to work in pairs and take longer to think about and write down their answers. When pairs have finished the questions, they swap with another pair and correct each other's work, with you monitoring and giving help and advice when needed.
  - You could set this task for homework / self-study.

**Answers**
1 a vet, a science teacher, a car mechanic and a marine biologist. Compound nouns: science teacher, car mechanic, marine biologist
2 A presenter. Personal qualities needed: (five from) to be enthusiastic (about people and their lives); have lots of energy; to be confident; to be good with children especially; to be friendly and calm; to be knowledgeable (so that you can interview people well).
3 The uniform is designed for a postman/woman. Features: (three from) it is like a tracksuit, dark blue with a green and white stripe. The top is a jacket with a zip and inside pockets and the post office logo; underneath is a blue t-shirt. The trousers are quite wide and made of waterproof material from the ankle to the knee. There are zips at the bottom and zipped pockets on the side. On their feet, the postmen or women wear trainers. They also wear a cap with a light at the front; a belt, pockets to carry things, including an alarm. The uniform design will suit people who are all shapes and sizes because the clothes are loose-fitting and stretchy.

4 Learners' own answers.
5 Example answers: (two sentences for each job from)
   Job 1: He/she is really good at science / astronomy / fascinated by / knowledgeable about space and planets / crazy about flying / interested in rockets, etc.
   Job 2: He/she is really good at design and technology / interested in / knowledgeable about science / fascinated by gadgets, etc.
   Job 3: He/she is really good at science / biology / natural science / fascinated by / knowledgeable about good with all kinds of animals, etc.
6 The piece of advice that is repeated is: *You can be anything but you must try, so never give up and reach for the sky.*

## Look what I can do!
**Aim:** To check learners have fulfilled the objectives for **Unit 7** (and to what degree).
- Present the objectives slide or poster from the introduction to **Unit 7** (in **Lesson 1**) and remind learners of the objectives from the start of the unit.
- Focus their attention on the '*I can ...*' statements and read through together. You could put these on a slide or write on the board. Ask learners if they feel they can now do these tasks after completing **Unit 7**. By this point, you should have a clear idea yourself of how well your learners have completed the tasks. However, ask them now to do an initial self-assessment.
- Put learners in pairs and ask them to look through their notebooks and portfolios to find evidence of their work for each of the statements. Then they give themselves a rating as follows:
  ✓ Yes, I can – no problem!
  ? A little – I need more practice.
  ☺ No – I need a lot more practice.
- Circulate and chat to learners about their self-assessment (some might be overly modest and you can point out that their rating could be higher). If you haven't already done so, make notes about areas that learners are not confident about for future reference (see **Teaching tip**).
- Conduct a general feedback at the end and find out which tasks learners found the most interesting / useful / challenging, etc.
- **Extend and challenge:** A mini-awards system: Customise the idea presented in **Unit 1** for **Unit 7** (see **Unit 1** page 38).

**Answers**
Learners' own answers.

 **Wrap up**
- As a class, look at the Big question again on a slide or written on the board: *How do people get to do the jobs they do? Why do they do their jobs?*
- Focus learners on the first question, *How do people get to do the jobs they do?* Then ask them to look at the following statements on the board or on a slide. Read through the statements and ask learners what

they think they are about; elicit or explain that they are things you have to do to get and keep a job.

*1 Answer a job advertisement.*
*2 Use your skills and personality to do the job well.*
*3 Get the job!*
*4 Work hard at school.*
*5 Go for an interview.*

- Ask learners to work in pairs and put the statements in the order that they think they happen.
- If you want to make this task more active, use the statements to do a running dictation (for instructions, see **Unit 2**, **Lesson 2**), placing them around the classroom in the above order and ask learners to dictate and copy them in that order. Once they have dictated and copied the five statements, they sit down together and decide on the best order.
- Now focus learners on the second question, *Why do they do their jobs?* Take them through examples in **Lessons 1** and **2** in **Unit 7** of people talking about why they like their jobs and why they do them in terms of skills and interests. Point to relevant pictures (eg the TV presenter of **Lesson 2**) and ask learners what they remember about why the person does the job they do (focusing on personal qualities, skills and interests given in the texts and listening extracts).
- If you want to add an extra challenge, ask learners to close their books, put them in small groups, ask a question (e.g. *Why does the TV presenter in Lesson 2 like her job? Why did the woman in Lesson 1 become a vet?*, etc), ask them to discuss and then award points for every piece of information they remember from the text. This activity would exercise memory and generate a lot of language as learners try to remember as many details as possible.
- Now ask learners to talk about personal examples of why people do their jobs, drawing on the interviews they did in **Activity 8** of **Lesson 2** and possibly in Project 2 (if they interviewed someone as part of their research for the presentation).

> **Answers**
> 4 / 1 / 5 / 3 / 2
> Learners' own answers.

## Activity Book

### Revision

### 1 Multiple-choice quiz

- Learners complete sentences 1–12 by choosing the correct answer, a–c. Sentences cover key grammar and vocabulary from **Lessons 1–6** in **Unit 7**.

> **Answers**
> 1 b    2 c    3 b    4 a    5 c    6 b
> 7 c    8 b    9 a    10 b   11 a   12 b

### My global progress

- Learners think about their own responses to topics and activities in the **Unit 7** lessons and answer the questions.

> **Answers**
> Learners' own answers.

**Teaching tip**

Review the learners' work and their own assessment of their progress, noting areas where learners demonstrate strength and confidence and areas where they need additional instruction and practice. Use this information to select areas for review and specific focus, as you continue to **Unit 8**.

# 8 Communication

**How do we communicate effectively with each other?**

## Unit overview

In this unit learners will:

- talk and read about ways of communicating in different places
- listen to different types of messages
- learn how to get your points across
- write a post for an online forum
- read a poem about a thank-you letter.

In **Unit 8**, learners will look at ways of communicating, focusing on different kinds of communication styles and methods rather than communication gadgets. They will explore how to get a message across effectively, either verbally or in writing, as well as the different ways in which methods of communication are used. Learners are presented with the Big question in **Lesson 1** and will understand that tasks and projects in the unit will contribute to answering the question.

The unit begins by focusing on different ways of communicating that are popular and commonly used, giving learners an accessible and familiar topic with which to start the unit. The main reading and speaking tasks give learners the opportunity to learn about and discuss culturally specific ways of communicating, offering an opportunity for personalisation and cross-cultural comparison. Learners then listen to a varied selection of messages and report the information contained in them, practising useful language for making arrangements. **Lesson 3** gives speaking practice in how we can effectively get our message across in a challenging situation and ease the problem through skilful communication, using appropriate language and techniques. Learners then look at appropriate online communication and how to contribute effectively to an online forum in terms of language and appropriate behaviour. Finally they read a thank you letter in the form of a poem, and practise using descriptive language and alliteration to create a short poem about something meaningful to them.

The **Photocopiable activities** provide practice in translating and using text message abbreviations in English (**15**) and discussing appropriate online behaviour (**16**).

### Language focus

Present continuous forms (for arrangements); polite requests: *could, would you mind...*

**Vocabulary topics:** Ways of communicating (verb-noun collocations); gestures for communication; functional language for discussion; words about the sun.

### Self-assessment

- I can talk about different ways to communicate.
- I can read and understand information about what gestures mean in different countries.
- I can listen to and understand different kinds of messages.
- I can use different phrases to explain something that has happened.
- I can write a post for an online discussion forum.
- I can read and talk about a thank you letter poem.

### Teaching tip

Help learners to adopt efficient reading habits before moving to secondary level by reiterating techniques such as skimming (for general sense and main points) and scanning (for details) and making sure they understand the difference. Adjust the techniques according to the task and the number of times they have read the text in question. Give time limits to control the way they manage the text using the techniques mentioned, i.e. they are more likely to skim a text, rather than hesitate over every word, if they have to read it quickly in a time limit. These techniques are integrated into an activity in **Unit 8**, **Lesson 4**.

# Lesson 1: Communication

Learner's Book pages: 110–111

Activity Book pages: 88–89

## Lesson objectives

**Reading:** Read about the meaning of physical gestures and body language in different countries and compare with your own country / culture.

**Speaking:** Talk about different ways of communicating; discuss gestures used in own country to communicate different messages.

**Critical thinking:** Compare gestures used in different countries to communicate common messages with own country / culture.

**Vocabulary:** Ways of communicating: *raise your hand, send an email / a text, write an email / text / note / blog, make a call, reply to an email / text*; physical gestures: *a handshake, make eye contact, shake the head, greet, press palms together, a nod, a bow, wave your hand*

**Materials:** poster paper or IWB slides; realia representing different ways of communicating (see **Warm up**)

## Learner's Book

###  Warm up

- To introduce the Big question, start by telling the class that this unit is going to be about communication. Explain that you are going to look at ways of communicating in what we say and how we say or write it, how to communicate effectively and get our message across. So the Big question is ... *How do we communicate effectively with each other?*
- Write the question on the board (for an electronic presentation, create a slide with interesting graphics). Tell learners that you are all going to do tasks and projects in the unit that will answer this question.
- Introduce the unit objectives to show learners what tasks are coming up. Present the objectives on a slide or large piece of poster paper to attach to the board.
- Tell learners that you will answer the Big question and look again at the objectives at the end of the unit. Keep the objectives slide / poster to revisit at the end of the unit.
- Tell learners that you are going to start by looking at ways of communicating. Introduce the topic with a bag of realia representing different ways of communicating and ask learners to guess what is in the bag. Your bag could include a mobile phone, a pen, some Post-its, a notebook, a newspaper or magazine, a letter (e.g. a utility bill), a postcard, a phone card, etc. Depending on resources available and practicalities, you could also include items such as a laptop, a tablet, a cordless microphone, i-pod – any gadget that allows communication.
- See how many of the items learners can guess and take them out as they guess them. If your bag

contains small items, you could allow learners to feel the bag and guess what's inside.

- Ask learners to look in their school bags and see what items are inside that allow them to communicate some kind of message (e.g. note from a parent to teacher or vice versa, as well as pens and notebooks).

## 1 💬 Talk about it

- Focus learners on the first question, How many ways do we communicate with each other? Elicit a couple of examples from the class, then put learners in pairs and ask them to write down as many ways as they can think of in a time limit (e.g. 30 seconds / one minute).
- When time is up, have the pair with the longest list read it out to the class. The others have to listen and tick any ideas that are the same on their own list. After, they can add any ideas that weren't mentioned by the first pair.
- Next focus learners on the second question, *How do you like to communicate with people? Why?* ask them to discuss in pairs.
- Conduct a short feedback, asking learners to share their favourite ways of communicating. *Do you prefer texting to making phone calls? Do you like instant messaging?* Stretch learners by asking them *why* they like particular methods of communicating.
- **Critical thinking:** Learners identify their own preferences. They can be challenged by being asked to give reasons too.

> **Answers**
> Learners' own answers +
> Suggestions:
> We communicate with people through speaking, writing and body language. There are many different ways within each method, e.g. speaking: chatting, shouting, whispering, laughing, crying etc; writing: emailing, texting, writing letters, writing notes, advertising, news reports etc; body language: eye contact, gestures, ways of sitting, standing, etc.

## 2 Talk

- Focus learners on the pictures in the Learner's Book and ask them what ways of communicating they can see. Elicit a noun or verb-noun phrase for each one.
- Then ask them to work in pairs and talk about when people use these communication methods and why you might choose one above the other. Encourage learners to use their own experience and preferences as examples or give your own examples, e.g. when you might send a text instead of an email and vice versa.

> **Answers**
> a sending a text – to send someone who is not nearby a short message (a reminder, invitation, ask a question, etc.)
> b sending an email – to send someone a short or long message who is not nearby (send information, invitations, etc.)
> c a note – to leave a message for someone nearby or to remind yourself to do something (at home, school, work).
> d raising hands – when you want to answer a question or ask the teacher something in class.
> e chatting / talking – when we want to tell someone something directly or face to face.

## 3 Word study

- Focus attention on the verbs and nouns in the box. Ask learners to match them, giving a time limit (e.g. one minute) to see how many correct combinations they can make. Ask them to do the task individually, then compare with their partner when the time is up. At this stage they can add any combinations they missed, to build up a complete list of combinations (16 in total).
- **Extend and challenge:** Having established the answers, you could play the ball game described in **Unit 7** (see **Unit 7**, **Lesson 2** for instructions). Write the verbs on the board (not the nouns) and say one when you throw the ball to the first learner. He / she adds a noun and throws the ball to another learner, saying a new verb ... that learner adds a noun and so on. If someone gives a wrong combination, or repeats a verb phrase that has already been said, they have to sit down.
- There are 16 possible combinations for the verbs and nouns in **Activity 3**. When learners have exhausted the list in **Activity 3**, ask them to think of new combinations from their own knowledge, using different verbs and nouns or adding new nouns to the existing verbs.

> **Answers**
> raise your hand
> send an email / a text / a note
> write an email / a text / a note / a blog
> make a call / a note
> reply to an email / a text / a note / a blog / a note / a call

## 4 Talk

- Focus learners on **Activity 4** and read the situations together. Ask them to talk with their partner about how they communicate in these situations, using the verb-noun phrases in **Activity 3**.

> **Answers**
> **Suggested answers:**
> 1 raise your hand
> 2 send an email / a text; make a call
> 3 make a call
> 4 reply to an email / a text / a call
> 5 write / make a note

 **For further practice, see Activities 1 and 2 in the Activity Book.**

## 5 Talk

- Introduce the word, *gestures* in **Activity 5** by asking learners if they can put all the ways of communicating discussed so far into three groups. If necessary, mime actions to elicit *speaking* (indicate your mouth), *writing* (make an action as if writing with a pen) and *gestures* (wave or make a gesture that learners are familiar with). Tell learners that you are now going to talk about ways of communicating by *gestures*.

- Put learners in pairs and focus them on the messages in **Activity 5**. Ask them to act them out (by doing the gesture that they associated with the messages).

> **Answers**
> Learners' own answers.

## 6 Read

- Focus learners on the text and the picture. Ask them to guess which country the people are from (Thailand) and what message they are communicating to each other (saying hello / greeting formally). Elicit the equivalent gesture in learners' own country.
- Then ask them to read the text and find examples of the gestures they talked about in **Activity 5**. When they have finished reading, they should compare answers with a partner.
- When learners have finished reading, ask them which information from the text they already knew and which surprised them.

> **Answers**
> Examples:
> *Hello* – a handshake (more formal), a hug (very informal), pressing palms together (formal or semi-formal), a nod and a bow.
> *Pleased to meet you* – a handshake, pressing palms together, a nod and a bow.
> *I don't understand* – waving your hand
> *Yes* – shaking the head from side to side.

## 7 Word study

- Now ask learners to read the text again and act out the words in blue with their partner. If they don't know what the word means, they should check with their partner or look in a dictionary.
- Circulate and monitor, helping learners with any unknown words (most of the words in blue can be demonstrated, rather than give definitions).

> **Answers**
> Definitions:
> A handshake – taking someone's hand and moving it up and down once or twice when you meet them.
> A hug (very informal) – to put your arms around someone in a gesture of affection when you meet.
> Make eye contact – to look someone directly in the eye when you are talking.
> Shaking the head – moving the head from side to side, either in agreement or disagreement (depending on culture).
> Greet – to say hello to someone or a group of people.
> Pressing palms together – putting the inside of your hands together with fingers pointing up (as if saying a prayer).
> A nod – to move your head up and down once while looking down or looking at someone, as a way of greeting them.
> A bow – to move the upper part of your body down and then up, whilst looking down, as a way of greeting someone.
> Waving your hand – moving your hand side to side with the palm facing outwards.

 **For further practice, see Activities 3 and 4 in the Activity Book.**

## 8  Talk

- Ask learners to discuss in pairs which of the gestures described in the **Activity 6** text are true for their country. For gestures that are not used, ask learners to identify which ones are used instead.

> **Answers**
> Learners' own answers.

### ☞ Wrap up

- To finish off, ask learners if they know of any other gestures for communication used in other countries or cultures. Ask them if they have ever visited any places where people communicated in a different way. Share your own experiences with the class too.

## Activity Book

### 1 Vocabulary

- Learners read short texts giving comments about ways of communicating. They underline six verb-noun phrases to describe ways of communicating.

> **Answers**
> 1 raise our hands
> 2 writes notes
> 3 wrote a blog
> 4 sending texts / make a call / have a chat
> 5 replying to emails

### 2 Over to you

- Learners use the target verb-noun phrases to write sentences about how they like to communicate.

> **Answers**
> Learners' own answers.

### 3 Vocabulary

- Learners match words and phrases describing gestures with pictures.

> **Answers**
> a a handshake
> b a bow
> c a hug
> d shake your head
> e wave your hand
> f make eye contact
> g a nod

### 4 Read

- Learners complete a multiple-choice set of questions about gestures used in their own country.

> **Answers**
> Learners' own answers.

## Lesson 2: Getting the message

Learner's Book pages: 112–113

Activity Book pages: 90–91

### Lesson objectives

**Listening:** Identify the main points and purpose of a series of messages; identify functional language.

**Speaking:** Talk about ways of sending messages; report a message; leave a message (with a purpose) for a friend.

**Language focus:** Present continuous forms (for making arrangements in the near future); functional phrases to introduce a message: *Please could you ...? Just to remind you that ...; Just wanted to invite you to ...; This is to let you know that ...*

**Materials:** Post-it notes or pieces of note paper (optional). Copies of **Photocopiable activity 15**.

### Learner's Book

### ☞ Warm up

- Start by playing the *Name 5* game to recycle and review vocabulary and themes from the previous lesson (for instructions, see extension to the *Name 3* game described in **Unit 7**, **Lesson 6**. Ask learners to brainstorm five ways of communicating in the categories of speaking, writing and gestures.

### 1  Talk about it

- Focus attention on the first three questions and ask learners to tell their partner about the last time they sent a message, the reason and how they sent it.
- Conduct a quick class feedback, to ascertain the most common ways of sending a message and variety of reasons.
- Ask learners the final question: *What ways are there of sending messages to people?* Ask them to write down, in pairs, as many ways as they can think of in 30 seconds.
- Stop learners after 30 seconds and ask the pair with the most answers to read out their list. Other learners listen and tick the same answers on their own lists and make further suggestions, if applicable.
- **Extend and challenge:** Extend the topic or give an alternative talking point by asking learners to tell each other about a funny message they received recently or at some point in the past. Give them an example from your own experience, if possible.
- **Critical thinking:** Learners activate their own knowledge and experience of the lesson topic.

## Answers

Learners' own answers +
Suggestions:
send texts / emails; leave a message (on voicemail)
send a note / letter; ask someone else to deliver a message for
you (verbally)
use instant messaging

## 2 Listen 48

- Tell learners that they are now going to listen to some interesting messages. Ask them to look at the pictures in the Learner's Book and tell you if they think the messages will be about good or bad news.
- Use the pictures to pre-teach *tarantula, rock-climbing* and *appointment* from the audioscript, if necessary.
- Then ask them to listen and match a message with a picture.
- After listening, ask them to compare their answers with their partner before checking as a class.
- **Extend and challenge:** After listening and matching messages to pictures, ask learners to look at each picture in pairs and talk about how much they understood about the content of each message after the first listening.

## Answers

All the messages are bad news!
Picture a – Message 4
Picture b – Message 1
Picture c – Message 2
Picture d – Message 3

## 3 Listen 48 [CD2 Track 16]

- Focus learners on **Activity 3** and read through the partial sentences. Tell them that they need to complete these sentences to get the main points of each message. Ask them to listen for these sentences within the messages and copy down to complete the message.
- Stop the audio after each message to give learners time to write. If necessary, elicit the sentence first, then ask learners to copy it down.
- **Additional support and practice:** If necessary, stop the audio after each target sentence (instead of waiting until the end of the message), elicit and then give learners time to write it down. Then play the message to the end.
- To make the activity more interactive, you could ask learners to shout out *Stop!* (or raise their hands) when they hear the target sentence.
- Ask learners to check their answers in pairs before going through the complete sentences as a class.
- Now read the message purposes (a – d) together and ask learners to work in pairs to match them to the main message points (1 – 4) they have just noted down.

## Audioscript: Track 48

**Message 1:** Hi Bruno, Billy here. I think I've left my pet tarantula at your house. He was in my backpack and I think he escaped while we were watching TV. If you find him, please could you catch him for me? Don't worry, he's very friendly and won't bite ... unless he's hungry ... I'm playing football after school tomorrow so I'll collect him on my way home. Thanks! Bye!

**Message 2:** Hello, this is a message for Mrs Smith at 11 New Road from Bob Bailey at Castro Constructions. Just to remind you that we're taking off your front door at 2 o'clock this afternoon. If you're not in, don't worry, we'll just carry on until you get home! Thank you, Mrs Smith! Bye now.

**Message 3:** Hi Mila, this is Mandy. Just wanted to invite you to my birthday on Sunday. We're going rock-climbing and we're meeting at the cafe next to the cliff at 10 o'clock. Really hope you can make it. Don't tell me you're scared of heights too. Three people have already dropped out – I don't know what everyone's scared of! Hope to see you there! Bye!

**Message 4:** Good morning, this is a message for Tom Nash. This is to let you know that we have changed your dental appointment. Dr Singh isn't seeing you on Friday. He's seeing you today at 4 o'clock. You are having two teeth taken out and a filling! It will probably take about a couple of hours. We look forward to seeing you later, Tom. Goodbye

## Answers

1 Please could you catch him for me? c
2 Just to remind you that we're taking off your front door at 2 o'clock this afternoon. a
3 Just wanted to invite you to my birthday on Sunday. We're going rock-climbing ... d
4 This is to let you know that we have changed your dental appointment. b

 **For further practice, see Activities 1 and 2 in the Activity Book.**

## 4 Talk

- Ask learners to discuss in pairs, which message they think is the worst one to receive and why.
- After chatting, encourage learners to share their thoughts with the class. You could take a vote on the worst message to receive.

## Answers

Learners' own answers.

## 5 Listen 48 [CD2 Track 16]

- Focus learners on the key words listed from message 1. Tell them that they are going to listen to the first message again and put these words in the order that they hear them. Also explain that afterwards, they will listen again and write down more key words so that they can remember and report the message in the next task (so learners know what they are aiming for at the beginning of the task).
- Ask learners to copy the words first into their notebooks or ask them to close their books and dictate the words. When they listen, ask them to number the words as they hear them.
- Listen to message 1 again, then ask them to check their order in pairs before going through the order as a class.
- Now tell learners to listen again and this time, note down more useful words as they listen. Remind them again that they will use these words to report the message in the next task (**Activity 6**).

- When they have listened and noted key words, ask them to compare with their partner and note down any other words from each other's notes that they missed.
- Conduct feedback around the class, asking learners to share their words and making a note on the board, so all learners have a comprehensive record of useful words for the next activity.
  **Note:** This activity type is commonly known as a *dictogloss*.

> **Answers**
> **Order: 1** tarantula  **2** house  **3** backpack  **4** escaped
> **5** catch  **6** football  **7** collect
> More useful words (suggestions): If you find him ... / friendly /
> won't bite / hungry / tomorrow
> + learners' own answers.

 For further practice, see Activities 3 and 4 in the Activity Book.

## 6  Talk

- Now ask learners to work in pairs to report as much of the message as they can by using the key words as prompts. Tell them that they don't have to reproduce the message exactly but their reported message should contain all the most important information from the original.
- After learners have finished, draw their attention to the listening strategy; tell them that key words can be used to help you remember whole chunks of information when you listen.

> **Answers**
> **Sample answer:**
> Billy says that he thinks he's left his pet tarantula at Bruno's house. He thinks he escaped from his backpack while they were watching TV. He says that if Bruno finds him, please could he catch him? The tarantula is very friendly and won't bite unless he's hungry. Billy says that he is playing football after school tomorrow so he'll collect him on his way home.

## 7 Use of English

- Ask learners to close their books now and look at the board. Ask them to tell you an arrangement that Billy (the sender of message 1) had for after school tomorrow. Elicit the following sentence, leaving gaps as indicated.
  *I _____ football after school tomorrow.*
- Now elicit the missing words and highlight in a different colour as per the **Use of English** example:
  *I'm playing football after school tomorrow.*
- Ask learners if they can remember one other arrangement from the messages and write another example on the board. Then elicit the following sentence (if it hasn't already been suggested), so learners have an example of the negative form. Leave gaps as indicated:
  *Dr Singh _____ you on Friday ...*
- Now elicit the missing words and highlight in a different colour:
  *Dr Singh isn't seeing you on Friday ...*

- Ask learners to tell you again what the sentences express (future arrangements). Ask them if they think the future plan is fixed or not (it's fixed).
  Now focus them on the form. Ask which tense we use here if your learners are familiar with grammar terms for tenses. In any case, ask them how we make sentences like this and indicate the form of the verb, *be* and the verb + *-ing*.
- Ask learners to talk in pairs and try to remember two more arrangements from the messages.
- If necessary, play the messages again and ask learners to shout *Stop!* or raise their hands when they hear an arrangement expressed in the present continuous.

> **Answers**
> **Example answers** (two from ...):
> ... we're taking off your front door at 2 o'clock this afternoon.
> We're going rock-climbing and we're meeting at the cafe next to the cliff at 10 o'clock.
> He's seeing you today at 4 o'clock. You are having two teeth taken out and a filling!

 For further practice, see Activities 5 and 6 in the Activity Book.

## 8 Listen 49 [CD2 Track 17]

- Now tell learners that they are going to listen to two message replies. They need to listen and match a reply to a message in **Activity 2** and identify the main point of each message.
- Ask learners to listen, then discuss in pairs which message the replies are for and what the main point was. Stress that they need only understand the basic message, not details.

> **Audioscript:** Track 49
>
> **1** Hello. This is a message for Bill Bailey from Mrs Brown at 11 New Road. I've just received your message and there has been a mistake! I haven't asked anyone to take off my front door at 2 o'clock today! You have mixed up my address and phone number with someone else! If I get home and my front door is gone, I will call the police! Goodbye!
>
> **2** Billy! This is Bruno. We've found your tarantula! It was in a saucepan in the kitchen. My mum nearly poured pasta sauce on it. Then she saw it, screamed and dropped the saucepan on her toe. My dad chased the spider and trapped it under a bowl. My parents are going crazy! They've called the fire service, the police and the local zookeeper. If you want your spider back, come and get it now before it gets arrested! Bye!

> **Answers**
> **Reply 1** – Message 2. Main point: The builder has got the wrong address and phone number!
> **Reply 2** – Message 1. Main point: Bruno has found Billy's tarantula (spider) and he wants him to collect it now!

## 9 Listen and write 50 [CD2 Track 18]

- Tell learners that they are going to listen to the second reply again; explain that you will ask them to note down key words and then *write* the reply this time (instead of speaking).

- Take them through the step-by-step instructions outlined in the Learner's Book. The process is a *dictogloss* activity, similar to **Activity 5**.
- Ask them to listen and, after noting down key words, work with a partner to construct the message in writing. Remind them that the message needs to be reported in the third person, e.g. *Bruno says that **he** has found Billy's tarantula. **His** mum ...*
- Tell them that the message doesn't have to be exactly the same as the original, but must contain as much of the original information as possible.
- Once learners have finished their drafts, play the message again for them to check.

> **Audioscript:** Track 50
>
> 2 Billy! This is Bruno. We've found your tarantula! It was in a saucepan in the kitchen. My mum nearly poured pasta sauce on it. Then she saw it, screamed and dropped the saucepan on her toe. My dad chased the spider and trapped it under a bowl. My parents are going crazy! They've called the fire service, the police and the local zoo keeper! If you want your spider back, come and get it now before it gets arrested! Bye!

> **Answers**
> Suggested main words:
> Billy / Bruno / found / tarantula / saucepan / kitchen / mum / pasta sauce / saw / screamed / dropped / saucepan / toe / dad / chased / spider / trapped / bowl / parents / crazy / fire service / police / zookeeper / spider / get / now / arrested

## 10 🐟 Talk

- Ask learners to think of a message to send to a friend in the class in English. Point out that the message must have a purpose (refer them to **Activity 3**) and can be funny or serious.
- Tell them to leave their messages on a phone, as either a voicemail or text message or write them on Post-it notes or note paper and give them directly to the recipient.
- If you choose the phone option, you could set the task for homework, asking them to report their friend's replies in the warm-up stage of the next lesson. However, if you prefer, you could ask them to write messages in the class on Post-it notes, and then the recipient sends back a reply in the same way.

> **Answers**
> Learners' own answers.

## 🖙 Wrap up

- If you choose the paper note option in **Activity 10**, finish the class by finding out who sent what type of message (e.g. a reminder, an invitation, etc.). You could also share messages and vote on the funniest.

## Activity Book

### 1 Read and Strategy check

- Learners complete a multiple-choice activity to check they have understood the reading strategy (using key

words). They then read a series of written messages and match to a message type.

> **Answers**
> Understand the main topic of the text by looking at pictures, headings, etc; then look for words that link to the topic. ✓
> Look for the words that express the most important information in the text. ✓
> 1 a text message   2 an email   3 a shopping list   4 a note

### 2 Read

- Learners read the messages in **Activity 1** again and match to a purpose.

> **Answers**
> 1 c   2 d   3 a   4 b

### 3 Read

- Learners look at underlined key words in the texts and underline two more key words in each message.

> **Answers**
> 1 Sat / 2 pm
> 2 can't / birthday
> 3 chicken / beans / rice
> 4 dish / oven

### 4 Write

- Learners make messages from key words given as prompts.

> **Answers**
> Learners' own answers.
> Suggestions for answers:
> 1 Please remember to finish your art projects by next Friday.
> 2 We're playing football at Mo's house at 5 pm on Tuesday. Do you want to join us?
> 3 I can't go to the cinema on Saturday – would you like to go next week instead?
> 4 Please do Activities 2 and 3 for English homework for Monday.

### 5 Use of English

- Learners complete a text (an email message) using the correct form of the verbs in the box.

> **Answers**
> 1 are meeting
> 2 are going
> 3 are having
> 4 Are / bringing
> 5 isn't coming

### 6 📝 Use of English

- Learners write sentences about themselves using the present continuous.

> **Answers**
> Learners' own answers.

**To practise translating and using text message abbreviations, see Photocopiable activity 15.**

# Lesson 3: Explaining something difficult

Learner's Book pages: 114–115

Activity Book pages: 92–93

## Lesson objectives

**Speaking:** Talk about the best way to communicate in a difficult situation; prepare and perform a role play about a difficult situation.

**Listening:** Listen to two dialogues, identify specific information and features of language.

**Critical thinking:** Thinking of and analysing the best way to communicate in a difficult situation; problem solving.

**Language focus:** Polite requests: *Could I ...? Would you mind if ...?*

**Materials:** Learner's Book, Activity Book.

## Learner's Book

###  Warm up

- If you chose the phone option in **Activity 10** in **Lesson 2**, and learners did the task for homework, you could set the task for homework, ask them to report their friend's replies in the warm-up stage of this lesson. Then move on to the following activity suggestion.
- You could introduce the topic of this lesson by telling a short anecdote about a time you got into trouble as a child and how you tried to explain the situation. Then learners could talk in pairs about the last time they got into trouble about something: what happened? Who were they in trouble with? How did they explain what they'd done? Did it make the situation any better?

### 1 Talk about it

- Ask learners as a class the questions in **Activity 1** and elicit responses around the room. If learners use the Internet for some parts of their homework, ask them if they ever have problems (e.g. with connectivity, availability, finding the right information, etc.).

> **Answers**
> Learners' own answers.

 **For further practice, see Activity 1 in the Activity Book.**

### 2 Listen 51 [CD2 Track 19]

- Tell learners that they are going to listen to a conversation about a problem with homework. Ask them to look at the picture and predict what the problem is (either as a class or in pairs). When learners have offered some predictions, read the gist questions in **Activity 2** together and tell learners

to focus on these questions when they listen to the conversation between Carl and his teacher.

- After listening to the audio once, ask learners to discuss the answers to the questions in pairs. Then conduct a class feedback.

> **Answers**
> Carl hasn't done his homework / handed in his science project and the teacher is annoyed.
> He couldn't finish the project because he had no internet connection at home at the weekend.

### 3 Listen 51 [CD2 Track 19]

- Ask learners to read the sentences 1–5 before listening again and speculate in pairs if they are true or false.
- Then ask learners to listen again to ascertain whether the statements are true or false.
- When they have listened for a second time, ask them to discuss the statements in pairs, correcting the ones that are false. Then conduct a class feedback.

> **Audioscript:** Track 51
>
> **Mr Simms:** Er, Carl, wait! Did you give me your Science project?
>
> **Carl:** Er, no Sir.
>
> **Mr S:** I didn't think so. Where is it?
>
> **C:** Er, I haven't got it, Sir. Can I give it to you tomorrow?
>
> **Mr S:** Why haven't you got it today?
>
> **C:** Well, we had no Internet at home on Sunday so I couldn't finish it. I had to look on that website you told us about to finish the questions for the project. We have lots of problems with our Internet in my house ... my mum keeps phoning but ...
>
> **Mr S:** Carl, I'm not interested in your Internet problems at home. I want to know why you didn't tell me sooner. You knew that you couldn't finish the project in time for the deadline. Why didn't you tell me before?
>
> **C:** Don't know Sir ...
>
> **Mr S:** That's why I'm angry, Carl. I'm angry because you didn't tell me about the problem sooner. I know there are problems with the Internet sometimes but ...

> **Answers**
> 1 true
> 2 false. He tells the teacher on the day of the deadline that the homework will be late.
> 3 true. Carl asks if he can hand his project in the next day.
> 4 false. The teacher is angry because Carl didn't tell him sooner that he couldn't hand in his homework on time.
> 5 false. Carl doesn't say sorry (or make any attempt to make the situation better).

### 4 Talk

- **Critical thinking:** Elicit from learners again Carl's problem and why the teacher was angry. Then ask them to discuss in pairs the two questions in **Activity 4**.

- After discussing, ask learners to share their answers with the class. For the second question, write good suggestions on the board for reference in the next listening activity.

> **Answers**
> Learners' own answers +
> Suggestions for making things better:
> Carl could have apologised for handing in the homework late. He could have told the teacher about the problem before the teacher had to call him back (instead he tried to leave the classroom without saying anything).

## 5 Talk

- **Critical thinking:** Tell learners that soon they are going to listen to another child with the same problem having a conversation with the same teacher. However, this child handles things differently. Ask them to look at Ben's notes in **Activity 5** and discuss with their partner how they think Ben's explanation will be different from Carl's. Ask them to predict what the teacher will say in this case.
- Ask learners to share their thoughts as a class and note down good suggestions for reference in the next activity.
- When learners have finished discussing the notes and you have conducted feedback, ask them why they think Ben wrote notes before he spoke to the teacher. Then draw their attention to the **Speaking tip**.

> **Answers**
> Learners' own answers +
> Ben's notes indicate that he is going to suggest an alternative date (Friday) to hand the homework in to the teacher (and that he has taken the time to think of a solution to the problem).

## 6 Listen 52 [CD2 Track 20]

- Now ask learners to listen to Ben's conversation with the teacher. Tell them to answer the question and check the predictions they made in **Activity 5**. Draw their attention to suggestions outlined on the board, especially to help learners who may have struggled to make their own predictions in the last activity.
- Listen and then ask learners to talk in pairs about the answer to the question and whether their predictions were mentioned in the conversation.

> **Answers**
> Ben explained that he couldn't finish the homework on Sunday (when he had planned to finish it) because there was no internet connection at home. He offered to hand the homework in on Friday instead, because he knew that he could get it finished by then.

## 7 Listen 52 [CD2 Track 20]

- Before listening again, ask learners in pairs to look at the phrases (a–f) in **Activity 7** and put them in the order that they appeared in the conversation.
- Now ask them to listen and check their order. When they listen, ask them to raise their hands when they hear a target phrase.

> **Audioscript:** Track 52
> **Ben:** Excuse me, Mr Simms. Could I talk to you about something?
>
> **Mr Simms:** Yes, of course, Ben. What is it?
>
> **B:** I need to ask for more time to do the Science Project. I'm sorry but I won't be able to give it to you in time for Tuesday.
>
> **Mr S:** Oh ... Why's that?
>
> **B:** The reason is because we had a problem with the internet at home this weekend. I tried to finish the project on Sunday, but where I live there was no Internet connection for most of the day. It's okay now but I haven't had time to finish the project. Would you mind if I handed it in on Friday instead? I know I can finish it by then.
>
> **Mr S:** OK, yes, in this case that's fine, Ben. Thanks for letting me know.
>
> **B:** Thanks very much, Mr Simms.

> **Answers**
> **1 / b** Could I talk to you about something?
> **2 / d** I need to ask for ...
> **3 / f** I'm sorry but ...
> **4 / a** The reason is because ...
> **5 / e** Would you mind if I ...
> **6 / c** Thanks very much

 For further practice, see Activity 1 in the Activity Book.

## 8 🗨 Talk

- **Critical thinking:** Read the questions in **Activity 8** as a class then ask learners to discuss in pairs.
- **Additional support and practice:** If you think learners might struggle to explain the things Ben did differently to Carl, write the following sentences on the board (or slide) and ask learners to fill in the gaps.
  *Ben told Mr Simms _____ that he hadn't done the homework (without Mr Simms having to 'chase' him).* (first)
  *Ben told Mr Simms about the problem _____ the homework deadline that he wouldn't be able to hand it in on time.* (before)
  *He said _____ for handing the homework in late.* (sorry)
  *He gave Mr Simms a simple _____ about what the problem was.* (explanation).
  *He told Mr Simms _____ he could hand in the homework* (when).
  *He _____ Mr Simms for agreeing to the new deadline.* (thanked)

## 9 Use of English

- Write the following sentence parts on the board and ask learners if they can remember the questions from the conversation.
  *Could I talk* _____?
  *Would you mind if* _____?
- Elicit or tell learners the remainder of the questions, then underline or highlight the verbs as indicated below.
  *Could I **talk** to you about something?*
  *Would you mind if I **handed** it in on Friday instead?*
- Focus learners on the questions in **Activity 9** and ask them to look at the examples on the board to help them answer.

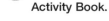 For further practice, see Activities 3 and 4 in the Activity Book.

## Present it!

- **Critical thinking:** Put learners into pairs and explain that they are going to write a dialogue together. Learner A explains what the problem is; Learner B listens and decides whether or not to accept Learner A's explanation.).
- Remind them of the functional language for navigating the conversation and making polite requests (see **Activity 7** and **9**). Elicit the phrases again on the board.
- **Additional support and practice:** To give learners extra support in writing the role play, write part of one together as a class. Choose a problem to discuss and elicit a simple dialogue line by line. Leave the dialogue on the board to give learners a structure. Or you could erase certain words, or just leave prompts, so they have to work a little harder to remember).
- Learners write their role play in pairs in their notebooks. Monitor the pairs, helping with language and vocabulary. Check the dialogues for grammar, vocabulary and organisation; however, the emphasis is on organisation and quality of ideas rather than perfectly accurate scripts.

- Now ask learners to choose a 'role': Learner A has to explain a problem to Learner B, who listens and decides whether or not to accept Learner A's explanation, depending on how well it is communicated. Ask learners to practise their role plays in pairs. Again, monitor the pairs, helping with pronunciation and sentence stress.
- **Delivery:** When learners have finished practising, you could either ask a few confident pairs to deliver their role plays, in front of the class, or move all learners into groups of six and have three pairs perform for each other. While pairs are performing their role plays, ask listeners to note down the explanation for each problem.
- If pairs are performing their dialogues in front of the class, generate a supportive atmosphere by having learners applaud each pair before and after each role play. When each pair finishes, make a positive comment about their dialogue before welcoming the next pair.
- **Extend and challenge:** As learners are delivering their role plays, note down main errors; either give to each pair a note of the errors to correct themselves, or write up on the board at the end for a class error correction session (without stating which learners made the errors).
  **Note:** This would come after plenty of positive feedback regarding the role plays. Positive feedback must always come first and be emphasised.

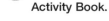 For further practice, see Activity 5 in the Activity Book.

## Wrap up

- **Critical thinking:** Ask learners to vote on the best explanation they heard.

## Activity Book

### 1 Read

- Learners read a gapped conversation between a student and a teacher and put target phrases in the correct place.

### 2 Read

- Learners answer a multiple-choice question about the dialogue in **Activity 1**.

## 3 Use of English

- Learners choose the correct form of the word to complete sentences.

> **Answers**
> 1 borrow    2 gave    3 didn't    4 join

## 4  Use of English

- Learners rewrite a series of requests to make them sound more polite.

> **Answers**
> 1 Could I ask you a big favour? Would you mind if I borrowed your smart phone?
> 2 Mr Diaz, would you mind if I had a week longer to finish my project?
> 3 Dad, could I ask you something? Could I do my homework on your laptop?
> 4 Would you mind if I didn't come to football practice tonight?
> 5 Could you lend me your textbook?

## 5 Challenge

- Learners write a dialogue from given information, making the explanation and request contained within the dialogue more polite.

> **Answers**
> Suggested answer:
> **Leah:** Hi Kate – could I talk to you about something?
> **Kate:** Yes, sure, what is it?
> **Leah:** I'm really sorry but I can't give you back your swimming goggles today …
> **Kate:** Oh … Why's that?
> **Leah:** The reason is because my little brother has broken them. I'm sorry but it was my fault – I let him play with them. But don't worry – my mum is going to buy you a new pair. Would you mind if I gave you the new ones at the weekend?
> **Kate:** Yes, that's fine, no problem.
> **Leah:** OK, thanks very much …

# Lesson 4: Getting your point across

Learner's Book pages: 116–117

Activity Book pages: 94–95

## Lesson objectives

**Reading:** Read an online forum for a group of students discussing a class issue; notice features of content, style and use of language.

**Writing:** Write a list of advice and tips about communicating appropriately online; write a forum post about a class or school topic or issue.

**Speaking:** Discuss the ideas in the forum and the supporting reasons.

**Critical thinking:** Discuss appropriate ways of communicating online; write an opinion in the form of an online post about a class or school topic or issue.

**Vocabulary:** Functional language for discussions: introducing a point; agreeing; partly agreeing; encouraging other people to respond; making a suggestion

**Materials:** Learner's Book, Activity Book. Copies of **Photocopiable activity 16.**

## Learner's Book

### Warm up

- Brainstorm ways of communicating online (e.g. email, forums, social networks, instant messaging, etc). Ask learners which they use and which are their favourite ways.
- When you have established the most popular methods in the class, brainstorm advantages and disadvantages of each one. Put ideas on the board for reference later.

## 1 Talk about it

- Focus learners on the three questions in **Activity 1** and read through them together. Elicit from learners what an online forum is. If possible, show them an example. If your school runs any kind of forum for students, look at the example here. Ask around the class if anyone has ever taken part in an online forum. What was the topic?

> **Answers**
> A forum is an organised space where people can discuss their views. Forums can be online or face-to-face situations. Learners' own answers.

## 2 Read

- Focus learners on the forum-style text in the Learner's Book and tell them they are going to read an online class forum. Read through the two questions together and tell learners to look for the answers in the text. Point out that this is the only information they need to look for at the moment – the topic of the discussion and what the teacher does. They should *scan* the text to find out the topic and *skim* to deduce the role of the teacher (see **Teaching tip**, **Unit 8** overview).
- Give learners a time limit to encourage them to read in an efficient way (e.g. two to three minutes). They will have a chance to read the text in more detail later.

> **Answers**
> The class are discussing how to spend the money they raised through their class activities at the school fair.
> The role of the teacher is to moderate/manage the forum. He/she sets the forum up, introduces the topic and then mediates between the students, encouraging them to express their views. The teacher makes some comments and guides the discussion but doesn't dominate.

## 3 Talk

- Now ask learners to read the forum text again, this time more slowly because they are looking for details. Read the questions and put learners into small groups (e.g. 3) to find the answers.
- Each group needs to be prepared to explain one idea and reason to the class during feedback at the end of the task.
- **Additional support and practice:** Instead of having all learners in the group identify all the ideas and reasons offered by the children, ask them to each focus on just one or two responses. There are five children taking part in the forum – learners could look closely at one

or two each (e.g. Nacho, Pablo / Mari, Daniel / Luisa) then share the information in their groups. However, they all need to read the whole text to understand how the responses link together (but can closely look at just one or two to give answers).

- Conduct feedback, asking each group to explain one idea and reason.
- **Extend and challenge:** Ask learners to discuss which idea they think is the best one and why and, if their class had this amount of money, what they would spend it on.

> **Answers**
> **Ideas and reasons:**
> Buy some new laptops for the computer room because, at the moment, students sometimes have to share computers.
> Buy new equipment for the after-school table tennis club because one of the tables has broken recently.
> An end-of-term celebration because everyone in the class would enjoy it.
> A school trip that would help with the history project next term.

## 4 Word study

- Focus learners on the phrases in blue in the text. Read the phrases together and ask them to work in the same small groups (as for **Activity 3**) to match them to a function (1–5). Do an example together as a class, by asking learners to look at the first phrase in blue in the text (*I think we should ...*) and match it to a function (1–5).
- Ask learners to record the phrases in their notebooks under the headings of the functions.

> **Answers**
> 1 introducing your point I think we should ...
> 2 agreeing I agree
> 3 partly agreeing I think it's a good idea to ... , but not ...
> 4 encouraging other people to respond What does everyone else think?
> 5 making a suggestion Maybe we could ...

 For further practice, see Activities 1, 2 and 3 in the Activity Book.

## 5  Talk

- First, ask learners to find more phrases in the text to match to the functions in **Activity 4**.
- Then draw their attention to the next part of the rubric and ask them to decide which of the adjectives best describes the way the teacher and students communicate with each other. Read the adjectives out and ask learners to say *yes* or *no* after each one, according to whether they think it describes the communication, e.g.
  (T): *Is it formal?* (Ls): No!
  **Note:** If learners are unsure about the difference between *formal* and *informal*, use examples to demonstrate. Ask them to compare writing an email to the head teacher to writing one to their best friend. How are the styles different? Then establish that the head teacher's email would be *formal* and the friend's would be *informal*.

- Ask learners to work in pairs or small groups to find examples of phrases that match the adjectives.
- Alternatively, you could quicken the pace by conducting this task as a reading race, awarding points to different groups who give correct answers to questions such as:
  *Find me an informal or friendly phrase that the teacher says at the beginning!* (Hello everyone / a huge thanks / Now the big question is / Over to you ...!)

> **Answers**
> **Adjectives to describe the forum communication:** Informal / polite / friendly
> **Examples:**
> **Informal / friendly:** *Hello everyone / a huge thanks / Now the big question is / Over to you ..! / Hi everyone / Hi Nacho* (addressing directly by name) / *Good points*
> **Polite:** *Thanks for your idea, Daniel .. / I can see your point but ... / Thanks for your comments / What does everyone else think? / We could go ...*

 For further practice, see Activity 4 in the Activity Book.

## 6 Write

- **Critical thinking:** Use the task in **Activity 5** to lead into the focus on appropriate online communication in **Activity 6**. Put learners into small groups and ask them to think of things you should and shouldn't do when communicating in an online forum. Elicit a couple of examples first from the class and then ask them to brainstorm in their groups and write down at least four points for each category. Give them a time limit.
  **Note:** This topic is extended and covered in more detail in the **Unit 8 Photocopiable activities** page 232. Here it can be covered quite briefly or extended using the photocopiable worksheet.

- During feedback, ask the first group to read out their list; other groups listen and tick any similar points. Then move around the class and ask learners to share any different points from their lists.

> **Answers**
> Learners' own answers.
> Suggestions:
> **Good:** Be polite and friendly.
> Acknowledge other points of view.
> Invite others to respond and share discussion.
> Make posts short and to the point.
> **Not good:** Don't write rude or aggressive posts even if you disagree with someone else's opinion.
> Don't write in capital letters – it will be interpreted by others as shouting.
> Try not to write anything that is not relevant to the topic.
> Don't dominate the discussion – let other people have space to respond.

## 7 Calculate

- Draw learners' attention back to the forum text and elicit again the topic and how much money the class has to spend. Talk through questions 1–3 together.
- Ask learners to write down the amount and then answer the questions in pairs.

- For question 3, find out the most-up-to date currency rate for your country against the US dollar and write the rate against 1 USD, to help learners with the calculations needed for question 3.

> **Answers**
> The class has $825 to spend.
> **1** $275    **2** $206.25    **3** Learners' own answers.

 **For further practice, see Activity 5 in the Activity Book.**

## Writing tip

Draw learners' attention to the **Writing tip** and emphasise to learners that writing online is the same as other forms of writing. They should be polite and remember that lots of people might read what they say. You should also remind them that what they write online can't easily be removed.

### 🗨 Write

- Put learners in groups of four and tell them that they are now going to practice writing in a forum type discussion. Read the two suggested topics together (*Is it better to have longer school days and longer holidays?* Or *A good school trip.)* and ask each group to decide which one to discuss. Alternatively, you may want to give them the option of choosing their own discussion question or suggest ones yourself that are more relevant to your class and school.
- Give each learner some paper and ask them to write the forum topic at the top. Tell them that they are going to write a comment about the topic on their paper, then pass it to the classmate on their left. The classmate on their right will in turn hand their paper to them. They must read the comment already on the paper and write a response.
- Elicit a phrase from **Activity 4** or **5** for *introducing your topic,* and tell all learners to start their writing task with this phrase. Elicit other phrases for the other functions in **Activity 4** and **5** and tell learners that they should try and use these phrases when they respond.
- Tell learners that they should also give *reasons* for their ideas or suggestions (ref. **Activity 3**).
- Remind them to communicate appropriately, keeping in mind the points made in **Activity 6**. Draw their attention to the points in the **Writing tip** as this applies to this writing task (because it is a simulation of an online form discussion).
- Learners will stop writing when they receive the paper with their original comment on the top. They should now read the responses.
- **Extend and challenge:** If it is possible to set up this activity as an actual forum online, then learners might benefit from the authentic experience.

> **Answers**
> Learners' own answers.

 **For further practice, see Activity 6 in the Activity Book.**

### ↪ Wrap up

- **Critical thinking:** Ask learners to share good points made about their chosen forum topic during the writing activity.

## Activity Book

### 1 Read

- Learners read an online forum text (with gaps for missing phrases) and match to a topic (the text is a continuation of the text that appears in the Learner's Book).

> **Answers**
> The topic is c.

### 2 Read

- Learners read the forum again and put phrases, (a–e), in the correct place in the text.

> **Answers**
> **1** b    **2** a    **3** d    **4** e    **5** c

### 3 Vocabulary

- Learners match phrases in **Activity 2** (a – e) with functions (1 – 5).

> **Answers**
> **1** b    **2** c    **3** d    **4** a    **5** e

### 4 📝 Read

- Learners write down four different types of school trip mentioned in the forum text and the reasons for each suggestion.

> **Answers**
> **1** A history trip: to help with the history project next term.
> **2** A science trip: because a lot of kids in the class find science difficult and need more help with it.
> **3** A trip to a theme park: to help the children relax.
> **4** A sports trip: because it would be good exercise and a new experience for everyone.

### 5 🔢 Calculate

- Learners read sentences containing information about numbers of students (referring to the fictitious class featured in the forum text) represented in the form of fractions. They calculate the number of learners represented by the fractions.

> **Answers**
> **1** 15 students.
> **2** 10 students.
> **3** 5 students.
> **4** 20 students.

### 6 📝 Challenge

- Learners write a post for an online class forum for two topics from a given list, making a suggestion and giving the reason why.

**For further practice, in discussing appropriate online behaviour, see Photocopiable activity 16.**

# Lesson 5: A thank you letter

Learner's Book pages: 118–119

Activity Book pages: 96–97

## Lesson objectives

**Listening and reading:** Listen to and read a 'thank you letter' to the sun, in the form of a poem. Answer questions about poem content and themes; look at features of language within the poem.

**Speaking:** Discuss poem themes and inferences; compare writer's stance with own feelings about the sun.

**Writing:** Write a 'thank you' verse about something that makes you feel happy.

**Critical thinking:** Discuss own feelings about the sun and compare to sentiments expressed in the poem; discuss ways to say 'thank you' to someone who does something kind for you.

**Vocabulary:** Words to describe the sun: *blazing, dawn, glow, sunset, ripening*

**Values:** Saying thank you.

**Materials:** dramatic images depicting the sun (optional for **Warm up**).

## Learner's Book

###  Warm up

- Ask learners to look at the illustrations in the book or show them some separate pictures and images of the sun (if you do this, try to show contrasts, e.g. beautiful sunset / parched cracked earth) and elicit the theme of the lesson (the sun). Tell them that before you start the lesson, you are going to play a quick dictation game.
- Put learners in small teams and set up the letter dictation activity. Tell them that you are going to dictate some words letter by letter without pausing. They should listen and copy the letters down in a long line.
- Dictate the following, letter by letter, so learners finish with a long continuous line of letters as below: b-o-i-l-i-n-g-w-e-t-g-l-o-o-m-y-d-r-y-b-r-i-g-h-t-l-i-g-h-t-f-r-e-e-z-i-n-g-d-a-r-k
- Dictate two or three times if necessary. **Note:** These words can be changed, increased or reduced according to the ability of your class (but they should include words relating to the sun and an equal number of unrelated words, so learners have to think about the contrast).
- Then ask learners to find eight words in the line. When they have found all the words they must match

them into opposites. Make this into a competition if you wish, with a time limit, giving points to the first group who manages to complete the task.
- When groups have finished, elicit which words can be used to describe the sun (or effects of the sun).

### 1 Talk about it

- Ask learners what kind of text they can see on pages 118–119. Elicit that it is a poem but it is also a thank you letter. Focus learners on the questions in **Activity 1**. Have them discuss these in pairs or the same small groups from the warm–up stage. Then share responses as a class.
  **Note:** If the country or culture you work in has different customs for saying 'thank you', adapt this activity accordingly. If learners are not familiar with the custom of sending thank you letters and notes, explain that, in some countries, this is a way to say thank you for kindnesses and gifts received, especially from a groups of people (e.g. children attending a party) or relatives and friends who live some distance away.

### 2 Talk

- Tell learners that they are going to read and listen to a poem called *Thank You Letter* by Eric Finney, expressing thank you to the sun. Beforehand, they are going to write down as many words and phrases about the sun as they can think of, adding to the words in the warm-up stage.
- **Critical thinking:** Have learners do this activity in pairs or small groups. Encourage them to generate words by making Mind Maps, as this will encourage them to think laterally and so produce words and phrases by association (rather than in a linear list, which might inhibit that process).
- Conduct a quick class feedback, asking groups to share some of the lexis they have produced. Focus in particular on interesting, descriptive words and phrases and ask challenge learners by asking them to explain any unusual associations.
- Now ask learners to look at their lists and underline positive things that the writer might *thank* the sun for.

### 3 Read 53 [CD2 Track 21]

- Now focus learners on the poem and ask them to read and listen to the audio. Their first task is to notice which of their ideas from **Activity 2** are mentioned in the poem (e.g. if they thought of and underlined the word, *sunset*, in their Mind Map in **Activity 2**, they should listen to see if this is something the writer thanks the sun for in his letter).
- Start the audio and tell learners to read the poem while listening.

- After reading / listening, ask learners to confer in their pairs or groups which of their ideas were mentioned. Then conduct a class feedback, writing ideas that were mentioned on the board, to help with comprehension (especially in the next activity). Encourage learners to tell you which lines corresponded with their ideas.

> **Audioscript:** Track 53
> See Learner's Book pages 118–119.

> **Answers**
> Learners' own answers.

## 4  Talk 53 [CD2 Track 21]

- Before listening and reading again, focus learners on questions 1–3 in **Activity 4** and read through together. Ask learners to pay special attention to these points when they listen and read a second time.
- Afterwards, ask them to discuss the questions in their groups. At this point, just ask them to focus on questions 1–3. Point out that they should be prepared to share their thoughts on all questions with the class afterwards.
- **Additional support and practice:** You could divide the questions up, giving some groups questions 1 and others, question 2. All learners should do questions 3 and 4.
- When you go through the answers as a class, keep drawing learners back to the poem by closely referring to the language, especially for answers to questions 1 and 2. For question 3, ask learners to tell you specifically which language led them to make their deductions about the kind of country the writer lives in.
- **Critical thinking:** Now draw learners' attention to question 4 and read through it together. Ask them first to write down adjectives that they personally associate with the sun and that describe their feelings about the sun. Do they have a positive or a negative feeling? Do they associate the sun with fun, holidays, being outside and suntans? Or do they associate it with having to stay inside because it is too hot? Too humid? Do they crave air-conditioning during hot weather? Then they should look at the things the writer *thanks* the sun for and ask themselves if they agree with his viewpoint, or do they have a different attitude towards the sun?
  Finally they should consider if there are any other aspects of the sun that they would include in a poem like this one, which offers a positive perspective (e.g. hot weather often means long school holidays, long evenings, etc.).
  **Note:** Attitudes to the sun tend to depend on the type of climate people have to endure on a constant basis; people in hot, humid or intensely hot and dry climates often don't have the same attitude to the sun as people who live in temperate climates.
- When you conduct class feedback for question 4, highlight similarities and differences in opinions.

This could be between learners, between you and the learners (especially if you are from another culture) or through an explanation about how people's attitude to the sun depends on the climate they live in (giving one or two examples). Use this opportunity to emphasise that it is possible to have very different viewpoints on the same topic, depending on your own experience, and this can be applied to other subjects and topics too.

> **Answers**
> **1 The writer thanks the sun for:** (Three from ...)
> Every day that it shines (*Thanks for this / And every day.*)
> Dawns and sunsets that always arrive at the same time (*Your dawns and sunsets / Are just great – / Bang on time, / Never late. / For sunsets – the / Loveliest things I know.*)
> Brightening grey, cold days (*On dismal days, / As grey as slate, / Behind a cloud / You calmly wait, / Till out you sail ...*)
> Bright, hot days on beaches (*Thanks for those / Blazing days on beaches,*)
> Ripening fruit and making it ready to eat (*For ripening apples, / Pears and peaches*)
> The beauty of sunlight (*For sharing out / Your noble glow;*)
>
> **2 Words and phrases to describe:**
> How the sun looks – *Your noble glow; / For sunsets – the / Loveliest things I know.*
> What it does – *Your dawns and sunsets / Are just great – / Bang on time, / Never late. / To put a smile / On the whole world's face / Blazing days on beaches, / For ripening apples, / Pears and peaches; / For sharing out / Your noble glow;*
> How it moves – *Till out you sail / With cheerful grace*
>
> **3** The poem indicates that the writer lives in a country with a temperate climate, which has cold, dull weather, as well as hot (*On dismal days, / As grey as slate,*). It is a country that grows apples, pears and peaches, (*For ripening apples, /Pears and peaches*), so could be a European country.
>
> **4** Learners' own answers.

> [AB] **For further practice, see Activity 1 in the Activity Book.**

## 5 Word study

- Focus learners on the poem again and draw their attention to the words highlighted in blue. Then read through the definitions, 1–5 and ask learners to match to the words in blue. Do the first one as an example if necessary.
- Tell learners to add the words in **Activity 5** to their Mind Maps or vocabulary lists under the theme of *the sun.*

> **Answers**
> 1 blazing
> 2 dawn
> 3 glow
> 4 sunset
> 5 ripening (verb – to ripen)

> [AB] **For further practice, see Activities 2 and 3 in the Activity Book.**

## 6 Pronunciation 54 [CD2 Track 22]

- Focus learners on **Activity 6**. Ask them to listen to and repeat the lines from the poem again. Which sounds are the same? Which sounds are similar? **Note:** At this point the focus of the lesson moves from words and meanings to *sounds*. Similar and matching sounds in a poem are used to make it engaging and memorable to read and listen to, as well as to enhance a mood or stress a theme. Learners will combine words and sounds in the following activities to create their own poems.

> **Audioscript:** Track 54
> Thanks for those
> Blazing days on beaches,

> **Answers**
> **Sounds**
> **Th**anks for **those**
> **Bl**azing d**a**ys on b**ea**ches
> Same sounds: 'b', 'a' sound.
> Similar: 'th' - soft (thanks) and hard 'th' sound (those).

## 7 Pronunciation 54 [CD2 Track 22]

- Ask learners to look for through the poem again and find other examples of similar and matching sounds in the poem. You could ask learners to do this in small groups and make it into a reading race, awarding points when learners find matching sounds or read the poem and ask learners to shout *Stop!* (or raise hands) when they hear a matching sound. However, ask learners to read aloud or listen to the lines afterwards to appreciate the way they sound and how this enhances the descriptive quality of the poem.

> **Answers**
> **Other lines with similar and matching sounds:**
> On **d**ismal **d**ays,
> As grey as slate,
>
> For **r**ipening **a**pples,
> **P**ears and **p**eaches;
>
> Your n**o**ble gl**o**w;

## 8 Pronunciation 55 [CD2 Track 23]

- Now ask them to look at the words in **Activity 8** and practise saying them. They then need to match the words that have the same sound, then listen to the audio and check.

> **Answers**
> **w**arm **w**onderful / **m**agical **m**akes / br**i**ght sh**i**ning

 **For further practice, see Activities 4 and 5 in the Activity Book.**

## 9 Write

- Now focus learners on the picture next to **Activity 9** and ask them what words come to mind when they see this picture, eliciting some words from **Activity 8**

and other ones learners suggest (especially ones that describe sunlight and colour, as depicted in the illustration).

- Now draw their attention to the verse and point out the gaps. Tell them that they are going to fill the gaps with words from **Activity 8**. They need to choose words with the same matching sound to complete each line. Do the first one as an example, eliciting which word has the same sound as bright (shining). Then read the completed line together:
  Thanks for
  *Your bright shining light.*
- Now ask them to complete the other lines in the same way, working collaboratively in pairs.
- During feedback, read out the completed verse, emphasising the matching sounds.

> **Answers**
> Thanks for
> Your bright shining light,
> In the morning
> Your warm wonderful glow
> In the evening
> That makes colours magical.

 **For further practice, see Activity 6 in the Activity Book.**

## 10 Write

- Now tell learners that they are going to write their own poem about something or someone that makes them feel happy. **Note:** Some of the topics suggested lend themselves better to learners working individually because they are personal, others (e.g. an activity or type of weather) could be done collaboratively. Decide if your learners would benefit more from working individually, so they can express their own ideas, or from the support of pair or group work.
- Give learners time to choose a topic and help them by eliciting and inputting ideas and suggestions for each one.
- When learners have thought of a topic ask them to brainstorm words associated with the topic to make descriptive phrases. Ask them to record these on a Mind Map. Monitor and circulate, helping with vocabulary and helping learners to make connections between words with the same or similar sounds.
- Ask learners to make phrases to describe their chosen topic and put them in a verse, using the same model and structure as the example in **Activity 9**. Tell them to start the verse as in the example (in **Activity 10**) and that it does not need to rhyme.
- When they have prepared a satisfactory first draft, ask them to write the verse on clean paper. Have them mount this on coloured paper and decorate with pictures to display on the classroom walls.
- Finally, ask learners to walk around the classroom and read each other's poems. They should note down two new and / or interesting words or phrases from each one (or ask them to note down, say, ten new words from their reading of all the poems, if there are a lot of texts).

| Answers |
| --- |
| Learners' own answers. |

## 11  Values

- Focus learners on the **Values** heading and read through the questions together. Then ask them in pairs to discuss the bullet pointed list of ways to say thank you. Which do they think is the best way of saying thank you? Can they think of any other ways to say thank you?

| Answers |
| --- |
| Depending on your culture and / or the conventions of the country you live in, ways to say thank you include: sending a thank-you card, saying thank you by text and email; making a phone call to say thanks; buying someone some flowers; giving chocolates; buying a small gift to show appreciation for something; doing something for someone in return; simply saying 'thank you' face to face. |

## Wrap up

- Have learners record the words or phrases they noted down in the last stage of **Activity 11**. They can record in vocabulary notebooks and / or on vocabulary cards for recycling and review activities.

## Activity Book

## 1 Read

- Learners read the poem, *Thank You Letter* by Eric Finney again, and choose the correct answer to complete sentences about the content of the poem.

| Answers |
| --- |
| **1** rises and goes down |
| **2** always on time |
| **3** makes grey days brighter |
| **4** making the whole world feel happy |
| **5** making beaches hot and bright |
| **6** making fruit ready to eat |
| **7** light |
| **8** valuable you are |

## 2 Vocabulary

- Learners read a set of sentences about the sun and replace underlined words with more descriptive words from the box.

| Answers |
| --- |
| **1** blazing |
| **2** at dawn |
| **3** glow |
| **4** sunset |
| **5** ripening |

## 3 Pronunciation 75 [CD2 Track 43]

- Learners listen to sets of words from the poem and identify which sound is the same or similar in each group.

**Audioscript:** Track 75

1

dismal

days

2

days

grey

late

slate

wait

3

late

slate

wait

| Answers |
| --- |
| **1** 'd' sound |
| **2** the vowel sound /eɪ/ |
| **3** 't' sound |

## 4 Pronunciation 76 [CD2 Track 44]

- Learners listen to the sets of words and identify the same or similar sounds in each group.

**Audioscript:** Track 76

1

funny

face

2

play

day

awake

3

cry

night

4

beautiful

baby

brother

| Answers |
| --- |
| **1** funny / face 'f' sound |
| **2** the vowel sound ('a') /eɪ/ |
| **3** the vowel sound ('i') /aɪ/ |
| **4** 'b' sound |

## 5 Write

- Learners use the matching words in **Activity 5** to complete the verse about a baby brother.

> **Answers**
> Dear baby brother,
> Just a line to say,
> Thanks for your big smile
> And funny face.
> You play all day,
> And cry at night,
> You keep me awake,
> But I love you anyway,
> My beautiful baby brother ...

## 6 Challenge

- Learners write their own short poem about one of three given topics, using a given structure and word prompts as a guide and words with similar or matching sounds.

> **Answers**
> Learners' own answers.

# Lesson 6: Choose a project

Learner's Book pages: 122–123

### Lesson objectives

**Speaking:** Participate in a discussion forum (depends on how Project 2 is set up) about an issue connected to your school, town / city or age group; revise unit themes; discuss **Unit 8** Big question.

**Writing:** Organise and prepare notes for a poster outlining points about communicating effectively in your country; add comments to a discussion forum (depends on how Project 2 is set up); revise unit themes.

**Critical thinking:** Select points about communicating effectively on your country; give opinions on a topic related to personal experience; apply new skills and language acquired in **Unit 8** to project work and revision activities.

**Language focus:** Recycling language points from **Unit 8**, i.e. present continuous forms (for arrangements); polite requests (*could; would you mind ... ?*).

**Vocabulary:** Ways of communicating (verb-noun collocations); gestures for communication; functional language for discussions; words about the sun

**Materials:** paper; poster paper or IWB slides

### Learner's Book

###  Warm up

- Play *Bingo* to revise key vocabulary from **Unit 8**, but ask learners to call out the words, rather than the teacher. Focus the game on a specific vocabulary area that you wish to revise from **Unit 8**, or play several rounds and cover a different topic in each one.

- Give each learner a handout with a bingo grid with nine squares (3 × 3). Choose a topic from **Unit 8** and do a quick brainstorm of key words / phrases around the class, e.g.
  *Ways of communicating: send a text / raise your hand / write a blog,* etc.
- Now ask learners to fill in the grid on their handout with a relevant word / phrase from the focus topic. They must write one word / phrase in each box.
- Explain that you are now going to move around the class and ask learners randomly to call out a word from their grid. Other learners must listen and cross out the word if it also appears on their grid. When they have three crosses in a row – either horizontally, vertically or diagonally – they shout *Bingo!* and win the round. Ask the winner to read out his or her winning line of three words.
- You can continue playing until you have a second and third learner who gains 'three in a row'. Alternatively, you could stop this round and have another round with a different topic and a new grid.
- Do a practice turn first to make sure learners are clear about the rules of the game. Ask one or two learners to call out a word and demonstrate with your own grid or a copy on the board how you would cross those words out if they appeared on your grid.
- Tell learners they are now going to choose from the two projects and follow the instructions below for the one they have decided on.

### 1  A communication poster

- Put learners in small groups and take them through the step-by-step instructions presented in the Learner's Book. Spend time helping them to generate ideas for the three categories listed in stage 1.
- When they are at the stage of choosing the ten most important points, give them assistance on how to select and prioritise. If they have made decisions, you could stretch some learners by asking them to explain why they have chosen some points above others.
- Circulate and give assistance with language expression and vocabulary.
- When learners have drafted ten points, ask them to check their work for grammar vocabulary and spelling, then ask them to copy the points onto a large piece of paper to make a poster. Allow them to decorate with pictures and different colours.
- When they have finished, ask learners to display their posters on the wall. Allow them to walk around and read other groups' posters. While they are reading, they should make a note of any points that are different to theirs.

> **Answers**
> Learners' own answers.

### Wrap up

- At the end, decide as a class on the ten most important pieces of advice about communication in their country.

## 2 👄 Create a discussion forum

- **Critical thinking:** Focus learners' attention on the topic areas and brainstorm ideas for each one. The aim here is that learners choose a discussion area that is topical, relevant and personal to them and their realm of immediate experience.
- Now establish the discussion forum. This can be online, if you have the facilities, or a class speaking activity (the same codes of interaction apply to both).
- Before they begin the discussion, ask them to write down some notes about the topic and their own thoughts and opinions. While they are doing this, monitor and circulate, helping with any questions about vocabulary and how to express certain points.
- When the forum is set up, tell learners that each person must make at least one comment. Remind them of appropriate ways of communicating and functional phrases to use (see **Lesson 4**).
- If you choose to conduct the discussion forum as a speaking activity, you could set it up either as a whole class debate, or ask learners to work in groups of about five or six (this way, learners may get more speaking practice).
- **Additional support and practice:** If the forum is conducted as a speaking activity, you could structure the use of functional language for interacting appropriately as follows: learners have a list of the target phrases in front of them (either in their notebooks or on a handout); as they use them in the discussion, they tick them off. Having to physically tick off ones they use will raise their awareness of their function and motivate them to actually incorporate the phrases. They obviously don't have to use all the phrases.

**Answers**
Learners' own answers.

## 👉 Wrap up

- At the end of the forum, ask learners to suggest which ideas they thought were the strongest and most interesting points. This can be done whether the forum is conducted online or as a speaking activity.

## 👄 Reflect on your learning

- These revision activities can be approached in different ways, according to the level and character of your class.
  - Questions 1–8 could be used as a class quiz, with learners in teams and a time limit given to write answers to each question.
  - Alternatively, you could conduct a revision session. Ask learners to work in pairs and take longer to think about and write down their answers. When pairs have finished the questions, they swap with another pair and correct each other's work, with you monitoring and giving help and advice when needed.
  - You could set this task for homework / self-study.

**Answers**
1 (Five from ... )
  raise your hand
  send an email /a text / a note
  write an email / a text / a note / a blog
  make a call / a note
  reply to an email / a text / a note / a blog / a note / a call
  Learners' own answers.
2 (Three from ... )
  Adults saying hello to each other with a handshake; good friends greeting each other with a hug; making eye contact when you are talking to someone.
  (Saudi Arabia), shaking the head from side to side means 'yes'.
  (Thailand), people greeting each other by pressing their palms together and bowing their heads.
  (China), people saying hello with a small nod and a bow.
  (Japan), waving your hand with the palm outwards, meaning 'I don't understand'.
  Learners' own answers.
3 Main point of each message / purpose:
  Message 1 – Billy tells Bruno that he's left his pet tarantula (spider) at his house. He asks him to catch it for him. (Purpose: asking someone to do something)
  Message 2 – Bob Bailey (a builder) reminds Mrs Smith that he is going to take her front door off this afternoon (Purpose: a reminder)
  Message 3 – Mandy invites Mila to go rock climbing for her birthday celebration on Sunday (Purpose: an invitation).
  Message 4 – The receptionist calls Tom to tell him that his dental appointment has been changed. (Purpose: giving information)
4 Ben and Carl handed their homework in late because they lost the internet connection in their homes (and so couldn't access a website they needed to finish the homework).
  **Differences between their explanations:** (three from ... )
  Ben tells the teacher first that he hasn't done the homework before the teacher has to 'chase' him/Carl tries to leave the classroom without mentioning it.
  Ben told Mr Simms *before* the homework deadline that his homework would be late/Carl told him on the day of the deadline.
  Ben said sorry for the late homework/Carl didn't. He apologised for having to hand the homework in late.
  Ben gave the teacher a simple direct explanation about the problem/Carl started rambling and going into unnecessary details.
  Ben told Mr Simms when he could hand in the homework (i.e. he offered a solution to the problem)/Carl didn't mention this or offer any alternatives.
5 The classmates discussed how to spend the money they raised through their class activities at the school fair.
  **Phrases:**
  introducing your point: I think we should ... I think it is (better to) ...
  partly agreeing: I think it's a good idea to ... , but not ... I can see your point but ...
  encouraging other people to respond: What does everyone else think? What do other people think? What do you all think?
6 A thank you letter.
7 What the writer liked about the sun: (four from ... )
  Dawns and sunsets.
  The way it brightens grey, cold days.
  The way it moves out from behind a cloud.
  Bright, hot days on beaches.
  The way it ripens fruit and makes it ready to eat.
  The beauty of sunlight.

**8** Words or phrases to describe the sun and what it does: (five from ...).

blazing
glow
sunset
dawn
ripening fruit
cheerful grace

## Look what I can do!

**Aim:** To check learners have fulfilled the objectives for **Unit 8** (and to what degree).

- Present the objectives slide or poster from the introduction to **Unit 8** (in **Lesson 1**) and remind learners of the objectives from the start of the unit.
- Focus their attention on the '*I can ...*' statements and read through together. You could put these on a slide or write on the board. Ask learners if they feel they can now do these tasks after completing **Unit 8**. By this point, you should have a clear idea yourself of how well your learners have completed the tasks. However, ask them to now do an initial self-assessment.
- Put learners in pairs and ask them to look through their notebooks and portfolios to find evidence of their work for each of the statements. Then they give themselves a rating as follows:
  ✓ Yes, I can – no problem!
  ? A little – I need more practice.
  ☹ No – I need a lot more practice.
- Circulate and chat to learners about their self-assessment (some might be overly modest and you can point out that their rating could be higher). Make notes about areas that learners are not confident about (if you haven't already done so) for future reference (see **Teaching tip**).
- Conduct a general feedback at the end and find out which tasks learners found the most interesting / useful / challenging, etc.

Answers
Learners' own answers.

## 👉 Wrap up

- As a class, look at the Big question again on a slide or written on the board: *How do we communicate effectively with each other?*
- Ask learners: *What are good ways to communicate with each other? How can we get our message across?* Elicit a couple of responses before asking learners to work in small groups, look through **Unit 8** and write down three ways that we can communicate effectively with each other. Point out to them that this is not about methods of communication such as speaking or texting, it is about *how* you communicate – the words you choose, your manner, etc.
- **Additional support and practice:** Instead of having learners come up with their own answers to the Big question, you could guide them by giving them the following sentences and ask them to sort into two

categories: *good / effective* and *bad / ineffective* ways of communicating. These sentences all correspond to themes and topics from the lessons in **Unit 8**; all good sentences are ticked (✓) below:
*Think about the words to use.* ✓
*Be polite and respect other people.* ✓
*Think that your opinion is the most important – other opinions don't matter.*
*Remember that people often communicate in different ways in different parts of the world.* ✓
*Use different ways to communicate according to the situation.* ✓
*Always use the same method of communication.*
*If there's a problem, say nothing – don't try to explain.*
*Think about what you say before saying it.* ✓
*Respect other points of view; try to see both sides.* ✓
*Say or write whatever you like even if it is rude or might hurt someone.*
*Say what you think without thinking first.*
*Listen to other people's opinions.* ✓

- These sentences can be written on the board or put on a slide for learners to categorise. Alternatively, you could ask them to write on strips of paper for learners to categorise in small groups at their tables/desks. You could also use them as a listening activity: read them out and ask learners to respond to each one by raising their hands (for good) or keeping hands down (for bad). They could also respond with signs, e.g. a green sign and smiley face for good, a red one for bad.

## Activity Book

### Revision

### 1 Vocabulary

- Learners read definitions and complete words drawn from **Lessons 1–6** in **Unit 8**.

Answers
1 blog
2 reply
3 raise
4 greet
5 shake
6 sunset

### 2 Use of English

- Learners complete a gapped email text with the correct form of the verbs in the box, focusing on language points from **Lessons 1–6**.

**Answers**
1 borrowed
2 am going
3 is choosing
4 are playing
5 is going
6 come

## 3 Over to you

- Learners write their own responses in the form of sentences and questions to given situations. This task utilises functional language covered in **Lessons 1–6**.

**Answers**
Learners' own answers.

## My global progress

- Learners think about their own responses to topics and activities in the units and answer the questions.

**Answers**
Learners' own answers.

### Teaching tip

Review the learners' work and their own assessment of their progress, noting areas where learners demonstrate strength and confidence and areas where they need additional instruction and practice. Use this information to select areas for review and specific focus, as you continue to **Unit 9**.

# Review 4

Learner's Book pages: 124–125

- Review 4 offers learners the opportunity to review and recycle key language and vocabulary items from **Units 7** and **8**, presented in similar contexts to themes that appeared in these units. All items are briefly covered in activities that are similar in type to those in the Activity Book. There is a range of activity types that cover all skills areas.
- Learners can do Review 4 activities either in class or for homework. However, there is a short speaking activity, which will need to be covered in class (see below for suggestion). The Review pages can also be used to occupy early finishers, provided learners have already covered the relevant language points in class.
- **Speaking activities:** If learners have done the Review 4 activities at home, the speaking activity could be carried out during a Review 4 feedback session, either at the beginning or end of the class.
- **Feedback:** Answers to the activities can be elicited from learners or displayed on the board or on a slide for learners to use to correct their work. To make the correction stage more interactive, ask learners to swap notebooks and correct each other's work.

## 1 Listen 56 [CD2 Track 24]

- Learners listen to four messages and match to a picture.

**Audioscript:** Track 56

**Message 1:** Hi Danny. This is Marcus. I've got a big favour to ask! I'm going cycling with my cousin on Saturday. Would you mind if I borrowed your helmet? The strap's broken on mine. I'll bring it back on Sunday morning. Could you let me know if that's OK? Thanks! Bye!

**Message 2:** Hi Freya, this is Eva. This is just to let you know that Ana and I are coming to your birthday lunch on Sunday at the pizza restaurant. Would you mind if we left the restaurant at 2.30 pm? It's a bit early, I know. Our aunt and uncle are arriving from Australia and we are going to the airport to meet them. Hope that's OK, see you on Sunday!

**Message 3:** Hi Mum, this is Yasmin. This is just to let you know that I'm playing basketball today after school. I thought it was tomorrow but it's today! Could you pick me up at 6.30? Thanks, Mum, bye!

**Message 4:** Hello, this is a message for Jamie from Mr Phillips. Just to let you know that we are not having football practice on Thursday morning this week – we're having it on Friday morning instead. And could you bring the money for the school trip in two weeks' time? Thanks, Jamie. Bye!

**Answers**
Message 1 – Picture c
Message 2 – Picture a
Message 3 – Picture d
Message 4 – Picture b

## 2 Listen 56 [CD2 Track 24]

- Learners listen to the messages again and identify the arrangements that each person has.

**Answers**
1 (Example) Marcus is going cycling with his cousin on Saturday.
2 Eva and Ana are coming/going to Freya's birthday lunch on Sunday and they are also going to meet their aunt and uncle at the airport.
3 Yasmin is playing basketball today after school.
4 Jamie is having football practice on Friday morning instead of Thursday morning.

## 3 Vocabulary

- Learners read descriptions and guess the words.

**Answers**
1 knowledgeable
2 an architect
3 voluntary work
4 a car mechanic
5 a reporter
6 confident
7 sleeve
8 a zip

## 4 Talk

• Learners tell a partner about personal arrangements they have for next week.

> **Answers**
> Learners' own answers.

## 5 Use of English

Learners choose the correct form of the verb or correct preposition to complete the job advertisement text.

> **Answers**
> **1** looking
> **2** about
> **3** with
> **4** is
> **5** in
> **6** on
> **7** will
> **8** could

## 6 Write

• Learners write an email to a friend inviting them to meet up at the weekend. Prompts are given to support the writing task.

> **Answers**
> Learners' own answers.

## 7 Talk

• Learners compare the poems in **Units 7** and **8**, saying which one they liked best and why.

> **Answers**
> Learners' own answers.

# 9 Travellers' tales

**Big question** What can we learn from travelling and holidays?

## Unit overview

In this unit learners will:
- talk about holiday activities
- read about a place to visit
- describe a special place
- write a poem about a dream holiday
- read and talk about a special journey.

In **Unit 9**, learners will explore the topic of travel and holidays, looking at how these activities and experiences make us feel and what we can learn from them. This is reflected in the Big question, which is presented in **Lesson 1**. As with all other units, learners will understand that themes, tasks and projects in the unit will contribute to answering this question at the end.

The unit begins by looking at interesting and unusual holiday activities, giving learners opportunities to talk about the type of activities that are popular in their own countries, but also consider new and unusual ones and whether they would like to experience them. From holiday activities, learners move on to holiday places, evaluating advantages and disadvantages and looking at how these are reflected in comments on an online forum. In **Lesson 3**, learners listen to a description of a special place, then use this as a model for their own account of a place which has special significance for them. In **Lesson 4**, they consider where they would go for a dream holiday and use their thoughts and feelings to write a simple poem. Finally, they explore the notion of other kinds of journeys by looking at a piece of literature which examines the journey made by light. There is an opportunity here to combine aspects of science with literature.

The **Photocopiable activities** provide a cross curricular focus in the form of a holiday-themed worksheet, practising calculations using dates (17), as well as conversation practice about holiday experiences, using a variety of structures (18).

### Language focus

Second conditional forms (review); *adjectives + prepositions*.

**Vocabulary topics:** Holiday activities (nouns with *-ing*); expressing preferences in imaginary situations; verbs describing senses (review); descriptive adjectives; expressions with *take*.

### Self-assessment
- I can talk about trying new holiday activities.
- I can read and discuss information about a place to visit.
- I can describe a place that is special to me.
- I can listen and understand other descriptions.
- I can write a poem about a dream holiday.
- I can read and talk about a story about a special journey.

### Teaching tip

**Revision tips:** At this stage in the course, you might be considering revision of key themes examined in the Stage 6 course and language and vocabulary items that have arisen. When organising revision activities, keep in mind different learning styles. For example, visual learners will respond to materials with colour and pictures: ask them to write important points on Post-its and stick around the classroom as constant reminders; revise points from coloured flashcards which can be turned over to test memory; or make Mind Maps with colour and simple diagrams. Auditory learners will respond well to verbalising their revision, i.e. talking through revision points with each other and the teacher. Kinaesthetic learners will respond well to a hands-on approach, e.g. activities which involve physically matching and categorising different items on pieces of card; or doing standard textbook revision activities on separate cards chosen from a pile in the middle of the table or on the teacher's desk (as opposed to working through in a linear fashion from a textbook).

# Lesson 1: Travellers' tales

Learner's Book pages: 126–127

Activity Book pages: 100–101

## Lesson objectives

**Listening:** Listen to children talking about holiday activities they would and wouldn't like to try and understand the reasons why; identify functional language expressing imaginary situations.

**Speaking:** Talk about holiday activities; talk about which activities you would and wouldn't like to try; play a guessing game about holiday activities with a partner.

**Critical thinking:** Express opinions and indicate preferences for holiday activities.

**Language focus:** 2nd conditional (review).

**Vocabulary:** Holiday activities (nouns with *–ing*): *rock-climbing, skiing, snorkelling, bungee-jumping, snowboarding, surfing*

**Materials:** poster paper or electronic slides, coloured pens; video clips of adventurous holiday activities (optional for **Warm up**).

## Learner's Book

###  Warm up

- To introduce the Big question, start by telling the class that this unit is going to be about travel and holiday activities, and that these activities give us interesting and sometimes powerful experiences that we can learn from. So the Big question is ... *What can we learn from travelling & holidays?*
- Write the question on the board (for an electronic presentation, create a slide with interesting graphics). Tell learners that you are all going to do tasks and projects in the unit that will answer this question.
- Introduce the unit objectives to show learners what tasks are coming up. Present the objectives on a slide or large piece of poster paper to attach to the board.
- Tell learners that you will answer the Big question and look again at the objectives at the end of the unit. Keep the objectives slide / poster to revisit at the end of the unit.
- Tell learners that you are going to start by looking at exciting and unusual holiday activities. If you have the facilities, show the class some video clips of some of the more dramatic activities featured in the Learner's Book such as bungee-jumping, surfing and snowboarding and elicit their reactions.
- Now focus learners on the pictures in the first page of the unit and ask if they can see any of the activities mentioned during the warm-up.
  **Note:** If you haven't shown learners video clips, simply move on to **Activity 1** in the Learner's Book and use the pictures in the book to engage them with the topic.

## 1  Talk about it

- Focus learners on the questions in **Activity 1** and look at the first one together, eliciting which holiday activities are popular in their country. Then look at the pictures and, if you think it is possible that they have tried any of the activities, elicit which ones and encourage learners to talk a little about the experience (*Where? When? Was it fun? How did you feel? Was it scary? Would you do it again?*).
- Now ask learners to discuss the last question: *Which activities would you like to try?* in pairs. At this point, don't worry if they make errors with the 2nd conditional structure, as long as they understand the sense of the question.
- Conduct a quick feedback to get a general idea of which activities appeal the most to learners.
- **Critical thinking:** Learners relate the topic to their own realm of experience and identify their own preferences from a choice of activities.

> **Answers**
> Learners' own answers.

## 2 Word study

- Focus attention on the words in the box and ask learners to match them to the pictures.
- As a class talk about which activities, if any can be done in your country and where.
- Do a quick focus on pronunciation and word stress. If necessary, tap or clap the stress pattern at the same time as saying the words. Have the class repeat and clap after you. If learners need further practice, ask them to do the same activity again in pairs. You could extend the activity (and help learners assimilate the words) by clapping out stress patterns and ask learners to guess the word (or words – if more than one word follows the same stress patterns). Ask them to turn over their books so they can't see the words for an extra challenge.

> **Answers**
> **a** rock-climbing (Stress pattern: Ooo)
> **b** skiing (Oo)
> **c** snorkelling (Ooo)
> **d** bungee-jumping (Oooo)
> **e** snowboarding (Ooo)
> **f** surfing (Oo)

[AB] **For further practice, see Activity 1 in the Activity Book.**

## 3 Listen 57 [CD2 Track 25]

- Tell the class that they are going to listen to four children talking about the activities in the pictures. They need to listen and identify which activities the children are talking about. Ask them to listen and find out too if the children have already done the activities or not.

- Play the listening text, pausing after each dialogue; learners listen for and write the activities mentioned from **Activity 2**.
- After listening to all four speakers once, check answers with the class. Establish that none of the children have done any of the activities before. If learners have understood this, challenge them by asking them *how* they know and eliciting that the speakers used the word, *would*, because they were *imagining* the situations.

---

**Audioscript:** Track 57

**Conversation 1**

**Boy 1:** ... Are you serious? I think you're crazy! You couldn't do it anyway, you're too young ... they wouldn't let you ... !

**Boy 2:** Yes, I know I'm too young now ... but I'd really like to try it when I'm older. It would be fantastic – like flying through the air!

**Boy 1:** No way! It's dangerous! You could break your leg! They tie the elastic cord around your ankles, then push you off a bridge ... .There is no way I'd do it!

**Boy 2:** OK, you have an elastic cord around your ankles but you also have a harness around the top part of your body. And the feeling you get is really fantastic ... it's really exciting and thrilling ... that's what I've heard anyway ...

**Boy 1:** Who told you that?

**Boy 2:** My aunt and uncle did it last year on holiday in New Zealand. They said it was the best thing ever and that everyone should do it once in their life time!

**Conversation 2**

**Girl 1:** I don't know ... I don't think I'd try it ... I'd be really scared ... I'd keep thinking I was going to fall off.

**Girl 2:** Yeah, you'd probably fall off a lot while you were learning ... It's all about balance I think – you'd need to have strong legs too. I'd love to have a go though ...

**Girl 1:** Yeah, maybe ... I suppose you could start by just lying on the board and getting used to moving on top of the waves. Then when you're ready you could try standing up ...

**Girl 2:** You'd have to be a good swimmer I think and not be scared of big waves.

**Girl 1:** Hmm, maybe I would have a go, if I had the chance. You have to try new things, don't you? Or you never find out what you can do!

---

**Answers**
The children are talking about:
**Part 1:** bungee-jumping
**Part 2:** snorkelling
None of the children have tried the activities (hence use of *2nd conditional*).

---

## 4 Listen 57 [CD2 Track 25]

- Focus learners on the questions in **Activity 4** and read through together. Learners may know some of the answers already; if they do, allow them to speculate, then ask them to listen and check.

- Ask all learners to listen again for the answers to questions 1 and 2. After listening, ask them to compare answers in pairs, then go through the answers as a class.
- When you conduct feedback, play the audio again if necessary, stopping after each comment and highlighting the parts of each comment needed for the answers.

---

**Answers**
1 The first boy thinks that the activity is dangerous and a crazy thing to do. The second boy thinks the activity would be 'fantastic' – exciting and thrilling, 'like flying through the air'.
2 The first girl is not sure at first if she would like to try the activity. She thinks she would be really scared. But by the end of the conversation she decides that she would probably try it after all, if she had the opportunity.

---

## 5 Listen 57 [CD2 Track 25]

- Tell learners that they are now going to listen for a third time, this time to focus specifically on the words and phrases the children use to give their opinions about the activities.
- Read through the phrases 1–6 first, highlighting the gaps. Ask learners to read again in pairs and discuss which words might be missing. Ask them to write the phrases in their notebooks with gaps in preparation for listening and completing.
- Now ask them to listen again, pausing after each target phrase, to either check their ideas or complete the missing words in their notebooks.
- **Additional support and practice:** This activity could obviously be simplified by stopping after each phrase rather than waiting to the end of each dialogue. If you do this, make the activity a little more challenging by having learners either call out *Stop!* or raise their hands when they hear a target phrase. Then pause the audio and allow them to complete the phrase.
- Go through the missing words as a class.

---

**Answers**
1 I'd really like to try it. It would be fantastic.
2 There is no way I'd do it!
3 It's really exciting and thrilling.
4 I don't think I would try it ... I'd be really scared.
5 I'd love to have a go.
6 Maybe I would have a go, if I had the chance.

---

## 6 Use of English

- Ask learners if the phrases in **Activity 5** express real or imaginary situations. *Have the children already done the activities?* (No, then the phrases are expressing *imaginary* situations). Ask if they know (or can remember) the name of the kind of structure that is used in these sentences, and elicit or tell them that it is the 2nd conditional.

## Answers
The phrases are 2nd conditional sentences. They express imaginary situations.

 **For further practice, see Activity 4 in the Activity Book.**

## 7 Talk

- At this point, elicit again the words to describe the activities in the pictures. As you go through them, make sure learners are clear about pronunciation and word stress, before they use the words in the speaking activity.
- Ask what they notice about the ending of all the words and elicit that they are all nouns ending in *-ing*. Next, draw their attention to the **Word study** box on page 126 and explain that nouns ending in *-ing* often describe actions. Look at the example sentences showing the use of more nouns ending in *-ing*.
- **Critical thinking:** Now ask learners to work in pairs and talk about the activities in the pictures. Encourage them to give their personal opinions about the activities, using the phrases in **Activity 5**, taken from the listening.
- First, go through the phrases, having learners repeat after you, paying attention to intonation (e.g. *There's no WAY I'd do it!*).
- **Additional support and practice:** Write the target phrases on the board or on a slide and use the *backchaining* method to drill the sentences (for instructions, see **Unit 1 Lesson 1 Additional support and practice**). Once learners are confidently pronouncing the phrases, help them to remember by doing a *disappearing drill* on the sentences until they can remember them by heart (for instructions, see **Unit 1, Lesson 1,** as above).
- For feedback, say an activity and elicit individual responses around the class, using the target phrases. E.g. Snowboarding : *I'd like to have a go! | Maybe I'd have a go if I had the chance ... | There's no way I'd do it!*
- **Extend and challenge:** When learners are using the target phrases in **Activity 5** in their pair work conversations, monitor and circulate, encouraging stronger learners to combine and vary the target phrases as follows:
  *There's no way I'd do it – I'd be really scared!*
  *I'd like to have a go, if I had the chance ...*
  *I think it would be really exciting but quite scary ..., etc*

## Answers
Learners' own answers.

 **For further practice, see Activity 5 in the Activity Book.**

## 8 Talk

- As a final consolidation activity, ask learners to work with a different partner and carry out a similar activity to the *20 questions* game (see **Unit 1, Lesson 4**). They should think of an activity and their partner has to guess what it is, asking yes / no questions.
- Tell them that their partner must ask at least three questions before asking a question naming an actual sport (e.g. *Is it snorkelling?*).
- Allow learners to think of any sport or activity to widen the scope and encourage more question practice. Stipulate, however, that learners need to choose an *-ing* activity, to focus them on this language point.

## Answers
Learners' own answers.

##  Wrap up

- To finish off, you could show more video clips and/ or ask learners to share experiences of more general holiday activities (e.g. cycling, horse-riding, etc.) not mentioned in this lesson.

## Activity Book

## 1 Vocabulary

- Learners complete words describing holiday activities and match to a picture.

## Answers
1 surfing  f
2 rock-climbing  a
3 snorkelling  c
4 bungee-jumping  d
5 snowboarding  e
6 skiing  b

## 2 Read

- Learners read a dialogue about holiday activities and identify which activities the children are talking about.

## Answers
snorkelling, bungee-jumping, skiing

## 3 Read

- Learners read the dialogue again and answer comprehension questions.

## Answers
1 no
2 snorkelling and skiing
3 snorkelling
4 bungee-jumping and skiing

## 4 Use of English

- Learners make sentences from given prompts using the 2nd conditional.

> **Answers**
> 1 Ollie would like to try/go snorkelling if he had the chance.
> 2 Tara's family would like to visit the Taj Mahal if they went to India.
> 3 If Luis had a choice, he would go to Disneyland.
> 4 My uncle would cycle around Europe if he had more time.
> 5 If Aisha went on holiday, she would go bungee-jumping.

## 5 Word study

- Learners finish sentences with personal responses, using target 2nd conditional phrases and words from **Activity 1**, and other vocabulary about holiday activities.

> **Answers**
> Learners' own answers.

# Lesson 2: Where shall we go?

Learner's Book pages: 128–129
Activity Book pages: 102–103

### Lesson objectives

**Reading:** Read opinions on a forum about a day out at a marine wildlife park; practise techniques to predict content and text type.

**Speaking:** Talk about places you like to visit on a day out; discuss positive and negative points about the marine park in the text, drawing conclusions about whether you'd like to visit.

**Writing:** Write a post for an online forum about a place that you have visited; compare comments with classmates who have visited the same place.

**Critical thinking:** Discuss positive and negative points and come to a conclusion.

**Vocabulary:** Places to visit: *an adventure playground, a wildlife park, a zoo, a museum, a theme park*

**Materials:** Learner's Book, Activity Book. Copies of **Photocopiable activity 17**.

## Learner's Book

### ⮕ Warm up

- Ask learners to think about the last day trip they went on, either with family, friends or on a school trip. Elicit the places and write on the board. Then ask learners to comment on the places: Who has been there? When? What did they like about it? Were there any bad points? Would they recommend it to someone else?
- Focus in particular on good and bad points about each place, to prepare learners for the tasks later in the lesson.

## 1 🗨 Talk about it

- Focus attention on the four questions and read through together. Read out the places in the box and ask learners to draw any comparisons with places mentioned in the warm-up stage. Then ask them to discuss the questions in pairs.
- When you conduct feedback, focus in particular on the last question. Elicit from learners what factors make them and their families decide where to go on a day trip (e.g. variety of things to do, cost, distance from home, facilities available, etc.). Write their suggestions on the board to refer to later in the lesson.
- **Critical thinking:** Giving an opinion and making deductions.

> **Answers**
> Learners' own answers.

## 2 Read

- Focus learners on the text on page 129 and ask them what type of text they think it is. Where *would they see it?* (online) *What kind of website would it appear on?* (a travel / country or city guide / holidays website) *What type of text is it?* (an Internet forum).
- Ask them what they think they will find out from the forum. Highlight such features as the stars and the highlighted quotes as headings.
- When learners have offered some suggestions as to what they might find out from the text, point out to them that they have already deduced quite a lot about the content of the text simply by looking at what type of text it is and making predictions. Draw their attention to the **Reading strategy** in the Learner's Book. Make learners aware that they can often guess the content of a reading text by looking at what *type* of text it is, as well as other more obvious clues such as pictures and headings.

> **Answers**
> The text is an online forum. You read it to find out people's opinions about a place and if they recommend it as a place to visit.

## 3 Read

- Now ask learners to read the text and match it to a place in the box in **Activity 1**. Remind them that they just need to scan the text at this point to find out that information and not worry about other details and words they don't know. Give them a time limit to encourage them to be focused.

## 4 📝 Read

- Ask learners now to draw a table in their notebooks, to note down good and bad points about the marine wildlife park, as follows:

| Place | Good points | Bad points |
|---|---|---|
| *Sol Marine Park* | | |

- Before they read, pre-teach the words, *disappointed, feeding time, downside, queue.* You could read out the following definitions (in the order below – the order the words appear in the text) and ask them to find the words in the text; or for more support, write the words on the board, read the definitions and ask learners to identify the words:
  *When something isn't as good as you thought it would be, or doesn't happen in the way you expected* (disappointed).
  *The time when animals get their food* (feeding time).
  *A bad point about something, a disadvantage* (downside).
  *When you stand in a line to wait for something, e.g. to get into the cinema* (a queue).
- Now tell them to read the forum text again, more slowly, looking specifically for good and bad points about the Marine Park. They should read and then discuss with a partner, before writing notes in the table.
- Conduct feedback, highlighting good and bad points on the board.

**Answers**

| Good points | Bad points |
|---|---|
| Feeding time at the dolphin arena. 'Fascinating facts' at marine life exhibition. Interesting film about endangered marine species. Underground aquarium – 'awesome'. | Crowds of people. Queues to get into attractions. Very expensive to get in. Have to pay extra for some attractions. Small choice of expensive takeaway food to eat inside. |

 For further practice, see Activities 1, 2 and 3 in the Activity Book.

## 5 💬 Talk

- **Critical thinking:** Ask learners to work in pairs and imagine that they live quite near to Sol Marine Park and their family is thinking of having a day out there. They should look at the good and bad points on their table and use the points to decide if they would like to go there or not.
- To help them decide, ask them to think about which points are the most important to them, e.g. would they like to see the underground aquarium even if there were a lot of crowds, or would that spoil the experience too much?

- **Extend and challenge:** If your learners are confident speakers, or if you want to stretch them further, use this opportunity to input natural, conversational phrases such as:
  *I'd like to see the underground aquarium, even if there were a lot of crowds.* (*even* is used here to emphasise the point that follows).
  *I think the Marine Park is too expensive. I would rather go somewhere quieter and cheaper.* (*rather* here means *prefer to*).
  *I don't mind if a place is crowded* (it *isn't important* to me).
- Ask learners to discuss in pairs; then do a quick feedback, eliciting different points of view from around the class.

**Answers**
Learners' own answers.

## 6 📝 Write

- Focus learners on **Activity 6** and ask them to look at the sentences in blue in the forum text. Ask them what they notice about the sentences. *Are they the same as other sentences? How are they different? Are they 'complete' sentences?* Elicit that the sentences have some words missing – they are *shortened* sentences.
- Put the shortened sentences on the board and ask for volunteers to come up and change them to make them into full sentences. Remind them to change the punctuation too (i.e. a word that started the sentence in the text becomes lower case in the full sentences, with other words preceding it – see Answers). If you have a team point system, award team points for volunteers who make correct changes to the sentences.

**Answers**
There wasn't enough time to ...
It was an incredible experience ....
We will definitely come again though ...
It was very expensive to get in;
There were also long tiring queues to get into most attractions

## 7 Use of English

- Ask learners why they think shortened sentences are used in the forum. Also ask them if they can think of other types of writing where shortened sentences can be used. If they are slow to respond, give them some extreme examples so they begin to understand the difference in style between sentences written in this way and other sentences, e.g. *Would you use shortened sentences in a school essay?* (No, not appropriate – you have to write in full sentences). *How about in an email to the head teacher?* (No, not appropriate – you need to write in a more formal, 'polite' way) *What about in a text message?* (Yes, that's OK because it's usually to a family member or friend, so it's informal).

**Note: Activities 6** and **7** are intended to raise learners' awareness of different writing styles and register.

> **Answers**
> Shortened sentences are used in a forum because the writers are writing quickly and spontaneously, in an informal, conversational style. Emails, text messages and notes are often written in the same way. Remind learners about the job advertisements in Unit 7, which also contained shortened sentences.

 **For further practice, see Activity 4 in the Activity Book.**

## 8 Write

- This activity aims to replicate an online forum discussing a place that is familiar to learners. Put learners into groups of about five or six and ask them to brainstorm places that they have all visited at some point in their lives, and that everyone has an opinion about. A place similar to the example is ideal but, if this isn't possible, a local swimming pool, a park or a local shopping centre is OK. Each group should try to think of a different place.
- **Critical thinking:** Ask learners to think individually about the positive and negative points about the place and give it a star rating (as in the example). Then ask them to imagine they are posting a comment about the place on a website that will be read by visitors from other cities and countries. What information would they want to know?
- Ask learners to write their thoughts down in their notebooks. Their first comment could reflect their strongest view on the place (e.g. *Great day out!*) or how they came to hear about it (*My best friend recommended the Plaza because ...*). They can use shortened sentences if they wish.
- When each group has written comments about their chosen place and rated it, ask them to copy their comments clearly onto strips of paper. Either arrange the comments, grouped according to place, to make a display on the wall, or hand them around to other groups to read. Keep all comments about one place together, so learners can read and compare the points of view.
- **Extend and challenge:** If your learners choose a well-known place to comment on, you could show them comments about the place on a real online forum on an English language website (e.g. Tripadvisor), if this is possible in your classroom. Let them read the comments and compare to their own. Even if they find the language on the forum challenging, they may be able to understand the general sense. **Note:** If you are going to show learners comments on a particular site, obviously check before the lesson that comments are appropriate in tone and content.

> **Answers**
> Learners' own answers – Portfolio opportunity.

 **Wrap up**

- After learners have read all the comments on several different places, vote as a class on the most and least attractive place to visit.

## Activity Book

### 1 Read and Strategy check

- Learners do a multiple-choice activity to support their understanding of the reading strategy (prediction). Then they read a text (a magazine review) comparing swimming pools in a city and identify the text type and the subject of the reviews.

> **Answers**
> Look at what *type* of text it is by noticing the design and layout. ✓
> Think about the kind of information you can find in specific types of text. ✓
> Reviews in a magazine about swimming pools.

### 2 Read

- Learners read comments about what facilities and features people look for if they are going to visit a swimming pool. They decide which pool described in the reviews would suit which person and match a pool to a comment.

> **Answers**
> 1 Hampton Baths
> 2 Wells Lido
> 3 Nova Swimming Park
> 4 Water Wonder
> 5 Water Wonder
> 6 Nova Swimming Park

### 3 Read

- Learners write down one negative point about the swimming pools mentioned in the reviews.

> **Answers**
> Water Wonder is expensive;
> Nova Swimming Park is 'not cheap' and often very crowded.
> Hampton Baths is small, basic, no separate pool for young kids.
> Wells Lido is only open May to September; children under 7 are not allowed in the main pool.

### 4 Write

- Learners look at the shortened sentences from the text and make them into full sentences by choosing a phrase from the box.

> **Answers**
> 1 There isn't a separate pool
> 2 There is fun for all the family
> 3 There are two water slides
> 4 It is good for serious swimmers
> 5 It isn't cheap

## 5 Over to you

- Learners write about which swimming pool in the reviews they would like to go to and why.

For a cross-curricular task relating to holiday activities, see **Photocopiable activity 17.**

# Lesson 3: Describing a special place

Learner's Book pages: 130–131
Activity Book pages: 104–105

## Lesson objectives

**Speaking:** Prepare and deliver a presentation describing a special place.

**Listening:** Listen to a presentation describing a special place; identify the order of information in the presentation, specific facts and phrases to describe feelings about the place.

**Critical thinking:** Identify interesting facts and describe feelings about a special place.

**Language focus:** Adjectives + prepositions: *surprised by; interested in; fascinated by, amazed by, sad about.*

**Materials:** images representing a special place (optional for **Warm up**). Copies of **Photocopiable activity 18.**

## Learner's Book

###  Warm up

- Introduce the lesson by showing learners a special place you've been to. Show them some images (photos or videos, if available) and ask them to guess the country and place (if it is well-known, e.g. the Taj Mahal), when you went and who with. Finally ask them if they can guess why the place is special for you.
- Tell them that they are now going to think of a place that is special to them.

### 1 🗩 Talk about it

- **Critical thinking:** First, ask learners to close their eyes and think of a special place that they have been to and what it means to them. Give them some guiding questions and prompts, e.g. *Have you ever been to a place that was really special? Where was it? When did you go? How often have you been? Who did you go with? What things did you see? What things did you do? How did you feel when you were there? What made it so interesting / so much fun / so beautiful?*
- Tell them that they don't have to write anything just yet, just sit and think.

- Now ask them to open their eyes and tell them that they have one minute to write down as many adjectives as they can think of, to describe the place.
- When time is up, ask them to compare their adjectives with their partner, then tell their partner which place they thought of and why they chose the adjectives to describe it. Show them the example in the book, or demonstrate using your own example from the warm-up stage, e.g. *amazing – the mountains were amazing because they were so huge.*
- Conduct a quick feedback, asking learners to share some initial ideas at this stage.

## 2 Talk

- Focus learners on the Learner's Book and the pictures of Pompeii in southern Italy. Tell them the name of the place (or elicit, if you think your learners might have heard of Pompeii) and ask them what they think happened there by looking at the pictures.
- Elicit learners' ideas and write on the board, for reference in the next activity.
- Use this stage to pre-teach or elicit words that will appear in the listening text: *volcano, erupt, ash cloud, poisonous.* Also ask learners when they think this event took place (in Roman times, nearly 2000 years ago). If learners have studied the ancient Romans in another subject, use this opportunity to link with other elements of the curriculum.

Answers
Facts about Pompeii for reference:
*In CE79, Mount Vesuvius, a huge volcano, erupted over the city of Pompeii and other towns and settlements in the south of Italy. It sent an infernal, poisonous ash cloud over Pompeii and the surrounding area. In 24 hours it covered the city, destroying buildings and killing thousands of people almost immediately. The ash cloud encased people and objects and turned to stone, thus preserving whole bodies and the objects around them. The submerged city was first discovered at the end of the 16th century; excavations have revealed valuable information about all aspects of Roman life.*
*Today you can visit the site and gain a dramatic insight into the tragedy of Pompeii by observing the stone figures of the people, who remain where they fell on the day of the eruption. The site also provides an insight into everyday Roman life through excavated buildings, frescoes and everyday objects.*

## 3 Listen 58 [CD2 Track 26]

- Tell learners that they are now going to listen to someone (Hannah) describing her visit to Pompeii. Tell them that Pompeii was a very special place for Hannah and her visit made a big impression on her. Ask them to listen to find out what happened in Pompeii and if their predictions (from **Activity 2**) were correct. Read through the points made in the previous stage, listed on the board, before you listen to the description.

- Listen to the description; then ask learners to discuss the answers in pairs before conducting general class feedback. Refer to the pictures in the Learner's Book when conducting feedback and the points made on the board, so learners can see how many of their initial predictions appeared in the listening text. **Note:** In this initial first listening, learners are not expected to understand all the points listed below, just gain a general sense of what happened in Pompeii. They may just pick up some of the points listed.

---

**Audioscript:** Track 58

**Part 1**

I'm going to tell you about a place that is special to me ...

In CE 79, nearly 2000 years ago, a huge volcano erupted in the south of Italy. The ash cloud that came from out of it was over 20 kilometres high. It was a poisonous mixture of ash and gas. In 24 hours it covered the city of Pompeii. The temperature of the ash cloud was 300°C. It destroyed houses and killed thousands of people almost immediately.

**Part 2**

Last summer, my dad and I visited Pompeii on our holiday in Italy. Dad took me there because he said it would be good research for my history project about the ancient Romans. I thought it would be a bit boring! But when we got there I was really amazed by what I saw ...

**Part 3**

Parts of the city are exactly as they were in the times of the ancient Romans. You can see rows of houses and shops. The ash covered people and objects and turned them to stone. People, animals and objects look exactly the same as when the ash hit them. So you can see whole families trying look after each other. You can also see normal objects that they used every day, like bread, bottles and cooking utensils. These things give us an idea of what life was like in those times.

**Part 4**

My visit to Pompeii made me feel so many different emotions. I was really interested in the history and information about how the people lived so long ago. I was fascinated by the stone figures of the people but I felt very sad about what I saw at the same time. Those people must have been so terrified. I felt sad about normal people like you and me doing normal everyday things ...

---

**Answers**

**Hannah's description of what happened in Pompeii.**
In CE 79, (nearly 2000 years ago), a huge volcano erupted in the south of Italy. The ash cloud from the volcano was over 20 kilometres high. It was a poisonous mixture of ash and gas, with a temperature of 300°C. In 24 hours it covered the city. It destroyed houses and killed thousands of people almost immediately. The ash covered people and objects and turned them to stone.

---

**4 Listen** 58 [CD2 Track 26]

- Now focus learners' attention on the headings in **Activity 4** and read through together. Tell them that you are going to play the description again, stopping after each section; they must write down the letter of the heading they think the section corresponds to.
- After listening, ask learners to compare answers, then conduct class feedback.

---

**Answers**
**Part 1** c (Interesting and surprising facts about Pompeii)
**Part 2** a (When Hannah visited Pompeii and who with)
**Part 3** d (What she saw there)
**Part 4** b (Her feelings about Pompeii)

---

**5 Listen** 58 [CD2 Track 26]

- Now ask learners if they can remember three surprising facts from the first part of Hannah's description. Write the following prompts on the board to help them and ask them to work in pairs to make three sentences:
*Nearly 2000 years ago ...    over 20 kilometres high ... ash and gas ...*
*24 hours ...    300°C*
**Note:** Stronger learners can be challenged to produce sentences using all the prompts.
- Elicit sentences from the prompts and ask learners why they think Hannah mentioned this information at the beginning of her description. Elicit or tell them that putting interesting or surprising information at the beginning of a description is a good technique to get the attention of the listener (or reader), and will make them want to hear more (reference **Speaking tip** in Learner's Book).
- Now ask them to listen to the first part again to hear the strategy in context and to check their sentences.

---

**Answers**
Surprising facts: (three from ... )
In CE79, nearly 2000 years ago, a huge volcano erupted in the south of Italy.
The ash cloud was over 20 kilometres high.
It was a poisonous mixture of ash and gas.
In 24 hours it covered the city of Pompeii.
The temperature of the ash cloud was 300°C.
It destroyed houses and killed thousands of people almost immediately.

---

**6 Use of English**

- Write the following sentences on the board and elicit from learners the missing words.
*Hannah was very interested ____ Pompeii.* (in)
*She felt sad about ____ the terrible things that happened.* (about)
- Write in the missing words in a different colour (or underline) and ask learners what kind of words they are (prepositions). Then ask them what kind of words come before the prepositions (adjectives). Circle or highlight the preceding adjectives, so the structure is clear.
- Elicit from learners what the sentences describe (Hannah's *feelings* about Pompeii); then draw their attention to the **Use of English** box in the Learner's Book, explaining that we often use phrases with an adjective and a preposition to talk about how we feel about something.
- Now ask learners to complete **Activity 6**. They need to match a preposition to an adjective, then complete sentences, 1–4 from the listening text. Allow them to work in pairs.

**Note:** Most of these phrases have appeared before in the Stage 6 course and the *adjectives + preposition* language point also appeared in **Unit 7**, so learners should already be quite familiar with this language.

- To check sentences 1–4, you could play the relevant parts of the listening text again, stop the audio when a target phrase is heard and elicit the phrase again. (Sentence 1 appears at the end of the second part of the listening and sentences 2–4 are all in the last part).

- **Extend and challenge:** Review some of the extraordinary elements of Pompeii described by Hannah and then ask learners to give personal reactions to the description, using the target phrases. Start by asking questions like:
*What can you see at Pompeii even now?* (rows of shops and houses) *Are they the same or different to how they were nearly 2000 years ago?* (the same) *Why did the people 'turn to stone'?* (because the ash from the volcano covered them). *Do you see just one or two people?* (No, lots of people, for example, whole families).
Now ask learners to work in pairs and talk about how the description made them feel.
**Note:** Depending on their language level, encourage them to follow the phrases with a noun (in italics below), to make the phrases easier to build.
*I was interested in the information about the buildings in Pompeii.*
*I felt sad about the story of how the people died ...*
*I was amazed by the power of the volcano ...*
If your learners need more support, you could elicit the most memorable parts of the description and formulate into noun phrases (e.g. *the heat of the volcano; the story of how people died,* etc.); then ask learners to match them to the *adjective + preposition* phrases, to express their reactions to the description.

---

**Answers**
I was fascinated by
I was really interested in
I was really amazed by
I felt very sad about
1 When we got there *I was amazed by* what I saw.
2 *I was fascinated by* the stone figures.
3 *I was really interested in* the history and information
4 *I felt very sad about* what I saw at the same time.

---

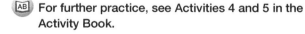 For further practice, see Activities 4 and 5 in the Activity Book.

## Present it!

- Tell learners that they are now going to prepare their own descriptions about a special place and go through the step-by-step instructions outlined in the Learner's Book. If some learners want to talk about the same place, this task could be done in small groups (in the same way as most of the other presentations in Stage 6). However, if you would like each learner to prepare their own description,

you could organise it so that learners present to small groups in the final stage, rather than the whole class, as this would be more time-efficient.

- First give learners time to prepare notes about a place that is special to them. Ask them to look again at the adjectives they wrote at the beginning of the class (**Activity 1**, **Talk about it**) to help them generate initial ideas.

- Ask learners to organise their description using the same headings as those in **Activity 4**, adapted for themselves and the place they want to describe. If necessary, give them time to research a little for 'interesting and surprising facts' (Part 1 / heading c) about their place.

- Ask them to find clear, enlarged (if possible) visual images to accompany their description.

- Ask learners to write out their presentation from their notes, either in class time or at home. Make sure they include some sentences that talk directly to the audience and show them the examples in the audioscript, e.g. *I'm going to tell you about a place ... You can see ...,* etc.

- Tell them to include some sentences using some of the *adjective + preposition* phrases in **Activity 6** to describe their feelings about the place.

- Check the scripts for grammar, vocabulary and organisation; however, the emphasis is on organisation and quality of ideas, rather than perfectly accurate scripts.

- Give learners the opportunity to practise their presentations together, whether they are presenting the descriptions individually or in groups. If they are presenting as a group, each member should deliver a part of the presentation.

- As learners practise, monitor the groups, making sure you spend some time with each, helping with any pronunciation difficulties.

- **Critical thinking:** Before learners either present to their group or to the class, give listeners a task by asking them to note down two interesting or surprising facts about each place.

- Ask learners to present their descriptions individually to a group of about 3 or 4, or in small groups in front of the class.

- **Additional support and practice:** Use of notes in delivery: stronger learners may be able to deliver without looking too closely at their notes; others may need to read from their notes at this stage. Use your discretion with regard to how much you allow this, taking into account ability and confidence levels in your class. Ultimately in later years, learners need to be able to deliver oral presentations without reading word for word from notes. Ideally, we should encourage them to get into this habit as soon as possible but learners will probably need the support of reading from their notes in these early stages.

- **Extend and challenge:** As learners are delivering their presentations, note down main errors; either give to each group a note of the errors to correct themselves, or write up on the board at the end for a class error correction session (without stating which group or individual made the errors). **Note:** This would come after plenty of positive feedback regarding the presentations. Positive feedback must always come first and be emphasised.

> **Answers**
> Learners' own answers.

 **For further practice, see Activity 6 in the Activity Book.**

 **Wrap up**

* **Critical thinking:** After listening to all the presentations, ask learners to share interesting and surprising facts that they noted about the descriptions they listened to.

## Activity Book

**1 Listen** 🔊 77 [CD2 Track 45]

* Learners listen to a boy describing his visit to a special place and put headings in the order of his description.

> **Audioscript:** Track 77
> **Part 1**
>
> I'm going to tell you about Jamaa El-Fna Square in Marrakesh, Morocco. This is a special place for the people of Marrakesh and for me too. It is famous all over the world. The square has been in movies, on TV programmes and in novels. Rock stars have recorded songs there too.
>
> **Part 2**
>
> I live quite a long way from Marrakesh, in a city called Safi and I went to Jamaa El-Fna Square last year with my family. It was an awesome experience and we had a lot of fun.
>
> During the day you can go shopping in the huge market. It is very colourful – full of traditional Moroccan crafts and bags full of spices that smell delicious. In the square, you can watch snake-charmers. They play tunes on musical instruments and large snakes dance in front of them! But later on the square really comes alive. You can watch acrobats and dancers. You can listen to musicians and storytellers and buy delicious dishes and snacks from lots of food stalls.
>
> **Part 3**
>
> I was fascinated by the square because there were so many exciting things to see, hear, smell and taste! I was really interested in all the food from different parts of my country. I was amazed by the acrobats and musicians. I was surprised by how fast the time went. And I felt sad about the fact that our trip was so short.

> **Answers**
> **a** 2    **b** 4    **c** 1    **d** 3

**2** 📝 **Listen** 🔊 77 [CD2 Track 45]

* Learners read four statements about the listening text. Then they listen to Part 1 again to find out whether the statements are true or false. They correct the false sentences.

> **Answers**
> **1** false. Jamaa El Fna Square is famous all over the world.
> **2** false. It has been in movies and on TV programmes.
> **3** true
> **4** true

**3 Listen** 🔊 77 [CD2 Track 45]

* Learners listen to Parts 2 and 3 again. They look at pictures and put them in the order that they hear them mentioned in the listening text.

> **Answers**
> **Order:** b / a / d / c

**4 Use of English** 🔊 78 [CD2 Track 46]

* Learners circle the correct preposition (from a choice of two) in four sentences from the listening text.

> **Answers**
> **1** by    **2** in    **3** by    **4** about

**5 Use of English**

* Learners make sentences using adjectives and prepositions about given topics, choosing adjectives from the box.

> **Answers**
> Learners' own answers.

**6** 📝 **Challenge**

* Learners answer questions about a special place for them. They then write a presentation, using their notes.

> **Answers**
> Learners' own answers.

**For further practice, in talking about holiday activities and experiences, see Photocopiable activity 18.**

## Lesson 4: My dream holiday

Learner's Book pages: 132–133
Activity Book pages: 106–107

### Lesson objectives

**Reading:** Read two short poems about dream holidays; notice features of content, style and use of descriptive language.

**Writing:** Write a short poem about a dream holiday using a given structure.

**Critical thinking:** Think of your own dream holiday; talk about which poem you like best and why; create a poem about a dream holiday.

**Vocabulary:** Verbs describing senses (review); *see, hear, touch, taste, smell*; descriptive adjectives; *shimmering, sapphire, salty, ancient, worn*

**Materials:** Learner's Book, Activity Book; images of teacher's choice of a dream holiday destination (for **Warm up**); various pictures of dream holiday destinations (4 or 5 per small group).

## Learner's Book

###  Warm up

- Introduce the theme of the lesson by showing learners some images of a place you would like to go on a dream holiday. Choose a place that is far removed from your current environment to emphasise the 'dream' aspect, e.g. on the other side of the world, in a completely different climate, reflecting a completely different lifestyle, etc. It could even be the moon or a space journey.
- Ask learners to guess the place and talk to them a little bit about why it represents your dream holiday.

### 1 👉 Talk about it

- Put learners in small groups and distribute some more pictures of dream destinations that you think would appeal to them. Make them varied to engage all learners, e.g. a picture of the New York skyline or Sydney harbour, Mount Everest, the surface of the moon, the Egyptian pyramids, Disneyland, a tropical island, etc.
  **Note:** You will need quite a large number of pictures, or copies, so each group has plenty to look at. You could ask learners beforehand to find dream holiday images at home and bring them to the lesson; then put the pictures together and distribute so each group has five or six pictures to look at. If each group has different pictures, ask them to pass them round.
- **Critical thinking:** Ask them to talk about where they would like to go on a dream holiday, using the pictures for inspiration. They also need to think of two reasons why they would choose that place.
- Conduct a class feedback, asking learners to share their thoughts on dream holiday destinations and the reasons why.
- Explain to learners that they are all going to write about their dream holiday in the lesson today.

Answers
Learners' own answers.

### 2 📝 Read

- Focus learners on the pictures in the Learner's Book and ask them to describe the places. Do they know where these places are? What do they know about them? Would they like to go there?

- Tell learners that you (the teacher) are going to read the two poems aloud. They must listen and read too, then match the pictures with the poems.
- When you have finished reading, ask them to compare their answers in pairs, then do a quick class feedback. Ask learners which words in the poems helped them to match to the pictures and write these on the board. If your learners are familiar with Machu Picchu, ask them what other words, besides the place name, helped them to match with picture d.
- Ask learners to look at the sentences used in the poems and read a couple of examples, emphasising the use of the second conditional, e.g.
  *If I **could go** anywhere in the whole wide world,*
  *I **would travel** to a tropical island by private plane ...*
  *I'**d see** shimmering white sand and giant flowers,*
  *And I'**d hear** toucans and humming birds.*
  Ask them what kind of sentence / structure is used (2nd conditional) and why (because the poems are talking about *dreams* – imaginary situations).

Answers
Poem 1 / pictures b and c
Poem 2 / picture d
Note: Machu Picchu is a 15th century Inca site located nearly 2500 metres above sea level in the Cusco region of Peru in South America. It is in the middle of a tropical mountain setting.

 **For further practice, see Activity 2 in the Activity Book.**

### 3 💬 Talk

- Ask learners to read the words on the board from **Activity 2**. Then either partially erase or erase completely and ask them work in pairs to remember as many details as they can about each poem.
- **Critical thinking:** Now ask learners to discuss which poem they like best and why. Give them an example yourself first, e.g.
  *I like the first poem best because I love quiet natural places where there are few people.*
  *I like the second poem best because I love ancient ruins and history.*
- **Feedback:** Elicit from the class which poem different learners like best and why.

Answers
Learners' own answers.

### 4 Word study

- Focus learners on the adjectives in the poems and read through them together. Then ask them to work in pairs to match them to the descriptions in **Activity 4**. If learners are unsure about the meanings, encourage them to look at the context and the meanings of the other words around the adjectives to help them understand.
- When you go through the answers as a class, use the pictures where possible to help learners understand

the meanings; also give them other examples of things that can be described by these adjectives, preferable things that are familiar (e.g. the grass at the side of the playground is **worn** because lots of students have been running on it).

**Answers**
1 ancient
2 salty
3 worn
4 sapphire
5 shimmering

 **For further practice, see Activity 3 in the Activity Book.**

## 5 Word study

- Now focus learners on the verbs in blue in the poems and read them together. Ask learners to think about the meanings of the verbs and then elicit what they all have in common. If learners are slow to respond, give them clues by indicating the senses they apply to (e.g. point to your eyes, ears, etc.).

**Answers**
All the verbs in blue describe the *five senses*.

 **For further practice, see Activity 1 in the Activity Book.**

## 6  Listen and write

- Tell learners that they are now going to write some notes that they will use to write their own poems. Explain that you are going to ask them some questions and that they should listen and write their thoughts in their notebooks. Show them the example responses (about Japan) in the Learner's Book.
- Tell learners that they can write just one or two responses to the questions, then there will be more time to add to their answers later.
- Read out the first question: *If you could go on holiday anywhere, where would you go?* and make sure that everyone writes an answer. Where possible, give learners a picture (from **Activity 1**) to match their dream place.
- **Critical thinking:** Read out the following questions, 2–7. Give learners time to write at least one or two responses after each one.
- When you have finished asking the questions, give learners a few minutes more to add to their notes. Circulate and monitor, helping with vocabulary.
- **Additional support and practice: Activity 4** in the Activity Book, **Lesson 4** provides a gap-fill exercise which could act as a bridging activity between learners reading the model poems and writing notes for their own poems. The content of this example poem may be more accessible and provide a more relatable model for some learners.

**Answers**
Learners' own answers.

 **For further practice, see Activity 4 in the Activity Book.**

##   Write

- **Critical thinking:** Explain to learners that they are now going to use their notes to write their own poems about a dream holiday and that they are going to write their poems using the same structure as in the model poems.
- To start them off, elicit from learners the first line of the poems and then add two or three further lines using your own ideas (or the example in the Learner's Book):
  *If I could go anywhere in the whole wide world,*
  *I'd travel to (PLACE) Japan by (TRANSPORT) supersonic jet plane ...*
  *I'd see ...*
- Point out to learners (by using the model on the board) that they need to use the same structure as the model poems – sentences in the 2nd conditional and the verbs describing the five senses.
- Now ask them to write first drafts of their poems. Circulate and monitor, helping with vocabulary and structure.
- When learners are ready, ask them to write final versions of their poems for display on the classroom wall. Let them decorate with pictures and photos.
- Display the poems and ask learners to walk around and read each other's. Ask them to write down three more places that they would like to visit after reading their classmate's poems.

**Answers**
Learners' own answers – Portfolio opportunity.

 **For further practice, see Activity 5 in the Activity Book.**

## Wrap up

- **Critical thinking:** Ask learners to share their thoughts about which places they would like to visit after reading each other's poems. If you have a team points or class reward system, you could give learners credits for 'most descriptive line', 'most unusual place', etc.

## Activity Book

## 1 Vocabulary

- Learners label a diagram with verbs describing senses from the box.

**Answers**
a see   b smell   c taste   d hear   e touch

## 2 Read

- Learners complete a gapped poem with given sentences, matching verbs describing senses with the relevant words in the sentences.

> **Answers**
> **1** d   **2** b   **3** e   **4** c   **5** a

## 3 Vocabulary

- Learners complete sentences with an adjective from the box.

> **Answers**
> **1** ancient   **2** shimmering   **3** Salty   **4** worn   **5** sapphire

## 4 Read

- Learners complete a poem with words from the box.

> **Answers**
> **1** theme park
> **2** rollercoasters
> **3** laughing
> **4** slides
> **5** pizzas
> **6** milkshakes
> **7** burgers
> **8** friends

## 5 Challenge

- Learners write a poem about a place or country that they would like to visit, using the models in **Activity 2** and **4**.

> **Answers**
> Learners' own answers.

# Lesson 5: Other kinds of journeys

Learner's Book pages: 134–135
Activity Book pages: 108–109

### Lesson objectives

**Listening and reading:** Listen to and read an extract (from a novel) about the journey of light to Earth.

**Speaking:** Talk about stars and the night sky; talk about story themes and inferences; answer questions using phrases with the verb, *take*; discuss advice given by family members.

**Critical thinking:** Discuss what you have learned from family members.

**Vocabulary:** Expressions with take: *how long / how many years / how much time does it take ...? take something in, take ages ...*

**Values:** Learning from family members.

**Materials:** Learner's Book, Activity Book.

## Learner's Book

### Warm up

- As a tentative link to the theme of space in the literature extract, you could start the lesson by showing learners a picture or a video clip of a rocket launching into space. Elicit from learners what kind of transport they can see in the picture or video clip and ask them what they think is the purpose of space journeys like this one (this also acts as a review of the space exploration theme touched on in **Unit 6**).

### 1  Talk about it

- Now ask learners to brainstorm what they can see when they look at the sky at night. Write their ideas on the board and add a few of your own if necessary (see Answers box for ideas).
- **Critical thinking:** Choose one or two examples from learners' ideas and ask them to have a guess at how far some of the things are from Earth. Allow learners to wildly speculate here, so that they get a sense of the vastness of space (in preparation for some of the themes in the literature extract).

> **Answers**
> Possible answers for what is visible in the night sky (depending on which part of the world you live in and weather conditions): the moon, stars, constellations (e.g. the Milky Way), planets, meteors, comets, eclipses, satellites, planes.

### 2 Read 59 [CD2 Track 27]

- Tell learners that they are now going to listen to and read a story that has a space theme, from a novel called *The Time and Space of Uncle Albert* by Russell Stannard. The story is from a chapter called *The Light Beam that Got Away*, and revolves around a conversation between a girl called Gedanken and her Uncle Albert. Introduce the characters by drawing learners' attention to the illustrations in the Learner's Book.
- Now focus learners on the question in **Activity 2** and read it together. Tell the class to listen and read the whole text, looking for the answer to this question. Stress that, at this point, they only need look for this information and not to worry about words they do not understand.
- Start the audio and tell learners to read the text while listening.

> **Audioscript:** Track 59
> See Learner's Book pages 134–136.

> **Answers**
> They are talking about the night sky because they are interested in how fast light travels from the stars to the Earth.

### 3 Read

- In preparation for learners reading the text again (to answer the comprehension questions), pre-teach the following words, paragraph by paragraph: *burst out laughing / very fond* (Part 1); *a bench / starlit / ladder* (Part 2); *get here / given out / Not quite / lamp bulb* (Part 3)

- Read out the word definitions and ask learners to find the corresponding word in the text (make sure they only focus on the part where the word appears). Conduct the activity as a reading race to stretch learners and keep them engaged.
  **Part 1:** *burst out laughing* – when you suddenly start laughing (this could be mimed)
  *very fond* – when you like someone or something very much
  **Part 2:** *a bench* – something you sit on outside, e.g. in a park
  *starlit* – an adjective that means the light from stars in the sky
  *ladder* – (show learners the ladder in the illustration in the Learner's Book)
  **Part 3:** *get here* – to arrive
  *given out* – produced
  *not quite* – this is a nice way of saying, '*No, that isn't right*'.
  *lamp bulb* – the object inside a lamp that gives light (show learners an example or draw a lamp bulb).
- Tell learners that they are going to read the story again, part by part to answer the questions after each part. They should read and then answer the questions in their notebooks.
- **Additional support and practice:** Learners could work in pairs to do the comprehension questions 1–10. Alternatively you could divide the questions up, so learners don't have to answer all of them but benefit from learning all answers in feedback later on. Put learners in A/B pairs: A answers the odd numbered questions, B, the even numbered ones, then ask them to share the answers at the end.
- After learners have written the answers for questions 1–10, put them in groups of four to check their answers together.
- Allow time for this before giving feedback on the answers. Where possible, use the pictures in the book to illustrate the answers.

> **Answers**
> 1 true
> 2 false. Her teacher's name is Mr Turner.
> 3 false. Uncle Albert is a scientist.
> 4 true
> 5 false. Gedanken hasn't decided on the topic of her science project.
> 6 true
> 7 false. When he was a boy, Uncle Albert climbed a ladder and tried to touch the stars.
> 8 true
> 9 false. It still takes a tiny amount of time for light to travel from the lamp bulb to the walls of a room.
> 10 false. Uncle Albert knows exactly how long it takes for light to travel from space to Earth ('Three hundred thousand kilometres a second.' Or 'A hundred and eighty-six thousand miles a second.')

 **For further practice, see Activities 1 and 2 in the Activity Book.**

## 4 Talk

- **Critical thinking:** Ask learners to work in pairs to answer the questions in **Activity 4**. They should discuss the questions and be prepared to give feedback to the class at the end.
- **Additional support and practice:** The questions in this speaking activity could be divided up, rather than have all learners answer all questions; e.g. put learners into groups of three and give each learner a question to think about and then share with the group. Or give small groups of learners just one question to discuss. At the end of this stage, each group would give feedback on a different question and others could listen and see if they agree or not with the answer given. Early finishers could then be given another question to discuss while others finish.
- Do a class feedback, asking volunteers or nominating learners to share their answers with the class. Help learners with the language they need to express their thoughts (especially for question 2) by reformulating sentences where appropriate and highlighting useful phrases on the board.

> **Answers**
> 1 Uncle Albert believed that stars were little lights stuck on to the inside of a big round roof. He thought he could touch the stars in the sky if he stood on the roof of his house and reached up.
> 2 Learners' own answers.
> 3 Project that Gedanken is most likely to choose (because of her conversation with her uncle):
> *The journey of light from space to Earth*

## 5 Write

- Focus learners on the written numbers in **Activity 5** and read them together. Put them in pairs and ask them to write the words as numbers. This could be done as a competition, with a time limit. When learners think they have the correct answers, ask them to come up and write the numbers on the board. Alternatively, you (the teacher) could write the numbers on the board, with an error, then ask learners to come up and correct them.
- Now ask learners to look back through the story and discuss, in pairs, why the numbers are important in the story.
- When you conduct feedback, establish the answer given in the Answers box and draw comparisons with other sections of your curriculum where learners might have studied similar points (e.g. Science; Physics; Maths).

> **Answers**
> These numbers show the speed that light travels from space to earth in kilometres and miles.
> 300 000 (kilometres a second)
> 180 000 (miles a second)

For further practice, see Activity 3 in the Activity Book.

## 6 Word study

- Focus learners' attention on the verb phrases, with *take*, highlighted in blue in the story. Ask learners to read the expressions out to you and list them on the board (or have them prepared on a slide). List the expressions as fully as possible, so the context is clear, e.g.
  *It's **taken that long** to get here.*
  *The **time it takes** for ...*
  *Their light **takes ages** to make the journey ...*
  *She still didn't seem to **take it in** ...*
  *It still **takes years** to get here ...*
- Ask learners to think about the meaning of the expressions, then to discuss in pairs which one is the odd-one-out (in terms of meaning). To quicken pace and keep learners engaged, give them a time limit and make it into a competition, awarding points for the correct answer, if you have a reward system in place in your classroom.
- When learners record these phrases in their vocabulary records, take this opportunity to reinforce the idea of recording vocabulary in 'chunks' like this, and that it is usually as easy to remember a short phrase as it is to remember one word (and much more useful).

> **Answers**
> **Odd-one-out:** *to take (something) in.* This phrase means to *understand* (and *absorb*) something; the other phrases with *take* are all about *length of time.*

## 7 Talk

- Focus learners on the questions in **Activity 7**, designed to give authentic practice using the target phrases derived from the text. Read through the questions together, then ask learners to answer them in pairs and to be prepared to share their answers with the class at the end.
- When you conduct feedback, nominate or ask for volunteers to give their answers to each of the questions. You could add an extra challenge by asking stronger learners to give feedback on their partner's answers instead of their own.

> **Answers**
> Learners' own answers.

 For further practice, see Activity 4 in the Activity Book.

## 8 Pronunciation 60 [CD2 Track 28]

- Focus learners on **Activity 8**. Ask them to listen to and repeat the words from the story, focusing on the pronunciation of the 'o' sound in each one.

- After listening, ask learners to tell you the difference between the pronunciation of the 'o' sound in the words.

> **Audioscript:** Track 60
> topic
> going
> fond
> so
> hoped
> sorry
> volcanoes

> **Answers**
> some are a long 'o' sound /əʊ/ some are a short 'o' sound /ɒ/

- Ask learners to write the words in two columns in their notebooks, according to the different 'o' sound. If your learners are familiar with the phonemic chart, you could use these symbols to differentiate the sounds. Encourage them to say the words before writing them down.
- Now ask them to listen again to check. Ask them also to identify the word which contains both 'o' sounds.

> **Answers**
> | /ɒ/ | /əʊ/ |
> |---|---|
> | topic | going |
> | fond | so |
> | sorry | hoped |
> **Both sounds:** v<u>o</u>lcan<u>oe</u>s

 For further practice, see Activities 5 and 6 in the Activity Book.

## 9  Values

- **Critical thinking:** Focus learners on the three questions and put them into small groups to discuss the answers. Tell them to be prepared to share their answers with the rest of the class at the end of the activity.
- During feedback, if you feel learners might struggle to express the answer to the first question, give them a false answer and ask them to correct it, e.g.,
  *Uncle Albert told Gedanken that the light we see in space is instant / has taken a short time to travel to Earth.*
  *The light we see at home, when we turn on a light, is instant.*
  *Light doesn't 'travel' – it's instant!*
- For the last question, you could create a list of 'good advice' on the board and discuss different situations that the various pieces of advice can be applied to.

**Answers**
1 From Uncle Albert, Gedanken learned that light always has to 'travel' – it doesn't appear instantly, even when we switch on a lamp bulb in a small room. The light that we see in space (e.g.from stars) has taken a long time to travel to Earth. Gedanken also learned the exact speed that light travels from space (in kilometres and miles).
This information will help her with Science, in particular Physics (and also Maths).
2 Learners' own answers.
3 Learners' own answers.

 **For further practice, see Activity 7 in the Activity Book.**

##  Wrap up

• Put learners into small teams. Find out some 'amazing facts' about how far different planets and stars are from Earth. Dictate the figures to learners and ask them to write down the numbers on A4 paper and hold it up when they think they have written it correctly. Give team points to the first teams with the correctly written numbers.

## Activity Book

### 1 Read

• Learners put sentences about the story in the correct order.

**Answers**
a 2    b 1    c 4    d 6    e 3    f 5

### 2 Read

• Learners choose the correct answer (from a choice of two) in sentences that describe some events in the story.

**Answers**
1 find information
2 is annoyed
3 uncle
4 didn't know
5 at his home
6 travel
7 hard

### 3 Read

• Learners complete a gapped explanation about how light travels, using words in the box.

**Answers**
1 night
2 years
3 far
4 Earth
5 fast
6 kilometres
7 five
8 home
9 room

## 4 Word study

• Learners complete sentences, using expressions with *take*, and make them true for them.

**Answers**
Learners' own answers.

## 5 Pronunciation 79 [CD2 Track 47]

• Learners listen and repeat two groups of words from the story and identify which sound for the letter 'o' they hear in each group.

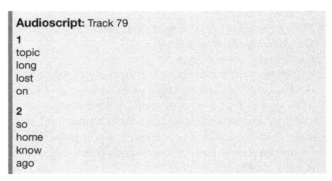

**Audioscript:** Track 79
1
topic
long
lost
on

2
so
home
know
ago

**Answers**
1 topic    long    lost    on    /ɒ/
2 so    home    know    ago    /əʊ/

## 6 Pronunciation 80 [CD2 Track 48]

• Learners listen and repeat more words from the story (featuring the letter, 'o'). They identify which 'o' sound, from groups 1 and 2 in **Activity 5**, they hear in each word.

**Audioscript:** Track 80
off
only
dome
folder
project
notice

**Answers**
off 1    only 2    dome 2    folder 1    project 1    notice 2

## 7 Values

• Learners write some useful information or advice they received from one of their family members.

**Answers**
Learners' own answers.

# Lesson 6: Choose a project

Learner's Book pages: 138–139

## Lesson objectives

**Speaking:** Conduct a survey about holiday activities and present findings to the class; revise unit themes; discuss **Unit 9** Big question.

**Writing:** Write a mini-report about the results of the survey; organise and prepare notes for a poster about a place you would like to visit; revise unit themes.

**Critical thinking:** Compare survey results with other groups; select a place you would like to visit and imagine aspects of the visit; apply new skills and language acquired in **Unit 9** to project work and revision activities.

**Language focus:** Recycling language points from **Unit 9**, i.e. 2nd conditional forms (review); adjective + preposition structure.

**Vocabulary:** Holiday activities (nouns with *–ing*); expressing preferences in imaginary situations; verbs describing senses (review); descriptive adjectives; expressions with *take*

**Materials:** paper; poster paper; electronic slides (optional).

## Learner's Book

### 👉 Warm up

- Play *Noughts and Crosses* (also known as *Three in a Row* or *Tic Tac Toe*) to revise key vocabulary and themes from **Unit 9**.
- Draw a 3 × 3 grid on the board and number each box 1–9, as follows:

| 1 | 2 | 3 |
|---|---|---|
| 4 | 5 | 6 |
| 7 | 8 | 9 |

- Put learners in two teams (*Noughts* and *Crosses*). Tell them that you have nine questions about **Unit 9** – one for each square on the grid; they have to choose a square and answer the question corresponding to that square. If they give a correct answer, they 'win' the square. The objective of the game is to win three squares in a row (horizontally, vertically or diagonally).
- Roll a dice or flip a coin to decide which team starts the game. If *Noughts* win a square, place a '0' in the square, if *Crosses* win, place a 'X'. Teams should soon realise that their choice of square may depend on how many the other team have 'won' and they must try to stop them winning three in a row.

- Ask questions that revise key vocabulary, language points and themes in **Unit 9**: you could focus on just one area (e.g. nine questions about vocabulary) or provide a mixture of questions covering all areas. Your questions could ask learners to give vocabulary lists; answer a definition; complete a short gapped sentence; answer a comprehension question about a text, etc. e.g.:
  1 *Name three holiday activities from Lesson 1.* (Three activities from the six featured in **Lesson 1**)
  2 *Name two activities you can do in the snow.* (Skiing and snowboarding)
  3 *What is the name of the sport where you jump off a high place tied to an elastic rope?* (Bungee-jumping)
  4 *Complete this phrase: There is _____ _____ I would try snowboarding!* (... no way ... )
  5 *Complete this phrase: I _____ _____ to try snorkelling – it would be fun!* (... would like ...)
  6 *What did Gedanken learn from her uncle in the story?* (About the speed of light)
  7 *What were the reviews about in Lesson 2?* (A marine wildlife park)
  8 *Give me an adjective which means very very old.* (*ancient*)
  9 *What were the poems about in Lesson 4?* (A tropical island and Machu Picchu)

  **Note:** Be aware that some questions might replicate questions that appear in the **Reflect on your learning** section later (although this could be used to provide added support for some learners).
  **Note:** Sometimes this game gets to a point where it is impossible to win three in a row. In this case, have a tenth question ready as a 'tie-breaker'.
- Do a practice turn first to make sure learners are clear about the rules of the game.
- Tell learners they are now going to choose from the two projects and follow the instructions below for the one they have decided on.

### 1 A survey and mini-report

- Focus learner's attention on the pie chart and explain the topic (holiday activities). Tell them that they are now going to carry out a similar survey, interviewing ten classmates.
- Put learners in pairs and take them through the step-by-step instructions. Ask them to write down the six holiday activities from **Lesson 1**, then work together to construct two questions to find out the bullet-pointed information. E.g. *Which activity would you like to try (that you haven't tried before)? Why would you like to try it?*
- Then do an example of the mini-interview on the board, focusing on the use of the 2nd conditional in the answer:

Q: *Which activity would you like to try?* → A: *(I'd like to try) rock-climbing.*
Q: *Why would you like to try it? | Why is that?* →
A: *Because I think it would be exciting and scary at the same time ...*
If necessary, drill the questions and possible answers to build learner confidence for the survey stage.
*Also point out to them that their answers should sound natural and that it is often not necessary to repeat part of the question.* (With this in mind, *Why is that?* might also be a more natural follow up question than *Why would you like to try it?*).

- Give learners a few minutes to think about their answers to the questions (as they will be answering questions as well as asking). Circulate and help with vocabulary if necessary.
- Now ask them to carry out the survey. Learners can do this all in pairs (as suggested) or all individually according to their ability. However, if learners conduct the mini-interviews in pairs, they can work together to construct the piecharts and write the mini-reports together too.
- When they have completed the surveys, looked at the results and created a piechart, draw their attention to the percentages and ask them to write a mini-report explaining the survey and results, e.g.
*Two classmates would like to try rock climbing because it would be exciting and scary at the same time.*
Encourage them to vary the language used to express numbers, e.g. *five students ...* → *half of the students would like to try ...*
- When learners are ready, ask them to make a poster showing their piechart and mini-report.
- At the end of the activity, choose some learners (or ask for volunteers) to present their findings to the class. When presenting, encourage learners to use some of the techniques and phrases from the presentation activities in other units, e.g. *As you can see ... This piechart shows ...*
- When the class has listened to a few presentations, ask them what similarities and differences they noticed about the results.
- **Extend and challenge:** Ask learners to give a personal reaction to the results of their survey. Which results did they predict? Which surprised them?

Answers
Learners' own answers.

 **Wrap up**

- Find out the activities that learners in your class would most like to try.

Answers
Learners' own answers.

## 2 Make a poster about a place you would like to visit

- Put learners in pairs or groups of threes and ask them to think of a place that everyone in the pair / group would like to visit (they could prepare this beforehand). Take them through the step-by-step instructions presented in the Learner's Book. Follow the necessary steps to ask them to research the place first (see **Teaching tip**, **Unit 2** overview).
- The note-making stage (see Project 2, stage 2) could be divided up between the pair of group of three, i.e. one learner could write the description, another could describe how to get there and where to stay, another could describe what they would do when they were there.
- When learners are writing up their notes into a first draft, circulate and give assistance with language expression and vocabulary.
- When drafts have been checked (by teacher and learners) ask them to copy the parts of the description onto a large piece of paper to make a poster. Allow them to decorate with pictures and different colours.
- When they have finished, ask learners to display their posters on the wall. Allow them to walk around and read other groups' posters. While they are reading, they should make a note of at least one interesting or surprising point from each poster.

Answers
Learners' own answers.

 **Wrap up**

- At the end, compare the places described by different pairs / groups in the class and have a 'superlatives' vote: which is the most unusual place, the most fun place, the most beautiful place, the most historical place?, etc.

Answers
Learners' own answers.

## 🗨 Reflect on your learning

- These revision activities can be approached in different ways, according to the level and character of your class.
  - Questions 1–7 could be used as a class quiz, with learners in teams and a time limit given to write answers to each question.
  - Alternatively, you could conduct a revision session – ask learners to work in pairs and take longer to think about and write down their answers. When pairs have finished the questions, they swap with another pair and correct each other's work, with you monitoring and giving help and advice when needed.
  - You could set this task for homework / self-study.

## Look what I can do!

**Aim:** To check learners have fulfilled the objectives for **Unit 9** (and to what degree).

• Present the objectives slide or poster from the introduction to **Unit 9** in **Lesson 1** and remind learners of the objectives from the start of the unit.

• Focus their attention on the '*I can ...*' statements and read through together. You could put these on a slide or write on the board. Ask learners if they feel they can now do these tasks after completing **Unit 9**. By this point, you should have a clear idea yourself of how well your learners have completed the tasks. However, ask them now to do an initial self-assessment.

• Put learners in pairs and ask them to look through their notebooks and portfolios to find evidence of their work for each of the statements. Then they give themselves a rating as follows:
  ✓ Yes, I can – no problem!
  ? A little – I need more practice.
  ☺ No – I need a lot more practice.

• Circulate and chat to learners about their self-assessment (some might be overly modest and you can point out that their rating could be higher).

• Conduct a general feedback at the end and find out which tasks learners found the most interesting / useful / challenging, etc.

• **Extend and challenge:** At the end of the unit, you could give 'mini-awards' or 'unit awards' to individual learners, pairs or groups who have worked well in specific areas. These could be a mixture of serious and informal / humorous and could cover skills other than language to include learners of all levels and aptitudes.
  *Good conversationalist/s*
  *Good writers*
  *Best description*
  *Most improved pronunciation*
  *Best art work /graphics*
  *Good presentation skills*
  *Most interesting presentation*

**Answers**
Learners' own answers.

## Wrap up

• As a class, look at the Big question again on a slide or written on the board: *What can we learn from travelling & holidays?*

• Learners may need guiding to help them make the connection between the question and the unit themes and tasks. Write these prompts on the board (or put on a slide).
  **Prompts:**
  *1 How to use our imaginations and describe a place in an interesting way.*
  *2 How places make us feel because of different things that we see and find out.*
  *3 Sometimes we can learn about history and how people lived many years ago.*
  *4 How to consider good and bad points about a place and make up our own minds.*
  *5 Important facts that can help us with our school work.*
  *6 How it would feel to try something new or different.*

• Ask learners: *What can we learn from looking at different kinds of holiday sports activities?* (Answer: 6)
  *What can we learn from reading or listening to other people's opinions about places to visit?* (4)
  *What can we learn from visiting interesting and beautiful places?* (2 and 3)
  *What can we learn from thinking about our dream holiday?* (1)
  *What can we learn from different kinds of journeys, like the one described in Lesson 5?* (5)
  (**Note:** Other answers might also possible for some of questions, depending on view point.)

• Alternatively, put learners in groups, print the prompts on different colour paper and give a set to each group; then call out the questions and ask them to hold up the answers.

## Activity Book

### Revision

### 1 Vocabulary

• Learners complete a crossword covering key grammar and vocabulary from **Lessons 1–6** in **Unit 9**.

**Answers**
**Across**
1 surfing  4 smell  6 theme  7 would  8 touch  9 by  10 in
**Down**
1 snorkelling  2 fascinated  3 take  5 about  7 way

### My global progress

• Learners think about their own responses to topics and activities in the unit and answer the questions.

**Answers**
Learners' own answers.

# Review 5

Learner's Book pages: 140–141

**Photocopiable activity 19**

- Review 5 offers learners the opportunity to review and recycle vocabulary items from **Units 1–9**. The short tasks are designed to be carried out as a quiz or as questions on a board game, which learners work through in pairs and earn points.
- Review 5 activities are intended to be done in class (as a pair work activity), and have been designed with end-of-term revision sessions in mind.
- Whether learners work through Review 9 tasks as a quiz or board game, circulate and monitor the activity to check responses and ensure that they stay on task. They can earn points for each task and learners will need to administer this themselves if the tasks are done in pairs, with one learner deciding if the other has successfully earned the points after completing the tasks. In this case, check that points are being awarded fairly.
- **Feedback:** Where vocabulary lists are required as answers, these can be elicited from learners or displayed on the board or on a slide. To make the correction stage more active, ask learners to come up to the board and write the word lists.

## 1 Vocabulary and speaking

- Learners act out four free-time activities and ask their partner to guess what they are. They then tell each other what they like / don't like doing in their free time.

> **Answers**
> Four from: play video games, painting, play football, take photos, meet up with my friends, play piano (other answers also possible).
> + Learners' own answers.

## 2 Vocabulary

- Learners change adjectives into nouns, paying attention to form and spelling.

> **Answers**
> amazement   bravery   beauty   fear   pride   excitement

## 3 Vocabulary and speaking

- Learners name as many school subjects as they can in one minute; then tell their partner which ones they are good at / like / don't like.

> **Answers**
> School subjects: National history, Arabic, Science, Art and Design, French, Islamic education, Social Studies, Spanish, Physical education (other answers also possible).
> + Learners' own answers.

## 4 Vocabulary and speaking

- Learners talk about which extra-curricular activities are available at their school, which ones they do and which they would like to do.

> **Answers**
> Learners' own answers.

## 5 Vocabulary and speaking

- Learners act out four sports that they have done or played in the last two years and say which ones they like best and why. Then they tell their partner what equipment they need to do these sports.

> **Answers**
> Learners' own answers.

## 6 Vocabulary, speaking and writing

- Learners write down six types of film, paying attention to spelling. Then they tell their partner about the last film they saw and if they would recommend the film or not.

> **Answers**
> Six from: animation, comedy, horror, science-fiction, adventure, drama, action, historical.
> + Learners' own answers.

## 7 Vocabulary and speaking

Learners name four gadgets or pieces of equipment that they use a lot and tell their partner which is their favourite and why.

> **Answers**
> Learners' own answers.

## 8 Vocabulary and speaking

Learners talk about where they would go if they could go on an exciting expedition, and why, and talk about what equipment they would need.

> **Answers**
> Learners' own answers.

## 9 Vocabulary, writing and speaking

- Learners write down six verb/noun phrases to describe ways of communicating and say which they have used in the last two days. They talk about their favourite way of communicating and the reason why.

> **Answers**
> Six from: *raise your hand, send an email / a text, write an email / text / note / blog, make a call, reply to an email / text* (other answers possible).
> + Learners' own answers.

## 10 Vocabulary and writing

Learners write down as many holiday activities as they can, (ending in -*ing*) in a one-minute time limit, paying attention to spelling.

> **Answers**
> rock-climbing, skiing, snorkelling, bungee-jumping, snowboarding, surfing (other answers possible).

- Make up a certificate for each learner using **Photocopiable activity 19**. Don't forget to celebrate their achievements!

# Photocopiable activities

## Photocopiable activity 1

**Conversation cards:** *Have you ever...?*
**(Present perfect simple)** *When / where / who did you ...?* **(Past simple)**

**Aim:** Learners use the conversation cards as prompts to ask each other questions about experiences. Further prompts encourage them to extend the conversation to find out more information.

**Preparation time:** 10 minutes

**Completion time:** 20 minutes

**Language focus:** Asking and answering present perfect simple questions: *Have you ever ... ?* Extending the conversation using past simple questions: *When / Where / Who did you ... ?*

**Materials:** One set of **Conversation cards** for each group or pair of learners.

### Procedure

- Put learners into pairs or small groups and give each a set of cards. Explain that they are going to find out about interesting things their classmates have done, using the cards to ask questions.
- Ask learners to find Card 1 and look at the prompt on the left hand side. Elicit the full question and answer:
  *Have you ever tried spicy food?*    *Yes, I have / No, I haven't.*
- Circle the 'Yes' answer and ask learners to look at the prompts on the right hand side. Ask them to think of a question to find out more. Elicit possible follow-on questions: e.g.
  *Where did you try it? What kind of food did you try? What was it like? Did you like it?*
- Now elicit a short dialogue: e.g.

  | | |
  |---|---|
  | *Have you ever tried spicy food?* | *Yes, I have.* |
  | *Really? Where did you try it?* | *At an Indian restaurant last year.* |
  | *Did you like it?* | *Yes, I did.* |

- Now delete some of the words and ask learners to remember and repeat the dialogue together (e.g. one half of the class says the dialogue on the left, the other half, the dialogue on the right). Delete more parts of the dialogue until the whole text has 'disappeared' and ask learners to repeat the procedure until they are confident (see **Unit 1**, **Lesson 1**, page 24 for instructions on the *Disappearing drill* technique).
- **Note:** If learners answer 'no', simply move on to the next question.
- If necessary, use the backchaining technique to give learners practice with pronunciation and intonation regarding the questions (see **Unit 1**, **Lesson 1**, page 23 for instructions).
- Now ask learners to follow the same steps in pairs or small groups. They should turn all the cards over and pick ones at random, then ask and answer questions. In small groups, one person can ask the questions to all other group members, first directing questions at one member, then drawing in others with the question, *What about you?* E.g.

  | | |
  |---|---|
  | *A: Have you ever tried spicy food?* | *B: Yes, I have.* |
  | *A: Really? Where did you try it?* | *B: At an Indian restaurant last year.* |
  | *A: Did you like it?* | *B: Yes, I did.* |
  | *A: What about you?* | *C: Yes, I have.* |
  | *A: And where did you try it?* | *C: At my aunt's house on her birthday ...* |

- While learners are talking, circulate giving assistance with grammar and vocabulary as needed. Note down common errors with form and pronunciation for feedback at the end.
- Give class feedback, praising good efforts and dealing with common errors in a collective error correction session at the end.

## Photocopiable activity 1

Conversation cards: *Have you ever ...?* (Present perfect simple)
*When / where / who did you ...?* (Past simple)

| | | | |
|---|---|---|---|
| 1<br>try / spicy food | • Where?<br>• Who?<br>• Like? | 2<br>ride / horse | • Where?<br>• When?<br>• Who? |
| 3<br>use / chopsticks | • Where?<br>• Why? | 4<br>be / aeroplane | • Where?<br>• When?<br>• Who? |
| 5<br>be / on TV | • Why?<br>• When? | 6<br>travel / ship | • Where?<br>• When?<br>• Who? |
| 7<br>cook / dinner | • When?<br>• Who?<br>• What? | 8<br>write / e-pal | • Where?<br>• Who?<br>• What? |
| 9<br>see / someone famous | • Who?<br>• Where?<br>• What? | 10<br>perform / on stage | • When?<br>• Where?<br>• What? |
| 11<br>play / school team | • Which?<br>• Who? | 12<br>go / concert | • Where?<br>• What?<br>• Who? |

## Photocopiable activity 2

### Picture description worksheet: *What was the family doing last night?* (Past continuous tense)

**Aim:** Learners increase their understanding of the past continuous tense by describing a picture in which many actions are happening at the same time, at a given point in time.

**Preparation time:** 5 minutes

**Completion time:** 15–20 minutes

**Language focus:** Past continuous sentences and questions.

**Materials**: One copy of the **Picture description worksheet** for each pair of learners.

### Procedure

- Distribute one copy of the worksheet to each pair of learners.
- Ask learners to look at the picture. Elicit an initial description, asking all the questions in the past tense. *Who was in this house last night? Which members of the family can you see? What time was this picture taken?*
- Next, ask learners to brainstorm verbs to describe the actions in the picture. To give learners more support in the activity later, write the verbs on the board (in the base form); do not write, if you want to stretch them more by having them remember.
- Choose one activity and elicit a model sentence, e.g. Teacher: *What was Ben doing at 6 o'clock last night?* Learners: *He was playing a game with Sasha.*
- Ask learners to work in pairs and make similar sentences to describe the activities. They can either write or say the sentences, depending on which skill you wish to focus on. For a speaking exercise, you could ask learners to ask and answer as follows (asking five questions each), e.g.
A: *What was Grandma doing at 6 o'clock last night?*
B: *She was knitting.*
A: *And what was Dan doing?*
B: *He was playing the guitar.*

- Circulate and check, helping learners with language use, vocabulary and pronunciation as appropriate.
- When you conduct feedback, present some false sentences and ask learners to correct as follows, to practise negative forms:
Teacher: *Dan was reading a book.*
Learners: *False! Dan wasn't reading a book, he was playing the guitar.*

> **Answers**
> Possible answers: At 6 o'clock last night …
> Dad was serving tea. / Grandma was knitting / Josh was playing with his toy train / Dan was playing the guitar / Jess was working on her laptop / sending emails / Sasha was playing with Ben / Mum was reading a book / talking to Dad / Granddad was reading the newspaper.

### Wrap up

- Ask learners to describe what was happening at their homes last night at 6 pm. You could also vary the focus by asking them to describe what was happening at school at 9 am this morning, what was happening at the shopping centre at 7 pm last night, at the train station at 4 pm yesterday, etc.

## Photocopiable activity 2

Picture description worksheet: *What was the family doing last night?* (Past continuous tense)

## Photocopiable activity 3

### First conditional dominoes

**Aim:** Learners practise making first conditional sentences (**Unit 2 Lesson 2**) of the Learner's Book by matching sentence halves.

**Preparation time:** 5 minutes

**Completion time:** 20 minutes + extension activity for high level learners only

**Language focus:** *If / unless ... , will / won't* to express likely future events.

**Materials:** One set of **First conditional dominoes**, cut up as indicated per pair of learners.

### Procedure

- Distribute one set of dominoes, cut up as indicated, to each pair of learners. Tell them that they are going to practise making sentences by matching sentence halves (playing *dominoes*).
- Pick up random dominoes, show the class and elicit whether they can go together.
- Choose a confident pair of learners to demonstrate the game. Learners mix up their dominoes and take six each. Player 1 plays a domino and Player 2 puts down a domino which completes a logical sentence. Players take turns to play a suitable domino. A player who doesn't have a suitable domino, misses a turn. The first player to put down all the dominoes is the winner.
- Allow time to play the game while you circulate, giving assistance.
- To give higher-level learners an extra challenge and possibilities for extension, photocopy one set of the **Blank modal dominoes** (available in Stage 4 Teacher's Resource page 162) and get them to fill them in with their own sentences. Cut the dominoes up and play as the main activity.

**Answers**

If you don't work hard, / .... you won't pass the exam.
Unless you have enough sleep, / ... you won't be able to concentrate.
If you eat lots of fruit, / ...you'll have more energy for studying.
If you drink lots of water, / ...you'll be able to concentrate better.
Unless you get enough exercise,/ ...you won't be able to study well.
If you eat a balanced diet, / ...you'll feel healthy and strong.
If you get lots of exercise,/ ...your memory will improve.
If you eat fish and green vegetables,/... these foods will help your brain to work well.
Chocolate won't do your brain any good,/ ...unless it's dark chocolate.
If you eat wholegrain food, / ...you'll have lots of energy throughout the day.
If you eat too much sugary food,/ ...your energy will drop.
If you eat nuts and berries,/ ... your brain will get lots of good vitamins.
[Other combinations also possible]

## Photocopiable activity  3(i)

**First conditional dominoes**

| | | | |
|---|---|---|---|
| ... your brain will get lots of good vitamins. | If you don't work hard, | ... you won't pass the exam. | Unless you have enough sleep, |
| ... you won't be able to concentrate. | If you eat lots of fruit, | ... you'll have more energy for studying. | If you drink lots of water, |
| ... you'll be able to concentrate better. | Unless you get enough exercise, | ... you won't be able to study well. | If you eat a balanced diet, |
| ... you'll feel healthy and strong. | If you get lots of exercise, | ... your memory will improve. | If you eat fish and green vegetables, |
| ... these foods will help your brain to work well. | Chocolate won't do your brain any good, | ... unless it's dark chocolate. | If you eat wholegrain food, |
| ... you'll have lots of energy throughout the day. | If you eat too much sugary food, | ... your energy will drop. | If you eat nuts and berries, |

## Photocopiable activity 4

### Modals prompt cards

**Aim:** Learners use modals prompt cards to make questions and sentences using modal verbs for expressing requests and advice and phrases for expressing suggestions.

**Preparation time:** 5 minutes

**Completion time:** 20–25 mins.

**Language focus:** Modal verbs, *would, should, could* for expressing requests and advice.

**Vocabulary:** Functional language for expressing suggestions: *How about* + (verb + *-ing*)? *You could* (+ verb) ...; *Why don't you* (+verb)? *If I were you, I would* (+ verb) ...

**Materials:** One set of **Modals prompt cards** cut up as indicated per small group of learners; one dice per pair or small group of learners.

### Procedure

- Make double-sided photocopies of pages 209 and 210, with one side containing the text from page 209 and the other the corresponding numbers from page 210.
- Cut them them up as indicated and hand out sets to small groups of learners.
- Tell learners to lay them on the table with the number side facing up, in six sets, each containing all three cards of the same number.
- Give a dice to each group. Tell Player A to roll the dice and look at the number that appears; then pick up a card that corresponds with that number. Player A then reads the instruction on the card and answers. The other learners listen to the answer and say whether it is satisfactory or not. Then Player B has a turn and follows the same procedure, and so on around the table, so each learner has a go.

- Demonstrate the activity with a group of confident learners first, then tell the class to follow the same procedure in their groups.
- When learners have answered the prompt card, ask them to put it to one side and continue until all the cards have been answered. When learners have answered all the cards in one pile, they should keep throwing the dice until a number appears for another pile with unanswered cards. They could continue until all the cards have been answered, or you could set a time limit.
- Higher-level learners or early finishers could make some more cards of their own and continue the exercise. They could use their knowledge from other subjects to expand the activity.
- **Note:** This activity could be used for writing practice rather than speaking, following the same procedure as above.

---

**Answers**

Cards that begin, *Tell your (head) teacher politely ...*, should be answered: *I / we would like to ...*

Cards that begin, *Make a suggestion ...*, should be answered with the phrases, *How about (+verb + -ing) ...?; You could (+ verb) ... Why don't you (+ verb) ...? If I were you, I would (+ verb) ...*

Cards that begin, *Give some advice about ...*, should be answered with *should / shouldn't*.

Cards that begin, *Ask your teacher ...*, should be answered with *Could ...?*

---

## Photocopiable activity 4

Modals prompt cards

| | | |
|---|---|---|
| **1**<br><br>Tell your headteacher politely that you want to start a badminton club after school and why. | **1**<br><br>Make a suggestion for next term's school trip. | **1**<br><br>Give some advice about treating your classmates fairly in class. |
| **2**<br><br>Make a suggestion for a good class game. | **2**<br><br>Ask your teacher if you can go to the toilet. | **2**<br><br>Ask your teacher politely for extra time to finish your homework. |
| **3**<br><br>Tell your teacher politely that you want to start a class blog about ... and why. | **3**<br><br>Make a suggestion to help your friend who doesn't understand the maths homework. | **3**<br><br>Give some advice about preparing for an exam. |
| **4**<br><br>Make a suggestion for an article for the school newsletter next month. | **4**<br><br>Ask your teacher if your class can play your favourite class game. | **4**<br><br>Ask your teacher if you can have a drink of water. |
| **5**<br><br>Make a suggestion for a poster or picture to go on your classroom wall. | **5**<br><br>Ask your teacher if you can change seats. Say the reason why. | **5**<br><br>Ask your teacher to explain the homework again. |
| **6**<br><br>Tell your headteacher politely that you want the computer club to happen more times each month and why. | **6**<br><br>Make a suggestion for a good website to help with learning English. | **6**<br><br>Give some advice to someone who is new to your class. |

| | | |
|---|---|---|
| 1 | 1 | 1 |
| 2 | 2 | 2 |
| 3 | 3 | 3 |
| 4 | 4 | 4 |
| 5 | 5 | 5 |
| 6 | 6 | 6 |

# Photocopiable activity 5

## Reporting an interview and writing a summary

**Aim:** Learners use the interview text on the handout to practise reporting questions and statements in the present and summary writing.

**Preparation time:** 5 minutes

**Completion time:** 20–25 minutes.

**Language focus:** Practice of reporting questions and statements in the present.

**Materials:** One **Reporting an interview and writing a summary** handout for each learner; notebooks for answers.

## Procedure

- Show learners a picture of Jerome Nash. Elicit which sport he plays (basketball) and his nationality (American). Ask learners which words they know which are connected to basketball and put their suggestions on the board. During this process, make sure you elicit *league*, *coach*, *inspiration* and *off-season* by asking the questions: *What do we call a group of sports clubs which organise a competition for a title?* (league), *What's the name of the person who trains players and athletes?* (coach), *What word do we use to describe someone or something that makes us want to do good things?* (inspiration) and *What do we call the time when basketball players don't play any games?* (off-season).
- Distribute one copy of the **Reporting an interview and writing a summary** handout to each learner.
- Elicit how many tasks there are on the handout (four tasks) and read through each one together.
- Point out that for question 2 they must just focus on the main points of each answer and write short answers to the questions.
- Tell learners to read the text and work their way through the questions. Circulate and offer support while learners complete the tasks.

**Answers**

1 Two things that have made Jerome successful are 'hard work and loving the sport'.

2

a When he was 7 years old.

b His parents.

c To work very hard, be confident and believe that you have a talent and to love the sport.

d Spending time with his family and girlfriend, (watching movies and walking the dog).

3 (Sample answer)
Jerome Nash started playing basketball seriously when he was 7 years old and his biggest inspiration is his parents. His advice to young players is to work very hard, be confident, believe in your own talent and love the sport. When he is not playing he likes spending time with his family and girlfriend. (54 words).

4

The interviewer wants to know who Jerome's biggest inspiration is.
The interviewer wants to know what advice he has for young players.
The interviewer wants to know what he likes doing when he isn't playing.
Jerome says that his biggest inspiration is his parents.
He says that his advice for young players is work really hard, be confident, believe in yourself and love the sport.
He says that he likes spending time with his family and girlfriend when he isn't playing.

**Unit 3**

## Photocopiable activity 5

### Reporting an interview and writing a summary

#### 1 Read

**Read the introduction to the interview with American basketball player, Jerome Nash, and write down two things that have made him successful. Then read the interview and answer the questions.**

Jerome Nash started playing basketball when he was seven years old and he has never looked back. Success for him has come from 'hard work and loving the sport'. This year's star player tells SportQuest about how he got to be top of his game ...

**1 When did you start playing basketball seriously?**

Well, my mum says that I started shooting a basketball as soon as I could walk! But I started playing seriously when I was seven years old. That's when I joined a junior league. I loved playing lots of ball games as a kid – football, baseball ... but my parents realised that I had a talent for basketball.

**2 Who is your biggest inspiration?**

I've had some great coaches, but my biggest inspiration is my mum and dad. They have always supported me and given me confidence since I was very young. They told me to never give up, even when times were hard.

**3 What advice do you have for other young players?**

If you are serious about the game, then you have to work really hard. There is a lot of competition out there! You must also be confident and believe in yourself. And you must really love the sport!

**4 And what do you like doing when you aren't playing?**

During the season, I'm really busy and I don't get much free time. Off-season, I spend a lot of time with my family and girlfriend, catching up. We love going to the movies and taking our dogs for long walks ...

#### 2 Read

**Read again and write down short answers to the interviewer's questions.**

**a** When did Jerome start playing basketball seriously? _____

**b** Who is Jerome's biggest inspiration? _____

**c** What advice does he have for other young players? _____

**d** What does he like doing when he isn't playing? _____

#### 3 Write

**Make your short answers for Activity 2 into complete sentences and write a summary of Jerome's interview in 50–60 words.**

#### 4 Use of English: Reported speech in the present

Look at the interviewer's questions and Jerome's replies for sections 2, 3 and 4. Report the interviewer's questions and Jerome's replies.

*The interviewer wants to know ...*

*Jerome says that he ...*

# Photocopiable activity 6

## Sports commentaries

**Aim:** Learners construct three examples of radio or TV sports commentaries by sorting jumbled sentences on the handout. They then identify words to be emphasised when the commentaries are read in the style of a TV or radio presenter and practise reading in this way.

**Preparation time:** 5 minutes

**Completion time:** 25 minutes

**Language focus:** Pronunciation: Emphasising key words to read with expression.

**Vocabulary:** Descriptive words: *awesome, blast, fire, cheer*

**Materials:** One **Sports commentaries** handout for each learner; notebooks for answers

## Procedure

- Distribute one copy of the **Sports commentaries** handout to each learner.
- Elicit from learners how many commentaries there are on each handout (3) and if the sentences are in the correct order (no).
- Ask them to read each commentary quickly and identify which sport the commentator is talking about.
- Next, ask learners to read the commentaries and put the sentences in the correct order, using the structure given in **Activity 2**.
- When learners have ordered the commentaries correctly, get them to practise reading the commentaries in pairs as if they are going to present it on the radio or TV. They should identify words to emphasise as if they are reading in an excited fast-paced style.
- Circulate and help learners with pronunciation and intonation.

## Wrap up

- To finish, ask some confident learners to read their commentaries in the style of a radio or TV presenter.

---

**Answers**

**1** Commentary A: 100 metres running (sprint) / Commentary B: Football / Commentary C: swimming.

**2** Commentary A: 2,4,3,1 Commentary B: 2,1,4,3 Commentary C: 4,2,1,3

**3** Suggestions for emphasised words:

**Commentary A**
fastest / world / blasting / track
touch / he
goes /across / record time
world record / stadium / today

**Commentary B**
best / striker / scored
fired / goal / past
best / player / world / today
certainly / tonight

**Commentary C**
here / Millennium Sports Stadium
cheering / young swimmer / blast / pool
surely / gold medal
done it / What / awesome victory / champion today

---

## Photocopiable activity 6

### Sports commentaries

**1 Read the jumbled sentences in each sports commentary. Which sport is the presenter talking about in each one?**

**Commentary A**

1 Another world record has been broken in the stadium today!
2 The fastest man in the world is blasting down the track!
3 And there he goes across the finishing line in record time!
4 No-one can touch this man in the 100 metres and he knows it!

**Commentary B**

1 Did you see how he fired that goal past the keeper?
2 Brazil's best striker has just scored again!
3 And he's certainly proved it here tonight!
4 This young man must be the best player in the world today!

**Commentary C**

1 She is surely on her way to a gold medal!
2 The crowds are cheering as we watch this young swimmer blast down the pool!
3 And she's done it! What an awesome victory for the 18-year-old champion today!
4 And here we are at the Millennium Sports Stadium in Sydney.

**2 Put the sentences in each commentary in the correct order.**

Use this order to help you:

1 Opening sentence
2 What's happening
3 Exciting finish

**3 Read each commentary in the correct order. Underline the words you want to emphasise and read your description to your partner, in an expressive way, like a radio presenter.**

# Photocopiable activity 7

## A film review with relative clauses: Tell me about *Madagascar 3* ...

**Aim:** Learners conduct an A/B pair work dictation activity to build a film review about the animation film, *Madagascar 3*. They then identify relative clauses within the completed text and finally write their own film reviews, using the text as a model.

**Preparation time:** 5 minutes

**Completion time:** 1 hour

**Language focus:** Relative clauses with *that, who, where, when*.

**Materials:** One handout (A or B) for each learner; notebooks or paper for writing film reviews.

## Procedure

- Divide learners into A/B pairs. Distribute one copy of handout A to each student A and one copy of handout B to each student B. Tell them that they are going to complete a film review about a famous film. Ask them to read the title on the handout and tell you the name of the film (*Madagascar 3*).
- Ask learners to sit so they are facing each other and tell them not to look at each other's handout. Tell them that Player A has information that Player B needs to complete his/her review and Player B has information that Player A needs. Player A will read the first sentence and Player B will listen and copy to fill in the space on his/her handout; then Player B will finish the sentence and Player A will listen and copy to fill in the space on his/her handout, and so on, until the reviews on both handouts are completed.
- Remind learners to use phrases such as: *Can you say that again please? How do you spell ... ?*, etc., if they need any help from their partner when listening to the dictated sentences. Also remind them to indicate punctuation, e.g. *full stop, comma*. They shouldn't look at each other's handouts at any time.

- When learners have completed the texts, ask them to underline all the relative clauses on their handout.
- Now tell them to write their own film reviews (either individually or in pairs), choosing a film that they have seen recently either at the cinema or on DVD at home. Ask them to follow the structure:
  *Type of film → Plot and setting → My opinion → Recommendation*
  Tell them to use the review of *Madagascar 3* to help them write their own reviews. The review follows the structure outlined above.
- Circulate and help learners with vocabulary and language structures.

## Wrap up

- To finish, read out some of the reviews (without saying the name of the film) and ask learners to guess which film is being described.

**Answers**

*Madagascar 3* is an animation film that was released in 2012. It is about four animals, <u>who travel across Europe and have lots of funny adventures.</u> They want to get back home to New York, <u>where they live in a zoo.</u> The animals are trying to escape from a wicked lady, <u>who is trying to catch them.</u> While they are travelling through Europe they join the circus, <u>where they soon become friends with the other animals.</u> They make the circus funnier and more exciting too.

My favourite scenes are <u>when the animals are with the circus.</u> There is also a funny scene <u>where the wicked lady nearly catches them.</u> I really enjoyed *Madagascar 3* and I would recommend it to anyone <u>who likes colourful animation films that have an exciting story and funny characters.</u>

Film review: Learners' own answers.

## Photocopiable activity 7

**A film review with relative clauses: Tell me about *Madagascar 3* ...**

✂ ------------------------------------------------------------------------------------------------

**Player A**

*Madagascar 3* is an animation film _____. It is about four animals, _____. They want to get back home to New York, _____. The animals are trying to escape from a wicked lady, _____. While they are travelling through Europe _____ where they soon become friends with the other animals. _____ and more exciting too.

_____ when the animals are with the circus.

_____ where the wicked lady nearly catches them.

_____ and I would recommend it to anyone

_____ that have an exciting story and funny characters.

✂ ------------------------------------------------------------------------------------------------

**Player B**

_____ that was released in 2012. _____ who travel across Europe and have lots of funny adventures.

_____ where they live in a zoo.

_____ who is trying to catch them.

_____ they join the circus, _____.

They make the circus funnier _____.

My favourite scenes are _____. There is also a funny scene _____. I really enjoyed *Madagascar 3* _____ who likes colourful animation films _____.

# Photocopiable activity 8

## Revision word search: *What's in a movie ...?*

**Aim:** Learners find words about movies in the word search to match the definitions. They then categorise the words into four groups and add to the lists from their own knowledge.

**Preparation time:** 5 minutes

**Completion time:** 15–20 minutes

**Vocabulary:** Parts of a film: *setting, characters, actors*; things in a cinema: *screen, popcorn*; types of film: *comedy, drama, animation*; adjectives to describe films: *gorgeous, amazing*

**Materials:** One **Revision word search** handout for each learner; notebooks for vocabulary extension activity.

## Procedure

- Distribute one copy of the handout to each learner.
- Ask learners to read the definitions and then look for the words in the word search. They should circle the word in the word search and then write it next to the definition on the handout. For learners who need more support, give them the target words first and ask them to find them in the word search and match to the definitions; for other learners, stretch them by getting them to read the definitions then try to find the words in the word search. You could give them the first letter of the target words for a little extra support if needed.
- When they have found all the words in the word search and written them next to the definitions, they should divide the words into categories as instructed in **Activity 2**. Ask learners to write the words in their notebooks or wherever they keep vocabulary records.
- Ask learners to work in pairs and add more words to each category. Stipulate how many words according to the level of your learners and the actual category (i.e. learners might be more able to add six more *adjectives* than six more *parts of a film*).

### Answers

| | | | | | | | | | | | |
|---|---|---|---|---|---|---|---|---|---|---|---|
| | S | | | | | | | | | | |
| | E | P | O | P | C | O | R | N | | | |
| | T | | | | | | | | | | C |
| | T | S | C | R | E | E | N | | | | O |
| | I | | | | | | | | | | M |
| A | N | I | M | A | T | I | O | N | | | E |
| C | G | | D | | | | | | | | D |
| T | | | R | | | | | | | | Y |
| O | C | H | A | R | A | C | T | E | R | S | |
| R | | A | M | A | Z | I | N | G | | | |
| S | | | A | | | | | | | | |
| G | O | R | G | E | O | U | S | | | | |

**1**

1 comedy
2 gorgeous
3 characters
4 setting
5 screen
6 actors
7 amazing
8 drama
9 animation
10 popcorn

**2**

Parts of a film: characters, actors, setting
Things in a cinema: screen, popcorn
Types of film: comedy, drama, animation
Adjectives to describe films: gorgeous, amazing

## Photocopiable activity 8

**Revision word search: *What's in a movie ...?***

| R | S | M | N | B | C | T | Q | F | G | H |
|---|---|---|---|---|---|---|---|---|---|---|
| P | E | P | O | P | C | O | R | N | C | S |
| K | T | N | B | P | M | C | T | R | N | C |
| M | T | S | C | R | E | E | N | K | L | O |
| O | I | P | T | K | H | Y | T | I | O | M |
| A | N | I | M | A | T | I | O | N | H | E |
| C | G | T | D | E | U | J | C | P | L | D |
| T | N | U | R | K | H | B | N | T | E | Y |
| O | C | H | A | R | A | C | T | E | R | S |
| R | W | A | M | A | Z | I | N | G | S | T |
| S | Y | X | A | R | V | T | V | C | Q | U |
| G | O | R | G | E | O | U | S | M | N | W |

**1  Read the clues and find the words in the word search. Write the word next to the clue.**

  **1** A type of film that is very funny. _____

  **2** An adjective that means *very beautiful*. _____

  **3** The people (or animals) that are part of the film plot. _____

  **4** The place where the film is set. _____

  **5** The place in the cinema where the film appears. _____

  **6** The people who play a role in the film. _____

  **7** An adjective that means *very surprising* or *impressive*. _____

  **8** A type of film that is sometimes quite sad and serious. _____

  **9** A type of film that is created with computer generated images (CGI) or with cartoon pictures. _____

**10** Something that you can often buy to eat in cinemas. _____

**2  Put the words from the word search into these categories in your notebook. Add three (or more) words to each category from your own knowledge.**

Parts of a film          Things in a cinema          Types of film          Adjectives to describe films

# Photocopiable activity 9

## Past habits: *When you were younger, what did you use to do?*

**Aim:** Learners make questions about past habits from prompts and then use the questions to interview their classmates, recording their answers in a table.

**Preparation time:** 5 minutes

**Completion time:** 20–30 mins.

**Language focus:** *Used to* (+ verb) for past habits; *What did you use to ...? I used to ...; I didn't use to ...*

**Materials:** One **Past habits** handout for each learner.

## Procedure

- Distribute one copy of the handout to each learner.
- Explain to learners that they are going to make six questions to ask their classmates about things they *used to* do when they were younger (e.g. five years old and younger). Focus them on the question prompts and the example in question 1. Use question 1 to check their understanding of the concept by asking, *Is the question in the past or present?* (past) *Did you play with the toy when you were much younger?* (yes) *Did you play with it regularly?* (yes) *Do you still play with the toy now?* (no) *So this question is asking about a habit in the past, something you used to do ...*
- Give learners some time to write the complete questions on the worksheet from the prompts. Monitor and circulate as appropriate. Then go through the answers as a class.
- Tell learners that they are now going to use the questions to interview their classmates. Demonstrate the activity first with a confident learner, showing positive and negative responses, e.g.
  A: *What toy did you use to play with?*
  B: *I used to play with a ... And what food did you use to hate?*
  A: *I didn't use to hate any food. I used to eat anything!*

- If necessary, drill the questions to prepare them for the interviewing stage.
- Tell learners to ask each question to two classmates. They must listen and record their answers in the table on the handout, in the appropriate box. Tell them that they must ask their partner a different question to the one that their partner asks them, e.g.
  A: *What toy did you use to play with when you were younger?*
  B: *I used to play with a ... And what TV programmes did you use to watch?*
  A: *I used to watch ...*
- Ask learners to stand up, mingle and interview at least two classmates for each question.
- When they have finished, have them sit down again and compare their notes with their partner.

## Wrap up

- Ask learners to compare their answers and, as a class, decide which was the most popular toy / place to visit / TV programme / story; the most common time to go to bed and what type of food most people hated.

---

**Answers**

**1**

**a** What toys did you use to play with?
**b** Where did you use to go with your family?
**c** What time did you use to go to bed?
**d** What food did you use to hate?
**e** What TV programmes did you use to watch?
**f** What story did you use to like?
**g** Learners' own answers.

**2** Learners' own answers.

---

**Unit 5**

## Photocopiable activity 9

**Past habits:** *When you were younger, what did you use to do?*

**1 Use the prompts to make questions to ask your classmates about things that they used to do when they were younger.**

*When you were younger ...*

**a** What toys / play with?

What toys did you use to play with?

**b** Where / go with your family?

_____

**c** What time / go to bed?

_____

**d** What food / hate?

_____

**e** What TV programmes / watch?

_____

**f** What story / like?

_____

**g** (Write your own questions here).

_____

_____

**2 Write your classmates' answers in the table.**

| a  *We used to play with ...* | b  *Places we used to go ...* | c  *We used to go to bed at ...* |
|---|---|---|
| d  *We used to hate ...* | e  *We used to watch ...* | f  *Stories we used to like ...* |

# Photocopiable activity 10

## Imaginary scenarios with the second conditional: *Imagine if ....*

**Aim:** Learners complete sentences and make questions about imaginary or 'dream' situations; they complete sentences with their own thoughts and then ask their partner about the same topics. Finally they compare their own and their partner's answers.

**Preparation time:** 5 minutes
**Completion time:** 20–25 mins.

**Language focus:** 2nd conditional forms to describe imaginary situations. *If I ..., I would ...; What would you do if ...?*

**Materials:** One **Imaginary scenarios** handout for each learner.

## Procedure

- Distribute one copy of the handout to each learner.
- Focus learners on the sentence halves in **Activity 1** and ask them if these sentences are going to be about real or imaginary situations (imaginary).
- Write the first partial sentence on the board and ask learners to guess how you (the teacher) might complete it. When eliciting an answer, highlight language form using different colour pens, e.g. If *I* had *a lot of money, I* would buy *my own island.*
- Now ask learners to complete the sentences with their own ideas. Circulate and monitor, helping with vocabulary and checking accuracy of 2nd conditional forms.
- Next, tell learners that they are now going to find out the same information about their partner by first completing the questions in **Activity 2** and then asking their partner. Focus them on **Activity 2** and do the first one together as a class (eliciting onto the board). Then give them some time to form the questions.

- Check the completed questions as a class. Then, if necessary, drill the questions to prepare them for the interviewing stage.
- Now put learners in pairs to interview each other. Tell them to interview each other as follows, to avoid the interaction sounding unnatural through both learners reading out the same question in full:
  Student A: *If you had a lot of money, what would you do?*
  Student B: *I'd buy a rollercoaster. What about you?* (avoid repetition of above question)
  Student A: *I think I'd buy a Ferrari!*
  Student B: *If you could invent something new, what would it be?*
  Student A: *I'd ... What about you?*
- Ask learners to record each other's answers in the box in **Activity 2**.

## Wrap up

- When learners have finished interviewing, share responses as a class and ask learners to nominate the most interesting and unusual ideas.

**Answers**
**1** Learners' own answers.
**2**
**a** If you had a lot of money, what would you do?
**b** If you could invent something new, what would it be?
**c** If you could meet someone famous, who would it be?
**d** If you could buy a new gadget, what would it be?
**e** If your family didn't have a TV, what would you do instead / for entertainment?
**f** If you had a new pet, what kind of pet would you have?
**g** Learners' own answers.

Unit 5

## Photocopiable activity 10

**Imaginary scenarios with the second conditional:** *Imagine if ...*

**1 Complete the sentences with your own ideas.**

**a** If I had a lot of money, I would _____

**b** If I could invent something new, it would be a _____

**c** If I could meet someone famous, I'd like to meet _____

**d** If I could buy a new gadget, it would be a _____

**e** If my family didn't have a TV, we would _____

**f** If I had a new pet, it would be a _____

**2 Now make questions to ask your partner to find out the same information. Write his/her answers in the box.**

**a** If you had a lot of money, what would you do?

**b** If you could invent something new, *what* _____?

**c** If you could meet someone famous, _____?

**d** If you could buy a new gadget, _____?

**e** If your family didn't have a TV, _____?

**f** If you had a new pet, _____?

**g** (Write your own question here)

_____

_____

_____

_____

_____

_____

_____

_____

_____

---

**My partner ...**

**a** *If he/she had a lot of money, he/she would*

**b** _____

**c** _____

**d** _____

**e** _____

**f** _____

**g** _____

---

# Photocopiable activity 11

## Question forms: *Interview with an astronaut*

**Aim:** Learners imagine a profile for an astronaut. They sort jumbled words to make six questions to ask their astronaut, then imagine the answers and write under the questions.

**Preparation time:** 5 minutes

**Completion time:** 20–25 mins

**Language focus:** Question forms: *How many / what* + noun.

**Vocabulary:** Voyages and exploration (depending on learners' answers)

**Materials:** One **Interview with an astronaut** handout for each learner; paper and pens for drawing (optional).

## Procedure

- Distribute one copy of the handout to each learner.
- Focus learners on **Activity 1** and ask them to imagine an astronaut by answering the prompt questions. They write their ideas in the box under the questions. They could also draw their astronaut, if time permits and you think your class would enjoy this.
- Now focus their attention on the jumbled questions in **Activity 2**. Look at the example in question a together. Write the jumbled words for question (a) on the board; ask learners to turn over their handouts (so they can't see the answer) and elicit the correct order of the question. Then ask them to do the same for questions (b–f), and write their own question (or questions, if you want to extend the activity) for g.
- Tell learners that they must also imagine and write the answers for each question using the boxes underneath each one. Circulate and monitor while they are writing to help with expression and vocabulary.

- When they have finished, have them read each other's answers to questions (a–g), and look for similarities and differences in the imagined astronaut profiles and answers.
- Alternatively, you could set this up as a role play by having pairs of learners assuming the identity of their imagined astronaut and answering their partner's questions in that role. Then, as a consolidation, they write the answers in the boxes after the speaking activity.

## Wrap up

- When learners have finished interviewing, share responses as a class. Focus in particular on reasons for the space missions (**Activity 1**) and what the astronauts are studying in space (**Activity 2**, question c), as a review of these themes in **Unit 6**.

**Answers**
1 Learners' own answers.
2
a What food do you eat in space? (+ learners' own answers).
b What clothes do you wear? (+ learners' own answers).
c What things do you study in space? (+ learners' own answers).
d What things do you talk about with the other astronauts? (+ learners' own answers).
e How many days have you been in space? (+ learners' own answers).
f What things do you miss from home? (+ learners' own answers).
g Learners' own answers

## Photocopiable activity 11

**Question forms: Interview with an astronaut**

1 Imagine your astronaut: Is he/she male or female? *What nationality is he/she? How old is he/she? What is the reason for his/her space mission?*

2 Sort the words to make questions to ask your astronaut. Imagine the answers and write in the box under the question.

a food / what / you / do / in space / eat? What food do you eat in space?

b wear / do / clothes / what / you? _____

c in space / do / things / study / what / you? _____

d things / the / do / other astronauts / what / you / with / talk about?
_____

e you / been / how many / in space / days / have? _____

f miss / home / things / do / what / you / from? _____

g (Write your own question here) _____

# Photocopiable activity 12

## Conversation cards: Describing expeditions

**Aim:** Learners use the prompt cards to talk about an expedition as part of a guessing activity; then they write a blog or journal entry about the expedition detailed on the card.

**Preparation time:** 5 minutes

**Completion time:** 45 minutes

**Vocabulary:** Voyages and exploration (depending on learners' answers)

**Materials:** One set of **Conversation cards** for each group; notebooks or separate paper for writing.

## Procedure

- Put learners in groups of four or five. Distribute one set of prompt cards per group, positioned face down on groups' tables.
- Introduce the activity theme: exciting expeditions. Tell learners that each card in the set on their tables contains a short description of an expedition. They have to imagine that they are taking part, and use the questions on the cards to build up a picture of what is happening on the expedition and the reasons for doing it.
- Tell each member of the group to take a card and not show it to anyone else in the group. Tell them to read the information on the card and think about answers to the questions to build up a picture of their expedition.
- Now tell learners that they are going to take it in turns to tell their group about their expedition, without mentioning where it is actually taking place. The rest of the group has to listen and guess.
- Tell learners to wait until their classmate has finished their description before guessing the answer.
- Choose one learner in each group to start the activity; then learners go around the table, describing their expeditions and guessing where they are taking place.
- If you feel your learners would need more support with guessing the places, write the different places on the board and have them listen to their classmate and then choose from the list. Otherwise stretch learners and tap into their knowledge of geography by getting them to listen and guess without clues.
- When learners have finished the speaking stage, have them write a blog or journal entry, based on the information on their card.

> **Answers**
> Learners' own answers.

## Photocopiable activity 12

### Conversation cards: Describing expeditions

- A plane has just dropped you in the middle of the **Antarctic**:
  *What can you see?*
  *What can you hear?*
  *What is the climate like?*
  *What equipment do you have?*
  *Why are you there?*
  *What do you miss from home?*

  **Now write a diary entry or blog.**

- You are trekking deep in the **Amazon Rainforest**:
  *What animals can you see?*
  *What can you hear?*
  *What is the climate like?*
  *What equipment do you have?*
  *Why are you there?*
  *Who are you with?*
  *What do you miss from home?*

  **Now write a diary entry or blog.**

- You are on a sailing ship in the **Indian Ocean**:
  *How long have you been on this voyage?*
  *Why are you there?*
  *Who are you with?*
  *Where are you going?*
  *What activities are you going to do from the ship (e.g. diving)?*

  **Now write a diary entry or blog.**

- You are travelling across the **Sahara Desert**:
  *What can you see?*
  *What can you hear?*
  *Who are you with?*
  *How are you travelling?*
  *What is the climate like?*
  *Why are you there?*
  *What do you have to eat?*

  **Now write a diary entry or blog.**

- You are exploring some **ancient ruins in Central America**:
  *What can you see?*
  *Why are you there?*
  *How old are the ruins?*
  *What equipment do you have?*
  *Who are you with?*
  *Does anyone live in or near the ruins?*

  **Now write a diary entry or blog.**

- You are **cycling across Africa**:
  *What can you see?*
  *What can you hear?*
  *How do you feel?*
  *What is the climate like?*
  *What equipment do you have?*
  *Who are you with?*
  *Where are you going to?*

  **Now write a diary entry or blog.**

# Photocopiable activity 13

## Creating a business idea: *Be your own boss*

**Aim:** Learners write down things they are good at and interested in and compare with a partner, noting similarities. They then use the skills and interests they have in common to create an idea for a business which they will run together.

**Preparation time:** 5 minutes

**Completion time:** 1 hour

**Language focus:** Adjective + preposition (+ noun): *good at, interested in, crazy about, knowledgeable about*.

**Materials:** One **Create a business idea** handout for each learner; poster paper and pens.

## Procedure

- Distribute one copy of the handout to each learner.
- Focus learners on Activity A and ask them to think about all the things they are good at and interested in. Point out that this includes things at school and outside of school too – so they should think about things they are good at at home, e.g. being tidy, looking after their younger brother; and things they are good at in their relationships with other people, e.g. being kind, making people laugh, etc. Give them some examples using yourself as a model.
- **Note:** Point out to learners that, as well as the *adjective + preposition + noun* model (outlined in the Learner's Book), they can also use the *adjective + preposition + verb +ing* structure to express their ideas, e.g. I am good at *playing* football, I am good at *tidying* my bedroom.
- Ask learners to complete section A. Monitor and circulate, helping with vocabulary and language structures. Tell learners to answer the questions completely and not be overly modest about their skills and knowledge (i.e. everyone is good at more than one or two things!).
- When they have completed section A, put them into pairs or groups of three and ask them to compare their answers. Tell them to circle all the answers that are the same or similar.

- Now tell them that they are going to get together and create a business that will incorporate one or more of the skills and / or interests that they have in common.
- Elicit from learners what a *business* is. Elicit or tell them that sometimes people think of an idea for something that they know other people will like and want to buy; so they create a business to sell it to them. This means that they don't work for a boss: they work for themselves and 'are their own bosses'.
- Explain that in order to start their business they will need to borrow some money. Ask learners who they think will lend them the money (the bank). Then tell them that they are now going to write down their business ideas and think of ways to convince the bank to lend them lots of money to start their business.
- Now give learners time to think of a business idea and record it in the table (section C) on the handout. Each person in the pair or group must fill in each section. (Groups of threes could take responsibility for a section each, if allocating duties works better with your learners).
- Monitor and circulate, helping with vocabulary and language to express ideas. You may need to talk some groups through section 3 on the table, and input some ideas, depending on their business idea.
- When learners have input their ideas on the table, ask them to make a poster to explain their business idea. The poster will incorporate the ideas on the handout and pictures to illustrate their idea.
- When posters are ready, ask learners to display them around the classroom so they can walk around and look at each other's ideas. One learner will stay by the poster and talk about the idea, while the others walk around and look at the other posters, noting down which idea they liked best.

## Wrap up

- Vote as a class on the best business idea.

> **Answers**
> Learners' own answers.

## Photocopiable activity 13

**Creating a business idea: *Be your own boss***

**A  All about you**

**1  Write six things you are good at.**

_____
_____
_____
_____
_____
_____

**2  Write five things you are interested in or crazy about.**

_____
_____
_____
_____
_____

**3  Write down something that you are very knowledgeable about.**

_____

**B  Compare with your partner**

Compare your lists above with your partner and circle the things you have in common.

**C  Be your own bosses**

Now think of an idea for a business that you can create together. Describe your idea in the table.

| **1  Our business idea** |
|---|
| Are you selling a product or a service? What kind of product or service? Why do you think people will like it? |
| **2  Reasons for our idea** |
| Why do you think you will be good at this business? What skills and interests do you have? |
| **3  How we will start our business** |
| What are the first four things you need to do to start your business? |

# Photocopiable activity 14

## Revision crossword: *Name that job!*

**Aim:** Learners complete the crossword and definitions with words to describe jobs.

**Preparation time:** 5 minutes

**Completion time:** 15 minutes.

**Vocabulary:** words to describe jobs: *mechanic, architect, artist, dentist, vet, biologist, plasterer, builder, teacher, pilot*

**Materials:** One **Revision crossword** handout for each learner; notebooks for vocabulary extension activity (optional).

**Answers**

**Down**
1 vet
2 biologist
4 plasterer
5 builder
6 teacher
8 pilot

**Across**
3 mechanic
7 artist
9 architect
10 dentist

## Procedure

- Distribute one copy of the handout to each learner.
- Ask learners to read the clues, think of the missing word and complete the crossword. If you feel your learners need more support, you could get them to do the crossword in pairs. Ask learners to complete the gaps in the clues with the target words too.
- This activity could be done as a competition with a time limit and points awarded to the first learner or pair who correctly complete the crossword.
- **Extension:** When learners have completed the crossword, you could extend the activity by asking learners to categorise the target words according to suffix or job type and add more words to the category. Learners could also create their own crossword or word search with other jobs or job-related vocabulary from **Unit 7**.

## Photocopiable activity 14

**Revision crossword:** *Name that job!*

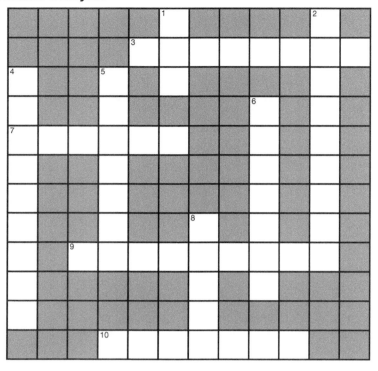

**1 Complete the crossword and write the missing words in the spaces.**

**Down ↓**

1 A _____ knows how to look after sick animals.

2 A marine _____ is fascinated by the wildlife in the sea.

4 A _____ knows how to make the walls in your house look smooth.

5 A _____ uses bricks and cement to make places to live.

6 A _____ is good with children and knowledgeable about lots of school subjects.

8 A _____ controls planes and takes passengers all over the world.


**Across →**

3 A _____ is knowledgeable about different types of engines.

7 An _____ is very talented at painting and drawing.

9 An _____ is very interested in how people live and work in buildings.

10 A _____ is knowledgeable about healthy gums and teeth.

# Photocopiable activity 15

## Worksheet: Text message abbreviations

**Aim:** Learners practise using texting abbreviations by first matching common abbreviations to full words and phrases, then decoding a text message exchange and finally sending a message using the abbreviations to another classmate.

**Preparation time:** 5 minutes

**Completion time:** 20 minutes

**Vocabulary:** Text message abbreviations (see handout)

**Materials:** One **Text message abbreviations** handout for each learner; slips of paper (optional)

## Procedure

- Distribute one copy of the handout to each learner.
- This activity could be introduced by asking learners if and when they send texts, who to and what kind of messages they usually send (e.g. making arrangements, asking someone to do something, just chatting, etc).
- First ask learners if they already know any texting abbreviations in English. Brainstorm the ones they already know and write on the board; then have them do the matching task in **Activity 1**.
- When they have matched all the abbreviations, go through the answers. Then ask them to decode the text message exchange in **Activity 2** and write the messages in full words and sentences in the space provided.

- Finally, have them write a message, using texting abbreviations, to another classmate. Ask them to write the message first in the box provided in **Activity 3**, so you can check the messages. Then have them either send the message by text (if this is an option) or by writing it on a Post-it or piece of paper and give it to the classmate. Ask learners to reply to the messages they receive using the texting abbreviations where appropriate.

**Note:** If you would like learners to send 'real' text messages and have a no-phones policy in school, ask them to send the message from home as a homework task. Tell them to show you the message they are going to send as written in the box in **Activity 3**.

---

**Answers**

**1**

| a 3 | b 5 | c 4 | d 8 | e 1 | f 12 | g 13 |
|------|------|------|------|------|------|------|
| h 2 | i 11 | j 15 | k 7 | l 14 | m 6 | n 10 | o 9 |

**2**

**A:** Do you want to go to the cinema later?
**B:** I can't go today – (I've got) too much to do!
**A:** No problem. Do you want to go tomorrow? (Do you want to go to the) film at 12.30?
**B:** Great! Do you want to meet before for chocolate at Dino's at 11 (o'clock)?
**A:** Great! See you tomorrow. Don't be late. (I've) got to go, bye!

**3** Learners' own answers.

---

## Unit 8

## Photocopiable activity 15

**Worksheet: Text message abbreviations**

**1 Match the texting abbreviations to the full words and phrases.**

| | |
|---|---|
| **a** thks / thx | **1** before |
| **b** 2moro | **2** no problem |
| **c** 2nite | **3** thanks |
| **d** gr8 | **4** tonight |
| **e** b4 | **5** tomorrow |
| **f** gnite | **6** See you later |
| **g** idk | **7** want to |
| **h** no prob | **8** great |
| **i** pls | **9** at |
| **j** w/ w/o | **10** Don't be late |
| **k** wanna | **11** please |
| **l** gtgb | **12** goodnight |
| **m** c u l8r | **13** I don't know |
| **n** dnbl8 | **14** I've got to go, bye! |
| **o** @ | **15** with / without |

**2 Write these text messages between two friends in full sentences.**

**A:** Wanna go 2 the cinema l8r?

**B:** I can't go 2day – 2 much 2 do!

**A:** No prob. Wanna go 2moro? Film at 12.30?

**B:** Gr8! Wanna meet b4 4 chocolate @ Dino's @ 11?

**A:** Gr8! C u tmoro. Dnbl8. Gtgb!

_____
_____
_____
_____
_____
_____
_____

**3 Use the texting abbreviations to write a message to another classmate.** First, write your message in the box; then send a real text message or write a message on a piece of paper and give it to your classmate.

My message to ..........................

# Photocopiable activity 16

## Worksheet: Communication via the Internet

**Aim:** Learners consider safe and appropriate ways to communicate online and use the Internet; they look at appropriate vocabulary to describe online usage and complete a text with modal verbs, giving advice about safe and appropriate online behaviour.

**Preparation time:** 5 minutes

**Completion time:** 1 hour

**Language focus:** Modal verbs; *should; shouldn't; mustn't* (Review from **Unit 3**).

**Vocabulary:** Things we do online: *post a comment; upload photos; download apps; message a friend; click on a link*

**Materials:** One handout for each learner; poster paper and coloured pens.

## Procedure

- Introduce the activity by asking learners how they use the Internet; use this stage to introduce some of the phrases in **Activity 1** on the handout in natural conversation, e.g. *Has anyone ever posted a comment? Do you message your friends online? Has anyone ever uploaded any photos?*
  **Note:** This stage is also important in finding out exactly how and to what extent your learners are communicating online at the moment, so that the materials on the handout can be tailored accordingly. You may feel that certain points warrant extra emphasis and need to be added to; or that some points can be touched on rather than dealt with in detail at this stage.
- Distribute one copy of the handout to each learner.
- Ask learners to do **Activity 1** in pairs. Tell them that they can use the words in the box more than once in some cases. Monitor and circulate, giving examples if learners are unsure about the meaning of some of the phrases.
- Then focus them on the title of the text in **Activity 2** and ask them to predict the points that might be mentioned; then ask them to read it quickly and highlight any phrases from **Activity 1**.
- Now focus them on the gaps showing the missing words. Tell them to read the article again and complete the points using the modal verbs in the box. Have them complete the gaps first and check with their partner.

- When you go through the answers, use this opportunity to talk about some of the points raised in the article, and relate the points to learners' personal experience of online usage, as appropriate. E.g. *What apps have members of the class downloaded? Who did they ask first? What can happen if you download apps without asking?* Use your discretion about how far to take the discussion, e.g. it might not be appropriate to ask if anyone has ever received an unkind online message, or it might be a good opportunity to have an open discussion, depending on the character of your class.
- Finally, ask learners to make posters describing good and bad online behaviour. This gives them the opportunity to tailor the information to make it most directly relevant to them and their current experience of communicating online and using the Internet. You could ask them to organise the posters in a *Dos and Don'ts* format (see example on handout) or to give further practice in modals (*You should / mustn't*, etc.) or the use of the zero or 1st conditional (*If you post a message, make sure ...*), etc.

### Answers

**1 a** *click on a link / a comment / photos*
  **b** *download photos / apps*
  **c** *upload photos / a comment*
  **d** *message a friend*
  **e** *post a comment / photos*

**2** It can be a lot of fun to use the Internet and communicate online. But there are some important things that you should remember so you can communicate safely and happily.

**3 1** You should remember that lots of people might read what you say online. You mustn't post messages that are rude or say things that might hurt someone.
  **2** Before you post a message, imagine that a member of your family or your teacher can read the message. If that makes you feel uncomfortable, then you shouldn't send it.
  **3** When we upload photos online, we should remember that lots of other people might see them, including people we don't know.
  **4** Before you download apps, you should ask your parents (or someone in charge) if this is okay.
  **5** When you are online, you mustn't click on any links or pop-ups, if you don't already know what they are.
  **6** If you see anything online or receive any messages that make you feel uncomfortable, you should tell your parents (or someone in charge) immediately.

Unit 8

## Photocopiable activity 16

### Worksheet: Communication via the Internet

#### 1 Things we do online

Use the verbs and the words in the box to make verb phrases to describe things we do online.
You can use the words more than once.

> a comment    a link    photos    apps    a friend

**a** click on ...

**b** download ...

**c** upload ...

**d** message ...

**e** post ...

#### 2 Communicating online

Read the article. How many phrases from **Activity 1** can you find in the text?

It can be a lot of fun to use the Internet and communicate online. But there are some important things that you _____ remember so you can communicate safely and happily.

**1** You _____ remember that lots of people might read what you say online.
You _____ post messages that are rude or say things that might hurt someone.

**2** Before you post a message, imagine that a member of your family or your teacher can read the message. If that makes you feel uncomfortable, then you _____ send it.

**3** When we upload photos online, we _____ remember that lots of other people might see them, including people we don't know.

**4** Before you download apps, you _____ ask your parents (or someone in charge) if this is OK.

**5** When you are online, you _____ click on any links or pop-ups, if you don't already know what they are.

**6** If you see anything online or receive any messages that make you feel uncomfortable, you _____ tell your parents (or someone in charge) immediately.

#### 3 Communicating online

Complete the article with the verbs in the box.

> mustn't    should    shouldn't

#### 4 Make a poster to give advice to other children about good ways to use the Internet and communicate online.

**Do** be polite and friendly        **Don't** write anything that is rude or aggressive

# Photocopiable activity 17

## Holiday dates worksheet: *Time to have fun!*

**Aim:** Learners make calculations with dates within the context of holiday activities (in the form of advertisements and descriptions of different holiday scenarios).

**Preparation time:** 5 minutes + time to calculate answers to handout tasks

**Completion time:** 20 minutes

**Vocabulary:** Holiday activities and places: *rock-climbing, snorkelling, bungee-jumping, surfing, skiing, camping, a theme park, a wildlife park*

**Materials:** One **Holiday dates** handout for each learner; one small calendar for each learner, showing current and following years (see small types that are available for children's calendar-making activities).

**Note:** Teachers will need to calculate answers to handout tasks 1–8 before the lesson, as answers are specific to the year in which the tasks are carried out.

## Procedure

- Distribute one copy of the handout and a calendar to each learner.
- Focus learners on the advertisements on the handout and elicit the text type. Look at question 1 together and do the task as a class. Ask learners to calculate the answer using their calendars. Explain that all the questions on the handout are about holiday activities and they will need to use their calendars in the same way for all the tasks.
- Ask learners to work through all the tasks in the same way. Monitor and circulate, giving support as appropriate. This activity could be presented as a competition (with a time limit), with learners working in pairs to calculate the answers.

## Wrap up

- Ask learners about their plans for different holiday activities and the dates that they will take place; or talk about the days for different school events that are coming up.

> **Answers**
> Answers will depend on the year in which these activities are carried out.

## Photocopiable activity 17

**Holiday dates worksheet: *Time to have fun!***

**Read the advertisements and write the dates or days for the activities.**

### Rock climbing club.

We meet on the fourth Saturday every month, February–November.
Come and join us! Visit our website for more information.

**1** When is the next meeting? _____

### Snorkelling trips

Snorkelling boat trips are available on Monday, Wednesday and Fridays for the next three months. Book early! Limited places available.

**2** Next month is the first month for the trips. Starting next month, how many boat trips will take place all together? _____

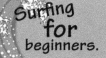

### Surfing for beginners.

Two-day surfing courses for beginners on Thursdays and Fridays, starting in July. Book your place now! Visit our website for more information.

**3** When is the next available date for a bungee-jump? _____

### Try bungee jumping!

Bungee-jumping across the Delphia Falls starts next month! Don't miss your chance! Weekend jumps have already sold out! Places available Mon–Fri.

**4** What are the dates for the next surfing course? _____

**5** Tom's school organises a skiing trip for Year 6 students in the second week of February every year. They go on a Monday and come back on a Saturday. What are the dates of the next trip? _____

**6** Fatima's class are going on a school trip to a wildlife park on the second Friday of next month. What date is the trip? _____

**7** At the wildlife park, you can usually watch a dolphin show every day. But last month it was cancelled for the last two days of the month. What day did it start again? _____

**8** Every year, Talia's family go camping in the third week of August, from Monday to Sunday. What are the dates of their next holiday? _____

236 Cambridge Global English Stage 6 Teacher's Resource © Cambridge University Press 2016

# Photocopiable activity 18

## Conversation cards: Talking about holidays

**Aim:** Learners use the prompt cards to ask and answer a range of questions about holiday experiences, using a range of tenses and structures.

**Preparation time:** 5 minutes

**Completion time:** 20–25 minutes.

**Language focus:** Question forms: past simple; present perfect simple; going to for future plans; 2nd conditional (review); adjectives + prepositions; *interested in*.

**Vocabulary:** Holiday activities and places: *rock-climbing, snorkelling, bungee-jumping, surfing, skiing, camping; a theme park, a wildlife park, a museum, an adventure playground*

**Materials:** One **Conversation card** for each learner; notebooks.

## Procedure

- Distribute one of the four prompt cards to each learner.
- Focus learners on the task and tell them that they have to form questions to find out the information on the card, then ask their classmates until they find someone who answers *yes* to the question. Then they write the classmate's name next to the question.
- Encourage stronger learners to elaborate on their answers or to continue the conversation with a second question: e.g.,
  A: *Have you ever been skiing?*
  B: *Yes, I have. I went to ... last year ...*
  A: *Did you enjoy it?*
  B: *Yes, it was great!*
- Before interviewing their classmates, ask learners to form the questions either orally or by writing it down on the prompt card or in a notebook. Monitor and circulate, checking that questions are structured correctly and that tenses are accurate.
- When learners are ready with their questions have them mingle and ask and answer questions. If a mingling activity is impractical in your classroom, you could ask learners to asking and answering questions in groups of four at their tables, with each learner using a different prompt card.

## Wrap up

- Ask learners to give feedback on the answers they received. Pick questions at random and elicit the answers learners found out, e.g. *Who would like to try bungee-jumping? Who visited somewhere interesting on holiday last year?* Ask learners which information they thought was the most interesting, surprising, etc.

**Answers**

**Card 1**
Would you like to try bungee-jumping?
Have you ever been skiing?
Did you go somewhere interesting on holiday last year?
Have you ever visited a historical place on holiday?
Would like to visit a city in another country?

**Card 2**
Have you ever been snorkelling?
Would you like to try snowboarding?
Did you go to a theme park last year?
Have you got a favourite museum?
Have you tried one of the activities in Lesson 1?

**Card 3**
Can you tell me about a special place you've visited?
Have you ever been to a wildlife park?
Would you like to try rock-climbing?
Are you going somewhere interesting on holiday this year?
Have you ever been on a camping holiday?

**Card 4**
Have you ever been on holiday without your parents?
Have you ever been to an adventure playground?
Which do you prefer - outdoor or indoor places?
Would you like to try surfing?
Which do you prefer - water sports or other sports?

## Unit 9

## Photocopiable activity 18

### Conversation cards: Talking about holidays

---

**Card 1**

**Find someone who ...**

... would like to try bungee-jumping.

*Would you like to try bungee-jumping?*

... has been skiing.

... went somewhere interesting on holiday last year.

... has visited a historical place on holiday.

... would like to visit a city in another country.

---

**Card 2**

**Find someone who ...**

... has been snorkelling.

*Have you ever been snorkelling?*

... would like to try snowboarding.

... went to a theme park last year.

... has a favourite museum.

... has tried one of the activities in Lesson 1.

---

**Card 3**

**Find someone who ...**

... can tell you about a special place they've visited.

*Can you tell me about a special place you've visited?*

... has been to a wildlife park.

... would like to try rock-climbing.

... is going somewhere interesting on holiday this year.

... has been on a camping holiday.

---

**Card 4**

**Find someone who ...**

... has been on holiday without their parents.

*Have you ever been on holiday without your parents?*

... has been to an adventure playground.

... prefers outdoor places to indoor places.

... would like to try surfing.

... prefers water sports to other sports.

---

**Photocopiable activity 19: Congratulations certificate for completing Stage 6 of *Cambridge Global English***

## Congratulations!

You have completed Stage 6 of *Cambridge Global English.*

Name: _____

Class: _____

Teacher: _____

# Word lists

| admire | amazement | an article |
|--------|-----------|------------|
| beauty | blind | bravery |
| brought up | can't stand | deaf |
| do research | excitement | give up on |
| go to college | hopeless at | meet up with (someone) |
| musician | painting | perform |
| pride | proud | raise money |
| receive an award | satisfaction | satisfying |
| since then | sold out | talented |
| terror | think of | to sum up |

| Arabic | Art and Design | as well as |
|---|---|---|
| belong to | berry | bully |
| day off | French | frightened |
| grade | hurry | instead of |
| Islamic education | join in with | laugh at |
| learn about | memory | mess about |
| National history | newsletter | Physical education |
| Science | shake | Social Studies |
| Spanish | stare | sugary |
| tell (someone) off | unless | vitamin |

| | | |
|---|---|---|
| a charity | a net | a racquet |
| a stick | ankle | athletics |
| awesome | badminton | court |
| equipment | goal | goalposts |
| goggles | hamstrings | heart |
| hip | hockey | judo |
| knees | muscles | pitch |
| score | shoulder | shuttlecock |
| spectators | sponsor | thighs |
| toes | trunks | volleyball |

| a (cinema) screen | a film projector | action |
| --- | --- | --- |
| adventure | amazing | an audience |
| animation | ask | characters |
| comedy | costume | dinosaur |
| drama | gorgeous | heart-breaking |
| hero | hilarious | historical |
| horror | imaginary | make up |
| plot | scene | science-fiction |
| setting | sigh | special effects |
| terrifying | thrilling | weight |

| a compass | a gadget | a laptop |
|---|---|---|
| a mobile phone | a tablet (computer) | a zip |
| appear | balance | bright |
| carefully | community | crash |
| demonstrate | depend on | failure |
| for these reasons | gently | in my opinion |
| invent | invention | inventor |
| prize | quickly | roughly |
| securely | sneer | such as |
| surf the Internet | tears | voucher |

| | | |
|---|---|---|
| a compass | a first aid kit | a laptop |
| amazed | amazing | as soon as |
| chew | circular | continent |
| destroy | discover | fifth |
| first | fourth | guard |
| increase | insect repellent | mission |
| sail | second | spot |
| tent | third | tiring |
| translate | until | valuable |
| voyage | waterproof clothing | while |

| | | |
|---|---|---|
| a florist | a builder | a dentist |
| a fire fighter | a hairdresser | a logo |
| a presenter | alarm | an actor |
| an architect | an artist | belt |
| calm | car mechanic | confident |
| conservation group | crazy about | enthusiastic |
| fascinated by | fascinating | friendly |
| interested in | knowledgeable | pocket |
| police officer | reporter | sleeve |
| stripe | voluntary work | work experience |

| | | |
|---|---|---|
| a blog | a bow | a handshake |
| a hug | a nod | a note |
| a text | aggressive | appointment |
| arrangement | cheerful | click on a link |
| dawn | download apps | escape |
| formal | gesture | greet |
| informal | make eye contact | message a friend |
| polite | post a comment | raise your hand |
| reply to | rude | send an email |
| sunset | upload photos | wave your hand |

| a theme park | a wildlife park | amazed by |
| --- | --- | --- |
| an adventure playground | ancient | annoying |
| bungee-jumping | childhood | disappointment |
| fascinated by | fond of | interested in |
| marine | mixture | poisonous |
| rock-climbing | sad about | salty |
| skiing | smell | snorkelling |
| snowboarding | species | stone |
| surfing | surprised by | taste |
| touch | volcano | worn |